Lecture Notes in Computer Science   10321

Commenced Publication in 1973
Founding and Former Series Editors:
Gerhard Goos, Juris Hartmanis, and Jan van Leeuwen

More information about this series at http://www.springer.com/series/7408

Ahmed Bouajjani · Alexandra Silva (Eds.)

Formal Techniques for Distributed Objects, Components, and Systems

37th IFIP WG 6.1 International Conference, FORTE 2017
Held as Part of the 12th International Federated Conference
on Distributed Computing Techniques, DisCoTec 2017
Neuchâtel, Switzerland, June 19–22, 2017
Proceedings

 Springer

Editors
Ahmed Bouajjani
University Paris Diderot
Paris
France

Alexandra Silva
University College London
London
UK

ISSN 0302-9743   ISSN 1611-3349   (electronic)
Lecture Notes in Computer Science
ISBN 978-3-319-60224-0   ISBN 978-3-319-60225-7   (eBook)
DOI 10.1007/978-3-319-60225-7

Library of Congress Control Number: 2017943019

LNCS Sublibrary: SL2 – Programming and Software Engineering

Printed on acid-free paper

This Springer imprint is published by Springer Nature
The registered company is Springer International Publishing AG
The registered company address is: Gewerbestrasse 11, 6330 Cham, Switzerland

Foreword

The 12th International Federated Conference on Distributed Computing Techniques (DisCoTec) took place in Neuchâtel, Switzerland, during June 19–22, 2017. It was organized by the Institute of Computer Science of the University of Neuchâtel.

The DisCoTec series is one of the major events sponsored by the International Federation for Information Processing (IFIP). It comprises three conferences:

- COORDINATION, the IFIP WG6.1 International Conference on Coordination Models and Languages
- DAIS, the IFIP WG6.1 International Conference on Distributed Applications and Interoperable Systems
- FORTE, the IFIP WG6.1 International Conference on Formal Techniques for Distributed Objects, Components and Systems

Together, these conferences cover a broad spectrum of distributed computing subjects, ranging from theoretical foundations and formal description techniques to systems research issues.

Each day of the federated event began with a plenary speaker nominated by one of the conferences. The three invited speakers were Prof. Giovanna Di Marzo Serugendo (UniGE, Switzerland), Dr. Marko Vukolić (IBM Research, Switzerland), and Dr. Rupak Majumdar (MPI, Germany).

Associated with the federated event were also three satellite events that took place during June 21–22, 2017:

- The 10th Workshop on Interaction and Concurrency Experience (ICE)
- The 4th Workshop on Security in Highly Connected IT Systems (SHCIS)
- The EBSIS-sponsored session on Dependability and Interoperability with Event-Based Systems (DIEBS)

Sincere thanks go to the chairs and members of the Program and Steering Committees of the aforementioned conferences and workshops for their highly appreciated efforts. The organization of DisCoTec 2017 was only possible thanks to the dedicated work of the Organizing Committee, including Ivan Lanese (publicity chair), Romain Rouvoy (workshop chair), Peter Kropf (finance chair), and Aurélien Havet (webmaster), as well as all the students and colleagues who volunteered their time to help. Finally, many thanks go to IFIP WG6.1 for sponsoring this event, Springer's *Lecture Notes in Computer Science* for their support and sponsorship, and EasyChair for providing the reviewing infrastructure.

April 2017

Pascal Felber
Valerio Schiavoni

Preface

This volume contains the papers presented at FORTE 2017, the 37th IFIP International Conference on Formal Techniques for Distributed Objects, Components and Systems. This conference was organized as part of the 12th International Federated Conference on Distributed Computing Techniques (DisCoTec) and was held during June 19–22, 2017, in Neuchâtel (Switzerland).

The FORTE conference series represents a forum for fundamental research on theory, models, tools, and applications for distributed systems. The conference encourages contributions that combine theory and practice, and that exploit formal methods and theoretical foundations to present novel solutions to problems arising from the development of distributed systems. FORTE covers distributed computing models and formal specification, testing, and verification methods. The application domains include all kinds of application-level distributed systems, telecommunication services, Internet, embedded, and real-time systems, as well as networking and communication security and reliability.

After careful deliberations, the Program Committee selected 17 papers for presentation, of which three are short papers and one is a tool paper. In addition to these papers, this volume contains an abstract of the invited talk by an outstanding researcher, Rupak Majumdar (Max Planck Institute for Software Systems, Kaiserslautern, Germany), on "Systematic Testing for Asynchronous Programs." We warmly thank him for his participation. We also thank all the authors for their submissions, their willingness to continue improving their papers, and their presentations!

Conferences like FORTE rely on the willingness of experts to serve in the Program Committee; their professionalism and their helpfulness were exemplary. We thank the members of the Program Committee and all the external reviewers for their excellent work. We would like also to thank the general chair, Pascal Felber (University of Neuchâtel, Switzerland), and the support of the Organizing Committee chaired by Valerio Schiavoni (University of Neuchâtel, Switzerland), and the publicity chair, Ivan Lanese (University of Bologna, Italy). We also thank the members of the Steering Committee for their helpful advice. For the work of the Program Committee and the compilation of the proceedings, the EasyChair system was employed; it freed us from many technical matters and allowed us to focus on the program, for which we are grateful.

April 2017

Ahmed Bouajjani
Alexandra Silva

Organization

Program Committee

Elvira Albert	Complutense University of Madrid, Spain
Luis Barbosa	Universidade do Minho, Portugal
Gilles Barthe	IMDEA Software Institute, Spain
Borzoo Bonakdarpour	McMaster University, Canada
Ahmed Bouajjani	IRIF, University of Paris Diderot, France
Franck Cassez	Macquarie University, Australia
Hana Chockler	King's College London, UK
Pedro D'Argenio	Universidad Nacional de Córdoba - CONICET, Argentina
Frank De Boer	CWI, The Netherlands
Mariangiola Dezani-Ciancaglini	Università di Torino, Italy
Cezara Dragoi	IST, Austria
Michael Emmi	Bell Labs, Nokia, USA
Carla Ferreira	CITI/DI/FCT/UNL, Portugal
Bart Jacobs	Katholieke Universiteit Leuven, Belgium
Sophia Knight	Uppsala University, Sweden
Annabelle McIver	Macquarie University, Australia
Stephan Merz	Inria Nancy, France
Stefan Milius	FAU Erlangen, Germany
Catuscia Palamidessi	Inria, France
Corina Pasareanu	CMU/NASA Ames Research Center, USA
Anna Philippou	University of Cyprus
Sanjiva Prasad	Indian Institute of Technology Delhi, India
Alexandra Silva	University College London, UK
Ana Sokolova	University of Salzburg, Austria
Marielle Stoelinga	University of Twente, The Netherlands

Additional Reviewers

Åman Pohjola, Johannes
Bacci, Giovanni
Brett, Noel
Chen, Tzu-Chun
Coppo, Mario
Dodds, Mike
Gerhold, Marcus
Gutkovas, Ramūnas

Göthel, Thomas
Isabel, Miguel
Jakšić, Svetlana
Jensen, Peter Gjøl
Klin, Bartek
Kouzapas, Dimitrios
Köpf, Boris
Lee, Matias David

Lienhardt, Michael
Luckow, Kasper
Madeira, Alexandre
Mamouras, Konstantinos
Maubert, Bastien
Meijer, Jeroen
Montenegro, Manuel
Monti, Raúl E.
Mousavi, Mohammadreza

Pang, Jun
Petrisan, Daniela
Proenca, Jose
Sammartino, Matteo
Schivo, Stefano
Schlatte, Rudolf
Siddique, Umair
Toninho, Bernardo

Systematic Testing
for Asynchronous Programs
(Invited Talk)

Rupak Majumdar

MPI-SWS, Kaiserslautern, Germany

Asynchronous programming is a generic term for concurrent programming with cooperative task management and shows up in many different applications. For example, many programming models for the web, smartphone and cloud-backed applications, server applications, and embedded systems implement programming in this style. In all these scenarios, while programs can be very efficient, the manual management of resources and asynchronous procedures can make programming quite difficult. The natural control flow of a task is obscured and the programmer must ensure correct behavior for all possible orderings of external events. Specifically, the global state of the program can change between the time an asynchronous procedure is posted and the time the scheduler picks and runs it.

In this talk, I will describe algorithmic analysis techniques for systematic testing of asynchronous programs. I will talk about formal models for asynchronous programs and verification and systematic testing techniques for these models. The results will use connections between asynchronous programs and classical concurrency models such as Petri nets, partial order reductions for asynchronous programs, as well as combinatorial constructions of small test suites with formal guarantees of coverage.

Contents

Session Types for Link Failures

Manuel Adameit, Kirstin Peters$^{(\boxtimes)}$, and Uwe Nestmann

TU Berlin, Berlin, Germany
`kirstin.peters@tu-berlin.de`

Abstract. We strive to use session type technology to prove behavioural properties of fault-tolerant distributed algorithms. Session types are designed to abstractly capture the structure of (even multi-party) communication protocols. The goal of session types is the analysis and verification of the protocols' behavioural properties. One important such property is progress, i.e., the absence of (unintended) deadlock. Distributed algorithms often resemble (compositions of) multi-party communication protocols. In contrast to protocols that are typically studied with session types, they are often designed to cope with system failures. An essential behavioural property is (successful) termination, despite failures, but it is often elaborate to prove for distributed algorithms.

We extend multi-party session types with optional blocks that cover a limited class of link failures. This allows us to automatically derive termination of distributed algorithms that come within these limits.

1 Introduction

Session types are used to statically ensure correctly coordinated behaviour in systems without global control. One important such property is progress, i.e., the absence of (unintended) deadlock. Like with every other static typing approach, the main advantage is that the respective properties are then provable without unrolling the process, i.e., without computing its executions. Thereby, the state explosion problem is avoided. Hence, after the often elaborate task of establishing a type system, they allow to prove properties of processes in a quite efficient way.

Session types describe global behaviours as *sessions*, i.e., units of conversations. The participants of such sessions are called *roles*. *Global types* specify protocols from a global point of view, whereas *local types* describe the behaviour of individual roles within a protocol. *Projection* ensures that a global type and its local types are consistent. These types are used to reason about processes formulated in a *session calculus*. Most of the existing session calculi are extensions of the well-known π-calculus [10] with specific operators adapted to correlate with local types. Session types are designed to abstractly capture the structure of (even multi-party) communication protocols [2,3]. The literature on session types provides a rich variety of extensions. *Nested* protocols were introduced by [7] as an extension of multi-party session types as defined e.g. in [2,3]. They offer the possibility to define sub-protocols independently of their parent protocols.

A. Bouajjani and A. Silva (Eds.): FORTE 2017, LNCS 10321, pp. 1–16, 2017.
DOI: 10.1007/978-3-319-60225-7_1

It is essentially the notion of nested protocols that led us to believe that session types could be applied to capture properties of distributed algorithms, especially the so-called round-based distributed algorithms. The latter are typically structured by a repeated execution of communication patterns by n distributed partners. Often such a pattern involves an exposed coordinator role, whose incarnation may differ from round to round. As such, distributed algorithms very much resemble compositions of nested multi-party communication protocols. Moreover, an essential behavioural property of distributed algorithms is (successful) termination [9,11], despite failures, but it is often elaborate to prove. It turns out that progress (as provided by session types) and termination (as required by distributed algorithms) are closely related. For these reasons, our goal is to apply session type technology to prove behavioural properties of distributed algorithms.

Particularly interesting round-based distributed algorithms were designed in a fault-tolerant way, in order to work in a model where they have to cope with system failures—be it links dropping or manipulating messages, or processes crashing with or without recovery. As the current session type systems are not able to cover fault-tolerance (except for exception handling as in [4,5]), it is necessary to add an appropriate mechanism to cover system failures.

While the detection of conceptual design errors is a standard property of type systems, proving correctness of algorithms despite the occurrence of uncontrollable system failures is not. In the context of distributed algorithms, various kinds of failures have been studied. Often, the correctness of an algorithm does not only depend on the kinds of failures but also of the phase of the algorithm in which they occur, the number of failures, or their likelihood. Here, we only consider a very simple case, namely algorithms that terminate despite arbitrarily many link failures that may occur at any moment in the execution of the algorithm.

Therefore, we extend session types with *optional blocks*, that specify chunks of communication that may at some point fail. This partial communication protocol is protected by the optional block, to ensure that no other process can interfere before the block was resolved and to ensure, that in the case of failure, no parts of the failed communication attempt may influence the further behaviour. In case a link fails, the ambition to guarantee progress requires that the continuation behaviour is not blocked. Therefore, the continuation of an optional block C can be parametrised by a set of values that are either computed by a successful termination of an optional block or are provided beforehand as default values, i.e., we require that for each value that C uses the optional block specifies a default value. An optional block can cover parts of a protocol or even other optional blocks. The type system ensures that communication with optional blocks requires an optional block as communication partner and that only a successful termination of a block releases the protection around its values. The semantics of the calculus then allows us to abort an unguarded optional block at any point. If an optional block models a single communication, its abortion represents a message loss. In summary, optional blocks allow us to automatically derive termination despite arbitrary link failures of distributed algorithms.

Related Work. Type systems are usually designed for scenarios that are free of system failures. An exception is [8] that introduces unreliable broadcast. Within such an unreliable broadcast a transmission can be received by multiple receivers but not necessarily all available receivers. In the latter case, the receiver is deadlocked. In contrast, we consider failure-tolerant unicast, i.e., communications between a single sender and a single receiver, where in the case of a failure the receiver is not deadlocked but continues using default values.

[4,5] extends session types with exceptions thrown by processes within TRY-and-CATCH-blocks. Both concepts—TRY-and-CATCH-blocks and optional blocks—introduce a way to structurally and semantically encapsulate an unreliable part of a protocol and provide some means to 'detect' a failure and 'react' to it. They are, however, conceptionally and technically different. An obvious difference is the limitation of the inner part of optional blocks towards the computation of values. More fundamentally these approaches differ in the way they allow to 'detect' failures and to 'react' to them.

Optional blocks are designed for the case of system errors that may occur non-deterministically and not necessarily reach the whole system or not even all participants of an optional block, whereas TRY-and-CATCH-blocks model controlled interruption requested by a participant. Hence these approaches differ in the source of an error; raised by the underlying system structure or by a participant. Technically this means that in the presented case failures are introduced by the semantics, whereas in [4] failures are modelled explicitly as THROW-operations. In particular we do not specify, how a participant 'detects' a failure. Different system architectures might provide different mechanisms to do so, e.g. by time-outs. As it is the standard for the analysis of distributed algorithms, our approach allows to port the verified algorithms on different systems architectures, provided that the respective structure and its failure pattern preserves correctness of the considered properties.

The main difference between these two approaches is how they react to failures. In [4] THROW-messages are propagated among nested TRY-and-CATCH-blocks to ensure that all participants are consistently informed about concurrent THROWS of exceptions. In distributed systems such a reaction towards a system error is unrealistic. Distributed processes usually do not have any method to observe an error on another system part and if a participant is crashed or a link fails permanently there is usually no way to inform a waiting communication partner. Instead abstractions (failure detectors) are used to model the detection of failures that can e.g. be implemented by time-outs. Here it is crucial to mention that failure detectors are usually considered to be local and can not ensure global consistency. Distributed algorithms have to deal with the problem that some part of a system may consider a process/link as crashed, while at the same time the same process/link is regarded as correct by another part. This is one of the most challenging problems in the design and verification of distributed algorithms.

In the case of link failures, if a participant is directly influenced by a failure on some other system part (a receiver of a lost message) it will eventually abort the respective communication attempt. If a participant does not depend (the sender in an unreliable link) it may never know about the failure or its nature. Distributed algorithms usually deal with unexpected failures that are hard to detect and often impossible to propagate. Generating correct algorithms for this scenario is difficult and error-prone, thus we need methods to verify them.

Overview. We present global types and restriction in Sect. 2, local types and projection in Sect. 3, and the session calculus in Sect. 4 with a mechanism to check types in Sect. 5. In Sect. 6 we discuss the properties of the type system. We conclude with Sect. 7. The missing proofs and some additional material can be found in [1].

2   Global Types with Optional Blocks

Throughout the paper we use G for global types, T for local types, l for communication labels, s, k for session names, a for shared channels, r for role identifiers, and v for values of a base type (e.g. integer or string). x, y are variables to represent e.g. session names, shared channels, or values. We formally distinguish between roles, labels, process variables, type variables, and names—additionally to identifiers for global/local types, protocols, processes, ... Formally we do however not further distinguish between different kinds of names but use different identifiers $(a, s, v, \dots)$ to provide hints on the main intended purpose at the respective occurrence. Roles and participants are used as synonyms. To simplify the presentation, we adapt set-like notions for tuples. For example we write $x_i \in \tilde{x}$ if $\tilde{x} = (x_1, \dots, x_n)$ and $1 \le i \le n$. We use $\cdot$ to denote the empty tuple.

Global types describe protocols from a global point of view on systems by interactions between roles. They are used to formalise specifications that describe the desired properties of a system. We extend the basic global types as used e.g. in [2,3] with a global type for optional blocks.

Definition 1 (Global Types). *Global types with optional blocks are given by*

$$G ::= r_1 \to r_2 : \sum_{i \in I} \left\{ l_i\left(\tilde{x}_i : \tilde{S}_i\right).G_i \right\} \quad | \quad \mathsf{opt}\left\langle r, \widetilde{\tilde{x}:\tilde{S}} \,|\, G \right\rangle.G'$$

$$| \quad G_1 \oplus^r G_2 \quad | \quad G_1 \,\|\, G_2 \quad | \quad \mu t.G \quad | \quad t \quad | \quad \mathbf{end}$$

$r_1 \to r_2 : \sum_{i \in I} \left\{ l_i\left(\tilde{x}_i : \tilde{S}_i\right).G_i \right\}$ is the standard way to specify a communication from role r_1 to role r_2, where r_1 has a direct choice between several labels l_i proposed by r_2. Each branch expects values $\tilde{x}_i$ of sorts $\tilde{S}_i$ and executes the continuation G_i. When I is a singleton, we write $r_1 \to r_2 : l\left(\tilde{x}:\tilde{S}\right)$. $G_1 \oplus^r G_2$ introduces so-called located (or internal) choice: the choice for one role r between two distinct protocol branches. The parallel composition $G_1 \,\|\, G_2$ allows to specify independent parts of a protocol. $\mu t.G$ and t are used to allow for recursion. $\mathbf{end}$ denotes the successful completion. We often omit trailing $\mathbf{end}$ clauses.

We add $\text{opt}\left\langle \widetilde{r, \tilde{x}{:}\tilde{S}} \mid G \right\rangle.G'$ to describe an optional block between the roles

$r_1, \ldots, r_n$, where $\widetilde{r, \tilde{x}{:}\tilde{S}}$ abbreviates the sequence $r_1, \tilde{x}_1 {:} \tilde{S}_1, \ldots, r_n, \tilde{x}_n {:} \tilde{S}_n$. Here G is the protocol that is encapsulated by the optional block and the $\tilde{x}_i$ are so-called default values that are used within the continuation G' of the surrounding parent session if the optional block fails. There is one (possibly empty) vector of default values $\tilde{x}_i$ for each role r_i. The inner part G of an optional block is a protocol that (in the case of success) is used to compute the vectors of return values. The typing rules ensure that for each role r_i the type of the computed vector coincides with the type $\tilde{S}_i$ of the specified vector of default values $\tilde{x}_i$. Intuitively, if the block does not fail, each participant can use its respective vector of computed values in the continuation G'. Otherwise, the default values are used.

Optional blocks capture the main features of a failure very naturally: a part of a protocol either succeeds or fails. They also encapsulate the source and direct impact of the failure, which allows us to study their implicit effect—as e.g. missing communication partners—on the overall behaviour of protocols. With that they help us to specify, implement, and verify failure-tolerant algorithms.

Using optional blocks we provide a natural and simple specification of an unreliable link c between the two roles src and trg, where in the case of success the value v_{src} is transmitted and in the case of failure a default value v_{trg} is used by the receiver.

Example 1 (Global Type of an Unreliable Link).

$$G_{\text{UL}}(\text{src}, v_{\text{src}}; \text{trg}, v_{\text{trg}}) = \text{opt}\langle \text{src}, \cdot, \text{trg}, v_{\text{trg}} {:} V \mid (\text{src} \to \text{trg} {:} c(v_{\text{src}} {:} V).\text{end})\rangle$$

Here we have a single communication step—to model the potential loss of a single message—that is covered within an optional block. In the term $G_{\text{UL}}(\text{src}, v_{\text{src}}; \text{trg}, v_{\text{trg}}).G'$ the receiver trg may use the transmitted value v_{src} in the continuation G' if the communication succeeds or else uses its default value v_{trg}. Note that the optional block above specifies the empty sequence of values as default values for the sending process src, i.e., the sender needs no default values.

Well-Formed. Following [7] we type all objects appearing in global types with *kinds* (types for types) $K ::= \text{Role} \mid \text{Val}$. Val are value-kinds, which are first-order types for values (like $\mathbb{B}$ for boolean) or data types. Role is used for identifiers of roles. We adopt the definition of *well-kinded* global types from [7] that basically ensures that all positions $r, r_1, r_2, \bar{r}_1, \bar{r}_2$ in global types can be instantiated only by objects of type Role. According to [7] a global type G is *projectable* if for each occurrence of $G_1 \oplus^r G_2$ in the type and for any free role $r' \neq r$ we have $G_1|_{r'} = G_2|_{r'}$. Additionally we require (similar to sub-sessions in [7]) for a global type G to be projectable that, for each optional block $\text{opt}\left\langle \widetilde{r, \tilde{x}{:}\tilde{S}} \mid G_1 \right\rangle.G_2$ in G, all roles in G_1 are contained in $\bar{r}$. A global type is *well-formed* when it is well-kinded and projectable, and satisfies the standard linearity condition [2]. For more intuition on the notion of well-formedness and examples for non-well-formed protocols we refer to [7]. In the examples, we use V as the type of values.

3 Local Types with Optional Blocks

Local types describe a local and partial point of view on a global communication protocol w.r.t. a single participant. They are used to validate and monitor distributed programs. We extend the basic local types as used e.g. in [2,3] with a local type for optional blocks.

Definition 2 (Local Types). *Local types with optional blocks are given by*

$$T ::= \text{get}[r]?_{i \in I} \left\{ l_i \left(\tilde{x}_i : \tilde{S}_i \right).T_i \right\} \quad | \quad \text{send}[r]!_{i \in I} \left\{ l_i \left(\tilde{x}_i : \tilde{S}_i \right).T_i \right\}$$

$$| \quad \text{opt}[\tilde{r}]\langle T\rangle \left(\tilde{x} : \tilde{S} \right).T' \quad | \quad T_1 \oplus T_2 \quad | \quad T_1 \parallel T_2 \quad | \quad \mu t.T \quad | \quad t \quad | \quad \text{end}$$

The first two operators specify endpoint primitives for communications with get for the receiver side—where r is the sender—and send for the sender side—where r denotes the receiver. Accordingly, they introduce the two possible local views of a global type for communication. $T_1 \oplus T_2$ is the local view of the global type $G_1 \oplus^r G_2$ for a choice determined by the role r for which this local type is created. $T_1 \parallel T_2$ represents the local view of the global type for parallel composition, i.e., describes independent parts of the protocol for the considered role. Again $\mu t.T$ and t are used to introduce recursion and end denotes the successful completion of a protocol. Again we usually omit trailing end clauses.

We add the local type $\text{opt}[\tilde{r}]\langle T\rangle \left(\tilde{x} : \tilde{S} \right).T'$. It initialises an optional block between the roles $\tilde{r}$ around the local type T, where the currently considered participant r (called *owner*) is a participant of this block, i.e., $r \in \tilde{r}$. After the optional block the local type continues with T'.

Projection. To ensure that a global type and its local types coincide, global types are projected to their local types. Accordingly we define the projection $(G) \Downarrow_{r_p}$ of a global type G on a role r_p for the case that G describes an optional block.

$$\left(\text{opt}\left\langle \widetilde{r, \tilde{x} : \tilde{S}} \mid G \right\rangle.G' \right) \Downarrow_{r_p} = \begin{cases} \text{opt}[\tilde{r}]\left\langle G \Downarrow_{r_p} \right\rangle \left(\tilde{x}_i : \tilde{S}_i \right).(G') \Downarrow_{r_p} & \begin{array}{l} \text{if } r_p = r_i \in \tilde{r} \\ \text{and } \tilde{x}_i \neq \cdot \end{array} \\[2ex] \text{opt}[\tilde{r}]\left\langle G \Downarrow_{r_p} \right\rangle(\cdot) \parallel (G') \Downarrow_{r_p} & \begin{array}{l} \text{if } r_p = r_i \in \tilde{r} \\ \text{and } \tilde{x}_i = \cdot \end{array} \\[2ex] G' \Downarrow_{r_p} & \text{else} \end{cases}$$

The projection rule for optional blocks has three cases. The last case is used to skip optional blocks when they are projected to roles that do not participate. The first two cases handle projection of optional blocks to one of its participants. A local optional block is generated with the projection of G as content.

The first two cases check whether the optional block indeed computes any values for the role we project onto. They differ only in the way that the continuation of the optional block and its inner part are connected. If the projected role does not specify default values—because no such values are required—the projected continuation $(G') \Downarrow_{r_p}$ can be placed in parallel to the optional block (second case). Otherwise, the continuation has to be guarded by the optional block and, thus, by the computation of the computed values (first case).

By distinguishing between these two first cases, we follow the same line of argument as used for sub-sessions in [7], where the projected continuation of a sub-session `call` is either in parallel to the projection of the `call` itself or connected sequentially. Intuitively, whenever the continuation depends on the outcome of the optional block it has to be connected sequentially. A complete list of all projection rules can be found in [1].

Example 2 (Projection of Unreliable Links).

$$G_{\mathsf{UL}}(\mathsf{src}, v_{\mathsf{src}}; \mathsf{trg}, v_{\mathsf{trg}}) \Downarrow_{\mathsf{src}} = T_{\mathsf{UL}\uparrow}(\mathsf{src}, v_{\mathsf{src}}, \mathsf{trg})$$
$$= \mathsf{opt}[\mathsf{scr}, \mathsf{trg}]\langle \mathsf{send}[\mathsf{trg}]! c(v_{\mathsf{src}} : V)\rangle(\cdot)$$
$$G_{\mathsf{UL}}(\mathsf{src}, v_{\mathsf{src}}; \mathsf{trg}, v_{\mathsf{trg}}) \Downarrow_{\mathsf{trg}} = T_{\mathsf{UL}\downarrow}(\mathsf{src}, v_{\mathsf{src}}; \mathsf{trg}, v_{\mathsf{trg}})$$
$$= \mathsf{opt}[\mathsf{src}, \mathsf{trg}]\langle \mathsf{get}[\mathsf{src}]? c(v_{\mathsf{src}} : V)\rangle(v_{\mathsf{trg}} : V)$$

When projected onto its sender, the global type for a communication over an unreliable link results in the local type $T_{\mathsf{UL}\uparrow}(\mathsf{src}, v_{\mathsf{src}}, \mathsf{trg})$ that consists of an optional block containing a send operation towards trg. Since the optional block for the sender does not specify any default values, the local type $T_{\mathsf{UL}\uparrow}(\mathsf{src}, v_{\mathsf{src}}, \mathsf{trg})$ will be placed in parallel to the projection of the continuation. The projection onto the receiver results in the local type $T_{\mathsf{UL}\downarrow}(\mathsf{src}, v_{\mathsf{src}}; \mathsf{trg}, v_{\mathsf{trg}})$ that consists of an optional block containing a receive operation from src. Here a default value is necessary for the case that the message is lost. So the type $T_{\mathsf{UL}\downarrow}(\mathsf{src}, v_{\mathsf{src}}; \mathsf{trg}, v_{\mathsf{trg}})$ has to be composed sequentially with the projection of the continuation.

4 A Session Calculus with Optional Blocks

Global types (and the local types that are derived from them) can be considered as specifications that describe the desired properties of the system we want to analyse. The process calculus, that we use to model/implement the system, is in the case of session types usually a variant of the π-calculus [10]. We extend a basic session-calculus as used e.g. in [2,3] with two operators.

Definition 3 (Processes). *Processes are given by*

$$P ::= a(\tilde{x}).P \quad | \quad \overline{a}\langle \tilde{s}\rangle.P \quad | \quad k?[r_1, r_2]_{i \in I}\{\ l_i(\tilde{x}_i).P_i\ \} \quad | \quad k![r_1, r_2]l\langle \tilde{v}\rangle.P$$
$$| \quad \mathsf{opt}[r; \tilde{v}; \tilde{r}]\langle P\rangle(\tilde{x}).P' \quad | \quad [r]\langle \tilde{v}\rangle$$
$$| \quad (\nu x)\,P \quad | \quad P_1 + P_2 \quad | \quad P_1\,|\,P_2 \quad | \quad \mu X\!:\!P \quad | \quad X \quad | \quad \mathbf{0}$$

The prefixes $a(\tilde{x}).P$ and $\overline{a}\langle \tilde{s}\rangle.P$ are inherited from the π-calculus and are used for external invitations. Using the shared channel a, an external participant can be invited with the output $\overline{a}\langle \tilde{s}\rangle.P$ transmitting the session channels $\tilde{s}$ that are necessary to participate and the external participant can accept the invitation using the input $a(\tilde{x}).P$. The following two operators introduce a branching input and the corresponding transmission on the session channel k from r_1 to r_2. These two operators correspond to the local types for get and send. Restriction $(\nu x)\, P$ allows to generate a fresh name that is not known outside of the scope of this operator unless it was explicitly communicated. For simplicity and following [6] we assume that only shared channels a for external invitations and session channels s, k for not yet initialised sub-sessions are restricted, because this covers the interesting cases[1] and simplifies the typing rules in Fig. 2. The term $P_1 + P_2$ either behaves as P_1 or P_2. $P_1 \mid P_2$ defines the parallel composition of the processes P_1 and P_2. $\mu X : P$ and X are used to introduce recursion. $\mathbf{0}$ denotes the successful completion.

To implement optional blocks, we add $\mathsf{opt}[r; \tilde{v}_d; \tilde{r}]\langle P\rangle(\tilde{x}).P'$ and $[r]\langle\tilde{v}\rangle$. The former defines an optional block between the roles $\tilde{r}$ around the process P with the default values $\tilde{v}_d$. We require that the owner r of this block is one of its participants $\tilde{r}$, i.e., $r \in \tilde{r}$. In the case of success, $[r]\langle\tilde{v}\rangle$ transmits the computed values $\tilde{v}$ from within the optional block to the continuation P' to be substituted for the variables $\tilde{x}$ within P'. If the optional block fails the variables $\tilde{x}$ of P' are replaced by the default values $\tilde{v}_d$ instead. Without loss of generality we assume that the roles $\tilde{r}$ of optional blocks are distinct. Since optional blocks can compute only values and their defaults need to be of the same kind, $[r]\langle\tilde{v}\rangle$ and the defaults cannot carry session names, i.e., names used as session channels. The type system ensures that the inner part P of a successful optional block reaches some $[r]\langle\tilde{v}\rangle$ and thus transmits computed values of the expected kinds in exactly one of its parallel branches. The semantics presented below ensures that every optional block can transmit at most one vector of computed values and has to fail otherwise. Similarly optional blocks, that use roles in their inner part P that are different from $\tilde{r}$ and are not newly introduced as part of a sub-session within P, cannot be well-typed. Since optional blocks open a context block around their inner part that separates P from the continuation P', scopes as introduced by input prefixes and restriction that are opened within P cannot cover parts of P'.

Example 3 (Implementation of Unreliable Links).

$$P_{\mathsf{UL}\uparrow}(\mathsf{p}_1, v_1, \mathsf{p}_2) = \mathsf{opt}[\mathsf{p}_1; \cdot; \mathsf{p}_1, \mathsf{p}_2]\langle s![\mathsf{p}_1, \mathsf{p}_2]c\langle v_1\rangle.\,[\mathsf{p}_1]\langle\cdot\rangle\rangle(\cdot)$$
$$P_{\mathsf{UL}\downarrow}(\mathsf{p}_1, \mathsf{p}_2, v_2) = \mathsf{opt}[\mathsf{p}_2; v_2; \mathsf{p}_1, \mathsf{p}_2]\langle s?[\mathsf{p}_1, \mathsf{p}_2]c(x).\,[\mathsf{p}_2]\langle x\rangle\rangle(y)$$

$P_{\mathsf{UL}\uparrow}(\mathsf{p}_1, v_1, \mathsf{p}_2)$ is the implementation of a single send action on an unreliable link and $P_{\mathsf{UL}\downarrow}(\mathsf{p}_1, \mathsf{p}_2, v_2)$ the corresponding receive action. Here a continuation of the sender cannot gain any information from the modelled communication; not even whether it succeeded, whereas a continuation of the receiver in the case of success obtains the transmitted value v_1 and else its own default value v_2.

Again we usually omit trailing $\mathbf{0}$. In Definition 3 all occurrences of x, $\tilde{x}$, and $\tilde{x}_i$ refer to bound names of the respective operators. The set $\mathrm{FN}(P)$ of free names of P is the set of names of P that are not bound. A substitution

---

[1] Sometimes it might be useful to allow the restriction of values, e.g. for security. For this case an additional restriction operator can be introduced.

$\{y_1/x_1, \ldots, y_n/x_n\} = \{\tilde{y}/\tilde{x}\}$ is a finite mapping from names to names, where the $\tilde{x}$ are pairwise distinct. The application of a substitution on a term $P\{\tilde{y}/\tilde{x}\}$ is defined as the result of simultaneously replacing all free occurrences of x_i by y_i, possibly applying alpha-conversion to avoid capture or name clashes. For all names $n \notin \tilde{x}$ the substitution behaves as the identity mapping. We use '.' (as e.g. in $a(\tilde{x}).P$) to denote sequential composition. In all operators the part before '.' guards the continuation after the '.', i.e., the continuation cannot reduce before the guard was reduced. A subprocess of a process is *guarded* if it occurs after such a guard, i.e., is the continuation (or part of the continuation) of a guard. Guarded subprocesses can be *unguarded* by steps that remove the guard. We identify processes up to a standard variant of structural congruence defined in [1].

$$(\mathsf{comS})\dfrac{j \in I}{E[k![r_1, r_2]l_j\langle \tilde{v}\rangle.P \mid k?[r_1, r_2]_{i\in I}\{\, l_i(\tilde{x}_i).P_i\,\}] \longmapsto E[P \mid P_j\{\tilde{v}/\tilde{x}_j\}]}$$

$$(\mathsf{choice})\dfrac{P_i \longmapsto P_i'}{E[P_1 + P_2] \longmapsto E[P_i']} \qquad (\mathsf{comC})\dfrac{}{E[\overline{a}\langle \tilde{s}\rangle.P_1 \mid a(\tilde{x}).P_2] \longmapsto E[P_1 \mid P_2\{\tilde{s}/\tilde{x}\}]}$$

$$(\mathsf{fail})\dfrac{}{E[\mathsf{opt}[r; \tilde{v}_d; \tilde{r}]\langle P\rangle(\tilde{x}).P'] \longmapsto E[P'\{\tilde{v}_d/\tilde{x}\}]}$$

$$(\mathsf{succ})\dfrac{}{E[\mathsf{opt}[r; \tilde{v}_d; \tilde{r}]\langle [r]\langle \tilde{v}\rangle\rangle(\tilde{x}).P] \longmapsto E[P\{\tilde{v}/\tilde{x}\}]}$$

$$(\mathsf{cSO})\dfrac{j \in I \quad \mathrm{roles}(C_{\mathsf{opt}}) \doteq \mathrm{roles}(C_{\mathsf{opt}}') \quad \mathrm{owner}(C_{\mathsf{opt}}) = r_1 \quad \mathrm{owner}(C_{\mathsf{opt}}') = r_2}{\begin{array}{c} E\big[E_{\mathsf{R}}[C_{\mathsf{opt}}[k![r_1, r_2]l_j\langle \tilde{v}\rangle.P]] \mid E_{\mathsf{R}}'\big[C_{\mathsf{opt}}'[k?[r_1, r_2]_{i\in I}\{\, l_i(\tilde{x}_i).P_i\,\}]]\big] \\ \longmapsto E\big[E_{\mathsf{R}}[C_{\mathsf{opt}}[P]] \mid E_{\mathsf{R}}'\big[C_{\mathsf{opt}}'[P_j\{\tilde{v}/\tilde{x}_j\}]]\big] \end{array}}$$

$$(\mathsf{cCO})\dfrac{\mathrm{roles}(C_{\mathsf{opt}}) \doteq \mathrm{roles}(C_{\mathsf{opt}}')}{E\big[E_{\mathsf{R}}[C_{\mathsf{opt}}[\overline{a}\langle \tilde{s}\rangle.P_1]] \mid E_{\mathsf{R}}'\big[C_{\mathsf{opt}}'[a(\tilde{x}).P_2]]\big] \longmapsto E\big[E_{\mathsf{R}}[C_{\mathsf{opt}}[P_1]] \mid E_{\mathsf{R}}'\big[C_{\mathsf{opt}}'[P_2\{\tilde{s}/\tilde{x}\}]]\big]}$$

Fig. 1. Reduction rules

Reduction Semantics. In [7] the semantics is given by a set of reduction rules that are defined w.r.t. evaluation contexts. We extend them with optional blocks.

Definition 4. $E ::= [\,] \quad | \quad P \mid E \quad | \quad (\nu x)\, E \quad | \quad \mathsf{opt}[r; \tilde{v}; \tilde{r}]\langle E\rangle(\tilde{x}).P'$

Intuitively an evaluation context is a term with a single hole that is not guarded. Additionally, we introduce two variants of evaluation contexts and a context for blocks that are used to simplify the presentation of our new rules.

Definition 5. $E_{\mathsf{R}} ::= [\,] \quad | \quad P \mid E_{\mathsf{R}} \quad | \quad \mathsf{opt}[r; \tilde{v}; \tilde{r}]\langle E_{\mathsf{R}}\rangle(\tilde{x}).P'$
$C_{\mathsf{opt}} ::= \mathsf{opt}[r; \tilde{v}; \tilde{r}]\langle E_{\mathsf{P}}\rangle(\tilde{x}).P', \text{ where } E_{\mathsf{P}} ::= [\,] \quad | \quad P \mid E_{\mathsf{P}}$

Accordingly, a C_{opt}-context consists of exactly one optional block that contains an E_{P}-context, i.e., a single hole that can occur within the parallel composition of arbitrary processes. We define the function roles($\mathsf{opt}[\mathsf{r}; \tilde{v}; \tilde{\mathsf{r}}]\langle E_\mathsf{P}\rangle(\tilde{x}).P') \triangleq \tilde{\mathsf{r}}$, to return the roles of the optional block of a C_{opt}-context, and the function owner($\mathsf{opt}[\mathsf{r}; \tilde{v}; \tilde{\mathsf{r}}]\langle E_\mathsf{P}\rangle(\tilde{x}).P') \triangleq \mathsf{r}$, to return its owner.

Figure 1 presents the reduction rules. The Rules (comS), (choice), and (comC) deal with the standard operators for communication, choice, and external invitations to sessions, respectively. Since evaluation contexts E contain optional blocks, these rules allow for steps within a single optional block. To capture optional blocks, we introduce the new Rules (fail), (succ), (cSO), and (cCO). Here $\doteq$ means that the two compared vectors contain the same roles but not necessarily in the same order, i.e., $\doteq$ checks whether the set of participants of two optional blocks are the same. The Rules (comS) and (comC) represent two different kinds of communication. They define communications within a session and external session invitations, respectively. In both cases communication is an axiom that requires the occurrence of two matching counterparts of communication primitives (of the respective kind) to be placed in parallel within an evaluation context. As a consequence of the respective communication step the continuations of both communication primitives are unguarded and the values transmitted in the communication step are instantiated (substituted) in the receiver continuation. (choice) allows the reduction of either side of a choice, if the respective side can perform a step.

The two rules (succ) and (fail) describe the main features of optional blocks, namely how they succeed (succ) and what happens if they fail (fail). (fail) aborts an optional block, i.e., removes it and unguards its continuation instantiated with the default values. This rule can be applied whenever an optional block is unguarded, i.e., there is no way to ensure that an optional block does indeed perform any step. In combination with (succ), it introduces the non-determinism that is used to express the random nature in that system errors may occur.

(succ) is the counterpart of (fail); it removes a successfully completed optional block and unguards its continuation instantiated with the computed results. To successfully complete an optional block, we require that its content has to reduce to a single occurrence of $[\mathsf{r}]\langle \tilde{v}\rangle$, where r is the owner of the block and accordingly one of the participating roles. Since (succ) and (fail) are the only ways to reduce $[\mathsf{r}]\langle \tilde{v}\rangle$, this ensures that a successful optional block can compute only a single vector of return values. Other parallel branches in the inner part of an optional block have to terminate with $\mathbf{0}$. This ensures that no confusion can arise from the computation of different values in different parallel branches. Since at the process-level an optional block covers only a single participant, this limitation does not restrict the expressive power of the considered processes. If the content of an optional block cannot reduce to $[\mathsf{r}]\langle \tilde{v}\rangle$ the optional block is doomed to fail.

The remaining rules describe how different optional blocks can interact. Here, we need to ensure that communication from within an optional block ensures isolation, i.e., that such communications are restricted to the encapsulated parts of other optional blocks. The E_R-contexts allow for two such blocks to be nested within different optional blocks. The exact definition of such a communication rule depends on the semantics of the considered calculi and their communication rules. Here there are the Rules (cSO) and (cCO). They are the counterparts of (comS) and (comC) and accordingly allow for the respective kind of communication step. As an example consider Rule (cSO). In comparison to (comS), Rule (cSO) ensures that communications involving the content of an optional block are limited to two such contents of optional blocks with the same participants. This ensures that optional blocks describe the local view-points of the encapsulated protocol.

Optional blocks do not allow for scope extrusion of restricted names, i.e., a name restricted within an optional block cannot be transmitted nor can an optional block successfully be terminated if the computed result values are subject to a restriction from the content of the optional block. Also values that are communicated between optional blocks can be used only by the continuation of the optional block and only if the optional block was completed successfully. If an optional block fails while another process is still waiting for a communication within its optional block, the latter optional block is doomed to fail. Note that the semantics of optional blocks is inherently synchronous, since an optional sending operation can realise the failing of its matching receiver (e.g. by $\mathsf{opt}[r_1; fail; r_2]\langle \ldots [r_1]\langle ok\rangle\rangle(x).P)$. Let $\longmapsto^+$ denote the transitive closure of $\longmapsto$ and let $\longmapsto^*$ denote the reflexive and transitive closure of $\longmapsto$, respectively.

5   Well-Typed Processes

Now we connect types with processes by the notion of well-typedness. A process P is *well-typed* if it satisfies a typing judgement of the form $\Gamma \vdash P \triangleright \Delta$, i.e., under the *global environment* Γ, P is validated by the *session environment* Δ. We extend environments defined in [7] with a primitive for session environments.

Definition 6 (Environments).

$$\Gamma ::= \emptyset \quad | \quad \Gamma, a{:}T[r] \quad | \quad \Gamma, s{:}G$$
$$\Delta ::= \emptyset \quad | \quad \Delta, s[r]{:}T \quad | \quad \Delta, s[r]^{\bullet}{:}T \quad | \quad \Delta, r{:}\tilde{S}^{\uparrow}$$

The global environment Γ relates shared channels to the type of the invitation they carry and session channels s to the global type G they implement. $a{:}T[r]$ means that a is used to send and receive invitations to play role r with local type T. The session environment Δ relates pairs of session channels s and roles r to local types T, where $s[r]^{\bullet}{:}T$ denotes the permission to transmit the corresponding s. We add the declaration $r{:}\tilde{S}^{\uparrow}$, to cover the kinds of the return values of an optional block of the owner r. A session environment is *closed* if it does not contain declarations $r{:}\tilde{S}^{\uparrow}$. We assume that initially session environments do not contain declarations $r{:}\tilde{S}^{\uparrow}$, i.e., are closed. Such declarations are introduced while typing the content of an optional block. Whereby the typing rules ensure that environments can never contain more than one declaration $r{:}\tilde{S}^{\uparrow}$.

Let $(\Delta, s[r]{:}\mathsf{end}) = \Delta$. If $s[r]$ does not appear in Δ, we write $\Delta(s[r]) = 0$. Following [7] we assume an operator $\otimes$ such that (1) $\Delta \otimes \emptyset = \Delta$, (2) $\Delta_1 \otimes \Delta_2 =$

$\Delta_2 \otimes \Delta_1$, (3) $\Delta_1 \otimes \left(\Delta_2, \mathsf{r} : \tilde{\mathsf{S}}^\uparrow\right) = \left(\Delta_1, \mathsf{r} : \tilde{\mathsf{S}}^\uparrow\right) \otimes \Delta_2$, (4) $\Delta_1 \otimes (\Delta_2, s[\mathsf{r}] : T) = (\Delta_1, s[\mathsf{r}] : T) \otimes \Delta_2$ if $\Delta_1(s[\mathsf{r}]) = 0 = \Delta_2(s[\mathsf{r}])$, and (5) $(\Delta_1, s[\mathsf{r}] : T_1) \otimes (\Delta_2, s[\mathsf{r}] : T_2) = (\Delta_1, s[\mathsf{r}] : T_1 \parallel T_2) \otimes \Delta_2$. Thus $\otimes$ allows to split parallel parts of local types. We write $\vdash v : \mathsf{S}$ if value v is of kind S.

In Fig. 2 we extend the typing rules of [7] with the Rules (Opt) and (OptE) for optional blocks. (Opt) ensures that (1) the process and the local type specify the same set of roles $\tilde{\mathsf{r}} \doteq \tilde{\mathsf{r}}'$ as participants of the optional block, (2) the kinds of the default values $\tilde{v}$, the arguments $\tilde{x}$ of the continuation P', and the respective variables $\tilde{y}$ in the local type coincide, (3) the continuation P' is well-typed w.r.t. the part Δ' of the current session environment and the remainder T' of the local type of $s[\mathsf{r}_1]$, (4) the content P of the block is well-typed w.r.t. the session environment $\Delta, s[\mathsf{r}_1] : T, \mathsf{r}_1 : \tilde{\mathsf{S}}^\uparrow$, where $\mathsf{r}_1 : \tilde{\mathsf{S}}^\uparrow$ ensures that P computes return values of the kinds $\tilde{\mathsf{S}}$ if no failure occurs, and (5) the return values of a surrounding optional block cannot be returned in a nested block, because of the condition $\nexists \mathsf{r}'', \tilde{\mathsf{K}}. \ \mathsf{r}'' : \tilde{\mathsf{K}}^\uparrow \in \Delta$. (OptE) ensures that the kinds of the values computed by a successful completion of an optional block match the kinds of the respective default values. Apart from that this rule is similar to (N) in Fig. 2. Since (OptE) is the only way to consume an instance of $\mathsf{r} : \tilde{\mathsf{S}}^\uparrow$, this rule checks that—ignoring the possibility to fail—the content of an optional block reduces to $[\mathsf{r}]\langle \tilde{v}\rangle$, if the corresponding local type requires it to do so. Combining these rules, (Opt) introduces exactly one occurrence of $\mathsf{r} : \tilde{\mathsf{S}}^\uparrow$ in the session environment, the function $\otimes$ in (Pa) for parallel processes in Fig. 2 ensures that this occurrence reaches exactly one of the parallel branches of the content of the optional block, and finally only (OptE) allows to terminate a branch with this occurrence. This

$$(\text{I})\frac{\Gamma \vdash P \triangleright \Delta, x[\mathsf{r}] : T \quad \Gamma(a) = T[\mathsf{r}]}{\Gamma \vdash a(x).P \triangleright \Delta} \qquad (\text{O})\frac{\Gamma \vdash P \triangleright \Delta \quad \Gamma(a) = T[\mathsf{r}]}{\Gamma \vdash \overline{a}\langle s \rangle.P \triangleright \Delta, s[\mathsf{r}]^\bullet : T} \qquad (\text{N})\frac{}{\Gamma \vdash \mathbf{0} \triangleright \emptyset}$$

$$(\text{C})\frac{\left(\Gamma \vdash P_i \triangleright \Delta, k[\mathsf{r}_2] : T_i \quad \vdash \tilde{y}_i : \tilde{\mathsf{S}}_i\right)_{i \in I}}{\Gamma \vdash k?[\mathsf{r}_1, \mathsf{r}_2]_{i \in I}\left\{\, l_i(\tilde{y}_i).P_i \,\right\} \triangleright \Delta, k[\mathsf{r}_2] : \mathbf{get}[\mathsf{r}_1]?_{i \in I}\left\{\, l_i\left(\tilde{x}_i : \tilde{\mathsf{S}}_i\right).T_i \,\right\}}$$

$$(\text{S1})\frac{\Gamma \vdash P_1 \triangleright \Delta, s[\mathsf{r}] : T_1 \quad \Gamma \vdash P_2 \triangleright \Delta, s[\mathsf{r}] : T_2}{\Gamma \vdash P_1 + P_2 \triangleright \Delta, s[\mathsf{r}] : T_1 \oplus T_2} \qquad (\text{S2})\frac{\Gamma \vdash P \triangleright \Delta, s[\mathsf{r}] : T_i \quad i \in \{1, 2\}}{\Gamma \vdash P \triangleright \Delta, s[\mathsf{r}] : T_1 \oplus T_2}$$

$$(\text{S})\frac{\Gamma \vdash P \triangleright \Delta, k[\mathsf{r}_1] : T_j \quad \vdash \tilde{v} : \tilde{\mathsf{S}}_j}{\Gamma \vdash k![\mathsf{r}_1, \mathsf{r}_2]l_j\langle \tilde{v}\rangle.P \triangleright \Delta, k[\mathsf{r}_1] : \mathbf{send}[\mathsf{r}_2]!_{i \in I}\left\{\, l_i\left(\tilde{x}_i : \tilde{\mathsf{S}}_i\right).T_i \,\right\}}$$

$$(\text{Pa})\frac{\Gamma \vdash P_1 \triangleright \Delta_1 \quad \Gamma \vdash P_2 \triangleright \Delta_2}{\Gamma \vdash P_1 \mid P_2 \triangleright \Delta_1 \otimes \Delta_2} \qquad (\text{R})\frac{\Gamma, x : T[\mathsf{r}] \vdash P \triangleright \Delta}{\Gamma \vdash (\nu x)P \triangleright \Delta} \qquad (\text{OptE})\frac{\vdash \tilde{v} : \tilde{\mathsf{S}}}{\Gamma \vdash [\mathsf{r}]\langle \tilde{v}\rangle \triangleright \mathsf{r} : \tilde{\mathsf{S}}^\uparrow}$$

$$(\text{Opt})\frac{\tilde{\mathsf{r}} \doteq \tilde{\mathsf{r}}' \quad \Gamma \vdash P \triangleright \Delta, s[\mathsf{r}_1] : T, \mathsf{r}_1 : \tilde{\mathsf{S}}^\uparrow \quad \nexists \mathsf{r}'', \tilde{\mathsf{K}}. \ \mathsf{r}'' : \tilde{\mathsf{K}}^\uparrow \in \Delta \qquad \Gamma \vdash P' \triangleright \Delta', s[\mathsf{r}_1] : T' \quad \vdash \tilde{x} : \tilde{\mathsf{S}} \quad \vdash \tilde{v} : \tilde{\mathsf{S}}}{\Gamma \vdash \mathbf{opt}[\mathsf{r}_1; \tilde{v}; \tilde{\mathsf{r}}]\langle P\rangle(\tilde{x}).P' \triangleright \Delta \otimes \Delta', s[\mathsf{r}_1] : \mathbf{opt}[\tilde{\mathsf{r}}']\langle T\rangle\left(\tilde{y} : \tilde{\mathsf{S}}\right).T'}$$

Fig. 2. Typing rules

ensures that—ignoring the possibility to fail—each block computes exactly one vector of return values $[r]\langle \tilde{v} \rangle$ (or, more precisely, one such vector for each choice-branch). For an explanation of the remaining rules we refer to [2,3,7]. Applying these typing rules is elaborate but straightforward and can be automated easily, since for all processes except choice exactly one rule applies and all parameters except for restriction are determined by the respective process. Thus, the number of different proof-trees is determined by the number of choices and the type of restricted channels can be derived using back-tracking.

6 Properties of the Type Systems

Subject reduction is a basic property of each type system. It is this property that allows us to reason statically about terms, by ensuring that whenever a process its well-typed then all its derivatives are well-typed as well. Hence, for all properties the type system ensures for well-typed terms, it is not necessary to compute executions but only to test for well-typedness of the original term. We use a strong variant of subject reduction that additionally involves the condition $\Delta \mapsto \Delta'$, in order to capture how the local types evolve alongside the reduction of processes. Therefore the effect of reductions on processes on the corresponding local types is captured within $\mapsto$ that can be found in [1].

Following [7] we use coherence to prove progress and completion. A session environment is *coherent* if it is composed of the projections of well-formed global types. Most of the reduction rules preserve coherence. The failing of optional blocks can however temporary invalidate this property. A failing optional block is not a problem for the process itself, because the continuation of the process is instantiated with the default value and this process with a corresponding session environment corresponds to the projection of the global type of the continuation. But a failing optional block may cause another part of the network, i.e., a parallel process, to lose coherence. If another, parallel optional block is waiting for a communication with the former, it is doomed to fail. This situation of a single optional block without its dual communication partner cannot result from the projection of a global type. Due to the interleaving of steps, an execution starting in a process with a coherent session environment may lead to a state in which there are several single optional blocks at the same time. However, coherence ensures that for all such reachable processes there is a finite sequence of steps that restores coherence and thus ensures progress and completion. A session environment Δ is *initially coherent* if it is obtained from a coherent environment, i.e., $\Delta_0 \mapsto^* \Delta$ for some coherent Δ_0, and does not contain optional blocks without their counterparts.

Progress ensures that well-typed processes cannot get stuck unless their protocol requires them to. In comparison to standard formulations of progress, we add that the respective sequence of steps does not require any optional blocks to be unreliable. We define an optional block as *unreliable* w.r.t. to a sequence of steps if it does fail within this sequence and else as *reliant*. In other words we ensure progress despite arbitrary (and any number of) failures of optional blocks.

Completion is a special case of progress for processes without infinite recursions. It ensures that well-typed processes, without infinite recursion, follow their protocol and then terminate. Similarly to progress, we prove that completion holds despite arbitrary failures of optional blocks but does not require any optional block to be unreliable.

A simple but interesting consequence of this formulation of completion is, that for each well-typed process there is a sequence of steps that successfully resolves all optional blocks. This is because we type the content of optional blocks and because the type system ensures that these contents reach exactly one success reporting message $[r]\langle \tilde{v} \rangle$ in exactly one of its parallel branches (and in each of its choice branches).

Theorem 1 (Properties).

Subject Reduction: *If* $\Gamma \vdash P \triangleright \Delta$ *and* $P \longmapsto P'$ *then there exists* Δ' *such that* $\Gamma \vdash P' \triangleright \Delta'$ *and* $\Delta \mapsto^* \Delta'$.

Progress: *If* $\Gamma \vdash P \triangleright \Delta$ *such that* Δ *is initially coherent, then either* $P = \mathbf{0}$ *or there exists* P' *such that* $P \longmapsto^+ P'$, $\Gamma \vdash P' \triangleright \Delta'$, *where* $\Delta \mapsto^* \Delta'$ *and* Δ' *is coherent, and* $P \longmapsto^+ P'$ *does not require any optional block to be unreliable.*

Completion: *If* $\Gamma \vdash P \triangleright \Delta$ *such that* Δ *is initially coherent and* P *does not contain infinite recursions, then* $P \longmapsto^* \mathbf{0}$, $\Gamma \vdash \mathbf{0} \triangleright \emptyset$, *and* $P \longmapsto^* \mathbf{0}$ *does not require any optional block to be unreliable.*

Reliance: *If* $\Gamma \vdash P \triangleright \Delta$ *such that* Δ *is initially coherent and* P *does not contain infinite recursions, then* $P \longmapsto^* \mathbf{0}$ *such that all optional blocks are successfully resolved in this sequence.*

The proofs of these properties can be found in [1]. They basically follow the same line of argument as used for similar type systems involving elaborate but straightforward structural inductions over the sets of rules.

Session types usually also ensure *communication safety*, i.e., freedom of communication error, and *session fidelity*, i.e., a well-typed process exactly follows the specification described by its global type. With optional blocks we lose these properties, because they model failures. As a consequence communications may fail and whole parts of the specified protocol in the global type might be skipped. In order to still provide some guarantees on the behaviour of well-typed processes, we however limited the effect of failures by encapsulation in optional blocks. It is trivial to see, that in the failure-free case, i.e., if no optional block fails, we inherit communication safety and session fidelity from the underlying session types in [2,3,7]. Even in the case of failing optional blocks, we inherit communication safety and session fidelity for the parts of protocols outside of optional blocks and the inner parts of successful optional blocks, since our extension ensures that all optional blocks that depend on a failure are doomed to fail and the remaining parts work as specified by the global type.

7   Conclusions

We extend standard session types with optional blocks with default values. Thereby, we obtain a type system for progress and completion/termination despite link failures that can be used to reason about fault-tolerant distributed algorithms. Our approach is limited with respect to two aspects: We only cover algorithms that (1) allow us to specify default values for all unreliable communication steps and (2) terminate despite arbitrary link failures. Accordingly, this approach is only a first step towards the analysis of distributed algorithms with session types. It shows however that it is possible to analyse distributed algorithms with session types and how the latter can solve the otherwise often complicated and elaborate task of proving termination. Note that, optional blocks can contain larger parts of protocols than a single communication step. Thus they may also allow for more complicated failure patterns than simple link failures/message loss.

We extend a simple type system with optional blocks. The (for many distributed algorithms interesting) concept of rounds is obtained instead by using the more complicated nested protocols (as defined in [7]) with optional blocks. Due to lack of space, the type systems with nested protocols/sub-sessions and optional blocks as well as more interesting examples with and without explicit (and of course overlapping) rounds are postponed to [1]. However the inclusion of sub-session is straightforward and does not require to change the above concept of optional blocks. In combination with sub-sessions our attempt respects two important aspects of fault-tolerant distributed algorithms: (1) The modularity as e.g. present in the concept of rounds in many algorithms can be expressed naturally, and (2) the model respects the asynchronous nature of distributed systems such that messages are not necessarily delivered in the order they are sent and the rounds may overlap.

Our extension offers new possibilities for the analysis of distributed algorithms and widens the applicability of session types to unreliable network structures. We hope to inspire further work in particular to cover larger classes of algorithms and system failures.

References

1. Adameit, M., Peters, K., Nestmann, U.: Session types for link failures. Technical report, TU Berlin (2017). https://arxiv.org
2. Bettini, L., Coppo, M., D'Antoni, L., Luca, M., Dezani-Ciancaglini, M., Yoshida, N.: Global progress in dynamically interleaved multiparty sessions. In: Breugel, F., Chechik, M. (eds.) CONCUR 2008. LNCS, vol. 5201, pp. 418–433. Springer, Heidelberg (2008). doi:10.1007/978-3-540-85361-9_33
3. Bocchi, L., Honda, K., Tuosto, E., Yoshida, N.: A theory of design-by-contract for distributed multiparty interactions. In: Gastin, P., Laroussinie, F. (eds.) CONCUR 2010. LNCS, vol. 6269, pp. 162–176. Springer, Heidelberg (2010). doi:10.1007/978-3-642-15375-4_12
4. Capecchi, S., Giachino, E., Yoshida, N.: Global escape in multiparty sessions. Math. Struct. Comput. Sci. **26**(2), 156–205 (2016)
5. Carbone, M., Honda, K., Yoshida, N.: Structured interactional exceptions in session types. In: Breugel, F., Chechik, M. (eds.) CONCUR 2008. LNCS, vol. 5201, pp. 402–417. Springer, Heidelberg (2008). doi:10.1007/978-3-540-85361-9_32

6. Demangeon, R.: Nested protocols in session types. Personal communication about an extended version of [7] that is currently prepared by R. Demangeon (2015)
7. Demangeon, R., Honda, K.: Nested protocols in session types. In: Koutny, M., Ulidowski, I. (eds.) CONCUR 2012. LNCS, vol. 7454, pp. 272–286. Springer, Heidelberg (2012). doi:10.1007/978-3-642-32940-1_20
8. Kouzapas, D., Gutkovas, R., Gay, S.J.: Session types for broadcasting. In: Proceedings of PLACES. EPTCS, vol. 155, pp. 25–31 (2014)
9. Lynch, N.A.: Distributed Algorithms. Morgan Kaufmann, Burlington (1996)
10. Milner, R., Parrow, J., Walker, D.: A calculus of mobile processes, part I and II. Inf. Comput. **100**(1), 1–77 (1992)
11. Tel, G.: Introduction to Distributed Algorithms. Cambridge University Press, Cambridge (1994)

Learning-Based Compositional Parameter Synthesis for Event-Recording Automata

Étienne André[1]([✉]) and Shang-Wei Lin[2]

[1] Université Paris 13, LIPN, CNRS, UMR 7030, Villetaneuse, France
eandre93430@lipn13.fr
[2] SCSE, Nanyang Technological University, Singapore, Singapore

Abstract. We address the verification of timed concurrent systems with unknown or uncertain constants considered as parameters. First, we introduce parametric event-recording automata (PERAs), as a new subclass of parametric timed automata (PTAs). Although in the non-parametric setting event-recording automata yield better decidability results than timed automata, we show that the most common decision problem remains undecidable for PERAs. Then, given one set of components with parameters and one without, we propose a method to compute an abstraction of the non-parametric set of components, so as to improve the verification of reachability properties in the full (parametric) system. We also show that our method can be extended to general PTAs. We implemented our method, which shows promising results.

1 Introduction

Verifying distributed systems involving timing constraints is notoriously difficult, especially when timing constants may be uncertain. This problems becomes even more difficult (often intractable) in the presence of timing parameters, unknown timing constants. Parametric reachability synthesis aims at synthesizing timing parameter valuations for which a set of (usually bad) states is reachable. Parametric timed automata (PTAs) [2] is a parametric extension of timed automata (TAs) to model and verify models involving (possibly parametric) timing constraints and concurrency. Its high expressiveness comes with the drawback that most interesting problems are undecidable [3].

Related Work. Despite undecidability of the theoretical problems, several monolithic (non-compositional) techniques for parametric reachability synthesis in PTAs have been proposed in the past, either in the form of semi-algorithms (a procedure that is correct but may not terminate), or using approximations. In [2], a basic semi-algorithm (called EFsynth in [14]) has been proposed: it explores

This work is partially supported by the ANR national research program "PACS" (ANR-14-CE28-0002).

A. Bouajjani and A. Silva (Eds.): FORTE 2017, LNCS 10321, pp. 17–32, 2017.
DOI: 10.1007/978-3-319-60225-7_2

the symbolic state space until bad states are found, and gathers the associated parameter constraints. In [12], approximated parametric reachability synthesis is performed using counter-example guided abstraction refinement (CEGAR) techniques for parametric linear hybrid automata, a class of models more expressive than PTAs. In [7], we proposed a point-based technique: instead of attacking the reachability synthesis in a brute-force manner, we iterate on (some) integer parameter valuations, and derive for each of them a constraint around this valuation that preserves the (non-)reachability of the bad locations. Although numerous iterations may be needed, each of them explores a much smaller part of the state space than the brute-force exploration of EFsynth, often resulting in a faster execution than EFsynth.

Distributed systems are often made of a set of components interacting with each other; taking advantage of the compositionality is a goal often desired to speed up verification. In [11], a learning-based approach is proposed to automate compositional verification of untimed systems modeled by labeled transition systems (LTS). For timed systems, we proposed a learning-based compositional verification framework [15] for event-recording automata (ERAs), a subclass of TAs for which language inclusion is decidable [1]. This approach showed to be much faster than monolithic verification.

The recent work [9] is close to our goal, as it proposes an approach for compositional parameter synthesis, based on the derivation of interaction and component invariants. The method is implemented in a prototype in Scala, making use of IMITATOR [5]. Whereas both [9] and our approach address reachability or safety properties, the class of PTAs of [9] is larger; conversely, we add no further restrictions on the models, whereas in [9] all clocks and (more problematically) parameters must be local to a single component and cannot be shared.

Contribution. In this work, we propose an approach relying on a point-based technique for parametric reachability synthesis, combined with learning-based abstraction techniques, for a subclass of PTAs, namely parametric event-recording automata. We propose this subclass due to the decidability of the language inclusion in the non-parametric setting. We consider a set of parametric components A (where parameters are dense in a bounded parameter domain D_0) and a set of non-parametric components B, with their parallel composition denoted by A $\parallel$ B. For each integer parameter valuation v not yet covered by a good or bad constraint, we try to compute, by learning, an abstraction $\widetilde{B}$ of B s.t. $v(A) \parallel$ B does not reach the bad locations. We then "enlarge" the valuation v using the abstract model A $\parallel \widetilde{B}$, which yields a dense good constraint; we prove the correctness of this approach. If the learning fails to compute an abstraction, we derive a counter-example, and we then replay it in the fully parametric model A $\parallel$ B, which allows us to derive very quickly a bad dense constraint. We iterate until (at least) all integer points in D_0 are covered. In practice, we cover not only all rational-valued in D_0, but in fact the entire parameter space (except for one benchmark for which we fail to compute a suitable abstraction).

We propose the following technical contributions:

1. we introduce a parametrization of event-recording automata (PERAs);
2. we show that the reachability emptiness problem is undecidable for PERAs;
3. we then introduce our approach that combines iteration-based synthesis with learning-based abstraction;
4. we implement our approach into a toolkit using IMITATOR and CV, and we demonstrate its efficiency on several case studies.

Outline. Section 2 introduces the necessary preliminaries. Section 3 recalls the parametric reachability preservation [7]. Section 4 introduces parametric event-recording automata, and proves the undecidability of the reachability emptiness problem. Section 5 introduces our main contribution, and Sect. 6 evaluates it on benchmarks. Section 7 concludes the paper.

2   Preliminaries

2.1   Clocks, Parameters and Constraints

Let $\mathbb{N}$, $\mathbb{Z}$, $\mathbb{Q}_+$ and $\mathbb{R}_+$ denote the sets of non-negative integers, integers, non-negative rational and non-negative real numbers respectively.

Throughout this paper, we assume a set $X = \{x_1, \ldots, x_H\}$ of *clocks*, real-valued variables that evolve at the same rate. A clock valuation is a function $\mu : X \rightarrow \mathbb{R}_+$. We write $\mathbf{0}$ for the clock valuation that assigns 0 to all clocks. Given $d \in \mathbb{R}_+$, $\mu + d$ denotes the valuation such that $(\mu + d)(x) = \mu(x) + d$, for all $x \in X$. Given $R \subseteq X$, we define the *reset* of a valuation μ, denoted by $[\mu]_R$, as follows: $[\mu]_R(x) = 0$ if $x \in R$, and $[\mu]_R(x) = \mu(x)$ otherwise.

We assume a set $P = \{p_1, \ldots, p_M\}$ of *parameters*, unknown rational-valued constants. A parameter *valuation* (or *point*) v is a function $v : P \rightarrow \mathbb{Q}_+$.

In the following, we assume $\lhd \in \{<, \leq\}$ and $\bowtie \in \{<, \leq, \geq, >\}$. Throughout this paper, lt denotes a linear term over $X \cup P$ of the form $\sum_{1 \leq i \leq H} \alpha_i x_i + \sum_{1 \leq j \leq M} \beta_j p_j + d$, with $\alpha_i, \beta_j, d \in \mathbb{Z}$. Similarly, plt denotes a parametric linear term over P, that is a linear term without clocks ($\alpha_i = 0$ for all i). A *constraint* C (a convex polyhedron) over $X \cup P$ is a conjunction of inequalities of the form $lt \bowtie 0$. Given a parameter valuation v, $v(C)$ denotes the constraint over X obtained by replacing each parameter p in C with $v(p)$. Likewise, given a clock valuation μ, $\mu(v(C))$ denotes the Boolean value obtained by replacing each clock x in $v(C)$ with $\mu(x)$.

A *guard* g is a constraint over $X \cup P$ defined by a conjunction of inequalities of the form $x \bowtie plt$.

A parameter constraint K is a constraint over P. We write $v \models K$ if $v(K)$ evaluates to true. $\perp$ (resp. $\top$) denotes the special parameter constraint containing no (resp. all) parameter valuations. We will sometime manipulate *non-convex* constraints over P, finite unions of parameter constraints. Such non-convex constraints can be implemented using finite lists of constraints, and therefore all definitions extend in a natural manner to non-convex constraints.

A *parameter domain* is a box parameter constraint, a conjunction of inequalities of the form $p \bowtie d$, with $d \in \mathbb{N}$. A parameter domain D is *bounded* if, for each parameter, there exists in D an inequality $p \lhd d$ (recall that, additionally, all parameters are bounded below from 0 as they are non-negative). Therefore D can be seen as a hypercube in M dimensions.

2.2 Parametric Timed Automata

Definition 1 (PTA). *A parametric timed automaton (hereafter PTA)* A *is a tuple* $(\Sigma, L, l_0, X, P, I, E)$, *where: (i)* Σ *is a finite set of actions, (ii)* L *is a finite set of locations, (iii)* $l_0 \in L$ *is the initial location, (iv)* X *is a finite set of clocks, (v)* P *is a finite set of parameters, (vi)* I *is the invariant, assigning to every* $l \in L$ *a guard* $I(l)$, *(vii)* E *is a finite set of edges* $e = (l, g, a, R, l')$ *where* $l, l' \in L$ *are the source and target locations,* $a \in \Sigma$, $R \subseteq X$ *is a set of clocks to be reset, and* g *is a guard.*

Given a PTA A and a parameter valuation v, we denote by $v(\mathsf{A})$ the non-parametric timed automaton where all occurrences of a parameter p_i have been replaced by $v(p_i)$.

As usual, PTAs can be composed by performing their parallel composition, their synchronized product on action names.

Definition 2 (Concrete semantics). *Given a PTA* $\mathsf{A} = (\Sigma, L, l_0, X, P, I, E)$, *and a parameter valuation* v, *the concrete semantics of* $v(\mathsf{A})$ *is given by the timed transition system* $(S, s_0, \rightarrow)$, *with* $S = \{(l, \mu) \in L \times \mathbb{R}_+^H \mid \mu(v(I(l))) \text{ is true}\}$, $s_0 = (l_0, \mathbf{0})$, *and* $\rightarrow$ *consists of the discrete and delay transition relations:*

- *discrete transitions:* $(l, \mu) \xrightarrow{e} (l', \mu')$, *if* $(l, \mu), (l', \mu') \in S$, *there exists* $e = (l, g, a, R, l') \in E$, $\mu' = [\mu]_R$, *and* $\mu(v(g))$ *is true.*
- *delay transitions:* $(l, \mu) \xrightarrow{d} (l, \mu + d)$, *with* $d \in \mathbb{R}_+$, *if* $\forall d' \in [0, d], (l, \mu + d') \in S$.

A *(concrete) run* is a sequence $\rho = s_0 \gamma_0 s_1 \gamma_1 \cdots s_n \gamma_n \cdots$ such that $\forall i, (s_i, \gamma_i, s_{i+1}) \in \rightarrow$. We consider as usual that concrete runs strictly alternate delays d_i and discrete transitions e_i and we thus write concrete runs in the form $\rho = s_0 \xrightarrow{(d_0, e_0)} s_1 \xrightarrow{(d_1, e_1)} \cdots$. The corresponding *timed word* is $(a_0, t_0), (a_1, t_1), \cdots$ where a_i is the action of e_i and $t_i = \sum_{j=0}^{i} d_j$. Given a state $s = (l, \mu)$, we say that s is reachable (or that $v(\mathsf{A})$ reaches s) if s belongs to a run of $v(\mathsf{A})$. By extension, we say that l is reachable in $v(\mathsf{A})$, if there exists a state (l, μ) that is reachable. Given $L^\circledcirc \subseteq L$, we say that $L^\circledcirc$ is reachable in $v(\mathsf{A})$ if $\exists l \in L^\circledcirc$ s.t. l is reachable.

Let $\rho = (l_0, \mu_0) \xrightarrow{(d_0, e_0)} (l_1, \mu_1) \xrightarrow{(d_1, e_1)} \cdots (l_n, \mu_n) \xrightarrow{(d_n, e_n)} \cdots$ be a run of $v(\mathsf{A})$. The *trace* of this run (denoted by $trace(\rho)$) is the sequence $e_0 e_1 \cdots e_n \cdots$, and the *untimed word* of this run is $a_0 a_1 \cdots a_n \cdots$, where a_i is the action of e_i for all i. The *trace set* of $v(\mathsf{A})$ is the set of traces associated with all runs of A.

Symbolic Semantics. Let us recall the symbolic semantics of PTAs (as in e.g., [4,14]). We define the *time elapsing* of a constraint C, denoted by $C^\nearrow$, as the constraint over X and P obtained from C by delaying all clocks by an arbitrary amount of time. That is, $C^{\nearrow} = \{(\mu, v) \mid \mu \models v(C) \land \forall x \in X : \mu'(x) = \mu(x) + d, d \in \mathbb{R}_+\}$. Given $R \subseteq X$, we define the *reset* of C, denoted by $[C]_R$, as the constraint obtained from C by resetting the clocks in R, and keeping the other clocks unchanged. We denote by $C{\downarrow}_P$ the projection of C onto P, obtained by eliminating the clock variables (e. g., using Fourier-Motzkin).

A *parametric zone* is a convex polyhedron over $X \cup P$ in which constraints are of the form $x \bowtie plt$, or $x_i - x_j \bowtie plt$, where $x_i, x_j \in X$ and plt is a parametric linear term over P.

A *symbolic state* is a pair $\mathbf{s} = (l, C)$ where $l \in L$ is a location, and C its associated parametric zone. The initial symbolic state of A is $\mathbf{s}_0 = (l_0, (\{\mathbf{0}\} \land I(l_0))^{\nearrow} \land I(l_0))$.

The symbolic semantics relies on the Succ operation. Given a symbolic state $\mathbf{s} = (l, C)$ and an edge $e = (l, g, a, R, l')$, $\mathsf{Succ}(\mathbf{s}, e) = (l', C')$, with $C' = ([(C \land g)]_R \land I(l'))^{\nearrow} \land I(l')$. The Succ operation is effectively computable, using polyhedra operations; also note that the successor of a parametric zone C is a parametric zone (see e. g., [14]).

A *symbolic run* of a PTA is an alternating sequence of symbolic states and edges starting from the initial symbolic state, of the form $\mathbf{s}_0 \overset{e_0}{\Rightarrow} \mathbf{s}_1 \overset{e_1}{\Rightarrow} \cdots \overset{e_{m-1}}{\Rightarrow} \mathbf{s}_m$, such that for all $i = 0, \ldots, m-1$, we have $e_i \in E$, and $\mathbf{s}_{i+1} = \mathsf{Succ}(\mathbf{s}_i, e_i)$.

Given a symbolic run $\mathbf{s}_0 \overset{e_0}{\Rightarrow} \mathbf{s}_1 \overset{e_1}{\Rightarrow} \cdots$, its *trace* is the sequence $e_0 e_1 \cdots$. Two runs (symbolic or concrete) are *equivalent* if they have the same trace.

3   Parametric Reachability Preservation

Let us briefly recall the parametric reachability preservation algorithm PRP [7]. Given a set of locations $L^{\ominus}$, $\mathsf{PRP}(\mathsf{A}, v, L^{\ominus})$ synthesizes a dense (convex) constraint K containing at least v and such that, for all $v' \in K$, $v'(\mathsf{A})$ preserves the reachability of $L^{\ominus}$ in $v(\mathsf{A})$. By preserving the reachability of $L^{\ominus}$ in $v(\mathsf{A})$, we mean that some locations of $L^{\ominus}$ are reachable in $v'(\mathsf{A})$ iff they are in $v(\mathsf{A})$. That is, if $v(\mathsf{A})$ is safe (it does not reach $L^{\ominus}$), then $v'(\mathsf{A})$ is safe too. Conversely, if $v(\mathsf{A})$ is unsafe ($L^{\ominus}$ is reachable for some runs), then $v'(\mathsf{A})$ is unsafe too.

Lemma 1 (Soundness of PRP [7]). *Let A be a PTA, v a parameter valuation, and $L^{\ominus}$ a subset of locations. Let $K = \mathsf{PRP}(\mathsf{A}, v, L^{\ominus})$.*

For all $v' \models K$, $v'(\mathsf{A})$ reaches $L^{\ominus}$ iff $v(\mathsf{A})$ reaches $L^{\ominus}$.

A specificity of PRP is that it does *not* aim at completeness; instead, it focuses on behaviors "similar" to that of $v(\mathsf{A})$ so as not to explore a too large part of the state space, and outputs valuations neighboring v. A sort of completeness can be achieved by iterating PRP on various parameter valuations: when $v(\mathsf{A})$ has computed K, the algorithm can be called again on a valuation v_2 "neighbor" of the result K, and so on until either the entire parameter space has been covered, or when a certain coverage of a bounded parameter domain has been achieved (e. g., 99 %). This iterated version is called PRPC (for PRP cartography), takes as input a PTA A and a bounded parameter domain D_0, and iteratively calls PRP on parameter valuations of D_0 with a given precision (e. g., at least all integer-valued). This gives a cartography of D_0 with a union K_{good} of safe constraints (valuations for which $L^\oplus$ is unreachable) and a union K_{bad} of unsafe constraints (for which $L^\oplus$ is reachable). Although only the coverage of the discrete points (e. g., integer-valued) can be theoretically guaranteed, PRPC often covers most (if not all) of the dense state space within D_0, and often outside too.

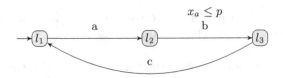

Fig. 1. An example of a PERA

4   Parametric Event-Recording Automata

Event-recording automata (ERAs) [1] are a subclass of timed automata, where each action label is associated with a clock such that, for every edge with a label, the associated clock is reset. We propose here a parametric extension of ERAs, following the parameterization of TAs into PTAs.

Formally, let Σ be a set of actions: we denote by X_Σ the set of clocks associated with Σ, $\{x_a \mid a \in \Sigma\}$. A Σ-guard is a guard on $X_\Sigma \cup P$.

Definition 3 (PERAs). *A parametric event-recording automaton (PERA) is a tuple $(\Sigma, L, l_0, P, I, E)$, where: (i) Σ is a finite set of actions, (ii) L is a finite set of locations, (iii) $l_0 \in L$ is the initial location, (iv) P is a finite set of parameters, (v) I is the invariant, assigning to every $l \in L$ a Σ-guard $I(l)$, (vi) E is a finite set of edges $e = (l, g, a, x_a, l')$ where $l, l' \in L$ are the source and target locations, $a \in \Sigma$, x_a is the clock to be reset, and g is a Σ-guard.*

Just as for ERAs, PERAs can be seen as a syntactic subclass of PTAs: a PERA is a PTA for which there is a one-to-one matching between clocks and actions and such that, for each edge, the clock corresponding to the action is the only clock to be reset.

Following the conventions used for ERAs, we do not explicitly represent graphically the clock x_a reset along an edge labeled with a: this is implicit.

Example 1. Figure 1 depicts an example of PERA with 3 actions (and therefore 3 clocks x_a, x_b and x_c), and one parameter p. Only clock x_a is used in a guard.

It is well-known that the EF-emptiness problem ("is the set of parameter valuations for which it is possible to reach a given location empty?") is undecidable for PTAs [2,6]. Reusing the proof of [6], we show below that this remains undecidable for PERAs.

Theorem 1. *The EF-emptiness problem is undecidable for PERAs, even with bounded parameters.*

Proof. The proof works by adapting to PERAs the proof of [6, Theorem 1].

This negative result rules out the possibility to perform exact synthesis for PERAs. Still, in the next section, we propose an approach that is sound, though maybe not complete: the synthesized valuations are correct, but some may be missing. More pragmatically, we aim at improving the synthesis efficiency.

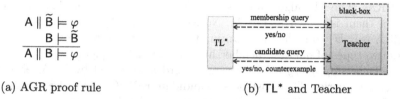

(a) AGR proof rule   (b) TL* and Teacher

Fig. 2. AGR proof rule (left) and TL* (right)

5   Compositional Parameter Synthesis for PERAs

Figure 2a recalls the common proof rule used in Assume-Guarantee Reasoning (AGR), which is one of the compositional verification techniques. Given two components A, B and a safety property φ, the proof rule tells us that if A can satisfy the property φ under an assumption $\tilde{B}$ and B can guarantee this assumption $\tilde{B}$, then we can conclude that A ∥ B satisfies φ.

5.1   Partitioning the System

The proof rule is presented in the context of two components. If a system consists of more than two components, an intuitive way is to partition the components into two groups to fit the proof rule. For example, if we have four components M_1, M_2, M_3, and M_4, we could partition them as A = M_1 ∥ M_2 and B = M_3 ∥ M_4. However, the number of possible partitions is exponential to the number of components. In addition, an investigation [10] showed that a good partition is very critical to AGR because it affects the verification performance significantly. In this work, we adopt the following heuristics:

1. If a component has timing parameters, it is collected in group A;
2. If a component shares common action labels with the property, the component is collected in group A.

Other components are collected in group B.

Heuristics 1 is required for our approach to be sound. Concerning heuristics 2, in AGR, the ideal case is when A satisfies the property with the weakest assumption $\widetilde{\mathsf{B}}$ that allows everything, A itself is sufficient to prove the property no matter how B behaves. Based on this observation, the rationale behind heuristics 2 is that if a component shares common action labels with the property, it is very likely to be necessary to prove the property. We will show that heuristics 2 indeed yields good performance in practice.

5.2   Computing an Abstraction via Learning

Let us explain how to automatically generate $\widetilde{\mathsf{B}}$ by learning for non-parametric timed systems. We adopt the TL* algorithm [15], which is a learning algorithm to infer ERAs. The TL* algorithm has to interact with a teacher. The interaction between them is shown in Fig. 2b. Notice that only the teacher knows about the ERA (say U) to be learned. During the learning process, the TL* algorithm makes two types of queries: membership and candidate queries.

A *membership query* asks whether a word is accepted by U. After several membership queries, TL* constructs a candidate ERA C, and makes a candidate query for it. A *candidate query* asks whether an ERA accepts the same timed language as U. If the teacher answers "yes", then the learning process is finished, and C is the ERA learned by TL*. If the candidate C accepts more (or less) timed words than U, the teacher answers "no" with a counterexample run ρ. TL* will refine the candidate ERA based on the counterexamples provided by the teacher until the answer to the candidate query is "yes". See [15] for details.

The two condition checkings in Fig. 3 ($\mathsf{A} \parallel \mathsf{C} \models \varphi$ and $\mathsf{B} \models \mathsf{C}$) can be done by model checking, and counterexamples given by model checking can also serve as counterexamples to the TL* algorithm. Figure 3 shows our overall procedure LearnAbstr(B, A, φ) that returns either an assumption (denoted by Abstraction($\widetilde{\mathsf{B}}$)) when it is proved that $\mathsf{A} \parallel \mathsf{B} \models \varphi$ holds, or a counterexample (denoted by Counterex(τ)) otherwise. Counterex and Abstraction are "tags" containing a value, in the spirit of data exchanged in distributed programming or types in functional programming; these tags will be used later on to differentiate between the two kinds of results output by LearnAbstr. Also note that, in our setting, we need a counterexample in the form of a trace τ, which is why LearnAbstr returns Counterex($trace(\rho)$).

Lemma 2. *Let* A, B *be two ERAs. Assume* LearnAbstr(B, A, φ) *terminates with result* Abstraction($\widetilde{\mathsf{B}}$). *Then* $\mathsf{A} \parallel \widetilde{\mathsf{B}} \models \varphi$ *and* $\mathsf{A} \parallel \mathsf{B} \models \varphi$.

Proof. Abstraction($\widetilde{\mathsf{B}}$) is returned only if $\mathsf{A} \parallel \widetilde{\mathsf{B}} \models \varphi$ and $\mathsf{B} \models \widetilde{\mathsf{B}}$. Thus, $\mathsf{A} \parallel \widetilde{\mathsf{B}} \models \varphi$ holds. In addition, according to Fig. 2a, we can conclude that $\mathsf{A} \parallel \mathsf{B} \models \varphi$. ∎

5.3   Replaying a Trace

In this section, we explain how to synthesize the exact set of parameter valuations for which a finite trace belongs to the trace set.

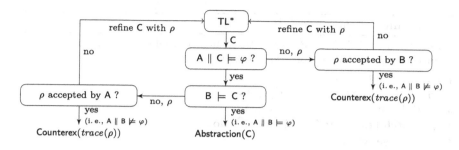

Fig. 3. LearnAbstr(B, A, φ)

Algorithm 1. ReplayTrace(A, τ)

---

input : PTA A, finite trace $\tau = e_0, e_1, \cdots e_{n-1}$
output : Constraint over the parameters

1 s = s_0
2 **for** $i = 0$ to $n - 1$ **do** s $\leftarrow$ Succ(s, e_i) ;
3 **return** s$\downarrow_P$

Replaying a trace is close to two undecidable problems for PTAs: *(i)* the reachability of a location is undecidable for PTAs [2], and therefore this result trivially extends to the reachability of a single edge; *(ii)* the emptiness of the set of valuations for which the set of untimed words is the same as a given valuation is undecidable for PTAs [8] (where a proof is provided even for a *unique* untimed word). Nevertheless, computing the set of parameter valuations for which a given *finite* trace belongs to the trace set can be done easily by exploring a small part of the symbolic state space as follows.

We give our procedure ReplayTrace(A, τ) in Algorithm 1. Basically, Replay-Trace computes the symbolic run equivalent to τ, and returns the projection onto P of the last symbolic state of that run. The correctness of ReplayTrace comes from the following results (proved in, e. g., [13]):

Lemma 3. *Let* A *be a PTA, and let* ρ *be a run of* A *reaching* (l, C). *Let* v *be a parameter valuation. There exists an equivalent run in* v(A) *iff* $v \models C\downarrow_P$.

Proof. From [13, Propositions 3.17 and 3.18].

Lemma 4. *Let* A *be a PTA, let* v *be a parameter valuation. Let* ρ *be a run of* v(A) *reaching* (l, μ). *Then there exists an equivalent symbolic run in* A *reaching* (l, C), *with* $v \models C\downarrow_P$.

Proof. From [13, Proposition 3.18].

Proposition 1. *Let* A *be a PTA, let* τ *a trace of* v_0(A) *for some* v_0. *Let* $K =$ ReplayTrace(A, τ). *Then, for all* v, τ *is a trace of* v(A) *iff* $v \models K$.

Algorithm 2. CompSynth($A, B, D_0, L^\circleddash$)

input : PERA A, ERA B, parameter domain D_0, subset $L^\circleddash$ of locations
output : Good and bad constraint over the parameters

1 $K_{bad} \leftarrow \perp$; $K_{good} \leftarrow \perp$
2 while $D_0 \cap \mathbb{N} \cap (K_{bad} \cup K_{good}) \neq \emptyset$ do
3 $\quad$ Pick v in $D_0 \cap \mathbb{N} \cap (K_{bad} \cup K_{good})$
4 $\quad$ switch LearnAbstr(B, v(A), $AG\neg L^\circleddash$) do
5 $\quad\quad$ case Abstraction($\widetilde{B}$)
6 $\quad\quad\quad$ $K_{good} \leftarrow K_{good} \cup$ PRP(A $\|$ $\widetilde{B}, v, L^\circleddash$)
7 $\quad\quad$ case Counterex(τ)
8 $\quad\quad\quad$ $K_{bad} \leftarrow K_{bad} \cup$ ReplayTrace(A $\|$ B, τ)

9 return (K_{good}, K_{bad})

Proof. τ is a trace of v_0(A) for some v_0, and therefore it corresponds to some run ρ of v_0(A). Then from Lemma 4 there exists an equivalent symbolic run in A reaching (l, C), with $v_0 \models C{\downarrow}_P$. Now, from Lemma 3, for all v, there exists an equivalent run in v(A) iff $v \models C{\downarrow}_P$. As ReplayTrace(A, τ) returns exactly $K = C{\downarrow}_P$ therefore τ is a trace of v(A) iff $v \models K$.

5.4 Exploiting the Abstraction and Performing Parameter Synthesis

We give our procedure in Algorithm 2: it takes as arguments a set of PERA components A, a set of ERA components B, a bounded parameter domain D_0 and a set of locations to be avoided. We maintain a safe non-convex parameter constraint K_{good} and an unsafe non-convex parameter constraint K_{bad}, both initially containing no valuations (line 1). Then CompSynth iterates on integer points: while not all integer points in D_0 are covered, do not belong to $K_{bad} \cup K_{good}$ (line 2), such an uncovered point v is picked (line 3). Then, we try to learn an abstraction of B w.r.t. v(A) (line 5) so that $L^\circleddash$ is unreachable ("$AG\neg L^\circleddash$" stands for "no run should ever reach $L^\circleddash$"). If an abstraction is successfully learned, then PRP is called on v and the abstract model A $\|$ $\widetilde{B}$ (line 6); the constraint K_{good} is then refined. Note that K_{good} is refined because, if an abstraction is computed, then necessarily the property is satisfied and therefore the (abstract) system is safe. Alternatively, if LearnAbstr fails to compute a valid abstraction, then a counterexample trace τ is returned (line 7); then this trace is replayed using ReplayTrace (line 8), and the constraint K_{bad} is updated.

5.5 Soundness

Proposition 2 (soundness). *Let* A $\|$ B *be a PERA and* D_0 *be a bounded parameter domain. Assume* CompSynth(A, B, $D_0, L^\circleddash$) *terminates with result* (K_{good}, K_{bad}).

Then, for all v (i) if $v \models K_{good}$ then $v(\mathsf{A} \parallel \mathsf{B})$ does not reach $L^{\circledcirc}$; (ii) if $v \models K_{bad}$ then $v(\mathsf{A} \parallel \mathsf{B})$ reaches $L^{\circledcirc}$.

Proof.

(i) Assume $v \models K_{good}$. From Algorithm 2, K_{good} is a finite union of convex constraints, each of them being the result of a call to PRP. Necessarily, $v \models K$, where K is one of these convex constraints, resulting from a call to $(\mathsf{A} \parallel \widetilde{\mathsf{B}}, v')$, for some v'. From Lemma 2, $v'(\mathsf{A}) \parallel \widetilde{\mathsf{B}} \models (AG\neg L^{\circledcirc})$. Since B and $\widetilde{\mathsf{B}}$ are non-parametric, we can write $v'(\mathsf{A} \parallel \widetilde{\mathsf{B}}) \models (AG\neg L^{\circledcirc})$, $v'(\mathsf{A} \parallel \widetilde{\mathsf{B}})$ does not reach $L^{\circledcirc}$. From Lemma 1, for all $v'' \models K$, $v''(\mathsf{A} \parallel \widetilde{\mathsf{B}})$ does not reach $L^{\circledcirc}$. Now, since $\widetilde{\mathsf{B}}$ is a valid abstraction of B (B $\models \widetilde{\mathsf{B}}$), therefore $\widetilde{\mathsf{B}}$ contains more behaviors than B. Therefore for all $v'' \models K$, $v''(\mathsf{A} \parallel \mathsf{B})$ does not reach $L^{\circledcirc}$ either. Since $v \models K$, therefore $v(\mathsf{A} \parallel \mathsf{B})$ does not reach $L^{\circledcirc}$.

(ii) Assume $v \models K_{bad}$. From Algorithm 2, K_{bad} is a finite union of convex constraints, each of them being the result of a call to ReplayTrace. Necessarily, $v \models K$, where K is one of these convex constraints, resulting from a call to ReplayTrace($\mathsf{A} \parallel \mathsf{B}, \tau$) for some trace τ reaching $L^{\circledcirc}$. This trace was generated by LearnAbstr for some v' and is a valid counter-example, this trace τ reaches $L^{\circledcirc}$ in $v'(\mathsf{A}) \parallel \mathsf{B}$. From Lemma 4, this trace is also a trace reaching $L^{\circledcirc}$ in $\mathsf{A} \parallel \mathsf{B}$. Then, from Proposition 1, for all $v'' \models K$, τ is a valid trace of $v''(\mathsf{A} \parallel \mathsf{B})$ which reaches $L^{\circledcirc}$ and therefore $v''(\mathsf{A} \parallel \mathsf{B})$ reaches $L^{\circledcirc}$. Since $v \models K$, then $v(\mathsf{A} \parallel \mathsf{B})$ reaches $L^{\circledcirc}$.

Proposition 3 (integer-completeness). *Let A be a PERA and D_0 be a bounded parameter domain. Assume* CompSynth$(\mathsf{A}, \mathsf{B}, D_0, L^{\circledcirc})$ *terminates with result* (K_{good}, K_{bad}).
Then, for all $v \in D_0 \cap \mathbb{N}$, $v \in K_{good} \cup K_{bad}$.

Proof. From Algorithm 2 (line 2).

Remark 1. Note that the integerness can be scaled down to, e. g., multiples of 0.1, or in fact arbitrarily small numbers. The time needed to perform the verification might grow, but the coverage of all these discrete points is still guaranteed.

6 Experiments

6.1 Handling General PTAs

So far, we showed that our framework is sound for PERAs. We now show that, since we address only reachability, any PTA can be transformed into an equivalent PERA, and therefore our framework is much more general. The idea is that, since we are interested in reachability properties, we can rename some of the actions so that the PTA becomes a PERA.

Basically, we remove any action labels along the edges, and we add them back as follows: *(1)* if clock x is reset along an edge, the action label will be a_x; *(2)* if no clock is reset along an edge, the action label will be na, where na is a (unique) label, the clock associated to which (say x_{na}) is never used (in guards and invariants) in the PERA; note that, by definition, x_{na} is reset along each edge labeled with na (although this has no impact in the PERA); *(3)* if more than one clock is reset along the edge, we split the edge into 2 consecutive edges in 0-time, where each clock is reset after the other, following the mechanism described above. Note that the 0-time can be ensured using an invariant $x \leq 0$, where x is the first clock to be reset.

Basically, our transformation leaves the structure of the PTA unchanged (with the exception of a few transitions in 0-time to simulate multiple simultaneous clock resets). For each parameter valuation, the resulting PERA has the same timed language as the original PTA – up to action renaming and with the introduction of some 0-time transitions (that could be considered as silent transitions if the language really mattered). Therefore, reachability is preserved.

Note that this construction provides an alternative proof for Theorem 1.

Example 2. Figure 4a shows a PTA, and Fig. 4b its translation into an equivalent PERA. (Recall that clock resets are implicit in PERAs.)

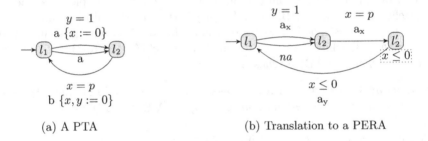

(a) A PTA   (b) Translation to a PERA

Fig. 4. General PTA and its translation to a PERA

Remark 2. In our benchmarks, although we only address reachability, action labels are not entirely useless: they are often used for action synchronization between components. Therefore, renaming all actions is not a valid transformation, as components may not synchronize anymore the way it was expected. In fact, we ensured that our models either only work using interleaving (no action synchronization) or, when various components of a PTA synchronize on an action label, at most one clock is reset along that transition for all PTAs synchronizing on this action label.

6.2   Experiments

We implemented our method in a toolkit made of the following components:

- IMITATOR [5] is a state of the art tool for verifying real-time systems modeled by an extension of PTAs with stopwatches, broadcast synchronization and integer-valued shared variables. IMITATOR is implemented in OCaml, and the polyhedra operations rely on the Parma Polyhedra Library (PPL).

- CV (Compositional Verifier) is a prototype implementation (in C++) of the proposed learning-based compositional verification framework for ERAs.

The architecture of our toolkit is shown in Fig. 5. The leading tool is IMITATOR, that takes the input model (in the IMITATOR input format), and eventually outputs the result. IMITATOR implements both algorithms CompSynth and ReplayTrace, while CV implements LearnAbstr. The interface between both tools is handled by a Python script, that is responsible for retrieving the abstraction of B computed by CV and re-parameterizing the components A. We used IMITATOR 2.9-alpha1, build 2212.[1] Experiments were run on a MacBook Pro with an i7 CPU 2.67 GHz and 3,7 GiB memory running Kubuntu 14.04 64 bits.

Benchmarks. We evaluated our approach using several benchmarks, with various (reachability) properties. We give in Table 1 the case studies, with the numbers of PERAs in parallel, of clocks (equal to the number of actions, by definition) and of parameters, followed by the specification number; then, we compare the computation time (in s) for EFsynth, PRPC, and CompSynth (for which we also give the number of abstractions and counter-examples generated

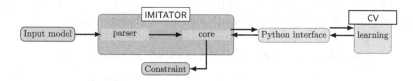

Fig. 5. Architecture of our toolkit

Table 1. Experiments: comparison between algorithms

Case study	#A	#X	#P	Spec	EFsynth	PRPC #iter	PRPC total	CompSynth #abs	CompSynth #c.-ex.	CompSynth learning	CompSynth total
FMS-1	6	18	2	1	0.299	2	0.654	1	1	0.074	**0.136**
				2	**0.010**	1	0.372	0	1	0.038	0.046
				3	0.282	1	0.309	1	0	0.090	**0.242**
FMS-2	11	37	2	1	T.O.	-	T.O.	1	1	84.2	**88.9**
				2	T.O.	-	T.O.	1	0	81.4	**85.2**
				3	**0.051**	-	T.O.	0	2	1.10	2.44
				4	**0.062**	-	T.O.	0	1	1.42	1.53
				5	T.O.	-	T.O.	1	0	31.4	**40.8**
				6	T.O.	-	T.O.	1	0	37.2	**42.4**
AIP	11	46	2	1	0.551	-	T.O.	0	1	0.086	**0.114**
				2	2.11	-	T.O.	0	1	1.22	**1.25**
				3	**3.91**	-	T.O.	0	1	8.50	8.54
				4	**0.235**	-	T.O.	1	1	8.39	8.42
				5	T.O.	-	T.O.	1	0	0.394	**0.871**
				6	T.O.	-	T.O.	1	0	5.32	**9.58**
				7	T.O.	-	T.O.	1	0	1.76	**3.19**
				8	T.O.	-	T.O.	1	0	1.13	**4.35**
				9	T.O.	-	T.O.	1	1	0.762	**1.84**
				10	**0.022**	-	T.O.	0	1	0.072	0.094
Fischer-3	5	12	2		**2.76**	4	14.0	0	1	-	T.O.
Fischer-4	6	16	2		T.O.	-	T.O.	0	1	-	T.O.

---

[1] Sources, binaries, models and results are available at imitator.fr/static/FORTE17.

by LearnAbstr, and the learning time required by LearnAbstr). "T.O." denotes a timeout (>600 s). FMS-1 and -2 are two versions of a flexible manufacturing system [15] (Fig. 1 depicts the conveyor component of FMS-1). AIP is a manufacturing system producing two products from two different materials [15]. Fischer-3 (resp. 4) is a PERA version of the mutual exclusion protocol with 3 (resp. 4) processes; it was obtained using the transformation in Sect. 6.1.

Comparison. Although reachability synthesis is intractable for PERAs (Theorem 1), CompSynth always terminates for our case studies (except for Fischer, for which the abstraction computation is too slow). In contrast, EFsynth does often not terminate. In addition, CompSynth always gives a complete (dense) result not only within D_0 but in fact in the entire parameter domain ($\mathbb{Q}_+^M$).

First, CompSynth outperforms PRPC for all but one benchmark: this suggest to use CompSynth instead of PRPC in the future.

Second, CompSynth is faster than EFsynth in 13/20 cases. In addition, whereas EFsynth often does not terminate, CompSynth always outputs a result (except for Fischer). In some cases (FMS-2:3, FMS-2:4, AIP:4), EFsynth is much faster because it immediately derives ⊥, whereas CompSynth has to compute the abstraction first. Even in these unfavorable cases, CompSynth is never much behind EFsynth: the worst case is AIP:4, with 8 s slower. This suggests that CompSynth may be preferred to EFsynth for PERAs benchmarks.

Table 2. Experiments: scalability w.r.t. the reference domain

Case study	#A	#X	#P	Spec	D_0	#abs	#c.-ex.	find next point	learning	total
FMS-2	11	37	2	1	2,500	1	1	0.0	81.0	85.7
					10,000	1	1	0.1	82.5	87.3
					250,000	1	1	2.2	82.0	89.0
					1,000,000	1	1	8.9	83.1	96.7
					25,000,000	1	1	221.2	83.1	309.0
					100,000,000	1	1	888.1	83.5	976.4

(CompSynth column heading spans #abs, #c.-ex., find next point, learning, total)

Interestingly, in almost all benchmarks, at most one abstraction (for good valuations) and one counter-example (for bad valuations) is necessary for CompSynth. In addition, most of the computation time of CompSynth (71 % in average) comes from LearnAbstr; this suggests to concentrate our future optimization efforts on this part. Perhaps an on-the-fly composition mixed with synthesis could help speeding-up this part; this would also solve the issue of constraints ⊥ synthesized only after the abstraction phase is completed (FMS-2:3, FMS-2:4, AIP:4).

For Fischer, our algorithm is very inefficient: this comes from the fact that the model is strongly synchronized, and the abstraction computation does not terminate within 600 s. In fact, in both cases, LearnAbstr successfully derives very quickly a counter-example that is used by CompSynth to immediately synthesize all "bad" valuations; but then, as LearnAbstr fails in computing an abstraction, the good valuations are not synthesized. Improving the learning phase for strongly synchronized models is on our agenda.

We were not able to perform a comparison with [9]; the prototype of [9] always failed to compute a result. In addition, our Fischer benchmark does not fit in [9] as Fischer makes use of shared parameters.

Size of the Parameter Domain. Algorithm 2 is based on an enumeration of integer points: although we could use an SMT solver to find the next uncovered point, in our implementation we just enumerate *all* points, and therefore the size of D_0 may have an impact on the efficiency of CompSynth. Table 2 shows the impact of the size of D_0 w.r.t. CompSynth. "find next point" is the time to find the next uncovered point (and therefore includes the enumeration of all points). The overhead is reasonable up to 1,000,000 points, but then becomes very significant. Two directions can be taken to overcome this problem for very large parameter domains: *(1)* using an SMT solver to find the next uncovered point; or *(2)* using an on-the-fly refinement of the precision (e. g., start with multiples of 100, then 10 for uncovered subparts of D_0, then 1 ... until $D_0 \subseteq K_{bad} \cup K_{good}$).

Partitioning. Finally, although the use of heuristic 2 is natural, we still wished to evaluate it. Results show that our partitioning heuristic yields always the best execution time, or almost the best execution time.

7 Conclusion and Perspectives

We proposed a learning-based approach to improve the verification of parametric distributed timed systems, that turns to be globally efficient on a set of benchmarks; most importantly, it outputs an exact result for most cases where the monolithic procedure EFsynth fails.

Among the limitations of our work is that the input model must be a PERA (although we provide an extension to PTAs), and that all parametric ERAs must be in the same component A. How to lift these assumptions is on our agenda.

Another perspective is the theoretical study of PERAs, their expressiveness and decidability (beyond EF-emptiness, that we proved to be undecidable).

Finally, addressing other properties than reachability is also on our agenda.

Acknowledgment. We warmly thank Lăcrămioara Aştefănoaei for her appreciated help with installing and using the prototype tool of [9].

References

1. Alur, R., Fix, L., Henzinger, T.A.: Event-clock automata: a determinizable class of timed automata. Theoret. Comput. Sci. **211**(1–2), 253–273 (1999)
2. Alur, R., Henzinger, T.A., Vardi, M.Y.: Parametric real-time reasoning. In: STOC, pp. 592–601. ACM (1993)
3. André, É.: What's decidable about parametric timed automata? In: Artho, C., Ölveczky, P.C. (eds.) FTSCS 2015. CCIS, vol. 596, pp. 52–68. Springer, Cham (2016). doi:10.1007/978-3-319-29510-7_3
4. André, É., Chatain, T., Encrenaz, E., Fribourg, L.: An inverse method for parametric timed automata. IJFCS **20**(5), 819–836 (2009)

5. André, É., Fribourg, L., Kühne, U., Soulat, R.: IMITATOR 2.5: a tool for analyzing robustness in scheduling problems. In: Giannakopoulou, D., Méry, D. (eds.) FM 2012. LNCS, vol. 7436, pp. 33–36. Springer, Heidelberg (2012). doi:10.1007/978-3-642-32759-9_6

6. André, É., Lime, D., Roux, O.H.: Decision problems for parametric timed automata. In: Ogata, K., Lawford, M., Liu, S. (eds.) ICFEM 2016. LNCS, vol. 10009, pp. 400–416. Springer, Cham (2016). doi:10.1007/978-3-319-47846-3_25

7. André, É., Lipari, G., Nguyen, H.G., Sun, Y.: Reachability preservation based parameter synthesis for timed automata. In: Havelund, K., Holzmann, G., Joshi, R. (eds.) NFM 2015. LNCS, vol. 9058, pp. 50–65. Springer, Cham (2015). doi:10.1007/978-3-319-17524-9_5

8. André, É., Markey, N.: Language preservation problems in parametric timed automata. In: Sankaranarayanan, S., Vicario, E. (eds.) FORMATS 2015. LNCS, vol. 9268, pp. 27–43. Springer, Cham (2015). doi:10.1007/978-3-319-22975-1_3

9. Aştefănoaei, L., Bensalem, S., Bozga, M., Cheng, C.-H., Ruess, H.: Compositional parameter synthesis. In: Fitzgerald, J., Heitmeyer, C., Gnesi, S., Philippou, A. (eds.) FM 2016. LNCS, vol. 9995, pp. 60–68. Springer, Cham (2016). doi:10.1007/978-3-319-48989-6_4

10. Cobleigh, J.M., Avrunin, G.S., Clarke, L.A.: Breaking up is hard to do: an evaluation of automated assume-guarantee reasoning. TOSEM 17(2), 7:1–7:52 (2008)

11. Cobleigh, J.M., Giannakopoulou, D., PǍsǍreanu, C.S.: Learning assumptions for compositional verification. In: Garavel, H., Hatcliff, J. (eds.) TACAS 2003. LNCS, vol. 2619, pp. 331–346. Springer, Heidelberg (2003). doi:10.1007/3-540-36577-X_24

12. Frehse, G., Jha, S.K., Krogh, B.H.: A counterexample-guided approach to parameter synthesis for linear hybrid automata. In: Egerstedt, M., Mishra, B. (eds.) HSCC 2008. LNCS, vol. 4981, pp. 187–200. Springer, Heidelberg (2008). doi:10.1007/978-3-540-78929-1_14

13. Hune, T., Romijn, J., Stoelinga, M., Vaandrager, F.W.: Linear parametric model checking of timed automata. JLAP 52–53, 183–220 (2002)

14. Jovanović, A., Lime, D., Roux, O.H.: Integer parameter synthesis for timed automata. Trans. Softw. Eng. 41(5), 445–461 (2015)

15. Lin, S.W., André, É., Liu, Y., Sun, J., Dong, J.S.: Learning assumptions for compositional verification of timed systems. TSE 40(2), 137–153 (2014)

Modularising Opacity Verification for Hybrid Transactional Memory

Alasdair Armstrong and Brijesh Dongol[(✉)]

Brunel University London, London, UK
{alasdair.armstrong,brijesh.dongol}@brunel.ac.uk

Abstract. Transactional memory (TM) manages thread synchronisation to provide an illusion of atomicity for arbitrary blocks of code. There are various implementations of TM, including hardware (HTM) and software (STM). HTMs provide high performance, but are inherently limited by hardware restrictions; STMs avoid these limitations but suffer from unpredictable performance. To solve these problems, hybrid TM (HyTM) algorithms have been introduced which provide reliable software fallback mechanisms for hardware transactions. The key safety property for TM is opacity, however a naive combination of an opaque STM and an opaque HTM does not necessarily result in an opaque HyTM. Therefore, HyTM algorithms must be specially designed to satisfy opacity. In this paper we introduce a modular method for verifying opacity of HyTM implementations. Our method provides conditions under which opacity proofs of HTM and STM components can be combined into a single proof of an overall hybrid algorithm. The proof method has been fully mechanised in Isabelle, and used to verify a novel hybrid version of a transactional mutex lock.

1 Introduction

By allowing programmers to mark blocks of arbitrary code as *transactions*, Transactional Memory (TM) aims to provide an easy-to-use synchronisation mechanism for concurrent access to shared data. Unlike coarse-grained locking, TM implementations are fine-grained, which improves performance. In recent years, TM has appeared as software libraries in languages such as Java, Clojure, Haskell and C++11, and received hardware support in processors (e.g., Intel's TSX).

Software Transactional Memory (STM), as provided by the aforementioned software libraries, offers a programmer-friendly mechanism for shared-variable concurrency. However, it suffers from unpredictable performance which makes it unsuitable for some applications. On the other hand, *Hardware Transactional Memory* (HTM), as implemented in modern Intel processors, offers high performance but comes with many limitations imposed by the constraints of the hardware itself. For example, HTM implementations do not guarantee progress for a transaction even in the absence of other concurrent transactions [11]. *Hybrid*

© IFIP International Federation for Information Processing 2017
Published by Springer International Publishing AG 2017. All Rights Reserved
A. Bouajjani and A. Silva (Eds.): FORTE 2017, LNCS 10321, pp. 33–49, 2017.
DOI: 10.1007/978-3-319-60225-7_3

TM (HyTM) implementations address these issues by integrating STM and HTM [10]. Recent work [2,3,18] has focused on providing software fallbacks for HTM, combining the performance benefits of HTM with the strong semantics and progress guarantees of STM.

Opacity [8,9] is the primary safety property for TM, which ensures that implementations have the familiar properties of database transactions: atomicity, consistency, and isolation. Opacity requires that all transactions (including aborting ones) can be serialised into some meaningful sequential order, so that no transaction witnesses an inconsistent state caused by the partial execution of any other transaction. Overall, this ensures that TM implementations execute with an *illusion of atomicity*.

HyTM algorithms, which are the focus of this paper, consist of STM (*slow-path*) transactions executing in parallel with HTM (*fast-path*) transactions. Since an execution may consist of only STM or only HTM transactions, one must ensure that slow-path and fast-path transactions are by themselves opaque. In addition, synchronisation between slow- and fast-path transactions must be introduced to ensure that executions consisting of arbitrary combinations of these transactions is opaque. It is already known that naively combining STM and HTM results in a non-opaque HyTM algorithm [2]. In this paper, we develop a modular verification method for proving opacity of HyTM algorithms—our method provides a means for independently proving opacity of both the STM slow path and the HTM fast path, and then combining them into a proof of opacity of the overall system.

To demonstrate our proof method, in Sect. 2, we develop a novel hybrid version of Dalessandro *et al.*'s Transactional Mutex Lock [4], extending it with a subscription mechanism described in [3]. Our algorithm, HyTML, combines an *eager* STM, where writes to the shared store are immediately committed to memory, with a *lazy* fast path HTM, where writes to the shared store are cached until the HTM executes a commit operation. Moreover, it improves concurrency in the original TML algorithm by allowing multiple concurrent writing HTM transactions; in the original algorithm, all transactions abort in the presence of *any* concurrent writing transaction.

Our proof method is an extension of previous work [6,14] that uses trace refinement of I/O automata (IOA) [17] to verify opacity via a TM specification known as TMS2 [7]. Unlike existing work, our methods enable one to verify HyTML in a modular manner (i.e., by combining *individual opacity proofs* of the fast-path and slow-path components) despite the monolithic structure of the algorithm. Our proof methods are influenced by compositional techniques [20] such as rely/guarantee [12]. However, unlike rely-guarantee, which focusses on composing processes, we focus on composition at the level of *components*, which themselves consist of multiple parallel processes.

We start by developing the notion of an *interference automaton* (Sect. 4), which specialises IOA by including transitions that take into account any potential interference from the environment. Parallel composition for interference automata is developed in Sect. 5, and the notion of *weak simulation* for parallel interference automata is given in Sect. 6. There we provide our main decomposition theorem, which describes how weak simulations can be combined to ensure trace refinement of the composed system. We apply our proof methods to verify HyTML in Sect. 7; we show how individual opacity proofs for the STM and HTM components can be combined, to avoid the complexity inherent in a monolithic proof. All the proofs in this paper, including our meta-theory, have been mechanised[1] in the Isabelle theorem prover [19].

2 Hybrid TML

Our running example is the *Hybrid Transaction Mutex Lock* (*HyTML*) algorithm given in Listing 1, which extends Dalessandro *et al.*'s TML algorithm [4] with a 2-counter subscription mechanism [3]. HyTML synchronises the software *slow path* with a hardware *fast path* using *glb* (which is *published* by software and *subscribed* by hardware) and *ctr* (which is *published* by hardware and *subscribed* by software).

The parity of *glb* indicates whether a writing software transaction is currently executing. Namely, a writing software transaction increments *glb* once at Line 31, where it effectively acquires the write lock, and again at Line 37, where it effectively releases the write lock. Thus, $\lfloor glb/2 \rfloor$ gives the total number of committed software transactions. TML, and by extension HyTML, has the property

---

Listing 1. A Hybrid Transactional Mutex Lock (HyTML) algorithm

1: **procedure** INIT	18: **procedure** SPBegin$_t$
2: *glb*, *ctr* ← 0, 0	19: **repeat**
	20: *loc$_t$* ← *glb*
3: **procedure** FPBegin$_t$	21: *lctr$_t$* ← *ctr*
4: XBegin()	22: **until** *even*(*loc$_t$*)
5: *loc$_t$* ← *glb*	
6: *writer$_t$* ← *false*	23: **procedure** SPRead$_t$(*a*)
7: **if** *odd*(*loc$_t$*) **then**	24: *v$_t$* ← *∗a*
8: XAbort()	25: **if** *glb* = *loc$_t$* **then**
	26: **if** *ctr* = *lctr$_t$* **then**
9: **procedure** FPRead$_t$(*a*)	27: **return** *v$_t$*
10: **return** *∗a*	28: **abort**
11: **procedure** FPWrite$_t$(*a*, *v*)	29: **procedure** SPWrite$_t$(*a*, *v*)
12: *writer$_t$* ← *true*	30: **if** *even*(*loc$_t$*) **then**
13: *∗a* ← *v*	31: **if** ¬*dcss*(&*glb*, *loc$_t$*, &*ctr*, *lctr$_t$*, *loc$_t$*+1)
14: **procedure** FPCommit$_t$	32: **then abort**
15: **if** *writer$_t$* **then**	33: **else** *loc$_t$*++
16: *ctr*++	34: *∗a* ← *v*
17: XEnd()	35: **procedure** SPCommit$_t$
	36: **if** *odd*(*loc$_t$*) **then**
	37: *glb* ← *loc$_t$* + 1

---

[1] The Isabelle files may be downloaded from [1].

that only a single software transaction can be writing at a time. The presence of a software writer causes all concurrently executing transactions, including fast-path transactions, to abort.[2] Unlike TML, HyTML allows more than one concurrent writing transaction via the fast path. Variable ctr is used to signal a completed hardware transaction and is incremented whenever a writing hardware transaction commits (Line 16). The total number of committed writing transactions is therefore given by $\lfloor glb/2 \rfloor + ctr$. Note that read-only transactions modify neither glb nor ctr.

Software Slow Path. The software slow path implementation is a conservative extension to the original TML algorithm [4] — we refer the interested reader to [4,5] for further details of the behaviour of TML. The implementation consists of operations SPBegin and SPCommit that start and end software transactions, respectively, as well as SPRead and SPWrite that perform (software) transactional reads and writes, respectively. Each operation and transaction-local variable is indexed by a transaction identifier t.

Procedure SPBegin_t repeatedly polls both glb and ctr, storing their values in local variables loc_t and $lctr_t$, respectively, until loc_t is even. This ensures that a software transaction cannot begin until there are no software writers. Procedure $\text{SPRead}_t(a)$ first reads the value in address a from memory and then checks (non-atomically) if glb and ctr are consistent with loc_t and $lctr_t$, respectively. The value of the address is returned if both checks succeed, otherwise it is likely that the transaction t has witnessed an inconsistent snapshot of the store, and hence it aborts.

Procedure SPWrite_t first checks the parity of loc_t. If loc_t is odd, then t must itself be the (unique) software writer, i.e., t had acquired the mutex lock from a previous call to SPWrite_t. Therefore, t can immediately proceed and eagerly update the value of $*a$ in the store to v. If loc_t is even, it contends with other writers to acquire the lock using a *double compare single swap* operation: $dccs$, which atomically checks both $lctr_t$ and loc_t against their global values and updates glb to $loc_t + 1$ if both are unmodified (which effectively acquires the mutex lock). The $dccs$ operation returns *true* iff it is successful. If either glb or ctr have changed since t first read their values within SPBegin_t, then t may go on to construct an inconsistent memory state, and hence, it must abort. Otherwise (i.e., if $dccs$ succeeds), loc_t is incremented (Line 33) to match the new value of glb. This makes the value of loc_t odd, allowing the expensive $dccs$ operation to be elided in future calls to SPWrite_t, as explained above, and allows future calls to SPRead_t to succeed.

Procedure SPCommit_t always succeeds. It checks to see if t is a writing transaction (i.e., loc_t is odd). If so, loc_t must be equal to glb, and hence, the update to glb at Line 37 is equivalent to an increment of glb that makes glb's value even. This second increment effectively releases the mutex lock.

---

[2] There are some exceptions, e.g., a read-only software transaction can successfully commit even in the presence of another writer if no more reads are performed [5].

Hardware Fast Path. Our implementation uses HTM primitives provided by an Intel x86 processor with TSX extensions. However, we keep the specifics of the hardware generic and assume as little as possible about the behaviour of the primitives, allowing our work to more easily be adapted to work with other HTMs. We use three basic primitives: XBegin, which starts a hardware transaction, XEnd, which ends (and attempts to commit) the hardware transaction, and XAbort, which explicitly aborts the hardware transaction. We assume that, once started, a hardware transaction may be forced abort at any time for any reason, which is consistent with Intel's specifications [11]. In addition, when interference on any variable that has been read is detected, a fast-path transaction *must* abort (details are provided below).

Procedure FPBegin$_t$ starts a fast-path transaction by calling XBegin, then *subscribes* to the software global version number, *glb*, by reading and recording its value in a local variable *loc$_t$*. A local flag *writer$_t$* (initially *false*) is used to indicate whether a fast-path transaction is a writer. Transaction *t* only begins if *loc$_t$* is even—if *loc$_t$* is odd, a slow-path writer is executing, and hence, the fast-path transaction aborts.

Note that because the read of *glb* occurs after XBegin, the underlying HTM will track the value of *glb* in memory, ensuring that the fast-path transaction aborts if *glb* changes. Such checks to *glb* are performed automatically by the HTM outside the control of the fast-path implementation, and hence, is not explicit in the code (Listing 1). This behaviour is captured in our model of the fast-path transactions by validating that the value of *glb* is equal to *loc$_t$* for every step of fast-path transaction *t*, and aborting whenever this validation fails.

The fast-path read and write operations, FPRead$_t$ and FPWrite$_t$ consist of standard memory operations, but the underlying HTM will ensures these writes are not visible outside *t* until *t* commits. In FPWrite$_t$, the flag *writer$_t$* is set to *true* to indicate that *t* is now a writer. Procedure FPCommit$_t$ updates *ctr* if *t* is a writer, which indicates to software transactions that a fast-path transaction is committing. Note that this increment to *ctr* will not cause other fast-path transactions to abort. Finally, FPCommit$_t$ calls XEnd, which, for a writer transaction, commits all the pending writes to the store and *publishes* the increment to *ctr*.

3   The TMS2 Specification

The basic principle behind the definition of opacity (and other similar definitions) compares a given concurrent history of transactional operations against a sequential one. Opacity requires it be possible for transactions to be serialised so that the real-time order of transactions is preserved. Within this serialisation order, read operations for all transactions, including aborted transactions, must be consistent with the state of the memory store, which is obtained from the initial store by applying the previously committed transactions in their serialised order [8,9]. We elide the formal definition of opacity here, focusing instead on an automata-based TM specification, TMS2 [7]. Lesani et al. [15] have mechanically verified that TMS2 is opaque, thus it is sufficient to show trace refinement against TMS2 to verify opacity of an implementation (cf [6,14]). TMS2 and the implementations we verify are modelled using input/output automata [16,17].

Definition 1. *An I/O automaton (IOA) is a labelled transition system A with a set of states states(A), a set of actions acts(A) (partitioned into internal and external actions), a set of start states start$(A) \subseteq$ states(A) and a transition relation trans$(A) \subseteq$ states$(A) \times$ acts$(A) \times$ states(A) (so that the actions label the transitions).*

TMS2 contains external transitions modelling operation invocations and responses, e.g., the invoke and respond actions for a write action are given below, where $status_t$ is a transaction-local variable that models control flow. The transition is *enabled* if all its preconditions, given after the keyword Pre, hold in the current state. State modifications (effects) of a transition are given as assignments after the keyword Eff.

$inv_t(\texttt{TMWrite}(a, v))$
Pre: $status_t = $ ready
Eff: $status_t := $ doWrite(a, v)

$resp_t(\texttt{TMWrite})$
Pre: $status_t = $ writeResp
Eff: $status_t := $ ready

TMS2 contains a pair of invocations and responses for begin, read, write and commit operations. In addition, a response is provided for aborting operations:

$resp_t(\texttt{TMAbort})$
Pre: $status_t \notin \{$notStarted, ready, commitResp, committed, aborted$\}$
Eff: $status_t := $ aborted

After invoking a write, read, or commit operation, a transaction may execute one of the 'do' actions in Fig. 1, which performs the corresponding abstract operation.

$\texttt{DoRead}_t(a, n)$
Pre: $status_t = $ doRead(a)
    $a \in dom(wrSet_t) \vee validIdx_t(n)$
Eff: **if** $a \in dom(wrSet_t)$ **then**
        $status_t := $ readResp$(wrSet_t(a))$
    else $v := memSeq(n)(a)$
        $status_t := $ readResp(v)
        $rdSet_t := rdSet_t \oplus \{a \mapsto v\}$

$\texttt{DoWrite}_t(a, v)$
Pre: $status_t = $ doWrite(a, v)
Eff: $status_t := $ writeResp
    $wrSet_t := wrSet_t \oplus \{a \mapsto v\}$

$\texttt{DoCommitRO}_t(n)$
Pre: $status_t = $ doCommit
    $dom(wrSet_t) = \emptyset$
    $validIdx_t(n)$
Eff: $status_t := $ commitResp

$\texttt{DoCommitW}_t$
Pre: $status_t = $ doCommit
    $rdSet_t \subseteq latestMem$
Eff: $status_t := $ commitResp
    $memSeq := memSeq \oplus newMem_t$

where $maxIdx \triangleq max(dom(memSeq))$
    $latestMem \triangleq memSeq(maxIdx)$
    $newMem_t \triangleq \{maxIdx + 1 \mapsto (latestMem \oplus wrSet_t)\}$
    $validIdx_t(n) \triangleq beginIdx_t \leq n \leq maxIdx \wedge rdSet_t \subseteq memSeq(n)$

Fig. 1. Internal actions of TMS2

TMS2 guarantees that transactions satisfy two critical requirements: (**R1**) all reads and writes of a transaction work with a *single consistent memory snapshot* that is the result of all previously committed transactions, and (**R2**) the *real-time order* of transactions is preserved. Full details of TMS2 may be found in [7]. Here, we give a brief overview of the requirements that our implementation must satisfy.

To ensure (**R1**), the state of TMS2 includes $\langle memSeq(0), \ldots memSeq(maxIdx) \rangle$, which is a sequence of all possible memory snapshots (the *stores sequence*). Initially the sequence consists of one element, the initial memory $memSeq(0)$. Committing writer transactions append a new memory $newMem$ to this sequence (cf. $\mathtt{DoCommitW}_t$), by applying the writes of the transaction to the last element $memSeq(maxIdx)$. To ensure that the writes of a transaction are not visible to other transactions before committing, TMS2 uses a *deferred update* semantics: writes are stored locally in the transaction t's write set $wrSet_t$ and only published to the shared state when the transaction commits. Note that this does not preclude TM implementations with eager writes, such as TML. However eager implementations must guarantee that writes are not observable until after the writing transaction has committed.

Each transaction t keeps track of all its reads from memory in a read set $rdSet_t$. A read of address a by transaction t checks that either a was previously written by t itself (**then** branch of $\mathtt{DoRead}_t(a)$), or that all values read so far, including a, are from the same memory snapshot n, where $beginIdx_t \leq n \leq maxIdx$ (predicate $validIdx_t(n)$ from the precondition, which must hold in the **else** branch). In the former case the value of a from $wrSet_t$ is returned, and in the latter, the value from $memSeq(n)$ is returned and the read set is updated. The read set of t is also validated when a transaction commits (cf. $\mathtt{DoCommitRO}_t$ and $\mathtt{DoCommitW}_t$). Note that when committing, a read-only transaction may read from a memory snapshot older than $memSeq(maxIdx)$, but a writing transaction must ensure that all reads in its read set are from most recent memory (i.e. *latestMem* $memSeq(maxIdx)$), since its writes will update the memory sequence with a new snapshot.

To ensure (**R2**), if a transaction t' commits before transaction t starts, then the memory that t reads from must include the writes of t'. Thus, when starting a transaction, t saves the current last index of the memory sequence, $maxIdx$, into a local variable $beginIdx_t$. When t performs a read, the predicate $validIdx_t(n)$ ensures that that the snapshot $memSeq(n)$ used has $beginIdx_t \leq n$, implying that writes of t' are included.

Our proof of opacity is based on *trace refinement* [16] between HyTML and TMS2, which ensures that every externally visible execution of HyTML is a possible externally visible execution of TMS2. Since every execution of TMS2 is known to be opaque [15], one can conclude that HyTML is itself opaque. We develop a proof method for trace refinement that exploits the fact that HyTML consists of two distinct sets of transactions: slow- and fast-path. Namely, our method proves opacity of each set of transactions independently, taking into account any possible interference from the other set.

4   Interference Automata

In this section, we formalise the concept of *interference automata* and the notions of trace refinement and forward simulation that we use. Interference automata specialise IOA by explicitly including transitions for *environment steps*, representing the potential interference from other components within the same system. In the context of the HyTM implementations we verify, an interference automaton will model the fast-path (slow-path) transactions with interference stemming from the slow-path (fast-path).

Definition 2 (Interference automata). *An* interference automaton *A consists of:*

- *P_A is an (infinite) set of process identifiers,*
- *sets local(A) and global(A) of local and global states,*
- *sets external(A) and internal(A) of external and internal actions, and*
- *an environment action $\epsilon \notin$ external$(A) \cup$ internal(A).*

We assume external$(A) \cap$ internal$(A) = \emptyset$, and use actions$(A) =$ external$(A) \cup$ internal$(A) \cup \{\epsilon\}$ to denote the actions of A. Furthermore:

- initialisation *of A is described by*
  - *lstart$(A) \subseteq P_A \rightarrow$ local(A), a set of local start states, and*
  - *gstart$(A) \in$ global(A), a global start state*
- transitions *of A are described by*
  - *ltrans$(A) \subseteq ($local$(A) \times$ global$(A)) \times$ actions$(A) \times ($local$(A) \times$ global$(A))$, which describes local transitions, and*
  - *env$(A) \subseteq$ global$(A) \times$ global(A), which is a reflexive relation that describes environment transitions.*

The overall state space of A is given by states$(A) = (P_A \rightarrow local(A)) \times global(A)$. That is, a state is a pair consisting of a local state for every possible process in P_A and a global state. For any state s, the local part of the state is denoted by s_l, and the global part by s_g, and hence, $s = (s_l, s_g)$.

An interference automaton A may perform an environment transition in $env(A)$, which may only modify the global state, or a local transition for a specific process $p \in P_A$, which may only modify the local state of p and the global state. For states s and s', action a, and process p, we denote an internal or external transition of A by $s \xrightarrow{a,p}_A s'$, where the action is paired with the process identifier executing the action. By construction, we have that the local state of process p' is unchanged after a transition of process p whenever $p \neq p'$. For global state s_g, s'_g, we use $s_g \xrightarrow{\epsilon}_A s'_g$ to denote an environment transition, which is lifted to the level of states in the obvious way. Namely, if s_l is a local state, we let $(s_l, s_g) \xrightarrow{\epsilon}_A (s_l, s'_g)$ denote an environment transition.

A *run* of an interference automaton A is an alternating sequence of states and actions starting from an initial state. The *traces* of A, denoted traces(A), are the runs of A restricted to external actions, and the *reachable states* of A, denoted reach(A), are states that can be reached by some run of A. For interference automata A and C, we say C is a *trace refinement* of A iff traces$(C) \subseteq$ traces(A).

Interference automata may be regarded as a special case of IOA, where the state is specialised and actions are split into internal and environment actions. Therefore, all theorems of IOA, including notions of simulation [16] are also applicable in this setting. Note that an interference automaton A represents the actions of an arbitrary amount of processes, which is why P_A must be infinite. As such, interference automata represent *systems of processes* and not specific sets of processes. A *forward simulation* is a standard way of verifying trace refinement between a concrete implementation and an abstract specification. For interference automata, this involves proving simulation between the external, internal, and environment steps.

Definition 3 (Forward simulation). *If A and C are interference automata such that $external(C) \subseteq external(A)$, we say $R \subseteq states(C) \times states(A)$ is a forward simulation between A and C iff each of the following hold:*

Initialisation. $\forall cs \in start(C) \bullet \exists as \in start(A) \bullet (cs, as) \in R$

External step correspondence
$\forall cs \in reach(C), as \in reach(A), a \in external(C), p \in P_C, cs' \in states(C) \bullet$
$\quad (cs, as) \in R \wedge cs \xrightarrow{a,p}_C cs' \implies$
$\quad \exists as' \in states(A) \bullet (cs', as') \in R \wedge as \xrightarrow{a,p}_A as',$

Internal step correspondence
$\forall cs \in reach(C), as \in reach(A), a \in internal(C), p \in P_C, cs' \in states(C) \bullet$
$\quad (cs, as) \in R \wedge cs \xrightarrow{a,p}_C cs' \implies (cs', as) \in R \vee$
$\quad \exists as' \in states(A), a' \in internal(A) \bullet (cs', as') \in R \wedge as \xrightarrow{a',p}_A as',$

Environment step correspondence
$\forall cs \in reach(C), as \in reach(A), cs'_g \in global(C) \bullet$
$\quad (cs, as) \in R \wedge cs_g \xrightarrow{\epsilon}_C cs'_g \implies$
$\quad \exists as'_g \in global(A) \bullet ((cs_l, cs'_g), (as_l, as'_g)) \in R \wedge as_g \xrightarrow{\epsilon}_A as'_g.$

Soundness of the forward simulation rule with respect to trace refinement has been checked in Isabelle [1].

Theorem 1 (Soundness). *If R is a forward simulation between interference automata A and C, then C is a trace refinement of A, i.e., $traces(C) \subseteq traces(A)$.*

In Sect. 5, we introduce the concept of parallel interference automata and in Sect. 6, we develop a theorem for decomposing parallel interference automata into proofs of individual sub-components. It turns out that our decomposition theorem only needs assume the existence of *weak forward simulation* of the components, in which environment step correspondence may not hold. The notion of a weak simulation is important here, as weak simulations correspond to our existing proofs of opacity for e.g. TML, since these proofs do not involve environment steps. As such, this facilitates the re-use of existing proofs of STM components in the parallel case with only minor modifications. Note that weak simulation between A and C ensures trace refinement for any automaton C in which $env(C)$ is the identity relation since the environment step correspondence proof is trivial.

5   Parallel Interference Automata

In this section, we define a notion of parallel composition for interference automata. The idea is that any possible interference from one component of the parallel composition is reflected as an environment transition in the other. Thus, the parallel composition $B\|C$ comprises an interleaving of the local (internal and external) actions of both B and C.

Two interference automata B and C can be composed iff they are *compatible*, which only requires that they share the same start state, i.e., $gstart(B) = gstart(C)$. We let $\uplus$ denote disjoint union with injections (or inclusion maps) ι_1 and ι_2.

Definition 4 (Parallel composition). *The* parallel composition *of two compatible interference automata B and C is constructed as follows:*

- $local(B\|C) = local(B) \uplus local(C)$,
- $global(B\|C) = global(B) \cup global(C)$,
- $P_{B\|C} = P_B \uplus P_C$,
- $lstart(B\|C) = \{f \cup g \bullet f \in lstart(B) \land g \in lstart(C)\}$,
- $gstart(B\|C) = gstart(B) = gstart(C)$ *as B and C are compatible,*
- $internal(B\|C) = internal(B) \uplus internal(C)$,
- $((\iota_n(s), g), \iota_n(a), (\iota_n(s'), g')) \in ltrans(B\|C)$ *iff* $((s, g), a, (s', g')) \in ltrans(B)$ *when $n = 1$ and* $((s, g), a, (s', g')) \in ltrans(C)$ *when $n = 2$, and*
- $env(A) = Id$, *where Id is the identity relation.*

Essentially this construction splits both the processes and the internal state space of the automaton into left and right processes and states, respectively. An invariant of any composed automaton is that left processes always act on left internal states, and vice versa. For the parallel composition $B\|C$, we typically refer to the automaton B as the left automaton and C as the right automaton. We use $\mathcal{L}$ to denote the projection function that takes a combined state of $B\|C$ and projects just to the part from the left automata B, and similarly for $\mathcal{R}$ and C.

Henceforth, we make the environment transitions of interference automata explicit. We introduce the notation $I \triangleright A$ for an interference automaton A where the environment is the relation I, i.e. $env(I \triangleright A) = I$. We write A when $env(A) = Id$ and refer to such A as an *interference-free automaton*. Note that we therefore have $Id \triangleright A = A$.

In Definition 4, the environment of the composed interference automaton $(I_C \triangleright B)\|(I_B \triangleright C)$ is set to be the identity relation Id, which is possible under the assumption that the local transitions of $I_C \triangleright B$ imply the environment transitions of C (namely I_B), and vice versa. To use this assumption in our proofs, we introduce the notion of a *guarantee condition* (inspired by rely/guarantee reasoning [12]). We say that an automaton $I \rhd B$ *guarantees* a relation J when

$$\forall s \in reach(I \rhd B), a \in actions(I \rhd B), p \in P_B \bullet s \xrightarrow{a,p}_{I \rhd B} s' \implies (s_g, s'_g) \in J.$$

This states that every reachable transition in $I \rhd B$ modifies the global state only as permitted by J. In other words, if $I_C \rhd B$ guarantees I_B and $I_B \rhd C$ guarantees I_C, then this ensures that every local transition of $I_C \rhd B$ can be matched with a environment step of $I_B \rhd C$, and vice versa.

As mentioned an (interference-free) interference automaton A represents the actions of zero or more transactions of type A. Similarly the parallel composition $A \| A$ also represents zero or more transactions of type A, with some labelled as from the left A and others from the right. In other words, parallel composition is idempotent for interference free interference automata. This can be shown via a re-labelling of process identifiers, and has been verified in Isabelle (see [1]).

Theorem 2. $traces(A \| A) = traces(A)$.

We will use this theorem in the proof of HyTML to split the interference-free IOA specification TMS2 into the parallel composition of two TMS2 components. Thus, to show that HyTML is a trace refinement of TMS2, it will be sufficient to show that the software and hardware components individually are refinements of TMS2.

6   Simulation Proofs for Parallel Interference Automata

For modular verification of a parallel interference automaton, we provide a way to build a simulation of a parallel composition from individual weak simulations of the sub-components. For example, in HyTML we consider the two concrete fast/slow paths, and prove both of them TMS2 independently. By Theorem 2, we have that $traces(\mathrm{TMS2}) = traces(\mathrm{TMS2} \| \mathrm{TMS2})$, and hence, for modular proofs of opacity, it is sufficient to consider abstract specifications of the form $A \| A$.

Consider interference automata $I_C \rhd B$ and $I_B \rhd C$, and an abstract interference automaton $I_A \rhd A$. Assume we have weak simulations R and S where

$$I_A \rhd A \text{ weakly simulates } I_C \rhd B \qquad \text{and,} \qquad I_A \rhd A \text{ weakly simulates } I_B \rhd C.$$

We aim to develop conditions such that $R \| S$ is a full (non-weak) simulation between $A \| A$ and $B \| C$, where

$$R \| S = \{(s, s') \bullet (\mathcal{L}(s), \mathcal{L}(s')) \in R \land (\mathcal{R}(s), \mathcal{R}(s')) \in S\}.$$

We now describe the weak simulations R and S, including the state projection functions $\mathcal{L}$ and $\mathcal{R}$, and their interaction with the non-weak simulation of the whole system. Graphically, we can visualise weak simulations R and S as

where the local states of the left (right) automaton $I_C \triangleright B$ (symmetrically $I_B \triangleright C$) combined with the global state is represented by $\oslash$ ($\oslash$). Thus, the left (right) simulation R (S) is over $\oslash$ ($\oslash$). Each state of the parallel automaton $B \| C$, denoted $\otimes$, contains both left and right processes, their local states, as well as the shared global state.

For the weak simulations R and S, we must construct a simulation $R \| S$ of the form:

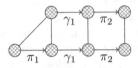

where the environment step ϵ of R must correspond to the appropriate program step of S, namely γ_1. However, we cannot prove this without some additional properties, because we do not know how actions of $I_B \triangleright C$ affect R, and similarly for $I_C \triangleright B$ and S. Note that establishing environment step correspondence (which would turn R and S into non-weak forward simulations) would not help. For example, consider R':

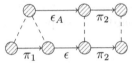

Because we have no way of guaranteeing that the abstract state after ϵ_A in R' is the same as the abstract state after γ_1 in S, we cannot naively construct a parallel forward simulation. Instead we use *non-interference* conditions which guarantee that C and B do not affect R and S, respectively. In essence, this enables us to 'stitch' together the two simulations R and S into a simulation of the parallel composition. In other words, the simulation relations used in both component proofs are preserved by the effects of both components' actions on the global state.

Definition 5. *The condition nonInterferenceLeft(R, S, B, C, A) holds iff*

$$\forall c_l, c_g, a_l, a_g, \pi_C, \pi_A, p \bullet$$
$$\mathcal{L}(c_l, c_g) \in reach(B) \land \mathcal{L}(a_l, a_g) \in reach(A) \land \mathcal{R}(c_l, c_g) \in reach(C)$$
$$\land (\mathcal{R}(c_l, c_g), \mathcal{R}(a_l, a_g)) \in R \land (\mathcal{L}(c_l, c_g), \mathcal{L}(a_l, a_g)) \in S$$
$$\land \mathcal{L}(c_l, c_g) \xrightarrow{\pi_B, p}_B \mathcal{L}(c_l', c_g') \land \mathcal{L}(a_l, a_g) \xrightarrow{\pi_A, p}_A \mathcal{L}(a_l', a_g')$$
$$\implies (\mathcal{R}(c_l, c_g'), \mathcal{R}(a_l, a_g')) \in R.$$

where π_A and π_C are corresponding actions. Symmetrically, we define a condition nonInterferenceRight(R, S, B, C, A).

The reason these conditions are needed is that our guarantee conditions talk purely about the state changes caused by the automaton itself, but not about the simulation relations between automata. While these non-interference conditions at first look complicated due to the amount of notation involved, notice that the local state c_l and a_l does not change between the pre- and post-condition for the simulation relation R. What this means is that we are really showing only that effects contained within the guarantee conditions do not affect the simulation relation, which means that these conditions turn out to be quite straightforward to prove in practice, as will be seen in Sect. 7.

Attempting to remove these non-interference conditions to make the method fully compositional might not be worthwhile in practice, as doing so would require full (rather than weak) simulations for each of the components. This proves to be difficult, as it requires induction on the amount of interference within the simulation proof of each component, and it would preclude easy reuse of existing opacity proofs for the fast and slow paths.

We can now state our simulation theorem for parallel interference automata. The theorem states that $R\|S$ can be strengthened to a forward simulation between $B\|C$ and $A\|A$ provided R (S) is a weak simulation between B (C) and A, and certain guarantee and non-interference conditions hold. This theorem has been verified in Isabelle [1].

Theorem 3 (Decomposition). *For two compatible interference automata B and C, if R is a weak forward simulation between $I_A \triangleright A$ and $I_C \triangleright B$, and S is a weak forward simulation between $I_A \triangleright A$ and $I_B \triangleright C$, where*

- *$I_B \triangleright C$ guarantees I_c, and $I_C \triangleright B$ guarantees I_B,*
- *$nonInterferenceRight(R, S, I_C \triangleright B, I_B \triangleright C, I_A \triangleright A)$,*
- *$nonInterferenceLeft(R, S, I_C \triangleright B, I_B \triangleright C, I_A \triangleright A)$.*

Then $R\|S$ is a (non-weak) forward simulation between $B\|C$ and $A\|A$, and hence $traces(B\|C) \subseteq traces(A\|A)$.

7 HyTML Proof and Mechanisation

In this section we discuss the proof of the HyTML algorithm, and its mechanisation in Isabelle. HyTML is equal to SP$\|$FP where SP and FP are the software slow-path and hardware fast-path components, respectively. Recall that we wish to prove $traces(\text{HyTML}) \subseteq traces(\text{TMS2})$. We prove that TMS2$\|$TMS2 weakly simulates HyTML via Theorem 3, and thus $traces(\text{HyTML}) \subseteq traces(\text{TMS2}\|\text{TMS2})$. By Theorem 2, $traces(\text{TMS2}) = traces(\text{TMS2}\|\text{TMS2})$, and hence the result follows by transitivity of $\subseteq$.

We start by defining environment relations for all the automata involved. The relation for the interference SP receives from FP, I_{FP} is

$$Id \cup \{(g, g') \bullet (odd(glb) \longrightarrow g = g') \wedge ctr' \geq ctr \wedge glb' = glb$$
$$\wedge (even(glb) \wedge store \neq store' \longrightarrow ctr' > ctr)\}.$$

In words, the fast-path guarantees that: (1) If glb is odd, then it will not affect the global state at all. (2) If glb is even, then any change to the store implies ctr

increased. (3) Even if the store remained the same, ctr may still increase, and, (4) The fast path never modifies glb (it only subscribes to it).

SP makes a much weaker guarantee to the FP; I_{SP} guarantees that

$$\{(g, g') \bullet ctr' = ctr \land glb' \geq glb\}.$$

In words, this means that the software only guarantees that it will not change the ctr variable, and that it only ever increments glb.

The interference from other TMS2 components on TMS2 is given by I_{TMS2}, which simply allows new stores to be added to the stores sequence (see **(R1)** in Sect. 3).

The proof that TMS2∥TMS2 weakly simulates HyTML is split into several sub-parts: First, we show weak simulation of both $I_{FP} \triangleright$ SP and $I_{SP} \triangleright$ FP against $I_{TMS2} \triangleright$ TMS2. The fast-path proof is much simpler than the slow-path, as the hardware transactional memory abstraction performs most of the fine-grained steps of atomically, which greatly simplifies the verification process. Third, we verify the guarantee conditions from Sect. 4. Fourth, we verify the non-interference properties in Sect. 4.

Mechanisation. For HyTM implementations we further specialise interference automata to model the components of a hybrid TM implementation. The set of process identifiers become transaction identifiers, and assuming L and V represent the set of all addresses and values, the set of external actions of a transactional automaton A are fixed, and given by:

$$external_T = \{\textbf{Begin}_I, \textbf{Begin}_R, \textbf{Commit}_I, \textbf{Commit}_R, \textbf{Abort}, \textbf{Write}_R\}$$
$$\cup \{\textbf{Read}_I(a) \mid a \in L\} \cup \{\textbf{Read}_R(v) \mid v \in V\}$$
$$\cup \{\textbf{Write}_I(a, v) \mid (a, v) \in L \times V\}$$

As mentioned in Sect. 2, we base our implementation of the underlying hardware transactional memory on Intel's TSX extensions. Therefore, we implement transitions for the XBegin, XEnd and XAbort actions within the hardware automaton. We assume that each hardware transaction is equipped with read and write sets representing the values held in the local processors cache. A simple validation predicate which checks if the values in the read and write set match those in main memory models the cache line invalidation used in the actual hardware. While this validation is more fine-grained than what the actual hardware can do (as it works on the level of cache lines), because the fast path automaton can abort non-deterministically at anytime, all the possible behaviour of the hardware is captured and shown to be opaque. Overly coarse-grained validation might force us to abort when the hardware could succeed, so we err on the side of caution. This behaviour should be generic enough to capture the behaviour of any reasonable hardware TM implementation, not just Intel's TSX. In particular, we do not assume that non-transactional reads and writes can occur within hardware transactions.

Proof in Isabelle. For full-details of our proofs, we refer the interested reader to our Isabelle theories. Here, we briefly comment on the complexity of our mechanisation. In Isabelle, formalising and proving the correctness of the TML slow-path required about 2900 lines, while formalising and proving the correctness of the hardware fast-path required around 600 lines. Proving the non-interference and guarantee conditions required only 450 lines; with the non-interference conditions taking 300 lines and the guarantee conditions requiring only around 70 lines. The formalisation of the transactional automata and requisite theorems took around 2000 lines of Isabelle. Although these are not perfect metrics, they show that the majority of the work was in proving that both HyTM paths satisfy TMS2. Once these individual proofs were completed, bringing the proofs together was fairly comparatively straightforward once the necessary theorems had been set up.

Proving that both HyTM paths are TMS2 is fairly mechanical, and involves detailed line-by-line simulations—showing that every possible step preserves the simulation relation even under interference from every other possible step. Our method enabled adapting our existing work verifying software TML and adapting it to the HyTM case. For simulation proofs of this nature, the number of subgoals grows geometrically with the number of lines in the algorithm, whereas the non-interference conditions only grow linearly in the modular case. However, we believe that both the conceptual benefits of splitting the proof into its logical sub-components, as well as the ability to re-use existing proofs are the main benefits to modularisation.

Our experience with Isabelle for these proofs was very positive. The powerful tools and tactics within Isabelle were very useful for automating many of the cases produced by the simulation rules.

8   Conclusion

In this paper we have developed a fully mechanised modular proof method for verifying opacity of HyTM algorithms. Verification of opacity has received considerable interest in recent years (see e.g., [5,13]). We leverage a simulation-based approach against the TMS2 specification [7] as well as the known result that TMS2 is itself opaque [15]. Our method supports adapting existing proofs of opacity (via TMS2) for both the fast- and slow-path into a HyTM system with only minor modifications to such existing proofs.

We develop the novel notion of interference automata, as well as notions of parallel composition and weak simulation for them. These concepts give us a proof method for combining weak simulations on individual interference automata into a single proof of trace refinement for their parallel composition. All of our meta theory has been checked using the Isabelle theorem prover. To show applicability of our methodology in the context of HyTM algorithms, we develop a novel hybrid extension to Dalessandro *et al.*'s TML [4], where we apply a 2-counter subscription mechanism [3]. Our new algorithm allows more concurrency than the original TML as it allows parallel hardware writers.

We conjecture the possibility of further optimisations to the algorithm by removing redundant checks on *glb* and *ctr* in the slow-path read operation if loc_t is odd. It may also be possible to replace the *dccs* operation by first acquiring a local value of *ctr* before acquiring the mutex lock *glb* using a compare and swap and then checking if the local value of *ctr* is still valid. However, we have chosen to present a conceptually simpler algorithm that nevertheless demonstrates our proof method. There are more complex HyTMs [2,3,18], some with more than two types of transactions; we leave verification of these for future work.

Acknowledgements. We thank Simon Doherty for his helpful comments on this work. Funding is provided by EPSRC grant EP/N016661/1.

References

1. Armstrong, A., Dongol, B.: Isabelle files for modularising opacity verification for hybrid transactional memory (2016). https://figshare.com/articles/Isabelle_files_for_verification_of_a_hybrid_transactional_mutex_lock/4868351
2. Calciu, I., Gottschlich, J., Shpeisman, T., Pokam, G., Herlihy, M.: Invyswell: a hybrid transactional memory for Haswell's restricted transactional memory. In: PACT, pp. 187–200. ACM, New York (2014)
3. Dalessandro, L., Carouge, F., White, S., Lev, Y., Moir, M., Scott, M.L., Spear, M.F.: Hybrid NOrec: a case study in the effectiveness of best effort hardware transactional memory. SIGPLAN Not. **46**(3), 39–52 (2011)
4. Dalessandro, L., Dice, D., Scott, M., Shavit, N., Spear, M.: Transactional mutex locks. In: D'Ambra, P., Guarracino, M., Talia, D. (eds.) Euro-Par 2010. LNCS, vol. 6272, pp. 2–13. Springer, Heidelberg (2010). doi:10.1007/978-3-642-15291-7_2
5. Derrick, J., Dongol, B., Schellhorn, G., Travkin, O., Wehrheim, H.: Verifying opacity of a transactional mutex lock. In: Bjørner, N., de Boer, F. (eds.) FM 2015. LNCS, vol. 9109, pp. 161–177. Springer, Cham (2015). doi:10.1007/978-3-319-19249-9_11
6. Doherty, S., Dongol, B., Derrick, J., Schellhorn, G., Wehrheim, H.: Proving opacity of a pessimistic STM. In: Jiménez, E. (ed.) OPODIS (2016, to appear)
7. Doherty, S., Groves, L., Luchangco, V., Moir, M.: Towards formally specifying and verifying transactional memory. Formal Asp. Comput. **25**(5), 769–799 (2013)
8. Guerraoui, R., Kapalka, M.: On the correctness of transactional memory. In: Chatterjee, S., Scott, M.L. (eds.) PPOPP, pp. 175–184. ACM (2008)
9. Guerraoui, R., Kapalka, M.: Principles of Transactional Memory. Synthesis Lectures on Distributed Computing Theory. Morgan & Claypool Publishers, San Rafael (2010)
10. Harris, T., Larus, J.R., Rajwar, R.: Transactional Memory. Synthesis Lectures on Computer Architecture, 2nd edn. Morgan & Claypool Publishers, San Rafael (2010)
11. Intel: Intel 64 and IA-32 Architectures Software Developers Manual (2016)
12. Jones, C.B.: Tentative steps toward a development method for interfering programs. ACM Trans. Program. Lang. Syst. **5**(4), 596–619 (1983)
13. Lesani, M.: On the correctness of transactional memory algorithms. Ph.D. thesis, UCLA (2014)
14. Lesani, M., Luchangco, V., Moir, M.: A framework for formally verifying software transactional memory algorithms. In: Koutny, M., Ulidowski, I. (eds.) CONCUR 2012. LNCS, vol. 7454, pp. 516–530. Springer, Heidelberg (2012). doi:10.1007/978-3-642-32940-1_36

15. Lesani, M., Luchangco, V., Moir, M.: Putting opacity in its place. In: Workshop on the Theory of Transactional Memory (2012)
16. Lynch, N.A.: Distributed Algorithms. Morgan Kaufmann, Burlington (1996)
17. Lynch, N.A., Tuttle, M.R.: Hierarchical correctness proofs for distributed algorithms. In: PODC, pp. 137–151. ACM (1987)
18. Matveev, A., Shavit, N.: Reduced hardware NOrec: a safe and scalable hybrid transactional memory. SIGPLAN Not. **50**(4), 59–71 (2015)
19. Paulson, L.C.: Isabelle - A Generic Theorem Prover. LNCS, vol. 828. Springer, Heidelberg (1994). (with a contribution by Nipkow, T.)
20. de Roever, W.P., de Boer, F.S., Hannemann, U., Hooman, J., Lakhnech, Y., Poel, M., Zwiers, J.: Concurrency Verification: Introduction to Compositional and Non-compositional Methods. Cambridge Tracts in Theoretical Computer Science, vol. 54. Cambridge University Press, New York (2001)

Proving Opacity via Linearizability: A Sound and Complete Method

Alasdair Armstrong[1], Brijesh Dongol[1(✉)], and Simon Doherty[2]

[1] Brunel University London, Uxbridge, UK
brijesh.dongol@brunel.ac.uk
[2] University of Sheffield, Sheffield, UK

Abstract. Transactional memory (TM) is a mechanism that manages thread synchronisation on behalf of a programmer so that blocks of code execute with the illusion of atomicity. The main safety criterion for transactional memory is opacity, which defines conditions for serialising concurrent transactions.

Verifying opacity is complex because one must not only consider the orderings between fine-grained (and hence concurrent) transactional operations, but also between the transactions themselves. This paper presents a sound and complete method for proving opacity by decomposing the proof into two parts, so that each form of concurrency can be dealt with separately. Thus, in our method, verification involves a simple proof of opacity of a coarse-grained abstraction, and a proof of linearizability, a better-understood correctness condition. The most difficult part of these verifications is dealing with the fine-grained synchronization mechanisms of a given implementation; in our method these aspects are isolated to the linearizability proof. Our result makes it possible to leverage the many sophisticated techniques for proving linearizability that have been developed in recent years. We use our method to prove opacity of two algorithms from the literature. Furthermore, we show that our method extends naturally to weak memory models by showing that both these algorithms are opaque under the TSO memory model, which is the memory model of the (widely deployed) x86 family of processors. All our proofs have been mechanised, either in the Isabelle theorem prover or the PAT model checker.

1 Introduction

Transactional Memory (TM) provides programmers with an easy-to-use synchronisation mechanism for concurrent access to shared data. The basic mechanism is a programming construct that allows one to specify blocks of code as *transactions*, with properties akin to database transactions [16]. Recent years have seen an explosion of interest in TM, leading to the implementation of TM libraries for many programming languages (including Java and C++), compiler support for TM (G++ 4.7) and hardware support (e.g., Intel's Haswell processor). This widespread adoption coupled with the complexity of TM implementations makes formal verification of TM an important problem.

© IFIP International Federation for Information Processing 2017
Published by Springer International Publishing AG 2017. All Rights Reserved
A. Bouajjani and A. Silva (Eds.): FORTE 2017, LNCS 10321, pp. 50–66, 2017.
DOI: 10.1007/978-3-319-60225-7_4

The main safety condition for TM is *opacity* [14,15], which defines conditions for serialising (concurrent) transactions into a sequential order and specifies which data values transactions may read. A direct proof of opacity must somehow construct an appropriate serialisation of the transactions. This is complicated by the fact that transactions are not constrained to read the most recently committed value at any given address. Because of this, several "snapshots" of the transactional memory must be made available to each transaction.

This situation may be contrasted with the well-known correctness condition *linearizability* [17]. Unlike opacity, linearizability proofs only need to consider a single value of the abstract object. Operations never "look back in time" to some earlier state, and linearizability proofs are therefore less complex. Furthermore, there is a rich literature on the verification of linearizability (see [12] for a survey), whereas the verification of opacity has received much more limited attention. Techniques exist for verifying linearizability using data-refinement [10,25], separation logic and other program logics [6,27], and model-checking [4,5,23]. With the possible exception of data refinement, none of these techniques are available for the verification of opacity.

These observations motivate us to explore methods for recasting the problem of verifying opacity to that of verifying linearizability, and this paper presents one such method. Briefly, our method involves the construction of a *coarse-grained abstraction* (CGA) that serves as an intermediate specification between the TM implementation to be verified and opacity itself. Our method requires us to prove that this CGA is opaque. But, as we shall see, the CGA features a coarse grain of atomicity and a simplified state space, relative to the original implementation. These features make verifying opacity of the CGA very straightforward. Importantly, we do not need to consider the complex interleaving and fine-grained synchronisation mechanisms of the original implementation in this part of the proof. Our method also requires us to prove the linearizability of the original TM implementation where the CGA becomes the abstract specification. Only at this point is it necessary to consider the fine-grained synchronization of the actual TM implementation. But for this linearizability proof we can leverage the powerful techniques for verifying linearizability that have been developed in recent years.

We adapt a result from [9] to prove that our method is *sound*: any verification using our technique guarantees opacity of the original algorithm. We also show that our method is *complete*: for any opaque TM implementation, there must exist an opaque CGA, such that the original implementation is linearizable with respect to the CGA. We use our method to prove opacity of two TM implementations: the Transactional Mutex Lock [7], and the more sophisticated and practical NORec algorithm [8]. In addition, we show that our method extends to weak memory models: we verify opacity of both TML and NORec under TSO memory.

For full details of our mechanisations see our extended report [2], which includes all mechanisations, and further descriptions of our proofs.

2 Transactional Memory

In this section, we describe the interface provided by the TM abstraction, and give an example of a transactional memory algorithm: the simple but efficient Transactional Mutex Lock (TML) by Dalessandro *et al.* [7]. Then we formalise *opacity* as defined by Guerraoui and Kapalka [15]. Our formalisation mainly follows Attiya *et al.* [3], but we explicitly include the prefix-closure constraint to ensure consistency with other accepted definitions [15,16,21].

To support transactional programming, TM provides a number of operations[1] to developers: operations to start (TXBegin) or to end a transaction (TXCommit), and operations to read or write shared data (TXRead, TXWrite). These operations can be invoked from within a program (possibly with some arguments, e.g., the address to be read) and then will return with a response. Except for operations that start transactions, all other operations can respond with a special *abort* value, thereby aborting the whole transaction.

Transactional Mutex Lock (TML). The TML algorithm is presented in Listing 1. It provides the four operations, but operation TXCommit in this algorithm never responds with abort. TML adopts a very strict policy for synchronisation among transactions: as soon as one transaction has successfully written to an address, other transactions running concurrently will be aborted if they subsequently invoke a TXRead or TXWrite operation on *any* address. For synchronisation, TML uses a global counter glb (initially 0), and each transaction t uses a local variable loc_t to store a local copy of glb. Variable glb records whether there is a *live writing transaction*, i.e., a transaction which has started, has neither committed nor aborted, and has executed a write operation. More precisely, glb is odd if there is a live writing transaction, and even otherwise. Initially, there are no live writing transactions and thus glb is even.

Listing 1. The Transactional Mutex Lock (TML) algorithm

```
1: procedure INIT              9: procedure TXRead_t(a)      14: procedure TXWrite_t(a, v)
2:    glb ← 0                  10:    v_t ← mem(a)           15:    if even(loc_t) then
                               11:    if glb = loc_t then    16:       if !cas(&glb, loc_t, loc_t+1)
3: procedure TXBegin_t         12:       return v_t          17:       then abort
4:    do loc_t ← glb           13:    else abort             18:       else loc_t++
5:    until even(loc_t)                                      19:    mem(a) ← v

6: procedure TXCommit_t
7:    if odd(loc_t) then
8:       glb ← loc_t + 1
```

---

[1] In this paper, we use the word 'operation' in two senses. Here, we mean 'operation' as a component of the TM interface. Later, we use 'operation' to mean the instance of an operation within an execution. Both senses are standard, and any ambiguity is resolved by the context.

Histories. As is standard in the literature, opacity is defined over *histories*, which are sequences of *events* that record all interactions between the TM and its clients. Each event is either the invocation or response of some TM operation. Possible invocations and their matching response events are given by the function M. For transaction t, address a and value v (taken from a set V), we have

$$M(\texttt{TXBegin}_t) = \{\overline{\texttt{TXBegin}_t}\}$$
$$M(\texttt{TXCommit}_t) = \{\overline{\texttt{TXCommit}_t}, \overline{\texttt{TXAbort}_t}\}$$
$$M(\texttt{TXWrite}_t(a, v)) = \{\overline{\texttt{TXWrite}_t}, \overline{\texttt{TXAbort}_t}\}$$
$$M(\texttt{TXRead}_t(a)) = \{\overline{\texttt{TXRead}_t}(v) \mid v \in V\} \cup \{\overline{\texttt{TXAbort}_t}\}$$

We let **TXBegin**$_t$ denote the two-element sequence $\langle \texttt{TXBegin}_t, \overline{\texttt{TXBegin}_t}\rangle$, let **TXWrite**$_t(x, v)$ denote $\langle \texttt{TXWrite}_t(x, v), \overline{\texttt{TXWrite}_t}\rangle$ and **TXRead**$_t(x, v)$ denote $\langle \texttt{TXRead}_t(x), \overline{\texttt{TXRead}_t}(v)\rangle$, and finally let **TXCommit**$_t$ denote $\langle \texttt{TXCommit}_t, \overline{\texttt{TXCommit}_t}\rangle$. We use notation '·' for sequence concatenation.

Example 1. The following history is a possible execution of the TML, where the address x (initially 0) is accessed by two transactions 2 and 3 running concurrently.

$$\langle \texttt{TXBegin}_3, \texttt{TXBegin}_2, \overline{\texttt{TXBegin}_3}, \overline{\texttt{TXBegin}_2}, \texttt{TXWrite}_3(x, 4)\rangle \cdot$$
$$\textbf{TXRead}_2(x, 0) \cdot \langle \overline{\texttt{TXWrite}_3}\rangle \cdot \textbf{TXCommit}_3$$

Note that operations overlap in this history. For example, the invocation $\texttt{TXBegin}_2$ appears between the invocation and response of transaction 3's TXBegin operation. This overlapping means that this history represents an execution with both concurrent transactions, and concurrent operations. There is an important subset of histories, called *alternating histories* that do not have overlapping operations. That is, a history h is *alternating* if $h = \varepsilon$ (the empty sequence) or h is an alternating sequence of invocation and matching response events starting with an invocation and possibly ending with an invocation. Alternating histories represent executions in which the TM operations are atomic. Note that transactions may still be interleaved in an alternating history; only concurrency *between* operations is prohibited.

For a history $h = \langle h_1, h_2, \ldots h_n\rangle$, let $h|t$ be the projection onto the events of transaction t and $h[i \ldots j]$ be the sub-sequence of h from h_i to h_j inclusive. We will assume that $h|t$ is alternating for any history h and transaction t. Note that this does not necessarily mean h is alternating itself. Opacity is defined for well-formed histories, which formalise the allowable interaction between a TM implementation and its clients. A projection $h|t$ of a history h onto a transaction t is *well-formed* iff it is ε or it is an alternating sequence of t-indexed invocations and matching responses, beginning with $\texttt{TXBegin}_t$, containing at most one each of $\texttt{TXBegin}_t$ and $\texttt{TXCommit}_t$, and containing no events after any $\overline{\texttt{TXCommit}_t}$ or $\overline{\texttt{TXAbort}_t}$ event. Furthermore, $h|t$ is *committed* whenever the last event is $\overline{\texttt{TXCommit}_t}$ and *aborted* whenever the last event is $\overline{\texttt{TXAbort}_t}$. In these cases, the transaction $h|t$ is *completed*, otherwise it is *live*. A history is *well-formed* iff $h|t$ is well-formed for every transaction t. The history in Example 1 is well-formed, and contains a committed transaction 3 and a live transaction 2.

Opacity. The basic principle behind the definition of opacity (and similar definitions) is the comparison of a given concurrent history against a sequential one.
Opacity imposes a number of constraints, that can be categorised into three
main types:

- *ordering constraints* that describe how events occurring in a concurrent history may be sequentialised;
- *semantic constraints* that describe validity of a sequential history *hs*; and
- a *prefix-closure constraint* that requires that each prefix of a concurrent history can be sequentialised so that the ordering and semantic constraints above
  are satisfied.

To help formalise these opacity constraints we introduce the following nota-
tion. We say a history h is *equivalent* to a history h', denoted $h \equiv h'$, iff $h|t = h'|t$
for all transactions $t \in T$. Further, the *real-time order* on transactions t and t'
in a history h is defined as $t \prec_h t'$ if t is a completed transaction and the last
event of t in h occurs before the first event of t'.

Sequential History Semantics. We now formalise the notion of sequentiality for
transactions, noting that the definitions must also cover live transactions. A well-
formed history h is *non-interleaved* if transactions do not overlap. In addition
to being non-interleaved, a sequential history has to ensure that the behaviour
is meaningful with respect to the reads and writes of the transactions. For this,
we look at each address in isolation and define the notion of a valid sequential
behaviour on a single address. To this end, we model shared memory by a set
A of addresses mapped to values denoted by a set V. Hence the type $A \rightarrow V$
describes the possible states of the shared memory.

Definition 1 (Valid history). *Let $h = \langle h_0, \ldots, h_{2n-1} \rangle$ be an alternating history ending with a response (recall that an alternating history is a sequence of
alternating invocation and response events starting with an invocation). We say
h is valid if there exists a sequence of states $\sigma_0, \ldots, \sigma_n$ such that $\sigma_0(a) = 0$ for
all addresses a, and for all i such that $0 \leq i < n$ and $t \in T$:*

1. *if $h_{2i} = \texttt{TXWrite}_t(a, v)$ and $h_{2i+1} = \overline{\texttt{TXWrite}}_t$ then $\sigma_{i+1} = \sigma_i[a := v]$; and*
2. *if $h_{2i} = \texttt{TXRead}_t(a)$ and $h_{2i+1} = \overline{\texttt{TXRead}}_t(v)$ then both $\sigma_i(a) = v$ and $\sigma_{i+1} = \sigma_i$ hold; and*
3. *for all other pairs of events $\sigma_{i+1} = \sigma_i$.*

A correct TM must ensure that all reads are consistent with the writes of the
executing transaction as well as all previously committed writes. On the other
hand, writes of aborted transactions must not be visible to other transactions.
We therefore define a notion of *legal* histories, which are non-interleaved histories where only the writes of successfully committed transactions are visible to
subsequent transactions.

Definition 2 (Legal history). *Let hs be a non-interleaved history, i an index
of hs, and hs' be the projection of $hs[0 \ldots (i-1)]$ onto all events of committed
transactions plus the events of the transaction to which hs_i belongs. We say hs is
legal at i whenever hs' is valid. We say hs is legal iff it is legal at each index i.*

This allows us to define sequentiality for a single history, which we additionally lift to the level of specifications.

Definition 3 (Sequential history). *A well-formed history hs is sequential if it is non-interleaved and legal. We let S denote the set of all well-formed sequential histories.*

Transactional History Semantics. A given history may be *incomplete*, i.e., it may contain pending operations, represented by invocations that do not have matching responses. Some of these pending operations may be commit operations, and some of these commit operations may have taken effect: that is, the write operations of a commit-pending transaction may already be visible to other transactions. To help account for this possibility, we must complete histories by (i) extending a history by adding responses to pending operations, then (ii) removing any pending operations that are left over. For (i), for each history h, we define a set $extend(h)$ that contains all histories obtained by adding to h response events matching any subset of the pending invocations in h. For (ii), for a history h, we let $[h]$ denote the history h with all pending invocations removed.

Definition 4 (Opaque history, Opaque object). *A history h is* final-state opaque *iff for some $he \in extend(h)$, there exists a sequential history $hs \in S$ such that $[he] \equiv hs$ and furthermore $\prec_{[he]} \subseteq \prec_{hs}$. A history h is* opaque *iff each prefix h' of h is final-state opaque; a set of histories $\mathcal{H}$ is* opaque *iff each $h \in \mathcal{H}$ is opaque; and a TM implementation is* opaque *iff its set of histories is opaque.*

In Definition 4, conditions $[he] \equiv hs$ and $\prec_{[he]} \subseteq \prec_{hs}$ establish the ordering constraints and the requirement that $hs \in S$ ensures the memory semantics constraints. Finally, the prefix-closure constraints are ensured because final-state opacity is checked for each prefix of $[he]$.

Example 2. The history in Example 1 is opaque; a corresponding sequential history is

$$\textbf{TXBegin}_2 \cdot \textbf{TXRead}_2(x, 0) \cdot \textbf{TXBegin}_3 \cdot \textbf{TXWrite}_3(x, 4) \cdot \textbf{TXCommit}_3$$

Note that reordering of TXRead$_2(x, 0)$ and TXBegin$_3$ is allowed because their corresponding transactions overlap (even though the operations themselves do not).

3   Proving Opacity via Linearizability

In this section, we describe our method in detail, and we illustrate it by showing how to verify the simple TML algorithm presented in Sect. 2. Briefly, our method proceeds as follows.

1. Given a TM implementation, we construct a *coarse-grained abstraction* (CGA). This intermediate abstraction supports the standard transactional operations (begin, read, write and commit), and the effect of each operation is atomic. The states of this abstraction are simplified versions of the states of the original implementation, since the variables that are used for fine-grained synchronisation can be removed.
2. We prove that this CGA is opaque. The coarse-grained atomicity and simplifed state space of this abstraction mean that this opacity proof is much simpler than the direct opacity proof of the original implementation. Importantly, we do not need to consider the fine-grained synchronisation mechanisms of the original implementation in this part of the proof.
3. We prove that the original TM implementation is linearizable with respect to the CGA. Only at this point is it necessary to consider the complex interleaving and fine-grained synchronization of the actual TM implementation. As we noted in the introduction, for this linearizability proof we can leverage the powerful techniques for verifying linearizability that have been developed in recent years.

Formally, we regard our TM implementations, and our CGAs as sets of histories (consistent with the definition of opacity). The histories of the TM implementation must model all possible behaviours of the algorithm, and therefore some of these histories may contain overlapping operations. However, because the operations of the CGA are atomic, all the histories of the CGA are alternating.

Because the histories of each CGA are alternating, it is possible to prove that the original TM implementation is linearizable with respect to the CGA. To show how this works, we briefly review the definition of linearizability [17]. As with opacity, the formal definition of linearizability is given in terms of histories: for every concurrent history an equivalent alternating history must exist that preserves the real-time order of operations of the original history. The *real-time order* on operations[2] o_1 and o_2 in a history h is given by $o_1 \lll_h o_2$ if the response of o_1 precedes the invocation of o_2 in h.

As with opacity, the given concurrent history may be incomplete, and hence, may need to be extended using *extend* and all remaining pending invocations may need to be removed. We say $lin(h, ha)$ holds iff both $[h] \equiv ha$ and $\lll_{[h]} \subseteq \lll_{ha}$ hold.

Definition 5 (Linearizability). *A history h is* linearized *by alternating history ha iff there exists a history $he \in extend(h)$ such that $lin(he, ha)$. A concurrent object is linearizable with respect to a set of alternating histories $\mathcal{A}$ (in our case a CGA) if for each concurrent history h, there is a history $ha \in \mathcal{A}$ that linearizes h.*

In the remainder of this section, we flesh out our technique by verifying the TML algorithm presented in Sect. 2.

---

[2] Note: this differs from the real-time order on transactions defined in Sect. 2.

A Coarse-grained Abstraction. Pseudocode describing the coarse-grained abstraction that we use to prove opacity of the TML is given in Listing 2. Like TML in Listing 1, it uses meta-variables loc_t (local to transaction t) and glb (shared by all transactions). Each operation is however, significantly simpler than the TML operations, and performs the entire operation in a single atomic step. The code for each operation is defined by wrapping the original code in an atomic block. However, the atomicity of the resulting method means that further simplifications can be made. For example, in the TXRead operation, the local variable v_t is no longer needed, and so can be removed. Likewise, CAS of the TXWrite operation is no longer required, and can also be dropped.

This basic strategy of making each operation atomic and then simplifying away any unnecessary state is sufficient for the examples we have considered. Indeed, when we apply our technique to the substantially more complicated NoRec algorithm, we find that the simplification step removes a great deal of complexity, including the entirety of NoRec's transactional validation procedure (Sect. 5).

Finding a CGA for any given TM algorithm is generally straightforward. We can provide three simple steps, or heuristics, that can be applied to find a useful CGA for any transactional memory algorithm. (1) We make every operation atomic in a naive way, essentially by surrounding the code in atomic blocks. (2) Much of the complexity in a transactional memory algorithm is often fine-grained concurrency control, such as locking, ensuring that each operation remains linearizable. This fine grained concurrency control can be removed in the CGA. (3) Concurrent/linearizable data structures in the implementation of the algorithm can be replaced by simple abstractions, that need not be implementable. For example, in the NORec algorithm (see Sect. 5) the write set and read sets are replaced with ordinary sets, and the validation routine becomes a predicate over these sets.

Opacity of the Coarse-grained Abstraction. We turn now to the question of proving that our CGA is opaque. While our TM implementations and CGAs are sets of histories, it is convenient to define these models operationally using labelled transition systems that generate the appropriate sets of histories (so

---

Listing 2. TML-CGA: Coarse-grained abstraction of TML

```
 1: procedure INIT            11: procedure ATXRead_t(a)      16: procedure ATXWrite_t(a,v)
 2:    glb ← 0                12:    atomic                   17:    atomic
                              13:       if glb = loc_t then   18:       if glb ≠ loc_t then
 3: procedure ATXBegin_t      14:          return mem(a)      19:          abort
 4:    atomic                 15:       else abort            20:       if even(loc_t) then
 5:       await even(glb)                                     21:          loc_t++; glb++
 6:       loc_t ← glb                                         22:          mem(a) ← v

 7: procedure ATXCommit_t
 8:    atomic
 9:       if odd(loc_t) then
10:          glb++
```

that the labels of the transition systems are invocation or response events). We do this for two reasons. First, the algorithms of interest work by manipulating state, and these manipulations can be mapped directly to labelled transition systems. The second reason relates to how we prove that our CGAs are opaque.

We prove that our CGAs are opaque using techniques described in [11]. This means we leverage two existing results from the literature: the TMS2 specification by Doherty *et al.* [11], and the mechanised proof that TMS2 is opaque by Lesani *et al.* [21]. Using these results, it is sufficient that we prove trace refinement (i.e., trace inclusion of visible behaviour) between TML-CGA and the TMS2 specification. The rigorous nature of these existing results means that a mechanised proof of refinement against TMS2 also comprises a rigorous proof of opacity of TML-CGA.

Although TMS2 simplifies proofs of opacity, using it to verify an implementation still involves a complex simulation argument [20]. On the other hand, using TMS2 to prove opacity of a coarse-grained abstraction (CGA) is simple: the operations of the CGA are atomic, and hence, each of its operations corresponds exactly one operation of TMS2. This one-one correspondence also makes the invariants and simulation relations needed for the proof straightforward to establish. There are at most four main proof steps to consider, corresponding to the main steps of the TMS2 specification.

Theorem 1. TML-CGA *is opaque.*

Linearizability Against the Coarse-grained Abstraction. Having established opacity of TML-CGA, we can now focus on linearizability between TML and TML-CGA, which by Theorem 2 will ensure opacity of TML. As with the opacity part, we are free to use any of the available methods from the literature to prove linearizability [12]. We opt for a model-checking approach; part of our motivation is to show that model checking indeed becomes a feasible technique for verifying opacity.

We use the PAT model checker [26], which enables one to verify trace refinement (in a manner that guarantees linearizability) without having to explicitly define invariants, refinement relations, or linearization points of the algorithm. Interestingly, the model checker additionally shows that, for the bounds tested, TML is *equivalent* to TML-CGA, i.e., both produce exactly the same set of observable traces (see Lemma 1 below).

PAT allows one to specify algorithms using a CSP-style syntax [18]. However, in contrast to conventional CSP, events in PAT are arbitrary programs assumed to execute atomically — as such they can directly modify shared state, and do not have to communicate via channels with input/output events. This enables our transactional memory algorithms to be implemented naturally. We obtain the following lemma, where constant *SIZE* denotes the size of the memory (i.e., number of addresses) and constant V for the possible values in these addresses.

Lemma 1. *For bounds* $N = 3$, *SIZE* $= 4$, *and* $V = \{0, 1, 2, 3\}$, *as well as* $N = 4$, *SIZE* $= 2$, *and* $V = \{0, 1\}$, *TML is equivalent to* TML-CGA.

4   Soundness and Completeness

We now present two key theorems for our proof method. Theorem 2, presented below, establishes soundness. That is, it states if we have an opaque CGA $\mathcal{A}$ (expressed as a set of alternating histories), and a TM implementation $\mathcal{H}$ (expressed as a set of concurrent histories) such that every history in $\mathcal{H}$ is linearizable to a history in $\mathcal{A}$, then every history in $\mathcal{H}$ is opaque. We prove Theorem 2 using the following lemma, which essentially states our soundness result for individual histories, rather than sets of histories.

Lemma 2 (Soundness per history [9]**).** *Suppose h is a concrete history. For any alternating history ha that linearizes h, if ha is opaque then h is also opaque.*

The main soundness theorem lifts this result to sets of histories. Its proof follows from Lemma 2 in a straightforward manner (see [2] for details).

Theorem 2 (Soundness). *Suppose $\mathcal{A}$ is a set of alternating opaque histories. Then a set of histories $\mathcal{H}$ is opaque if for each $h \in \mathcal{H}$, there exists a history $ha \in \mathcal{A}$ and an $he \in extend(h)$ such that $lin(he, ha)$.*

The next two results establish completeness of our proof method. Theorem 3 states that given an opaque TM implementation $\mathcal{H}$ (expressed as a set of concurrent histories) we can find a set of alternating opaque histories $\mathcal{A}$ such that every history in $\mathcal{H}$ can be linearized to a history in $\mathcal{A}$. Here, $\mathcal{A}$ is the CGA of our method. We prove this theorem using Lemma 3, which essentially states our completeness result for individual histories.

Lemma 3 (Existence of linearization). *If h is an opaque history then there exists an alternating history ha such that $lin(h, ha)$ and ha is final-state opaque.*

Proof. From the assumption that h is opaque, there exists an extension $he \in extend(h)$ and a history $hs \in \mathcal{S}$ such that $[he] \equiv hs$ and $\prec_{[he]} \subseteq \prec_{hs}$. Our proof proceeds by transposing operations in hs to obtain an alternating history ha such that $lin(he, ha)$. Our transpositions preserve final-state opacity, hence ha is final-state opaque.

We consider pairs of operations o_t and $o_{t'}$ such that $o_t \lll_{hs} o_{t'}$, but $o_{t'} \prec \prec_{[he]} o_t$, which we call *mis-ordered pairs*. If there are no mis-ordered pairs, then $lin(he, hs)$, and we are done. Let o_t and $o_{t'}$ be the mis-ordered pair such that the distance between o_t and $o_{t'}$ in hs is least among all mis-ordered pairs. Now, hs has the form $\ldots o_t g o_{t'} \ldots$. Note that g does not contain any operations of transaction t, since if there were some operation o of t in g, then because opacity preserves program order and $o_t \lll_{hs} o$, we would have $o_t \lll_{[he]} o$. Thus $o, o_{t'}$ would form a mis-ordered pair of lower distance, contrary to hypothesis. For a similar reason, g does not contain any operations of t'. Thus, as long as we do not create a new edge in the opacity order $\prec_{hs}$, we can reorder hs to (1) $\ldots g o_{t'} o_t \ldots$ or (2) $\ldots o_{t'} o_t g \ldots$ while preserving opacity. A new edge can be created only by reordering a pair of begin and commit operations so that the commit precedes the begin. If o_t is not a begin operation, then we choose option (1). Otherwise, note that $o_{t'}$ cannot be a commit, because since $o_{t'} \prec_{[he]} o_t$, $t' \prec t$, and thus t could not have been serialised before t'. Since $o_{t'}$ is not a commit, we can choose option (2). Finally, we show that the new history has no new mis-ordered pairs. Assume we took option (1). Then if there is some o in g such that $o_t \prec_{[he]} o$ we would have $o_{t'} \prec_{[he]} o$, and thus $o, o_{t'}$ would form a narrower mis-ordered pair. The argument for case (2) is symmetric. Thus, we can repeat this reordering process and eventually arrive at a final-state opaque history ha that has no mis-ordered pairs, and thus $lin(he, ha)$.   □

Theorem 3 (Completeness). *If $\mathcal{H}$ is a prefix-closed set of opaque histories, then there is some prefix-closed set of opaque alternating histories $\mathcal{A}$ such that for each $h \in \mathcal{H}$ there is some $h' \in \mathcal{A}$ such that $lin(h, ha)$.*

Proof. Let $\mathcal{A} = \{h'.h'$ is final-state opaque and $\exists h \in \mathcal{H}.lin(h, h')\}$. Note that both the set of all opaque histories and the set of linearizable histories of any prefix-closed set are themselves prefix-closed. Thus, $\mathcal{A}$ is prefix closed. Because $\mathcal{A}$ is prefix-closed, and each element is final-state opaque, each element of $\mathcal{A}$ is opaque. For any $h \in \mathcal{H}$, Lemma 3 implies that there is some $ha \in \mathcal{A}$ that linearizes h.   □

Note that the proof of Theorem 3 works by constructing the CGA $\mathcal{A}$ as a set of alternating histories. To construct the operational model that generates this set, we use the heuristics described in Sect. 3.

5   The NORec Algorithm

In this section, we show that the method scales to more complex algorithms. In particular, we verify the NORec algorithm by Dalessandro *et al.* [8] (see Listing 3), a popular and performant software TM.

The verification for NORec proceeds as with TML. Namely, we construct a coarse-grained abstraction, NORec-CGA (see Listing 4), verify that NORec-CGA is opaque, then show that NORec linearizes to NORec-CGA. As with TML, we do not perform a full verification of linearizability, but rather, model check the linearizability part of the proof using PAT. The proof that NORec-CGA is opaque proceeds via forward simulation against a variant of TMS2 (TMS3), which does not require read-only transactions to validate during their commit, matching the behaviour of NORec more closely. We have proved (in Isabelle) that despite this weaker precondition for read-only commits, TMS2 and TMS3 are equivalent by proving each refines the other. Further details of TMS3 and proofs (including mechanisation) may be found in our extended paper [2]. The following theorem (proved in Isabelle) establishes opacity of NORec-CGA.

Theorem 4. NORec-CGA *is opaque.*

Next, we have a lemma that is proved via model checking [2].

Listing 3. NORec pseudocode

```
 1: procedure TXBegin_t                          21: procedure TXWrite_t(a, v)
 2:   do loc_t ← glb                              22:   wrSet_t ← wrSet_t ⊕ {a ↦ v}
 3:   until even(loc_t)                           23: procedure TXRead_t(a)
 4: procedure Validate_t                          24:   if a ∈ dom(wrSet_t) then
 5:   while true do                               25:     return wrSet_t(a)
 6:     time_t ← glb                              26:   v_t ← mem(a)
 7:     if odd(time_t) then goto 6                27:   while loc_t ≠ glb do
 8:     for a ↦ v ∈ rdSet_t do                    28:     loc_t ← Validate_t
 9:       if mem(a) ≠ v then abort                29:     v_t ← mem(a)
10:     if time_t = glb then return time_t        30:   rdSet_t ← rdSet_t ⊕ {a ↦ v_t}
11: procedure TXCommit_t                          31:   return v_t
12:   if wrSet_t = ∅ then return
13:   while !cas(glb, loc_t, loc_t + 1) do
14:     loc_t ← Validate_t
15:   for a ↦ v ∈ wrSet_t do
16:     mem(a) ← v
17:   glb ← loc_t + 2
```

Listing 4. NORec-CGA: Coarse-grained abstraction of NORec

```
 1: procedure ATXBegin_t                           9: procedure ATXWrite_t(a, v)
 2:   return                                      10:   wrSet_t ← wrSet_t ⊕ {a ↦ v}

 3: procedure ATXCommit (t)                       11: procedure ATXRead_t(a)
 4:   atomic                                      12:   atomic
 5:     if wrSet_t = ∅ then return                13:     if a ∈ dom(wrSet_t) then
 6:     else if rdSet_t ⊆ mem then                14:       return wrSet_t(a)
 7:       mem ← mem ⊕ wrSet_t                     15:     else if rdSet_t ⊆ mem then
 8:     else abort                                16:       rdSet_t ← rdSet_t ⊕ {a ↦ v}
                                                  17:       return mem(a)
                                                  18:     else abort
```

Lemma 4. *For bounds $N = 2$, $SIZE = 2$ and $V = \{0, 1\}$, NORec is equivalent to NORec-CGA.*

TMS3 and NORec-CGA are similar in many respects. They both use read and write sets in the same way, and write-back lazily during the commit. The only additional information needed in the simulation is keeping track of the number of successful commits in NORec-CGA. Thus, the simulation relation used in the proof of Theorem 4 above is straightforward (see [2]). On the other hand, proving opacity of the fine-grained NoRec implementation directly would be much more difficult as we would need to concern ourselves with the locking mechanism employed during the commit to guarantee that the write-back occurs atomically. However, this locking mechanism is effectively only being used to guarantee linearizability of the NORec commit operation, so it need not occur in the opacity proof. Lesani *et al.* have directly verified opacity of NORec [20]. In comparison to our approach, they introduce several layers of intermediate automata, with each layer introducing additional complexity and design elements of the NORec algorithm. Overall, their proofs are much more involved than ours.

6   Weak Memory Models

We now demonstrate that our method naturally extends to reasoning about opacity of TM implementations under weak memory. We will focus on TSO in this Section, but our arguments and methods could be extended to other memory models. Note that we cannot employ a data-race freedom argument [1] to show that TML or NORec running on TSO are equivalent to sequentially consistent versions of the algorithms. This is because transactional reads can race with the writes of committing transactions (this is true even when we consider the weaker *triangular-race freedom* condition of [24]). This racy behaviour is typical for software transactional memory implementations.

There are two possibilities for verifying our TM algorithms on TSO. (1) Leveraging a proof of opacity of the implementation under sequential consistency then showing that the weak memory implementation refines this sequentially consistent implementation. (2) Showing that the implementation under weak memory linearizes to the coarse-grained abstraction directly. This approach simply treats an implementation executing under a particular memory model as an alternative implementation of the CGA algorithm in question.

In this paper, we follow the second approach, which shows that model checking linearizability of TSO implementations against a coarse-grained abstraction is indeed feasible. We verify both TML and NORec under TSO within the PAT model checker.

Due to the transitivity of trace inclusion, the proof proceeds by showing that the concrete implementation that executes using relaxed memory semantics linearizes to its corresponding coarse-grained abstraction. We use constant *BSIZE* to bound the maximum size of the local buffer for each transaction.

Lemma 5. *For bounds* $N = 2$, *SIZE* $= 2$, *BSIZE* $= 2$ *and* $V = \{0, 1\}$, TML *under TSO is equivalent to* TML-CGA *and* NORec *under TSO is equivalent to* NORec-CGA.

7   Conclusions

Our main contributions for this paper are as follows. **(1)** We have developed a complete method for proving opacity of TM algorithms using linearizability. This allows one to reuse the vast literature on linearizability verification [12] (for correctness of the fine-grained implementation), as well as the growing literature on opacity verification (to verify the coarse-grained abstractions). **(2)** We have demonstrated our technique using the TML algorithm, and shown that the method extends to more complex algorithms by verifying the NORec algorithm. **(3)** We have developed an equivalent variation of the TMS2 specification, TMS3 that does not require validation when read-only transactions commit. Because

Listing 5. Abstraction used to verify TML in [9] is not opaque

1: **procedure** Begin$_t$	
2: **return**	6: **procedure** Commit$_t$
	7: **return**
3: **procedure** Write$_t(a, v)$	
4: **atomic**	8: **procedure** Read$_t(a)$
5: **return abort or** $mem(a) \leftarrow$ v	9: **atomic**
	10: **return** $mem(a)$ **or return abort**

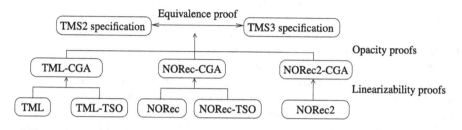

Fig. 1. Overview of proofs

TMS3 specifies equivalent behaviour to TMS2 while simplifying its preconditions, it is a preferable model for performing simulation proofs. **(4)** We have shown that the decomposition makes it possible to cope with relaxed memory by showing that both TML and NORec are opaque under TSO.

An overview of our proofs is given in Fig. 1. The equivalence proof between TMS2 and TMS3 as well as the opacity proofs between the CGAs and TMS2/3 specifications have been mechanised in Isabelle, whereas the linearizablity proofs are via model checking in PAT. We note that during our work, we developed a variation of NORec (called NORec2) which allows read operations to lookup values in the read set rather than querying shared memory, and demonstrated that this variation aborts less often than the existing NORec algorithm. We were able to quickly verify this modified algorithm. For more details, see [2].

Related Work. Derrick *et al.* give a proof method that inductively generates a linearized *history* of a fine-grained implementation and shows that this linearized history is opaque [9]. Although checking opacity of a linearized history is simpler than a proof of opacity of the full concurrent history, one cannot consider their proof method to be a decomposition because the main invariant of the implementation must explicitly assert the existence of an opaque history (see Sect. 7). However, these methods suggest a crucial insight: that linearizability provides a sound method for proving opacity.

The basic idea of using a linearized history to verify opacity appears in [9], but their proof technique has little in common with ours. The abstraction that Derrick *et al.* use to motivate linearizability is given in Listing 5. Note that the read and commit operations in this abstraction perform no validation, and this abstraction is not opaque by itself. Therefore, it cannot be as a genuine intermediate specification. Instead, the steps of this abstraction are explicitly coupled with the *linearization points* of the fine-grained TML implementation, and it is this coupled system that is shown to be opaque. It is currently unclear if such a method could scale to more complex algorithms such as NORec, or to include weak memory algorithms.

Lesani and Palsberg have developed a technique that allows opacity to be checked by verifying an invariant-like condition called *markability* [22]. Lesani *et al.* have developed a second method [20] that proves opacity using the intermediate TMS2 specification [11,21] using stepwise refinement against several intermediate layers of abstraction. Guerraoui *et al.* have developed an approach, where a set of *aspects* of an algorithm are checked, followed by model checking over a *conflict-freedom* condition that implies opacity [13]. Koskinen and Parkinson [19] have a technique where they describe a push/pull model of transactions, and note that opaque transactions are a special case of push/pull transactions that do not pull during execution. This allows opacity to be proven via mapping the algorithm to the rules of the push/pull automata, which are stated in terms of commutativity conditions. In the context of our work, one could see such push/pull automata as an alternative to TMS2—one could use their proof technique to prove that our CGAs are opaque, and then use traditional linearizability verification techniques. As such, our work allows for an additional degree of proof decomposition. A key advantage of our method is that it is agnostic as to the exact techniques used for both the linearizability and opacity verifications, allowing for full verification by any method, or as in our case a mix of full verification and model-checking.

Experiences. Our experiences suggest that our techniques do indeed simplify proofs of opacity (and their mechanisation). Opacity of each coarse-grained abstraction is generally trivial to verify (our proofs are mechanised in Isabelle), leaving one with a proof of linearizability of an implementation against this abstraction. We emphasise that the method used for the second step is limited only by techniques for verifying linearizability. We have opted for a model checking approach using PAT, which enables linearizability to be checked via refinement. It is of course also possible to perform a full verification of linearizability. Furthermore, we note that we were able to use the model-checking approach to quickly test small variants of the existing algorithms.

Future Work. Our work suggests that to fully verify a TM algorithm using coarse-grained abstraction, the bottleneck to verification is the proof of linearizability itself [12]. It is hence worthwhile considering whether linearizability proofs can be streamlined for transactional objects. For example, Bouajjani *et al.* have shown that for particular inductively-defined data structures, linearizability can be reduced to state reachability [4]. Exploration of whether such methods apply to transactional objects remains a topic for future work. Establishing this link would be a useful result — it would allow one to further reduce a proof of opacity to a proof of state reachability.

Acknowledgements. We thank John Derrick for helpful discussions and funding from EPSRC grant EP/N016661/1.

References

1. Adve, S.V., Aggarwal, J.K.: A unified formalization of four shared-memory models. IEEE Trans. Parallel Distrib. Syst. **4**(6), 613–624 (1993)
2. Armstrong, A., Dongol, B., Doherty, S.: Reducing opacity to linearizability: a sound and complete method. arXiv e-prints (October 2016). https://arxiv.org/abs/1610.01004
3. Attiya, H., Gotsman, A., Hans, S., Rinetzky, N.: A programming language perspective on transactional memory consistency. In: Fatourou, P., Taubenfeld, G. (eds.) PODC 2013, pp. 309–318. ACM (2013)
4. Bouajjani, A., Emmi, M., Enea, C., Hamza, J.: On reducing linearizability to state reachability. In: Halldórsson, M.M., Iwama, K., Kobayashi, N., Speckmann, B. (eds.) ICALP 2015. LNCS, vol. 9135, pp. 95–107. Springer, Heidelberg (2015). doi:10.1007/978-3-662-47666-6_8
5. Černý, P., Radhakrishna, A., Zufferey, D., Chaudhuri, S., Alur, R.: Model Checking of linearizability of concurrent list implementations. In: Touili, T., Cook, B., Jackson, P. (eds.) CAV 2010. LNCS, vol. 6174, pp. 465–479. Springer, Heidelberg (2010). doi:10.1007/978-3-642-14295-6_41
6. Chakraborty, S., Henzinger, T.A., Sezgin, A., Vafeiadis, V.: Aspect-oriented linearizability proofs. Logical Methods Comput. Sci. **11**(1) (2015)
7. Dalessandro, L., Dice, D., Scott, M., Shavit, N., Spear, M.: Transactional mutex locks. In: D'Ambra, P., Guarracino, M., Talia, D. (eds.) Euro-Par 2010. LNCS, vol. 6272, pp. 2–13. Springer, Heidelberg (2010). doi:10.1007/978-3-642-15291-7_2
8. Dalessandro, L., Spear, M.F., Scott, M.L.: NORec: streamlining STM by abolishing ownership records. In: Govindarajan, R., Padua, D.A., Hall, M.W. (eds.) PPoPP, pp. 67–78. ACM (2010)
9. Derrick, J., Dongol, B., Schellhorn, G., Travkin, O., Wehrheim, H.: Verifying opacity of a transactional mutex lock. In: Bjørner, N., de Boer, F. (eds.) FM 2015. LNCS, vol. 9109, pp. 161–177. Springer, Cham (2015). doi:10.1007/978-3-319-19249-9_11
10. Doherty, S., Groves, L., Luchangco, V., Moir, M.: Formal verification of a practical lock-free queue algorithm. In: Frutos-Escrig, D., Núñez, M. (eds.) FORTE 2004. LNCS, vol. 3235, pp. 97–114. Springer, Heidelberg (2004). doi:10.1007/978-3-540-30232-2_7
11. Doherty, S., Groves, L., Luchangco, V., Moir, M.: Towards formally specifying and verifying transactional memory. Formal Asp. Comput. **25**(5), 769–799 (2013)
12. Dongol, B., Derrick, J.: Verifying linearisability: a comparative survey. ACM Comput. Surv. **48**(2), 19 (2015)
13. Guerraoui, R., Henzinger, T.A., Singh, V.: Model checking transactional memories. Distrib. Comput. **22**(3), 129–145 (2010)
14. Guerraoui, R., Kapalka, M.: On the correctness of transactional memory. In: Chatterjee, S., Scott, M.L. (eds.) PPoPP, pp. 175–184. ACM (2008)
15. Guerraoui, R., Kapalka, M.: Principles of Transactional Memory. Synthesis Lectures on Distributed Computing Theory. Morgan & Claypool Publishers, San Rafael (2010)
16. Harris, T., Larus, J.R., Rajwar, R.: Transactional Memory. Synthesis Lectures on Computer Architecture, 2nd edn. Morgan & Claypool Publishers, San Rafael (2010)
17. Herlihy, M., Wing, J.M.: Linearizability: a correctness condition for concurrent objects. ACM TOPLAS **12**(3), 463–492 (1990)

18. Hoare, C.A.R.: Communicating sequential processes. Commun. ACM **21**(8), 666–677 (1978)

19. Koskinen, E., Parkinson, M.: The push/pull model of transactions. In: PLDI. PLDI 2015, vol. 50, pp. 186–195. ACM, New York, NY, USA, June 2015

20. Lesani, M., Luchangco, V., Moir, M.: A framework for formally verifying software transactional memory algorithms. In: Koutny, M., Ulidowski, I. (eds.) CONCUR 2012. LNCS, vol. 7454, pp. 516–530. Springer, Heidelberg (2012). doi:10.1007/978-3-642-32940-1_36

21. Lesani, M., Luchangco, V., Moir, M.: Putting opacity in its place. In: Workshop on the Theory of Transactional Memory (2012)

22. Lesani, M., Palsberg, J.: Decomposing opacity. In: Kuhn, F. (ed.) DISC 2014. LNCS, vol. 8784, pp. 391–405. Springer, Heidelberg (2014). doi:10.1007/978-3-662-45174-8_27

23. Liu, Y., Chen, W., Liu, Y.A., Sun, J., Zhang, S.J., Dong, J.S.: Verifying linearizability via optimized refinement checking. IEEE Trans. Softw. Eng. **39**(7), 1018–1039 (2013)

24. Owens, S.: Reasoning about the implementation of concurrency abstractions on x86-TSO. In: D'Hondt, T. (ed.) ECOOP 2010. LNCS, vol. 6183, pp. 478–503. Springer, Heidelberg (2010). doi:10.1007/978-3-642-14107-2_23

25. Schellhorn, G., Derrick, J., Wehrheim, H.: A sound and complete proof technique for linearizability of concurrent data structures. ACM TOCL **15**(4), 31:1–31:37 (2014)

26. Sun, J., Liu, Y., Dong, J.S., Pang, J.: PAT: towards flexible verification under fairness. In: Bouajjani, A., Maler, O. (eds.) CAV 2009. LNCS, vol. 5643, pp. 709–714. Springer, Heidelberg (2009). doi:10.1007/978-3-642-02658-4_59

27. Vafeiadis, V.: Modular fine-grained concurrency verification. Ph.D. thesis. University of Cambridge (2007)

On Futures for Streaming Data in ABS
(Short Paper)

Keyvan Azadbakht[(✉)], Nikolaos Bezirgiannis, and Frank S. de Boer

Centrum Wiskunde & Informatica (CWI), Amsterdam, Netherlands
{k.azadbakht,n.bezirgiannis,f.s.de.boer}@cwi.nl

Abstract. Many modern distributed software applications require a continuous interaction between their components exploiting streaming data from the server to the client. The Abstract Behavioral Specification (ABS) language has been developed for the modeling and analysis of distributed systems. In ABS, concurrent objects communicate by calling each other's methods asynchronously. Return values are communicated asynchronously too via the return statement and so-called futures. In this paper, we extend the basic ABS model of asynchronous method invocation and return in order to support the streaming of data. We introduce the notion of a "Future-based Data Stream" to extend the ABS. The application of this notion and its impact on performance are illustrated by means of a case study in the domain of social networks simulation.

Keywords: Future · Streaming · Cooperative scheduling · Active object · Programming language · Social network

1 Introduction

Streaming data is a client/server pattern used in many distributed applications. It consists of a continuous generation of data by the server where the generated data is processed by the client sequentially and incrementally. The Abstract Behavioral Specification (ABS) language [1] has been developed for formal modeling and analysis of distributed systems. In ABS, concurrent objects represent processes that execute in parallel and interact via asynchronous communication of messages. A message specifies a call to one of the methods of the called object. Return values are communicated asynchronously via so-called futures [2]. Futures are dynamically generated references for checking the availability of the return value and its reading.

In this paper, we extend this basic model of asynchronous method invocation and return to support the streaming of data between the server and the client. We introduce the notion of "Future-Based Data Stream" by extending the syntax with a *yield* statement which returns a value specified by its argument *without* terminating the execution of the method, which thus proceeds as specified. The generated values can be obtained incrementally and sequentially by querying the

A. Bouajjani and A. Silva (Eds.): FORTE 2017, LNCS 10321, pp. 67–73, 2017.
DOI: 10.1007/978-3-319-60225-7_5

future corresponding to this method invocation. The standard return statement terminates the method execution and is used to signal the end of the generated stream of data.

As a proof of concept, we also present the impact of the above-mentioned feature on performance in the implementation of distributed application for the generation of social networks.

Related Work. There are different programming constructs for streaming data. *Asynchronous generators* as specified in [3], enable the streaming of data in an asynchronous method invocation. This includes, on the callee side, yielding the data, and on the caller side receiving them as an asynchronous iterator or raising an exception if there is no further yielded data. These generators are defined in the context of the multithreaded model of concurrency, where asynchrony are provided by spawning a thread for a method call. *Akka Streams* [4] provide an API to specify a streaming setup between actors which allows to adapt behavior to the underlying resources in terms of both memory and speed. There are also languages which utilize the notion of a *channel* as a means of communication, inspired by the model of *Communicating Sequential Processes* (CSP). For instance, *JCSP* [5] is a library in Java that provides CSP-like elements, e.g., processes and channels with read and write possibilities.

Similarly to asynchronous generators, as proposed below streaming data is fully integrated with asynchronous method invocation, i.e., it is not a separate orthogonal concept like channels are. But its integration with the ABS language allows for an additional loose coupling between the producer and consumer of data streams: by means of cooperative scheduling of tasks the consumption of data can be interleaved with other tasks on demand. Moreover, the notion of data streaming abstracts from the specific implementation of ABS. In our case, we make use of the distributed Haskell backend of ABS [6] for the case study on future-based data streams reported in this paper.

This paper is organized as follows: a brief description of the ABS programming language is given in Sect. 2. The notion of Future-Based Data Stream is specified as an extension of ABS in Sect. 3. In Sect. 4, a case study on social network simulation is discussed, which uses the proposed notion of streams. Finally we conclude in Sect. 5.

2   The ABS Programming Language

Here we briefly highlight the main features of ABS relevant to our work in this paper. In ABS, parallel (or concurrent) processes are generated by asynchronous method calls of the form $f = o!m(\bar{e})$, where f is a future used as a reference to the return value of the asynchronous call of the method m, o is an expression denoting the called object, and $\bar{e}$ are the actual parameters. Such a call generates a process for the execution of the invoked method in the (unique) *concurrent object group* (cog) to which the called object belongs. Within such a group at most one process is executing. The executing process of a cog is however executing in parallel with all the executing processes of the other groups. A cog is created by the expression **new** C, where C denotes a class. The statement **new local** C adds a new instance of class C to the group of the object that creates this instance.

Further, ABS features synchronous method calls and a high-level synchronization mechanism (i.e., cooperative scheduling) which allows a cog to suspend the execution of the current process and schedule another (enabled) process for execution, by means of *await* and *suspend* statements. The *await f?* suspends the current process of the active object if the future f is not resolved yet, or it skips otherwise. The *await b* similarly suspends the current process if the boolean guard b evaluates to *false*. Finally, the *suspend* statement blocks the current process unconditionally. The process to be activated next is selected in a cog based on the scheduling policy. The *f.get* also queries the resolution of the future f and reads its value if it is resolved or it blocks the whole cog otherwise.

3   Future-Based Data Streams

In this section, future based data streaming is specified in the context of the ABS language which exploits the notion of cogs and cooperative scheduling.

The simple code example in Fig. 1 illustrates how data streams can be used in an ABS program extended by this feature. The program is comprised of two classes **Producer** and **Consumer** which implement the **IProd** and **ICons** interfaces, respectively, followed by the main block of the program. First, the runtime system instantiates two cogs, each of which contains one active object, i.e. the objects **prod** and **con**. The main cog then calls asynchronously the **process** method of the object **con**. The **process** method calls asynchronously the method **primes** which basically generates the first n prime numbers. The **primes** method is a *streamer method*, that is, its return type is **Str<Int>** and the method specification is allowed to contain the **yield** statement which is, roughly speaking, a non-terminating **return** statement.

Therefore, the prime numbers generated by the **primes** are streamed to the caller via a data stream. The last value by **return** statement is followed by a special token (e.g., *eof*) to state that there is no further value to be streamed. On the caller side, the return values are assigned to the variable **r** which is a stream buffer enabling the above-mentioned streaming of return values from the callee to the caller process. The **StrFut<T>** can only type a variable which is assigned by an asynchronous method call where the callee is a streamer method returning values of type **T**.

The **awaitAll** statement of the **Consumer** class is a mechanism to retrieve all the prime numbers from the stream **r**. Based on the state of the stream, the statement behaves in three different ways: (1) if there is at least one value in the stream then the first value will be retrieved, assigned to x, and removed from the stream buffer. The following block of the statement will be also executed. This will repeat until the buffer is empty. (2) If there is no value in the buffer but there may be more values to be received (i.e., *eof* is not buffered yet), then the process cooperatively releases control so that another process of the **consumer** is activated. The process will be activated later once the stream is not empty. (3) If there is no value in the buffer and the *eof* is in the stream then the statement will skip.

```
interface IProd {                      interface ICons {
   Str<Int> primes(Int n);                Unit process(IProd o);
}                                      }

class Producer implements IProd        class Consumer implements ICons
{                                      {
   Str<Int> primes(Int n) {               Unit process(IProd o){
      Int i = 1;                             StrFut<Int> r = o!primes(1000);
      Int j = 2;                             awaitAll r? in x
      while(i<n)                             {
      {                                          // process x
         yield j;                            }
         j = nextPrime(j);                }
         i = i + 1;                     }
      }                              // main block
      return j;                      {
   }                                    IProd prod = new Producer();
                                        ICons con = new Consumer();
   Int nextPrime(Int x) {               con ! process(prod);
      // return the smallest prime > x  }
   }
}
```

Fig. 1. An example in ABS extended by future-based data streams

Syntax. The syntax of our proposed extension of ABS, i.e., that of future-based data streams, is specified in Fig. 2. The only syntactic extension on the callee side is the **yield** statement, that can only be used in the specification of a *streamer* method. The rest of the statements are related to the specification of a caller to a streamer method.

awaitAll is already described in the above example. The **await-catch** statement is a single-fetch version of the repetitive **awaitAll**: (1) If there is at least one value in the stream buffer then it retrieves the head of the buffer and assigns it to x. It also removes the value from the buffer, but not repetition takes places. (2) As before, if there is no value in the buffer then the process releases the control cooperatively. (3) If there is *eof* in the stream buffer then, deviating from **awaitAll**, the statement s is executed. The **getAll** and **get-catch** coincide semantically to the **awaitAll** and **await-catch** respectively, except for releasing control, where the whole cog is suspended rather than the current process.

$$s ::= \textbf{yield } e \mid \textbf{awaitAll } e? \textbf{ in } x \; \{s\} \mid \textbf{await } e? \textbf{ in } x \textbf{ catch } \{s\} \mid$$
$$e.\textbf{getAll in } x\{s\} \mid e.\textbf{get in } x \textbf{ catch } \{s\}$$

Fig. 2. Syntax

4   Case Study

Simulation of massive social networks is of great importance. Typically, larger networks are structurally different from the smaller networks generated based on the same models [7]. Analysis of social networks is relevant to many scientific domains, e.g., data-mining, network sciences, physics, and social sciences [8]. In this section, we briefly investigate social network simulation based on so-called Preferential Attachment [9].

Modeling and implementation of the above-mentioned system is for standard ABS already extensively investigated for both multi-core [10] and distributed [11] architectures in the ABS language. Here we focus on how our proposed notion of streams influences the performance of the system presented in [11]. To adopt data streams, we have modified the communication pattern of the active objects, where instead of one request per message, a batch of requests is sent to an active object via one method invocation and the return values are streamed to the caller via data streaming. The performance gain, discussed below, can be attributed almost entirely to the batching responses instead of sending one packet per return value. Note, such a batching mechanism is integrated naturally in the context of data streams.

In graph-theoretical terms the problem of Preferential Attachment considers an initial graph of $d+1$ nodes for some small number d and seeks to extend the graph with n nodes, for some $n \gg d$, by adding nodes one-by-one such that each new node will have degree d. The d target nodes are selected preferentially where the preference is the degree, that is, the higher the degree of a node, the higher the probability to be attached to the new node.

4.1   Experimental Results

The case study on massive social network simulation has been implemented in Cloud ABS [6], which is a source-to-source transcompiler from ABS code down to Cloud Haskell [12] runnable on distributed machines. Beside a higher level of abstraction at the programming level thanks to our proposed feature, the distributed runtime system provides more than 6× speed-up performance compared to the same implementation without using the feature, presented in [11]. The results are illustrated in Fig. 3.

The distribution overhead increases the execution time for two machines, which is compensated by the parallelism achieved through adding more VMs. As shown in Table 1, the memory consumption decreases when adding more VMs, which enables generating extra-large graphs which cannot fit in centralized-memory architectures. We ran the implementation on a distributed cloud environment kindly provided by the Dutch SURF foundation. The hardware consisted of identical VMs interconnected over a 10Gbps ethernet network; each VM was a single-core Intel Xeon E5-2698, 16GB RAM running Ubuntu 14.04 Server edition. Finally, we provided an online repository[1] containing the ABS code for the case study and instructions for installing the ABS Haskell backend.

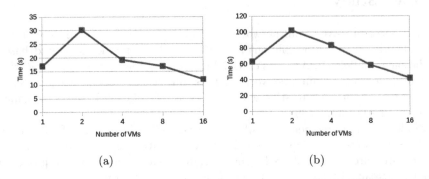

(a)   (b)

Fig. 3. Performance results of the distributed PA in ABS-Haskell for graphs of $n = 10^7$ nodes with $d =$ (a) 3, (b) 10.

Table 1. Maximum memory residency (in MB) per virtual machine.

	Total number of VMs				
Graph size	1	2	4	8	16
$n = 10^6, d = 3$	306	266	212	155	114
$n = 10^6, d = 10$	899	1028	547	354	221
$n = 10^7, d = 3$	2123	3242	1603	967	621
$n = 10^7, d = 10$	6260	9668	6702	3611	1905

5   Conclusion and Future Work

In the extended ABS, the proposed type strFut<T> of asynchronous data streams is similar to that of simple futures in the sense that a value of its type T can be passed around. However, shared data streams in general will give rise to race conditions because, by definition, processing an element from the stream implies its removal. Different standard techniques can be used to control race conditions, like ownership types. Alternatively, in future work we will investigate monotonically increasing streams whose generated elements are persistent. This will involve some additional cursor mechanism for local reading devices for different users and requires auxiliary garbage collection techniques.

Work is well under way addressing the type system and operational semantics of the proposed notion as an extension of ABS.

---

[1] http://github.com/abstools/distributed-PA/streams.

Acknowledgments. This research is partly funded by the EU project FP7-612985 UpScale: From Inherent Concurrency to Massive Parallelism through Type-based Optimizations (http://www.upscale-project.eu). This work was carried out on the Dutch national HPC cloud infrastructure, a service provided by the SURF Foundation (http://www.surf.nl). We also thank Erik de Vink for his constructive comments.

References

1. Johnsen, E.B., Hähnle, R., Schäfer, J., Schlatte, R., Steffen, M.: ABS: a core language for abstract behavioral specification. In: Aichernig, B.K., de Boer, F.S., Bonsangue, M.M. (eds.) FMCO 2010. LNCS, vol. 6957, pp. 142–164. Springer, Heidelberg (2011). doi:10.1007/978-3-642-25271-6_8

2. de Boer, F.S., Clarke, D., Johnsen, E.B.: A complete guide to the future. In: Nicola, R. (ed.) ESOP 2007. LNCS, vol. 4421, pp. 316–330. Springer, Heidelberg (2007). doi:10.1007/978-3-540-71316-6_22

3. Selivanov, Y.: Asynchronous generators (2016). https://www.python.org/dev/peps/pep-0525/

4. Streams - version 2.5.0 (2017). http://doc.akka.io/docs/akka/2.4/scala/stream/index.html

5. Welch, P., Brown, N.: Communicating Sequential Processes for Java^{tm} (JCSP) (2014). https://www.cs.kent.ac.uk/projects/ofa/jcsp/

6. Bezirgiannis, N., de Boer, F.: ABS: a high-level modeling language for cloud-aware programming. In: Freivalds, R.M., Engels, G., Catania, B. (eds.) SOFSEM 2016. LNCS, vol. 9587, pp. 433–444. Springer, Heidelberg (2016). doi:10.1007/978-3-662-49192-8_35

7. Leskovec, J.: Dynamics of large networks. ProQuest (2008)

8. Bader, D., Madduri, K.: Parallel algorithms for evaluating centrality indices in real-world networks. In: International Conference on Parallel Processing 2006, pp. 539–550. IEEE (2006)

9. Barabási, A.L., Albert, R.: Emergence of scaling in random networks. Science **286**(5439), 509–512 (1999)

10. Azadbakht, K., Bezirgiannis, N., de Boer, F.S., Aliakbary, S.: A high-level and scalable approach for generating scale-free graphs using active objects. In: 31st Annual ACM Symposium on Applied Computing, pp. 1244–1250. ACM (2016)

11. Azadbakht, K., Bezirgiannis, N., de Boer, F.S.: Distributed network generation based on preferential attachment in ABS. In: Steffen, B., Baier, C., Brand, M., Eder, J., Hinchey, M., Margaria, T. (eds.) SOFSEM 2017. LNCS, vol. 10139, pp. 103–115. Springer, Cham (2017). doi:10.1007/978-3-319-51963-0_9

12. Epstein, J., Black, A.P., Peyton-Jones, S.: Towards Haskell in the cloud. ACM SIGPLAN Not. **46**, 118–129 (2011). ACM

Session-Based Concurrency, Reactively

Mauricio Cano[1], Jaime Arias[2], and Jorge A. Pérez[3(✉)]

[1] University of Groningen, Groningen, The Netherlands
[2] Inria Grenoble Rhône-Alpes, Montbonnot-Saint-Martin, France
[3] University of Groningen and CWI, Amsterdam, The Netherlands
`j.a.perez@rug.nl`

Abstract. This paper concerns formal models for the analysis of communication-centric software systems that feature *declarative and reactive behaviors*. We focus on *session-based concurrency*, the interaction model induced by session types, which uses (variants of) the π-calculus as specification languages. While well-established, such process models are not expressive enough to specify declarative and reactive behaviors common in emerging communication-centric software systems. Here we propose the *synchronous reactive programming* paradigm as a uniform foundation for session-based concurrency. We present correct encodings of session-based calculi into ReactiveML, a synchronous reactive programming language. Our encodings bridge the gap between process specifications and concurrent programs in which session-based concurrency seamlessly coexists with declarative, reactive, timed, and contextual behaviors.

1 Introduction

In this paper, we introduce the *synchronous reactive programming* paradigm as a practical foundation for *communication-centric* software systems. Our motivation is twofold. First, synchronous reactive programming allows us to uniformly integrate point-to-point communications (as in the π-calculus) with declarative, reactive, timed, and contextual behaviors—this is an elusive combination for process models such as the π-calculus. Second, by relying on ReactiveML (a synchronous reactive programming language with a formal semantics), we may bridge the gap between π-calculus *processes* and actual concurrent *programs*, thus bringing a rigorous communication model to programmers.

Large software systems are deployed as aggregations of distributed interacting components, which are built using a myriad of different programming platforms and/or made available as black-boxes that expose minimal interaction interfaces. In these complex, heterogeneous systems *communication* emerges as the key unifying glue. Certifying that interacting components conform to their prescribed protocols is thus an important but challenging task, and is essential in ensuring overall system correctness.

Besides protocol conformance, analyzing communication-centric software systems entails addressing additional challenges, which can be seen as related to

© IFIP International Federation for Information Processing 2017
Published by Springer International Publishing AG 2017. All Rights Reserved
A. Bouajjani and A. Silva (Eds.): FORTE 2017, LNCS 10321, pp. 74–91, 2017.
DOI: 10.1007/978-3-319-60225-7_6

the increasing ubiquity of these systems. Indeed, communication-centric software appears in emerging trends (e.g., collective adaptive systems) and as such is subject to various classes of requirements that are orthogonal to communication correctness. We focus on communication-centric software systems featuring *declarative, reactive, timed,* and *contextual* behaviors. (In Sect. 2 we illustrate these intended systems, using a transactional protocol subject to failures.) By stipulating governing conditions (rather than *how* to implement such conditions), declarative approaches naturally specify, e.g., security policies. Closely intertwined, constructs modeling reactivity, time, and context-awareness are at the heart of mechanisms that enforce, e.g., self-adaptation and fault-tolerance in dependable systems. Therefore, while not directly connected to protocol specifications, declarative, reactive, timed, and contextual behaviors (and their interplay) do influence communication and should be integrated into the analysis of protocol conformance.

Process calculi (such as the π-calculus [17]) have long offered a principled basis for the compositional analysis of message-passing programs. Within these approaches, our work concerns *session-based concurrency*, the interaction model induced by *session types* [11], which organize protocols as *sessions* between two or more participants. In session-based concurrency, a session type describes the contribution of each partner to the protocol. Interactions are structured, and always occur in matching pairs; e.g., when one partner sends, the other receives; when one partner offers a selection, the other chooses. Different session type theories for *binary* (two-party) and *multiparty* protocols have been developed [12]; here we focus on binary sessions.

Binary and multiparty session types rely on π-calculi with session constructs. These session calculi have been extended with declarative, reactive, timed, and contextual behaviors, but none of these extensions captures all these features. For instance, session calculi with *assertions* (logical predicates) [3,5] may describe certain declarative requirements, but do not account for reactive and contextual behaviors. Frameworks with time-related conditions, such as [1,4], have similar limitations. The framework in [13] supports contextual information through *events*, but does not represent reactive, declarative behaviors. Integrating these extensions into a single process framework seems rather difficult, for they rely on different languages and often conflicting assumptions.

Here we pursue a different approach: we embed session-based concurrency within the synchronous reactive programming (SRP) model for reactive, timed systems [2,10]. Hence, rather than extending session π-calculi with declarative, reactive, timed, and contextual features, we encode session-based communication into a setting where these features (and their interplay) are already well understood. We consider ReactiveML, a programming language based on SRP [15,16], as target language in our developments. ReactiveML is a general purpose functional language with a well-defined formal semantics. Our **technical contributions** are two correct encodings of session π-calculi into ReactiveML. In a nutshell, we use *signals* in ReactiveML to mimick *names* in session π-calculi. Our encodings enable us to integrate, in a seamless and uniform way, session-based constructs as "macros" in ReactiveML programs with declarative and reactive constructs. Moreover, since our encodings are executable (well-typed) ReactiveML programs, our results have a direct practical character, which serves to bridge the gap between specifications in process models and actual concurrent programs.

This paper is structured as follows. Section 2 illustrates our approach via an example. Section 3 summarizes the syntax and semantics of a session π-calculus and of ReactiveML. In both cases, we consider languages with synchronous and asynchronous (queue-based) communication. Section 4 presents our two encodings and states their correctness. Section 5 collects closing remarks. An online appendix includes further examples and technical details (omitted definitions and proofs) [7].

2 A Motivating Example

We use a toy example to illustrate (i) the limitations of session π-calculi in representing structured communications with declarative/reactive behaviors, and (ii) how our approach, based on encodings into ReactiveML, can neatly overcome such limitations.

A Ride Protocol. Suppose a conference attendee who finds himself in a foreign airport. To get in time for his presentation, he uses a mobile app in his phone to request a ride to the conference venue. The intended protocol may be intuitively described as follows:

1. *Attendee* sends his current location and destination to a neighbouring *Driver*.
2. *Driver* receives these two pieces of information and offers three options to *Attendee*: a ride right *now*, a ride at a *later* time, or to *abort* the transaction.
3. *Attendee* is in a hurry, and so he selects to be picked up right now.
4. *Driver* replies by sending an estimated arrival time at *Attendee*'s location.

Using session π-calculus processes (as in, e.g., [18]), this protocol may be implemented as a process $S = (\nu xy)(A(x) \mid D(y))$, where processes $A(x)$ and $D(y)$ abstract the behavior of *Attendee* and *Driver* as follows:

$$A(x) = x\langle loc\rangle.x\langle des\rangle.x \triangleleft \mathsf{now}.x(e).\mathbf{0}$$
$$D(y) = y(l).y(d).y \triangleright \{\mathsf{now} : y\langle eta\rangle.\mathbf{0}, \mathsf{later} : y(t).y\langle ok\rangle.\mathbf{0}, \mathsf{quit} : Close_y\}$$

where process $Close_y$ denotes an unspecified sub-protocol for closing the transaction. Above, we write $x\langle z\rangle.P$ (resp. $x(w).P$) to denote the output (resp. input) along name x with continuation P. Processes $x \triangleleft l.P$ and $x \triangleright \{l_i : P_i\}_{i \in I}$ denote internal and external labeled choices, respectively. Above, now, later, and quit denote labels. Process $\mathbf{0}$ denotes inaction. Process $(\nu xy)P$ declares x and y as dual *session endpoints* in P. This way, S says that $A(x)$ and $D(y)$ play complementary roles in the session protocol.

The Need for Richer Behaviors. Session-based concurrency assumes that once a session is established, communication may proceed without interruptions. This is unrealistic in most real-life scenarios, where established sessions are prone to failures or interruptions. For instance, a connectivity issue in the middle of the protocol with *Driver* may leave *Attendee* stuck in the airport. In such cases, notions of *contextual information, reactivity,* and *time* become essential:

Contextual Information such as, e.g., external events signalling a malfunction, allows relating the system with its environment. For instance, we may like to relate $A(x)$ and $D(y)$ with a connectivity manager that triggers warning events.

Reactivity serves to detect unforeseen circumstances (e.g., failures) and to define appropriate system behaviors to run in such cases. For instance, we may like to define $A(x)$ so that another driver is requested if a failure in a protocol with $D(y)$ arises.

Time allows to track the instant in which a failure occurred, and also to establish a deadline within which the failure should be resolved. For instance, in case of failure $A(x)$ may try contacting alternative drivers only until k time instants after the failure.

As mentioned above, the session π-calculus does not support these features, and proposed extensions do not comprehensively address them. We rely on synchronous reactive programming (SRP) and ReactiveML, which already have the ingredients for seamlessly integrating declarative, reactive behavior into session-based concurrency.

ReactiveML. ReactiveML extends OCaml with reactive, timed behavior. Time is modelled as discrete units, called *instants*; reactivity arises through *signals*, which may carry values. In ReactiveML, expression signal x in e declares a new signal x. We use constructs emit s v and await $s(x)$ in e to emit and await a signal s, respectively. Preemption based on signals is obtained by the expression do (e_1) until $s \rightarrow (e_2)$, which executes e_1 until signal s is detected, and runs e_2 in the next instant. Moreover, ReactiveML can encode the parallel composition of expressions e_1 and e_2, denoted $e_1 \parallel e_2$.

Embedding Sessions in ReactiveML. Our first encoding, denoted $[\![\cdot]\!]_f$ (cf. Definition 14), translates session π-calculus processes into ReactiveML expressions; we use substitution f to represent names in the session π-calculus using (fresh) signals in ReactiveML. Our second encoding, denoted $(\![\cdot]\!)$ (cf. Definition 17), supports an asynchronous semantics.

We illustrate $[\![\cdot]\!]_f$ by revisiting our example above. Let us define a concurrent reactive program in which $[\![A(x)]\!]_f$, $[\![D(y)]\!]_f$, and $[\![D'(w)]\!]_f$ represent ReactiveML snippets that implement session-based communication. We consider a simple possibility for failure: that *Driver* $(D(y))$ may cancel a ride anytime or that communication with *Attendee* $(A(x))$ fails and cannot be recovered. Ideally, we would like a new driver $D'(w)$, whose implementation may be the same as $D(y)$, to continue with the protocol, without disrupting the protocol from

$$\lfloor \text{COM} \rfloor \ (\pmb{\nu}xy)(x\langle v\rangle.P \mid y(z).Q) \longrightarrow (\pmb{\nu}xy)(P \mid Q\{v/z\})$$

$$\lfloor \text{SEL} \rfloor \ (\pmb{\nu}xy)(x \triangleleft l_j.P \mid y \triangleright \{l_i{:}Q_i\}_{i\in I}) \longrightarrow (\pmb{\nu}xy)(P \mid Q_j) \ (j \in I)$$

$$\lfloor \text{REP} \rfloor \ (\pmb{\nu}xy)(x\langle v\rangle.P \mid *y(z).Q) \longrightarrow (\pmb{\nu}xy)(P \mid Q\{v/z\} \mid *y(z).Q)$$

$$\lfloor \text{IFT} \rfloor \ \texttt{tt?}\,(P){:}(Q) \longrightarrow P \qquad \lfloor \text{IFF} \rfloor \ \texttt{ff?}\,(P){:}(Q) \longrightarrow Q$$

Fig. 1. Reduction relation for π processes (contextual congruence rules omitted).

the perspective of $A(x)$. This could be easily expressed in ReactiveML as the expression $S' = \text{signal } w_1, w_2 \text{ in } (RA \parallel RD)$ where:

$$RA = \text{do } ([\![A(x)]\!]_{\{x\leftarrow w_1\}}) \text{ until } \textit{fail} \rightarrow (\text{await } w_2(z) \text{ in } [\![A(x)]\!]_{\{x\leftarrow z\}})$$
$$RD = \text{do } ([\![D(y)]\!]_{\{y\leftarrow w_1\}}) \text{ until } \textit{fail} \rightarrow (BD)$$
$$BD = \text{signal } w_3 \text{ in } (\text{emit } w_2 \ w_3; [\![D'(w)]\!]_{\{w\leftarrow w_3\}})$$

S' declares two signals: while signal w_1 connects a reactive attendee RA and the reactive driver RD, signal w_2 connects RA with a backup driver BD. If no failure arises, RA and RD run their expected session protocol. Otherwise, the presence of signal $\textit{fail}$ will be detected by both RA and RD: as a result, the attendee will await a new signal for restarting the session; process $[\![D(y)]\!]$ stops and BD will become active in the next instant. After emitting a fresh signal w_3, BD can execute the protocol with RA.

3 Preliminaries

A Session ***π-calculus.*** Our presentation follows closely that of [18]. We assume a countable infinite set of variables $\mathcal{V}_s$, ranged over by $x, y, \dots$. A variable represents one of the two *endpoints* of a session. We use $v, v', \dots$ to range over *values*, which include variables and the boolean constants $\texttt{tt}, \texttt{ff}$. Also, we use $l, l', \dots$ to range over *labels*. We write $\widetilde{x}$ to denote a finite sequence of variables (and similarly for other elements).

Definition 1 (π). *The set π of session processes is defined as:*

$$P, Q ::= x\langle v\rangle.P \mid x(y).P \mid x \triangleleft l.P \mid x \triangleright \{l_i : P_i\}_{i\in I} \mid v?\,(P){:}(Q) \mid P \mid Q \mid \mathbf{0}$$
$$\mid (\pmb{\nu}xy)P \mid *x(y).P$$

Process $x\langle v\rangle.P$ sends value v over x and then continues as P; dually, process $x(y).Q$ expects a value v on x that will replace all free occurrences of y in Q. Processes $x \triangleleft l_j.P$ and $x \triangleright \{l_i : Q_i\}_{i\in I}$ define a labeled choice mechanism, with labels indexed by the finite set I: given $j \in I$, process $x \triangleleft l_j.P$ uses x to select l_j and trigger process Q_j. We assume pairwise distinct labels. The conditional process $v?\,(P):(Q)$ behaves as P if v evaluates to $\texttt{tt}$; otherwise it behaves as Q. Parallel composition and inaction are standard. We often write $\prod_{i=1}^{n} P_i$ to stand for $P_1 \mid \cdots \mid P_n$. The *double restriction* $(\pmb{\nu}xy)P$ binds together x and y in P, thus indicating that they are the two endpoints of a session. Process $*x(y).P$

$\lfloor\text{SEND}\rfloor$ $x\langle v\rangle.P \mid x[i : \widetilde{m_1}, o : \widetilde{m_2}] \longrightarrow_{\mathbb{A}} P \mid x[i : \widetilde{m_1}, o : \widetilde{m_2} \cdot v]$

$\lfloor\text{SEL}\rfloor$ $x \triangleleft l.P \mid x[i : \widetilde{m_1}, o : \widetilde{m_2}] \longrightarrow_{\mathbb{A}} P \mid x[i : \widetilde{m_1}, o : \widetilde{m_2} \cdot l]$

$\lfloor\text{COM}\rfloor$ $x[i : \widetilde{m_1}, o : m \cdot \widetilde{m_2}] \mid \overline{x}[i : \widetilde{m_1}, o : \widetilde{m_2}] \longrightarrow_{\mathbb{A}} x[i : \widetilde{m_1}, o : \widetilde{m_2}] \mid \overline{x}[i : \widetilde{m_1} \cdot m, o : \widetilde{m_2}]$

$\lfloor\text{RECV}\rfloor$ $x(y).P \mid x[i : v \cdot \widetilde{m_1}, o : \widetilde{m_2}] \longrightarrow_{\mathbb{A}} P\{v/y\} \mid x[i : \widetilde{m_1}, o : \widetilde{m_2}]$

$\lfloor\text{BRA}\rfloor$ $x \triangleright \{l_i : P_i\}_{i \in I} \mid x[i : l_j \cdot \widetilde{m_1}, o : \widetilde{m_2}] \longrightarrow_{\mathbb{A}} P_j \mid x[i : \widetilde{m_1}, o : \widetilde{m_2}]$ $(j \in I)$

$\lfloor\text{IFT}\rfloor$ $\text{tt}?(P){:}(Q) \longrightarrow_{\mathbb{A}} P$ $\lfloor\text{IFF}\rfloor$ $\text{ff}?(P){:}(Q) \longrightarrow_{\mathbb{A}} Q$

Fig. 2. Reduction relation for aπ processes (contextual congruence rules omitted).

denotes a replicated input process, which allows us to express infinite server behaviors. In $x(y).P$ (resp. $(\nu yz)P$) occurrences of y (resp. y, z) are bound with scope P. The set of free variables of P, denoted $\text{fv}(P)$, is as expected.

The operational semantics for π is given as a *reduction relation* $\longrightarrow$, the smallest relation generated by the rules in Fig. 1. Reduction expresses the computation steps that a process performs on its own. It relies on a *structural congruence* on processes, denoted $\equiv_S$, which identifies processes up to consistent renaming of bound variables, denoted $\equiv_\alpha$. Formally, $\equiv_S$ is the smallest congruence that satisfies the axioms:

$$P \mid \mathbf{0} \equiv_S P \quad P \mid Q \equiv_S Q \mid P \quad P \equiv_S Q \text{ if } P \equiv_\alpha Q$$
$$(P \mid Q) \mid R \equiv_S P \mid (Q \mid R) \quad (\nu xy)(\nu wz)P \equiv_S (\nu wz)(\nu xy)P$$
$$(\nu xy)\mathbf{0} \equiv_S \mathbf{0} \quad (\nu xy)P \mid Q \equiv_S (\nu xy)(P \mid Q) \quad \text{if } x, y \notin \text{fv}(Q)$$

We briefly comment on the rules in Fig. 1. Reduction requires an enclosing restriction $(\nu xy)(\cdots)$; this represents the fact that a session connecting endpoints x and y has been already established. Rule $\lfloor\text{COM}\rfloor$ represents the synchronous communication of value v through endpoint x to endpoint y. While Rule $\lfloor\text{SEL}\rfloor$ formalizes a labeled choice mechanism, in which communication of a label l_j is used to choose which of the Q_i will be executed, Rule $\lfloor\text{REPL}\rfloor$ is similar to Rule $\lfloor\text{COM}\rfloor$, and used to spawn a new copy of Q, available as a replicated server. Rules $\lfloor\text{IFT}\rfloor$ and $\lfloor\text{IFF}\rfloor$ are self-explanatory. Rules for reduction within parallel, restriction, and $\equiv_S$ (not given in Fig. 1) are as expected.

The following notion will be useful in stating properties of our translations.

Definition 2 (Contexts for π). *The syntax of (evaluation) contexts in π is given by the following grammar:* $E ::= [\cdot] \mid E \mid P \mid P \mid E \mid (\nu xy)(E)$, *where P is a π process and '$[\cdot]$' represents a 'hole'. We write $C[\cdot]$ to range over contexts* $(\nu \widetilde{xy})([\cdot] \mid P_1 \mid \ldots \mid P_n)$, *with $n \geq 1$. $E[P]$ (resp. $C[P]$) will denote the process obtained by filling $[\cdot]$ with P.*

An Asynchronous Session π-calculus (aπ). Following [13], we now define aπ, a variant of π with asynchronous (queue-based) semantics. The syntax of aπ includes variables $x, y, \ldots$ and *co-variables*, denoted $\overline{x}, \overline{y}$. Intuitively, x and $\overline{x}$ denote the two endpoints of a session, with $\overline{\overline{x}} = x$. We write $\mathcal{V}_a$ to denote the set of variables and co-variables; k, k' will be used to range over $\mathcal{V}_a$. As before, values include booleans and variables. The syntax of processes is as follows:

Definition 3 (aπ and aπ*). *The set* aπ *of asynchronous session processes is defined as:*

$$P, Q ::= k\langle v \rangle.P \mid k(y).P \mid k \triangleleft l.P \mid k \triangleright \{l_i : P_i\}_{i \in I} \mid v?(P){:}(Q) \mid P \mid Q \mid \mathbf{0}$$
$$\mid (\boldsymbol{\nu}x)P \mid \mu X.P \mid X \mid k[i : \widetilde{m}; o : \widetilde{m}]$$

We write aπ* *to denote the sub-language of* aπ *without queues.*

Differences with respect to Definition 1 appear in the second line of the above grammar. The usual (single) restriction $(\boldsymbol{\nu}x)P$ is convenient in a queue-based setting; it binds both x and $\overline{x}$ in P. We consider recursion $\mu X.P$ rather than input-guarded replication. Communication in aπ is mediated by queues of messages m (values v or labels l), one for each endpoint k; these queues, denoted $k[i : \widetilde{m}; o : \widetilde{m}]$, have output and input parts. Synchronization proceeds as follows: the sending endpoint first enqueues the message m in its own output queue; then, m is moved to the input queue of the receiving endpoint; finally, the receiving endpoint retrieves m from its input queue. We will use ϵ to denote the empty queue. Notions of free/bound (recursive) variables are as expected.

The operational semantics of aπ is defined as a reduction relation coupled with a structural congruence relation $\equiv_\mathsf{A}$. The former is defined by the rules in Fig. 2, which either follow the above intuitions for queue-based message passing or are exactly as for π; the latter is defined as the smallest congruence on processes that considers standard principles for parallel composition and inaction, together with the axioms:

$$(\boldsymbol{\nu}x)(\boldsymbol{\nu}y)P \equiv_\mathsf{A} (\boldsymbol{\nu}y)(\boldsymbol{\nu}x)P \qquad (\boldsymbol{\nu}x)\mathbf{0} \equiv_\mathsf{A} \mathbf{0} \quad \mu X.P \equiv_\mathsf{A} P\{\mu X.P/X\}$$
$$k[i : \epsilon; o : \epsilon] \equiv_\mathsf{A} \mathbf{0} \qquad (\boldsymbol{\nu}x)P \mid Q \equiv_\mathsf{A} (\boldsymbol{\nu}x)(P \mid Q) \text{ if } x \notin \mathsf{fv}(Q).$$

The notion of contexts for aπ includes unary contexts E and binary contexts C:

Definition 4 (Contexts for aπ). *The syntax of contexts in* aπ *is given by the following grammar:* $E ::= [\cdot] \mid E \mid P \mid P \mid E \mid (\boldsymbol{\nu}x)E$, *where* P *is an* aπ *process and '$[\cdot]$' represents a 'hole'. We write* $C[\cdot_1, \cdot_2]$ *to denote binary contexts* $(\boldsymbol{\nu}\widetilde{x})([\cdot_1] \mid [\cdot_2] \mid \prod_{i=1}^n P_i)$ *with* $n \geq 1$. *We will write* $E[P]$ *(resp.* $C[P, Q]$*) to denote the* aπ *process obtained by filling the hole in* $E[\cdot]$ *(resp.* $C[\cdot_1, \cdot_2]$*) with* P *(resp.* P *and* Q*).*

Both π and aπ abstract from an explicit phase of session initiation in which endpoints are bound together. We thus find it useful to identify aπ processes which are *properly initialized (PI)*: intuitively, processes that contain all queues required to reduce.

Definition 5 (Properly Initialized Processes). *Let* $P \equiv_\mathsf{A} (\boldsymbol{\nu}\widetilde{x})(P_1 \mid P_2)$ *be an* aπ *process such that* P_1 *is in* aπ* *(i.e., it does not include queues) and* $\mathsf{fv}(P_1) = \{k_1, \ldots, k_n\}$. *We say* P *is properly initialized (PI) if* P_2 *contains a queue for each session declared in* P_1, *i.e., if* $P_2 = k_1[i : \epsilon, o : \epsilon] \mid \cdots \mid k_n[i : \epsilon, o : \epsilon]$.

ReactiveML: A Synchronous Reactive Programming Language. Based on the reactive model given in [6], ReactiveML [16] is an extension of OCaml that allows unbounded time response from processes, avoiding causality issues present in other SRP approaches. ReactiveML extends OCaml with *processes*: state machines whose behavior can be executed through several *instants*. Processes are the reactive counterpart of OCaml functions, which ReactiveML executes instantaneously. In ReactiveML, synchronization is based on *signals*: events that occur in one instant. Signals can trigger reactions in processes; these reactions can be run instantaneously or in the next instant. Signals carry values and can be emitted from different processes in the same instant.

We present the syntax of ReactiveML following [14], together with two semantics, with synchronous and asynchronous communication. We will assume countable infinite sets of variables $\mathcal{V}_r$ and names $\mathcal{N}_r$ (ranged over by x_1, x_2 and n_1, n_2, respectively).

Definition 6 (RML). *The set* RML *of ReactiveML expressions is defined as:*

$$
\begin{aligned}
v, v' ::=\ & c \mid (v, v) \mid n \mid \lambda x.e \mid \mathsf{process}\ e \\
e, e' ::=\ & x \mid c \mid (e, e) \mid \lambda x.e \mid e\ e \mid \mathsf{rec}\ x = v \\
& \mid\ \mathsf{match}\ e\ \mathsf{with}\ \{c_i \to e_i\}_{i \in I} \mid \mathsf{let}\ x = e\ \mathsf{and}\ x = e\ \mathsf{in}\ e \mid \mathsf{run}\ e \mid \mathsf{loop}\ e \\
& \mid\ \mathsf{signal}_e\ x : e\ \mathsf{in}\ e \mid \mathsf{emit}\ e\ e \mid \mathsf{pause} \mid \mathsf{process}\ e \\
& \mid\ \mathsf{present}\ e?\ (e) : e \mid \mathsf{do}\ e\ \mathsf{when}\ e \mid \mathsf{do}\ (e)\ \mathsf{until}\ e(x) \to (e)
\end{aligned}
$$

Values $v, v', \dots$ include constants c (booleans and the unit value $()$), pairs, names, abstractions, and also processes, which are made of expressions. The syntax of expressions e, e' extends a standard functional substrate with match and let expressions and with process- and signal-related constructs. Expressions run e and loop e follow the expected intuitions. Expression $\mathsf{signal}_g\ x : d$ in e declares a signal x with default value d, bound in e; here g denotes a *gathering function* that collects the values produced by x in one instant. When d and g are unimportant (e.g., when the signal will only be emitted once), we will write simply signal x in P. We will also write signal $x_1, \dots, x_n$ in e when declaring $n > 1$ distinct signals in e. If expression e_1 transitions to the name of a signal then emit $e_1\ e_2$ emits a signal carrying the value from the instantaneous execution of e_2. Expression pause postpones execution to the next instant. The conditional expression $\mathsf{present}\ e_1?\ (e_2) : (e_3)$ checks the presence of a signal: if e_1 transitions to the name of a signal present in the current instant, then e_2 is run in the same instant; otherwise, e_3 is run in the next instant. Expression do e when e_1 executes e only when e_1 transitions to the name of a signal present in the current instant, and suspends its execution otherwise. Expression $\mathsf{do}\ (e_1)\ \mathsf{until}\ e(x) \to (e_2)$ executes e_1 until e transitions into the name of a signal currently present that carries a value which will substitute x. If this occurs, the execution of e_1 stops at the end of the instant and e_2 is executed in the next one. Using these basic constructs, we may obtain the useful derived expressions reported in Fig. 3, which include the parallel composition $e_1 \parallel e_2$. We will say that an expression with no parallel composition operator at top level is a *thread*.

$$e_1 \parallel e_2 \overset{\Delta}{=} \mathsf{let}\ \_ = e_1\ \mathsf{and}\ \_ = e_2\ \mathsf{in}\ () \qquad e_1; e_2 \overset{\Delta}{=} \mathsf{let}\ \_ = ()\ \mathsf{and}\ \_ = e_1\ \mathsf{in}\ e_2$$

$$\mathsf{await}\ e_1(x)\ \mathsf{in}\ e_2 \overset{\Delta}{=} \mathsf{do}\ (\mathsf{loop\ pause})\ \mathsf{until}\ e_1(x) \to (e_2)$$

$$\mathsf{let\ rec\ process}\ f\ x_1 \ldots x_n = e_1\ \mathsf{in}\ e_2 \overset{\Delta}{=} \mathsf{let}\ f = (\mathsf{rec}\ f = \lambda x_1 \ldots x_n.\mathsf{process}\ e_1)\ \mathsf{in}\ e_2\ \ (n \geq 1)$$

$$\mathsf{if}\ e_1\ \mathsf{then}\ e_2\ \mathsf{else}\ e_3 \overset{\Delta}{=} \mathsf{match}\ e_1\ \mathsf{with}\ \{\mathsf{tt} \to e_2 \mid \mathsf{ff} \to e_3\}$$

Fig. 3. Derived RML expressions.

We write $\equiv_R$ to denote the smallest equivalence that satisfies the following axioms: (i) $e \parallel () \equiv_R e$; (ii) $e_1 \parallel e_2 \equiv_R e_2 \parallel e_1$; (iii) $(e_1 \parallel e_2) \parallel e_3 \equiv_R e_1 \parallel (e_2 \parallel e_3)$.

A Synchronous Semantics for RML. Following [14], we define a big-step operational semantics for RML. We require some auxiliary definitions for *signal environments* and *events*. Below, $\uplus$ and $\sqsubseteq$ denote usual multiset union and inclusion, respectively.

Definition 7 (Signal Environment). *Let* $\mathcal{D}, \mathcal{G}, \mathcal{M}$ *be sets of default values, gathering functions, and multisets, respectively. A* signal environment *is a function* $S : \mathcal{N}_r \to (\mathcal{D} \times \mathcal{G} \times \mathcal{M})$, *denoted* $S \overset{\Delta}{=} [(d_1, g_1, m_1)/n_1, \ldots, (d_k, g_k, m_k)/n_k]$, *with* $k \geq 1$.

We use the following notations: $S^d(n_i) = d_i$, $S^g(n_i) = g_i$, and $S^m(n_i) = m_i$. Also, $S^v = fold\ g_i\ m_i\ d_i$ where *fold* recursively gathers multiple emissions of different values in the same signal; see [14,16] for details. An event E associates a signal n_i to a multiset m_i that represents the values emitted during an instant:

Definition 8 (Events). *An* event *is defined as a function* $E : \mathcal{N}_r \to \mathcal{M}$, *i.e.*, $E \overset{\Delta}{=} [m_1/n_1, \ldots, m_k/n_k]$, *with* $k \geq 1$. *Given events* E_1 *and* E_2, *we say that* E_1 *is* included *in* E_2 *(written* $E_1 \sqsubseteq_E E_2$*) if and only if* $\forall n \in Dom(E_1) \cup Dom(E_2) \Rightarrow E_1(n) \sqsubseteq E_2(n)$. *The* union E_1 *and* E_2 *(written* $E_1 \sqcup_E E_2$*) is defined for all* $n \in Dom(E_1) \cup Dom(E_2)$ *as* $(E_1 \sqcup_E E_2)(n) = E_1(n) \uplus E_2(n)$.

We now define the semantics of RML expressions. A big-step transition in RML captures reactions within a single instant, and is of the form $e \xrightarrow[S]{E,b} e'$ where S stands for the smallest signal environment (wrt $\sqsubseteq_E$ and S^m) containing input, output, and local signals; E is the event made of signals emitted during the reaction; $b \in \{\mathsf{tt}, \mathsf{ff}\}$ is a boolean value that indicates termination: b is false if e is stuck during that instant and is true otherwise. At each instant i, the program reads an input I_i and produces an output O_i. The reaction of an expression obeys four conditions: (C1) $(I_i \sqcup_E E_i) \sqsubseteq_E S_i^m$ (i.e., S must contain the inputs and emitted signals); (C2) $O_i \sqsubseteq_E E_i$ (i.e., the output signals are included in the emitted signals); (C3) $S_i^d \subseteq S_{i+1}^d$; and (C4) $S_i^g \subseteq S_{i+1}^g$ (i.e., default values and gathering functions are preserved throughout instants).

Figure 4 gives selected transition rules; see [7] for a full account. Rules ⌊L-PAR⌋ and ⌊L-DONE⌋ handle let expressions, distinguishing when (a) at least

$$\lfloor\text{L-PAR}\rfloor \ \dfrac{e_1 \xrightarrow[S]{E_1,b_1} e_1' \quad e_2 \xrightarrow[S]{E_2,b_2} e_2' \quad b_1 \wedge b_2 = \mathbf{ff}}{\text{let } x_1 = e_1 \text{ and } x_2 = e_2 \text{ in } e_3 \xrightarrow[S]{E_1 \sqcup_E E_2,\mathbf{ff}} \text{let } x_1 = e_1' \text{ and } x_2 = e_2' \text{ in } e_3}$$

$$\lfloor\text{L-DONE}\rfloor \ \dfrac{e_1 \xrightarrow[S]{E_1,\mathbf{tt}} v_1 \quad e_2 \xrightarrow[S]{E_2,\mathbf{tt}} v_2 \quad e_3\{v_1,v_2/x_1,x_2\} \xrightarrow[S]{E_3,b} e_3'}{\text{let } x_1 = e_1 \text{ and } x_2 = e_2 \text{ in } e_3 \xrightarrow[S]{E_1 \sqcup_E E_2 \sqcup_E E_3,b} e_3'}$$

$$\text{RUN}\rfloor \ \dfrac{\xrightarrow[S]{E_1,\mathbf{tt}} \text{process } e' \quad e' \xrightarrow[S]{E_2,b} e''}{\text{run } e \xrightarrow[S]{E_1 \sqcup_E E_2,b} e''}$$

$$\lfloor\text{LP-STU}\rfloor \ \dfrac{e \xrightarrow[S]{E,\mathbf{ff}} e'}{\text{loop } e \xrightarrow[S]{E,\mathbf{ff}} e'; \text{loop } e}$$

$$\lfloor\text{LP-UN}\rfloor \ \dfrac{e \xrightarrow[S]{E_1,\mathbf{tt}} v \quad \text{loop } e \xrightarrow[S]{E_2,b} e'}{\text{loop } e \xrightarrow[S]{E_1 \sqcup_E E_2,b} e'}$$

$$\text{SIG-DEC}\rfloor \ \dfrac{e_1 \xrightarrow[S]{E_1,\mathbf{tt}} v_1 \quad e_2 \xrightarrow[S]{E_2,\mathbf{tt}} v_2 \quad e_3\{n/x\} \xrightarrow[S]{E_3,b} e_3' \quad n \text{ fresh} \quad S(n) = (v_1, v_2, m)}{\text{signal}_{e_2}\ x : e_1 \text{ in } e_3 \xrightarrow[S]{E_1 \sqcup_E E_2 \sqcup_E E_3,b} e_3'}$$

$$\lfloor\text{EMIT}\rfloor \ \dfrac{e_1 \xrightarrow[S]{E_1,\mathbf{tt}} n \quad e_2 \xrightarrow[S]{E_2,\mathbf{tt}} v}{\text{emit } e_1\ e_2 \xrightarrow[S]{E_1 \sqcup_E E_2 \sqcup_E [\{v\}/n],\mathbf{tt}} ()}$$

$$\lfloor\text{PAUSE}\rfloor \ \dfrac{}{\text{pause} \xrightarrow[S]{\emptyset,\mathbf{ff}} ()}$$

$$\lfloor\text{SIG-P}\rfloor \ \dfrac{e_1 \xrightarrow[S]{E_1,\mathbf{tt}} n \quad n \in S \quad e_2 \xrightarrow[S]{E_2,b} e_2'}{\text{present } e_1?\,(e_2):(e_3) \xrightarrow[S]{E,\mathbf{ff}} e_2'}$$

$$\lfloor\text{SIG-NP}\rfloor \ \dfrac{e_1 \xrightarrow[S]{E,\mathbf{tt}} n \quad n \notin S}{\text{present } e_1?\,(e_2):(e_3) \xrightarrow[S]{E,\mathbf{ff}} e_3}$$

$$\text{DU-END}\rfloor \ \dfrac{e_2 \xrightarrow[S]{E_2,\mathbf{tt}} n \quad e_1 \xrightarrow[S]{E_1,\mathbf{tt}} v}{\mathbf{o}\,(e_1) \text{ until } e_2(x) \to (e_3) \xrightarrow[S]{E_1 \sqcup_E E_2,\mathbf{tt}} v}$$

$$\lfloor\text{DU-P}\rfloor \ \dfrac{e_2 \xrightarrow[S]{E_2,\mathbf{tt}} n \quad n \in S \quad e_1 \xrightarrow[S]{E_1,\mathbf{ff}} e_1'}{\mathbf{do}\,(e_1) \text{ until } e_2(x) \to (e_3) \xrightarrow[S]{E_1 \sqcup_E E_2,\mathbf{ff}} e_3\{S^v(n)/x\}}$$

$$\lfloor\text{DU-NP}\rfloor \ \dfrac{e_2 \xrightarrow[S]{E_2,\mathbf{tt}} n \quad n \notin S \quad e_1 \xrightarrow[S]{E_1,\mathbf{ff}} e_1'}{\mathbf{do}\,(e_1) \text{ until } e_2(x) \to (e_3) \xrightarrow[S]{E_1 \sqcup_E E_2,\mathbf{ff}} \mathbf{do}\,(e_1') \text{ until } e_2(x) \to (e_3)}$$

Fig. 4. Big-step semantics for RML expressions (selection).

one of the parallel branches has not yet terminated, and (b) both branches have terminated and their resulting values can be used. Rule $\lfloor\text{RUN}\rfloor$ ensures that declared processes can only be executed while they are preceded by run. Rules $\lfloor\text{LP-STU}\rfloor$ and $\lfloor\text{LP-UN}\rfloor$ handle loop expressions: the former decrees that a loop will stop executing when the termination boolean of its body becomes $\mathbf{ff}$; the latter executes a loop until Rule $\lfloor\text{LP-STU}\rfloor$ is applied. Rule $\lfloor\text{SIG-DEC}\rfloor$ declares a signal by instantiating it with a fresh name in the continuation; its default value and gathering function must be instantaneous expressions. Rule $\lfloor\text{EMIT}\rfloor$ governs signal emission. Rule $\lfloor\text{PAUSE}\rfloor$ suspends the process for an instant. Rules $\lfloor\text{SIG-P}\rfloor$ and $\lfloor\text{SIG-NP}\rfloor$ check for presence of a signal n: when n is currently present, the body e_2 is run in the same instant; otherwise, e_3 is executed in the next instant. Rules $\lfloor\text{DU-END}\rfloor$, $\lfloor\text{DU-P}\rfloor$, and $\lfloor\text{DU-NP}\rfloor$ handle expressions $\mathbf{do}\,(e_1)$ until $e_2(x) \to (e_3)$. Rule $\lfloor\text{DU-END}\rfloor$ says that if e_1 terminates

$\lfloor\text{Put-Q}\rfloor$

$\langle\text{put } q\ v;\ \Sigma, q:\widetilde{h}\rangle \xrightarrow[S]{\emptyset,\text{tt}} \langle();\ \Sigma, q:\widetilde{h}\cdot v\rangle$

$\lfloor\text{Pop-Q}\rfloor$

$\langle\text{pop } q;\ \Sigma, q: v\cdot\widetilde{h}\rangle \xrightarrow[S]{\emptyset,\text{tt}} \langle v;\ \Sigma, q:\widetilde{h}\rangle$

$\lfloor\text{NEmpty}\rfloor$

$\langle\text{isEmpty } q;\ \Sigma, q:\widetilde{h}\rangle \xrightarrow[S]{\emptyset,\text{tt}} \langle();\ \Sigma, q:\widetilde{h}\rangle$

$\lfloor\text{Pop-Q}_\epsilon\rfloor$

$\langle\text{pop } q;\ \Sigma, q:\epsilon\rangle \xrightarrow[S]{\emptyset,\text{ff}} \langle\text{pop } q;\ \Sigma, q:\epsilon\rangle$

$\lfloor\text{Empty}\rfloor\ \langle\text{isEmpty } q;\ \Sigma, q:\epsilon\rangle \xrightarrow[S]{\emptyset,\text{ff}} \langle\text{isEmpty } q;\ \Sigma, q:\epsilon\rangle$

Fig. 5. Big-step semantics for RMLq: queue-related operations.

instantaneously, then the whole expression terminates. Rule $\lfloor\text{DU-P}\rfloor$ says that if e_2 transitions to a currently present signal n, then e_3 is executed in the next instant, substituting x with the values gathered in n. Rule $\lfloor\text{DU-NP}\rfloor$ executes e_1 as long as e_2 does not reduce to a currently present signal. We shall rely on a simple notion of equality.

Definition 9 (Equality with case normalization). *Let* $\hookrightarrow_R$ *denote the extension of* $\equiv_R$ *with the axiom* match c_j with $\{c_i \to P_i\}_{i\in I} \hookrightarrow_R P_j$*, where* c_j *is a constant and* $j \in I$.

RMLq: *ReactiveML with a Queue-Based Semantics.* We extend RML with an explicit store of queues that keeps the state of the executed program. Unlike signals, the store of queues is preserved throughout time. The syntax of RML is extended with constructs that modify the queues located in the store; the resulting language is called RMLq.

Definition 10 (RMLq). RMLq *expressions are obtained by extending the grammar of values in Definition 6 with the following forms:*

$$v ::= \cdots \mid \text{pop} \mid \text{put} \mid \text{isEmpty}.$$

The new constructs allow RMLq programs to modify queues, which are ranged over by $q, q', \dots$. Construct put receives a queue and an element as parameters and pushes the element into the end of the queue. Construct pop takes a queue and dequeues its first element; if the queue is empty in the current instant the process will block the current thread until an element is obtained. Construct isEmpty blocks a thread until the instant in which a queue stops being empty.

The semantics of RMLq includes a *state* $\Sigma, \Sigma' ::= \emptyset \mid \Sigma, q:\widetilde{v}$ (i.e., a possibly empty collection of queues) and *configurations* $K, K' ::= \langle e;\ \Sigma\rangle$. The big-step semantics then has transitions of the form $\langle e;\ \Sigma\rangle \xrightarrow[S]{E,b} \langle e';\ \Sigma'\rangle$, where S is a signal environment, b is a termination boolean, and E is an event. The corresponding transition system is generated by rules including those in Fig. 5 (see also [7]).

Most transition rules for RMLq are interpreted as for RML; we briefly discuss queue-related rules in Fig. 5. Rule $\lfloor\text{Put-Q}\rfloor$ pushes an element into a queue and terminates instantaneously. Rule $\lfloor\text{POP-Q}\rfloor$ takes the first element from the queue (if not empty) and terminates instantaneously. Rule $\lfloor\text{NEMPTY}\rfloor$ enables isEmpty to terminate instantaneously if the queue is not empty. Rule $\lfloor\text{POP-Q}_\epsilon\rfloor$ keeps the thread execution stuck for at least one instant if the queue is empty; Rule $\lfloor\text{EMPTY}\rfloor$ is similar. We rule out programs with parallel pop/put operations along the same session in the same instant.

4 Expressiveness Results

We present our main results: correct translations of π into RML and of $\mathsf{a}\pi$ into RMLq.

The Formal Notion of Encoding. We define notions of language, translation, and encoding by adapting those from Gorla's framework for relative expressiveness [9].

Definition 11 (Languages and Translations). *A language $\mathcal{L}$ is a tuple $\langle \mathsf{P}, \longrightarrow, \approx \rangle$, where P is a set of processes, $\longrightarrow$ denotes an operational semantics, and $\approx$ is a behavioral equality on P. A translation from $\mathcal{L}_s = \langle \mathsf{P}_s, \longrightarrow_s, \approx_s \rangle$ into $\mathcal{L}_t = \langle \mathsf{P}_t, \longrightarrow_t, \approx_t \rangle$ (each with countably infinite sets of variables V_s and V_t, respectively) is a pair $\langle [\![\cdot]\!], \psi_{[\![\cdot]\!]} \rangle$, where $[\![\cdot]\!] : \mathsf{P}_s \to \mathsf{P}_t$ is a mapping, and $\psi_{[\![\cdot]\!]} : \mathsf{V}_s \to \mathsf{V}_t$ is a renaming policy for $[\![\cdot]\!]$.*

We are interested in *encodings*: translations that satisfy certain correctness criteria:

Definition 12 (Encoding). *Let $\mathcal{L}_s = \langle \mathsf{P}_s, \longrightarrow_s, \approx_s \rangle$ and $\mathcal{L}_t = \langle \mathsf{P}_t, \longrightarrow_t, \approx_t \rangle$ be languages; also let $\langle [\![\cdot]\!], \psi_{[\![\cdot]\!]} \rangle$ be a translation between them (cf. Definition 11). We say that such a translation is an* encoding *if it satisfies the following criteria:*

1. ***Name invariance:*** *For all $S \in \mathsf{P}_s$ and substitution σ, there exists σ' such that $[\![S\sigma]\!] = [\![S]\!]\sigma'$, with $\psi_{[\![\cdot]\!]}(\sigma(x)) = \sigma'(\psi_{[\![\cdot]\!]}(x))$, for any $x \in \mathsf{V}_s$.*
2. ***Compositionality:*** *Let $\text{res}_s(\cdot,\cdot)$ and $\text{par}_s(\cdot,\cdot)$ (resp. $\text{res}_t(\cdot,\cdot)$ and $\text{par}_t(\cdot,\cdot)$) denote restriction and parallel composition operators in P_s (resp. P_t). Then, we define: $[\![\text{res}_s(\widetilde{x}, P)]\!] = \text{res}_t(\psi_{[\![\cdot]\!]}(\widetilde{x}), [\![P]\!])$ and $[\![\text{par}_s(P, Q)]\!] = \text{par}_t([\![P]\!], [\![Q]\!])$.*
3. ***Operational correspondence,*** *i.e., it is sound and complete: (1) **Soundness:** For all $S \in \mathsf{P}_s$, if $S \longrightarrow_s S'$, there exists $T \in \mathsf{P}_t$ such that $[\![S]\!] \Longrightarrow_t T$ and $T \approx_t [\![S']\!]$. (2) **Completeness:** For all $S \in \mathsf{P}_s$ and $T \in \mathsf{P}_t$, if $[\![S]\!] \Longrightarrow_t T$, there exists S' such that $S \Longrightarrow_s S'$ and $T \approx_t [\![S']\!]$.*

While name invariance and compositionality are *static correctness criteria*, operational correspondence is a *dynamic correctness criterion*. Notice that our notion of compositionality is less general than that in [9]: this is due to the several important differences in the structure of the languages under comparison (π vs. RML and $\mathsf{a}\pi$ vs. RMLq).

We shall present translations of π into RML and of $\mathsf{a}\pi$ into RMLq, which we will show to be encodings. We instantiate Definition 11 with the following languages:

Definition 13 (Concrete Languages). *We shall consider:*

- $\mathcal{L}_\pi$ *will denote the tuple* $\langle \pi, \longrightarrow, \equiv_S \rangle$*, where* π *is as in Definition 1;* $\longrightarrow$ *is the reduction semantics in Fig. 1; and* $\equiv_S$ *is the structural congruence relation for* π*.*

- $\mathcal{L}_{\mathsf{RML}}$ *will denote the tuple* $\langle \mathsf{RML}, \xrightarrow[S]{E,b}, \hookrightarrow_R \rangle$*, where* RML *is as in Definition 6;* $\xrightarrow[S]{E,b}$ *is the big-step semantics for* RML*; and* $\hookrightarrow_R$ *is the equivalence in Definition 9.*

- $\mathcal{L}_{\mathsf{a}\pi}$ *will denote the tuple* $\langle \mathsf{a}\pi, \longrightarrow_A, \equiv_A \rangle$*, where* $\mathsf{a}\pi$ *is as in Definition 3;* $\longrightarrow_A$ *is the reduction semantics in Fig. 2; and* $\equiv_A$ *is the structural congruence relation for* $\mathsf{a}\pi$*.*

- $\mathcal{L}_{\mathsf{RMLq}}$ *will denote the tuple* $\langle \mathsf{RMLq}, \dashrightarrow[S]{E,b}, \equiv_R \rangle$*, where* RMLq *is as in Definition 10;* $\dashrightarrow[S]{E,b}$ *is the big-step semantics for* RMLq*; and* $\equiv_R$ *is the equivalence for* RML*.*

When events, termination booleans, and signal environments are unimportant, we write $P \longmapsto Q$ instead of $P \xrightarrow[S]{E,b} Q$, and $K \vdash\!\dashrightarrow K'$ instead of $K \dashrightarrow[S]{E,b} K'$.

Encoding $\mathcal{L}_\pi$ into $\mathcal{L}_{\mathsf{RML}}$. Key aspects in our translation of $\mathcal{L}_\pi$ into $\mathcal{L}_{\mathsf{RML}}$ are: (i) the use of value carrying signals to model communication channels; and (ii) the use of a continuation-passing style (following [8]) to model variables in π using RML signals.

Definition 14 (Translating $\mathcal{L}_\pi$ into $\mathcal{L}_{\mathsf{RML}}$). *Let* $\langle [\![\cdot]\!]_f, \psi_{[\![\cdot]\!]_f} \rangle$ *be a translation where: (1)* $\psi_{[\![\cdot]\!]_f}(x) = x$*, i.e., every variable in* π *is mapped to the same variable in* RML*. (2)* $[\![\cdot]\!]_f : \mathcal{L}_\pi \to \mathcal{L}_{\mathsf{RML}}$ *is as in Fig. 6, where* f *is a substitution function.*

Function f in $[\![\cdot]\!]_f$ ensures that fresh signal identifiers are used in each protocol action. The translation of $x\langle v \rangle.P$ declares a new signal x' which will be sent paired with value v through signal x; process $[\![P]\!]_{f,\{x \leftarrow x'\}}$ is executed in the next instant. Dually, the translation of $x(y).P$ awaits a signal carrying a pair, composed of a value and the signal name that to be used in the continuation, which is executed in the next instant. Translations for selection and branching are special cases of those for output and input. Restriction $(\nu xy)P$ is translated by declaring a fresh signal w, which replaces x,y in $[\![P]\!]_f$. Conditionals, parallel composition and inaction are translated homomorphically. Input-guarded replication is a special case of recursion, enabling at most one copy of the spawned process in the same instant; such a copy will be blocked until the process that spawned it interacts with some process. In Fig. 6, α, β denote variables inside the declaration of a recursive process, distinct from any other variables.

We state our first technical result: the translation of $\mathcal{L}_\pi$ into $\mathcal{L}_{\mathsf{RML}}$ is an encoding. In the proof, we identify a class of *well-formed* π processes that have at most one output and selection per endpoint in the same instant; see [7] for details.

$$\llbracket x\langle v\rangle.P\rrbracket_f \triangleq \text{signal } x' \text{ in } (\text{emit } f_x \ (v,x'); \text{pause}; \llbracket P\rrbracket_{f,\{x\leftarrow x'\}})$$

$$\llbracket x(y).P\rrbracket_f \triangleq \text{await } f_x(y,w) \text{ in } \llbracket P\rrbracket_{f,\{x\leftarrow w\}}$$

$$\llbracket x \triangleleft l.P\rrbracket_f \triangleq \text{signal } x' \text{ in } (\text{emit } f_x \ (l,x'); \text{pause}; \llbracket P\rrbracket_{f,\{x\leftarrow x'\}})$$

$$\llbracket x \triangleright l_j\{l_i : P_i\}_{i\in I}\rrbracket_f \triangleq \text{await } f_x(l,w) \text{ in match } l \text{ with } \{l_i \to \llbracket P_i\rrbracket_{f,\{x\leftarrow w\}}\}$$

$$\llbracket v? (P):(Q)\rrbracket_f \triangleq \text{if } v \text{ then } (\text{pause}; P) \text{ else } (\text{pause}; Q)$$

$$\llbracket (\nu xy)P\rrbracket_f \triangleq \text{signal } w \text{ in } \llbracket P\rrbracket_{f,\{x\leftarrow w, y\leftarrow w\}}$$

$$\llbracket * x(y).P\rrbracket_f \triangleq \text{let rec process } repl\ \alpha\ \beta =$$
$$\text{signal } x' \text{ in}$$
$$\text{do (loop present } f_\alpha? (\text{emit } x'; \text{pause}) : (())) \text{ until } f_\alpha(y,w)$$
$$\to (\text{run } \beta_{\{\alpha\leftarrow w\}})$$
$$\parallel \text{await } x' \text{ in run } (repl\ \alpha\ \beta)$$
$$\text{in run } repl\ x\ (\text{process } \llbracket P\rrbracket_f)$$

$$\llbracket P \mid Q\rrbracket_f \triangleq \llbracket P\rrbracket_f \parallel \llbracket Q\rrbracket_f \qquad\qquad \llbracket 0\rrbracket_f \triangleq ()$$

Fig. 6. Translation from $\mathcal{L}_\pi$ to $\mathcal{L}_{\mathsf{RML}}$ (Definition 14). Notice that f_x is a shorthand for $f(x)$.

Theorem 1. *Translation* $\langle\llbracket\cdot\rrbracket_f, \psi_{\llbracket\cdot\rrbracket_f}\rangle$ *is an encoding, in the sense of Definition 12.*

Encoding $\mathcal{L}_{\mathsf{a}\pi}$ into $\mathcal{L}_{\mathsf{RML}}$. The main intuition in translating aπ into RMLq is to use the queues of RMLq coupled with a *handler process* that implements the output-input transmission between queues. We start by introducing some auxiliary notions.

Notation 1. *Let* $P \equiv_{\mathsf{A}} (\nu\widetilde{x})(\prod_{i\in\{1,\dots,n\}} Q_i \mid \prod_{k_j\in\widetilde{k}} k_j[i:\epsilon, o:\epsilon]$ *be PI (cf. Definition 5) with variables* $\widetilde{k}$. *We will write* P *as* $C_l[Q_l, \mathcal{K}(\widetilde{k})]$, *where* $l \in \{1,\dots,n\}$, $C_l[\cdot_1, \cdot_2] = \prod_{j\in\{1,\dots,n\}\setminus\{l\}} Q_j \mid [\cdot_1] \mid [\cdot_2]$, *and* $\mathcal{K}(\widetilde{k}) = \prod_{k_j\in\widetilde{k}} k_j[i:\epsilon, o:\epsilon]$.

This notation allows us to distinguish two parts in a PI process: the non-queue processes and the queue processes $\mathcal{K}(\widetilde{k})$. We now define the key notion of *handler process*:

Definition 15 (Handler process). *Given* $\widetilde{k} = \{k_1,\dots,k_n\}$, *the handler process* $\mathcal{H}(\widetilde{k})$ *is defined as* $\prod_{i\in\{1,\dots,n\}} I(k_i) \parallel O(k_i)$, *where* $I(k)$ *and* $O(k)$ *are as in Fig. 7.*

Given an endpoint k, a handler defines parallel processes I^k and O^k to handle input and output queues. Transmission is a handshake where both O^k and $I^{\overline{k}}$ (or viceversa) must be ready to communicate. If ready, O^k sends a pair containing the message (pop k_o) and a fresh signal for further actions (α'). Once the pair is received, it is enqueued in $\overline{k}_i$ (i.e., the dual $I^{\overline{k}}$). The process is recursively called in the next instant with the new endpoints. The translation of aπ^* into RMLq requires a final auxiliary definition:

$I(k) \triangleq$ let rec process I α =
    (present ack^{α}? (emit $ack^{\overline{\alpha}}$; await $\alpha(x, \alpha')$ in (put x k_i); run I $\overline{\alpha'}$) : (I α)
    in run I k
$O(k) \triangleq$ let rec process O α =
    signal α' in isEmpty α_o; emit $ack^{\overline{\alpha}}$;
    (present ack^{α}? (emit $\overline{\alpha}$ ((pop k_o), α'); pause ; run O α') : (run O α)
    in run O k

Fig. 7. Components of handler processes (Definition 15)

$$\{x(y).P\} \triangleq \text{let } y = \text{pop } x_i \text{ in } \{P\} \qquad \{x\langle v\rangle.P\} \triangleq \text{put } x_o \text{ } v; \{P\}$$
$$\{x \triangleright \{l_i : P_i\}_{i\in I}\} \triangleq \text{let } y = \text{pop } x_i \text{ in} \qquad \{x \triangleleft l.P\} \triangleq \text{put } x_o \text{ } l; \{P\}$$
$$\text{match } l \text{ with } \{l_i : \{P_i\}\}_{i\in I} \qquad \{P \mid Q\} \triangleq \{P\} \parallel \{Q\}$$
$$\{b? (P):(Q)\} \triangleq \text{if } b \text{ then } \{P\} \text{ else } \{Q\} \qquad \{(\nu x)P\} \triangleq \text{signal } x, \overline{x} \text{ in } \{P\}$$
$$\{\mu X.P\} \triangleq \text{let rec process } \alpha_X = \{P\} \text{ in} \qquad \{X\} \triangleq \text{pause}; \text{run } \alpha_X$$
$$\text{run } \alpha_X \qquad \{\mathbf{0}\} \triangleq ()$$

Fig. 8. Auxiliary translation from aπ^* into RMLq (Definition 17).

Definition 16. *We define $\delta(\cdot)$ as a function that maps* aπ *processes into* RMLq *states:*

$$\delta(k[i : \widetilde{h}; o : \widetilde{m}]) = \{k_i : \widetilde{h}, k_o : \widetilde{m}\} \quad \delta(P \mid Q) = \delta(P) \cup \delta(Q) \quad \delta((\nu x)P) = \delta(P)$$

and as $\delta(P) = \emptyset$ for every other aπ *process.*

Definition 17 (Translating $\mathcal{L}_{a\pi}$ into $\mathcal{L}_{RMLq}$). *Let $\langle (\![\cdot]\!), \psi_{(\![\cdot]\!)} \rangle$ be a translation where:*

- $\psi_{(\![\cdot]\!)}(k) = k$, *i.e., every variable in* aπ *is mapped to the same variable in* RMLq.
- $(\![\cdot]\!) : \mathcal{L}_{a\pi} \to \mathcal{L}_{RMLq}$ *is defined for properly initialized* aπ *processes $C[Q, \mathcal{K}(\widetilde{k})]$, which are translated into* RMLq *configurations as follows:*

$$(\![C[Q, \mathcal{K}(\widetilde{k})]]\!) = \langle \{C[Q, \mathbf{0}]\} \parallel \mathcal{H}(\widetilde{k}) ; \delta(\mathcal{K}(\widetilde{k})) \rangle$$

where $\{\cdot\} : \mathcal{L}_{a\pi^*} \to \mathcal{L}_{RMLq}$ is in Fig. 8; $\mathcal{H}(\widetilde{k})$ is in Definition 15; and $\delta(\cdot)$ is in Definition 16.

Two key ideas in translation $(\![\cdot]\!)$ are: *queues local to processes* and *compositional (queue) handlers*. Indeed, communication between an endpoint k and its queues k_i, k_o proceeds instantaneously, for such queues should be local to the process implementing session k. Queue handlers effectively separate processes/behavior from data/state. As such, it is conceivable to have handlers that have more functionalities than those of $\mathcal{H}(\widetilde{k})$. In [7] we provide an example of a handler more sophisticated than $\mathcal{H}(\widetilde{k})$.

Translation $(\![\cdot]\!)$ is in two parts. First, $\{\![\cdot]\!\}$ translates non-queue processes: output and input are translated into queuing and dequeuing operations, respectively. Selection and branching are modeled similarly. Translations for the conditional, inaction, parallel, and recursion is as expected. Recursion is limited to a pause-guarded tail recursion in $\{\![\cdot]\!\}$ to avoid loops of instantaneous expressions and nondeterminism when accessing queues. Second, $(\![\cdot]\!)$ creates an RML configuration by composing the RMLq process obtained via $\{\![\cdot]\!\}$ with appropriate handlers and with the state obtained from the information in aπ queues. Because of this two-part structure, static correctness properties are established for $\{\![\cdot]\!\}$ (for this is the actual translation of source processes), whereas operational correspondence is established for $(\![\cdot]\!)$ (which generates an RMLq configuration).

Theorem 2 (Name invariance and compositionality for $\{\![\cdot]\!\}$). *Let* P, σ, x, *and* $E[\cdot]$ *be an* a$\pi^\star$ *process, a substitution, a variable in* a$\pi^\star$, *and an evaluation context (cf. Definition 4), respectively. Then: (1)* $\{\![P\sigma]\!\} = \{\![P]\!\}\sigma$, *and (2)* $\{\![E[P]]\!\} = \{\![E]\!\}[\{\![P]\!\}]$.

Theorem 3 (Operational correspondence for $(\![\cdot]\!)$). *Given a properly initialized* aπ *process* $C[Q, \mathcal{K}(\widetilde{k})]$, *it holds that:*

1. **Soundness:** *If* $C[Q, \mathcal{K}(\widetilde{k})] \longrightarrow_\mathsf{A} C[Q', \mathcal{K}'(\widetilde{k})]$ *then*

   $(\![C[Q, \mathcal{K}(\widetilde{k})]]\!) \vdash\!\dashrightarrow (\![C'[Q'', \mathcal{K}''(\widetilde{k})]]\!)$, *for some* $Q'', \mathcal{K}''(\widetilde{x}), C'$ *where*
   $C[Q, \mathcal{K}(\widetilde{x})] \longrightarrow_\mathsf{A} C[Q', \mathcal{K}'(\widetilde{x})] \longrightarrow_\mathsf{A}^* (\boldsymbol{\nu}\widetilde{x})C'[Q'', \mathcal{K}''(\widetilde{x})]$.

2. **Completeness:** *If* $(\![C[Q, \mathcal{K}(\widetilde{x})]]\!) \vdash\!\dashrightarrow R$ *then there exist* $Q', C', \mathcal{K}'(\widetilde{x})$ *such that* $C[Q, \mathcal{K}(\widetilde{x})] \longrightarrow_\mathsf{A}^* (\boldsymbol{\nu}\widetilde{x})C'[Q', \mathcal{K}'(\widetilde{x})]$ *and* $R = (\![C'[Q', \mathcal{K}'(\widetilde{x})]]\!)$.

In soundness, a single RMLq step mimicks one or more steps in aπ, i.e., several source computations can be grouped into the same instant. This way, e.g., the interaction of several outputs along the same session with their queue (cf. Rule $\lfloor \textsc{Send} \rfloor$) will take place in the same instant. In contrast, several queue synchronizations in the same session (cf. Rule $\lfloor \textsc{Com} \rfloor$) will be sliced over different instants. Conversely, completeness ensures that our encoding does not introduce extraneous behaviors: for every RMLq transition of a translated process there exists one or more corresponding aπ reductions.

5   Closing Remarks

We have shown that ReactiveML can correctly encode session-based concurrency, covering both synchronous and asynchronous (queue-based) communications.[1] Our encodings are *executable*: as such, they enable to integrate session-based concurrency in actual RML programs featuring declarative, reactive, timed, and contextual behavior. This is an improvement with respect to previous works, which extend the π-calculus with some (but not all) of these features and/or

---

[1] *Synchronous communication* as in the (session) π-calculus should not be confused with the *synchronous programming* model of ReactiveML.

lack programming support. Interestingly, since ReactiveML has a well-defined semantics, it already offers a firm basis for both foundational and practical studies on session-based concurrency. Indeed, ongoing work concerns the principled extension of our approach to the case of multiparty sessions.

We have not considered types in source/target languages, but we do not foresee major obstacles. In fact, we have already shown that our encoding $[\![\cdot]\!]_f$ supports a large class of well-typed π processes in the system of [18], covering a typed form of operational correspondence but also *type soundness*: if P is a well-typed π process, then $[\![P]\!]_f$ is a well-typed RML expression—see [7]. We conjecture a similar result for $(\!|\cdot|\!)$, under an extension of [18] with queues. On the ReactiveML side, we can exploit the type-and-effect system in [14] to enforce *cooperative* programs (roughly, programs without infinite loops). Since $[\![\cdot]\!]_f$ and $(\!|\cdot|\!)$ already produce well-typed, executable ReactiveML expressions, we further conjecture that they are also cooperative, in the sense of [14].

Acknowledgements. We thank Ilaria Castellani, Cinzia Di Giusto, and the anonymous reviewers for useful remarks and suggestions. This work has been partially sponsored by CNRS PICS project 07313 (SuCCeSS) and EU COST Actions IC1201 (BETTY), IC1402 (ARVI), and IC1405 (Reversible Computation).

References

1. Bartoletti, M., Cimoli, T., Murgia, M., Podda, A.S., Pompianu, L.: Compliance and subtyping in timed session types. In: Graf, S., Viswanathan, M. (eds.) FORTE 2015. LNCS, vol. 9039, pp. 161–177. Springer, Cham (2015). doi:10.1007/978-3-319-19195-9_11
2. Benveniste, A., Caspi, P., Edwards, S.A., Halbwachs, N., Guernic, P.L., de Simone, R.: The synchronous languages 12 years later. Proc. IEEE **91**(1), 64–83 (2003)
3. Bocchi, L., Honda, K., Tuosto, E., Yoshida, N.: A theory of design-by-contract for distributed multiparty interactions. In: Gastin, P., Laroussinie, F. (eds.) CONCUR 2010. LNCS, vol. 6269, pp. 162–176. Springer, Heidelberg (2010). doi:10.1007/978-3-642-15375-4_12
4. Bocchi, L., Yang, W., Yoshida, N.: Timed multiparty session types. In: Baldan, P., Gorla, D. (eds.) CONCUR 2014. LNCS, vol. 8704, pp. 419–434. Springer, Heidelberg (2014). doi:10.1007/978-3-662-44584-6_29
5. Bonelli, E., Compagnoni, A.B., Gunter, E.L.: Correspondence assertions for process synchronization in concurrent communications. J. Funct. Program. **15**(2), 219–247 (2005)
6. Boussinot, F., de Simone, R.: The SL synchronous language. IEEE Trans. Softw. Eng. **22**(4), 256–266 (1996)
7. Cano, M., Arias, J., Pérez, J.A.: Session-based Concurrency, Reactively (Extended Version) (2017). http://www.jperez.nl/publications
8. Dardha, O., Giachino, E., Sangiorgi, D.: Session types revisited. In: Proceedings of the PPDP 2012, pp. 139–150 (2012)
9. Gorla, D.: Towards a unified approach to encodability and separation results for process calculi. Inf. Comput. **208**(9), 1031–1053 (2010)
10. Halbwachs, N., Lagnier, F., Ratel, C.: Programming and verifying real-time systems by means of the synchronous data-flow language LUSTRE. IEEE Trans. Softw. Eng. **18**(9), 785–793 (1992)

11. Honda, K., Vasconcelos, V.T., Kubo, M.: Language primitives and type discipline for structured communication-based programming. In: Hankin, C. (ed.) ESOP 1998. LNCS, vol. 1381, pp. 122–138. Springer, Heidelberg (1998). doi:10.1007/BFb0053567

12. Hüttel, H., Lanese, I., Vasconcelos, V.T., Caires, L., Carbone, M., Deniélou, P.-M., Mostrous, D., Padovani, L., Ravara, A., Tuosto, E., Vieira, H.T., Zavattaro, G.: Foundations of session types and behavioural contracts. ACM Comput. Surv. **49**(1), 3:1–3:36 (2016)

13. Kouzapas, D., Yoshida, N., Hu, R., Honda, K.: On asynchronous eventful session semantics. Math. Struct. Comput. Sci. **26**(2), 303–364 (2016)

14. Mandel, L., Pasteur, C.: Reactivity of cooperative systems. In: Müller-Olm, M., Seidl, H. (eds.) SAS 2014. LNCS, vol. 8723, pp. 219–236. Springer, Cham (2014). doi:10.1007/978-3-319-10936-7_14

15. Mandel, L., Pasteur, C., Pouzet, M.: ReactiveML, ten years later. In: Falaschi, M., Albert, E. (eds.) Proceedings of the PPDP 2015, pp. 6–17. ACM (2015)

16. Mandel, L., Pouzet, M.: ReactiveML: a reactive extension to ML. In: Proceedings of the PPDP 2005, pp. 82–93. ACM (2005)

17. Milner, R., Parrow, J., Walker, D.: A calculus of mobile processes, I. Inf. Comput. **100**(1), 1–40 (1992)

18. Vasconcelos, V.T.: Fundamentals of session types. Inf. Comput. **217**, 52–70 (2012)

Procedural Choreographic Programming

Luís Cruz-Filipe[(✉)] and Fabrizio Montesi

University of Southern Denmark, Odense, Denmark
{lcf,fmontesi}@imada.sdu.dk

Abstract. Choreographic Programming is an emerging paradigm for correct-by-construction concurrent programming. However, its applicability is limited by the current lack of support for reusable procedures. We propose Procedural Choreographies (PC), a choreographic language model with full procedural abstraction. PC includes unbounded process creation and name mobility, yielding a powerful framework for writing correct concurrent algorithms that can be compiled into a process calculus. This increased expressivity requires a typing discipline to ensure that processes are properly connected when enacting procedures.

1 Introduction

Choreographic Programming [20] is a paradigm for programming concurrent software that is deadlock-free by construction, by using an "Alice and Bob" notation to syntactically prevent mismatched I/O communications in programs (called choreographies) and using an EndPoint Projection to synthesise correct process implementations [2,4,24]. Choreographies are found in standards [1,26], languages [6,14,23,25], and specification models [2,4,17]. They are widely used as a design tool in communication-based software [1,23,25,26], since they describe interactions unambiguously and thus help ensure correctness [19].

Driven by these benefits, research on applicability of choreographic programming has recently gained in breadth, ranging from service programming [2,4] to runtime adaptation [11]. We focus on another important aspect: modular programming. Writing procedures that can be arbitrarily instantiated and composed into larger programs is still unsupported. The absence of full procedural abstraction disallows the creation of libraries that can be reused as "black boxes".

Example 1. We discuss a parallel version of merge sort, written as a choreography. Although this is a toy example, it cannot be written in any previous model for choreographic programming. We present more realistic and involved examples in the remainder. We make the standard assumption that we have concurrent processes with local storage and computational capabilities. In this example, each process stores a list and can use the following local functions: split1 and split2, respectively returning the first or the second half of a list; is_small, which tests if a list has at most one element; and merge, which combines two

© IFIP International Federation for Information Processing 2017
Published by Springer International Publishing AG 2017. All Rights Reserved
A. Bouajjani and A. Silva (Eds.): FORTE 2017, LNCS 10321, pp. 92–107, 2017.
DOI: 10.1007/978-3-319-60225-7_7

sorted lists into one. The following (choreographic) procedure, MS, implements merge sort on the list stored at its parameter process p.[1]

```
MS(p) = if p.is_small then 0
        else p start q1,q2; p.split1 -> q1; p.split2 -> q2;
             MS<q1>; MS<q2>; q1.* -> p; q2.* -> p.merge
```

Procedure MS starts by checking whether the list at process p is small, in which case it does not need to be sorted (0 denotes termination); otherwise, p starts two other processes q1 and q2 (p start q1,q2), to which it respectively sends the first and the second half of the list (p.split1 -> q1 and p.split2 -> q2). The procedure is recursively reapplied to q1 and q2, which independently (concurrently) proceed to ordering their respective sub-lists. When this is done, MS stores the first ordered half from q1 to p (q1.* -> p, where * retrieves the data stored in q1) and merges it with the ordered sub-list from q2 (q2.* -> p.merge).

Procedure MS in Example 1 cannot be written in current choreography models, because it uses two unsupported features: *general recursion*, allowing procedure calls to be followed by arbitrary code; and *parametric procedures*, which can be reused with different processes (as in MS<q1> and MS<q2>).

We present Procedural Choreographies (PC), a model for choreographic programming that captures these features (Sect. 2). PC has a simple syntax, but its semantics is expressive enough to infer safe out-of-order executions of choreographic procedures – for example, in MS<q1>; MS<q2>, the two calls can be run in parallel because they involve separate processes and are thus non-interfering.

We also illustrate the expressivity of PC with a more involved parallel downloader, showing how our semantics infers parallel executions in a complex scenario of concurrent data streams. This example makes use of additional features: mobility of process names (networks with connections that evolve at runtime) and propagation of choices among processes.

The interplay between name mobility and procedure composition requires careful handling, because of potential dangling process references. We prevent such errors using a decidable typing discipline (Sect. 3) that supports type inference.

PC includes an EndPoint Projection (EPP) that synthesises correct concurrent implementations in terms of a process calculus (Sect. 4). This process calculus is an abstraction of systems where processes refer to one another's locations or identifiers (e.g., MPI [22] or the Internet Protocol).

Full definitions, proofs, and further extensions are given in [9]. Additional examples can be found in [8] (which is based on a pre-print of this article).

2   Procedural Choreographies (PC)

Syntax. The syntax of PC is displayed in Fig. 1. A procedural choreography is a pair $\langle \mathcal{D}, C \rangle$, where C is a choreography and $\mathcal{D}$ is a set of procedure definitions.

---

[1] In this work, we use a `monospaced` font for readability of our concrete examples, and other fonts for distinguishing syntactic categories in our formal arguments as usual.

$$C ::= \eta; C \mid I; C \mid 0 \qquad\qquad \eta ::= \mathsf{p}.e \to \mathsf{q}.f \mid \mathsf{p} \to \mathsf{q}[l] \mid \mathsf{p}\,\mathsf{start}\,\mathsf{q}^T \mid \mathsf{p} \colon \mathsf{q} \mathrel{<\!\!-\!\!>} \mathsf{r}$$

$$\mathcal{D} ::= X(\widetilde{\mathsf{q}^T}) = C, \mathcal{D} \mid \emptyset \qquad I ::= \mathsf{if}\ \mathsf{p}.e\ \mathsf{then}\ C_1\ \mathsf{else}\ C_2 \mid X\langle \widetilde{\mathsf{p}} \rangle \mid 0$$

Fig. 1. Procedural choreographies, syntax.

Process names $(\mathsf{p}, \mathsf{q}, \mathsf{r}, \dots)$, identify processes that execute concurrently. Each process is equipped with a memory cell that stores a single value of a fixed type. Specifically, we consider a fixed set $\mathbb{T}$ of datatypes (numbers, lists, etc.); each process p stores only values of type $T_\mathsf{p} \in \mathbb{T}$. Statements in a choreography can either be communication actions (η) or compound instructions (I), both of which can have continuations. Term 0 is the terminated choreography, which we often omit in examples. We call all terms but $0; C$ *program terms*, or simply programs, since these form the syntax intended for developers to use for writing programs. Term $0; C$ is necessary only for the technical definition of the semantics, to capture termination of procedure calls with continuations, and can appear only at runtime. It is thus called a *runtime term*.

Processes communicate through direct references (names) to each other.[2] In a value communication $\mathsf{p}.e \to \mathsf{q}.f$, process p sends the result of evaluating expression e (replacing the placeholder $*$ at runtime with the data in its memory) to q. When q receives the value from p, it applies to it the (total) function f and stores the result. The definition of f may also access the contents of q's memory.

In a selection term $\mathsf{p} \to \mathsf{q}[l]$, p communicates to q its choice of label l, which is a constant. This term is intended to propagate information on which internal choice has been made by a process to another (see Remark 2 below).

In term $\mathsf{p}\,\mathsf{start}\,\mathsf{q}^T$, process p spawns the new process q, which stores data of type T. Process name q is bound in the continuation C of $\mathsf{p}\,\mathsf{start}\,\mathsf{q}^T; C$.

Process spawning introduces the need for name mobility. In real-world systems, after execution of $\mathsf{p}\,\mathsf{start}\,\mathsf{q}^T$, p is the only process that knows q's name. Any other process wanting to communicate with q must therefore be first informed of its existence. This is achieved with the introduction term $\mathsf{p} \colon \mathsf{q} \mathrel{<\!\!-\!\!>} \mathsf{r}$, read "$\mathsf{p}$ introduces q and r" (with p, q and r distinct). As its double-arrow syntax suggests, this action represents *two* communications – one where p sends q's name to r, and another where p sends r's name to q. This is made explicit in Sect. 4.

In a conditional term $\mathsf{if}\ \mathsf{p}.e\ \mathsf{then}\ C_1\ \mathsf{else}\ C_2$, process p evaluates e to choose between the possible continuations C_1 and C_2.

The set $\mathcal{D}$ contains global procedures. Term $X(\widetilde{\mathsf{q}^T}) = C_X$ defines a procedure X with body C_X, which can be used anywhere in $\langle \mathcal{D}, C \rangle$ – in particular, inside C_X. The names $\widetilde{\mathsf{q}}$ are bound to C_X, and they are exactly the free process names in C_X. Each procedure can be defined at most once in $\mathcal{D}$. Term $X\langle \widetilde{\mathsf{p}} \rangle$ calls (invokes) procedure X by passing $\widetilde{\mathsf{p}}$ as parameters. Procedure calls inside definitions must be guarded, i.e., they can only occur after some other action.

We assume the Barendregt convention and work up to α-equivalence in choreographies, renaming bound variables as needed when expanding procedure calls.

---

[2] PC thus easily applies to settings based on actors, objects, or ranks (e.g., MPI).

Example 2. Recall procedure MS from our merge sort example in the Introduction (Example 1). If we annotate the parameter p and the started processes q_1 and q_2 with a type, e.g., **List**(T) for some T (the type of lists containing elements of type T), then MS is a valid procedure definition in $\widetilde{PC}$, as long as we allow two straightforward syntactic conventions: (i) p start $\tilde{q}^T$ stands for the sequence p start $q_1^{T_1}; \ldots;$ p start $q_n^{T_n}$; (ii) a communication of the form p.e -> q stands for p.e -> q.id, where id is the identity function: it sets the content of q to the value received from p. We adopt these conventions also in the remainder.

Remark 1 (Design choices). We comment on two of our design choices.

The introduction action (p : q <-> r) requires a three-way synchronization, essentially performing two communications. The alternative development of PC with asymmetric introduction (an action p : q -> r whereby p sends q's name to r, but not conversely) would be very similar. Since in our examples we always perform introductions in pairs, the current choice makes the presentation easier.

The restriction that each process stores only one value of a fixed type is, in practice, a minor constraint. As shown in Example 2, types can be tuples or lists, which mimics storing several values. Also, a process can create new processes with different types – so we can encode changing the type of p by having p create a new process p' and then continuing the choreography with p' instead of p.

Remark 2 (Label Selection) We motivate the need for selections (p -> q[l]). Consider the choreography if p.coinflip then (p. * -> r) else (r. * -> p). Here, p flips a coin to decide whether to send a value to r or to receive a value from r. Since processes run independently and share no data, only p knows which branch of the conditional will be executed; but this information is essential for r to decide on its behaviour. To propagate p's decision to r, we use selections:

$$\text{if p.coinflip then (p -> r[L]; p. * -> r) else (p -> r[R]; r. * -> p)}$$

Now r receives a label reflecting p's choice, and can use it to decide what to do.

Selections are needed only for compilation (see Sect. 4): the first choreography above is not projectable, whereas the second one is. They can be inferred, and thus could be removed from the user syntax, but it is useful to be able to specify them manually (see Remark 4). See also Example 5 at the end of this section.

Semantics. We define a reduction semantics $\rightarrow_{\mathscr{D}}$ for PC, parameterised over $\mathscr{D}$ (Fig. 2, top). Given a choreography C, we model the state of its processes with a state function σ, with domain pn(C), where $\sigma(p)$ denotes the value stored in p. We assume that each type $T \in \mathbb{T}$ has a special value $\bot_T$, representing an uninitialised process state. We also use a connection graph G, keeping track of which processes know each other. In the rules, p $\stackrel{G}{\longleftrightarrow}$ q denotes that G contains an edge between p and q, and $G \cup \{p \leftrightarrow q\}$ denotes the graph obtained from G by adding an edge between p and q (if missing).

Executing a communication action p.e -> q.f in rule $\lfloor C|Com\rfloor$ requires that: p and q are connected in G; e is well typed; and the type of e matches that expected

$$\frac{\mathsf{p} \stackrel{G}{\longleftrightarrow} \mathsf{q} \quad e[\sigma(\mathsf{p})/*] \downarrow v \quad f[\sigma(\mathsf{q})/*](v) \downarrow w}{G, \mathsf{p}.e \rightarrow \mathsf{q}.f; C, \sigma \;\rightarrow_{\mathscr{D}}\; G, C, \sigma[\mathsf{q} \mapsto w]} \lfloor C|\mathrm{Com} \rceil$$

$$\frac{\mathsf{p} \stackrel{G}{\longleftrightarrow} \mathsf{q}}{G, \mathsf{p} \rightarrow \mathsf{q}[l]; C, \sigma \;\rightarrow_{\mathscr{D}}\; G, C, \sigma} \lfloor C|\mathrm{Sel} \rceil$$

$$\frac{}{G, \mathsf{p}\,\mathrm{start}\,\mathsf{q}^T; C, \sigma \;\rightarrow_{\mathscr{D}}\; G \cup \{\mathsf{p} \leftrightarrow \mathsf{q}\}, C, \sigma[\mathsf{q} \mapsto \perp_T]} \lfloor C|\mathrm{Start} \rceil$$

$$\frac{\mathsf{p} \stackrel{G}{\longleftrightarrow} \mathsf{q} \quad \mathsf{p} \stackrel{G}{\longleftrightarrow} \mathsf{r}}{G, \mathsf{p}: \mathsf{q} <\!\!-\!\!> \mathsf{r}; C, \sigma \;\rightarrow_{\mathscr{D}}\; G \cup \{\mathsf{q} \leftrightarrow \mathsf{r}\}, C, \sigma} \lfloor C|\mathrm{Tell} \rceil$$

$$\frac{i = 1 \text{ if } e[\sigma(\mathsf{p})/*] \downarrow \mathsf{true}, \quad i = 2 \text{ otherwise}}{G, (\mathrm{if}\ \mathsf{p}.e\,\mathrm{then}\ C_1\,\mathrm{else}\ C_2); C, \sigma \;\rightarrow_{\mathscr{D}}\; G, C_i \,\mathring{,}\, C, \sigma} \lfloor C|\mathrm{Cond} \rceil$$

$$\frac{C_1 \preceq_{\mathscr{D}} C_2 \quad G, C_2, \sigma \;\rightarrow_{\mathscr{D}}\; G', C_2', \sigma' \quad C_2' \preceq_{\mathscr{D}} C_1'}{G, C_1, \sigma \;\rightarrow_{\mathscr{D}}\; G', C_1', \sigma'} \lfloor C|\mathrm{Struct} \rceil$$

$$\frac{\mathrm{pn}(\eta)\#\mathrm{pn}(\eta')}{\eta; \eta' \equiv_{\mathscr{D}} \eta'; \eta} \lfloor C|\mathrm{Eta\text{-}Eta} \rceil \qquad \frac{\mathrm{pn}(I)\#\mathrm{pn}(I')}{I; I' \equiv_{\mathscr{D}} I'; I} \lfloor C|\mathrm{I\text{-}I} \rceil$$

$$\frac{X(\widetilde{\mathsf{q}^T}) = C_X \in \mathscr{D}}{X\langle \tilde{\mathsf{p}} \rangle; C \preceq_{\mathscr{D}} C_X[\tilde{\mathsf{p}}/\tilde{\mathsf{q}}] \,\mathring{,}\, C} \lfloor C|\mathrm{Unfold} \rceil$$

Fig. 2. Procedural choreographies, semantics and structural precongruence (selected rules).

by the function f at the receiver. The last two conditions are encapsulated in the notation $e \downarrow v$, read "e evaluates to v". Choreographies can thus deadlock (be unable to reduce) because of errors in the programming of communications; this issue is addressed by our typing discipline in Sect. 3.

Rule $\lfloor C|\mathrm{Sel} \rceil$ defines selection as a no-op for choreographies (see Remark 2).

Rule $\lfloor C|\mathrm{Start} \rceil$ models the creation of a process. In the reductum, the starter and started processes are connected and can thus communicate with each other. This rule also extends the domain of the state function σ accordingly. Rule $\lfloor C|\mathrm{Tell} \rceil$ captures name mobility, creating a connection between two processes q and r when they are introduced by a process p connected to both.

Rule $\lfloor C|\mathrm{Cond} \rceil$ uses the auxiliary operator $\mathring{,}$ to obtain a reductum in the syntax of PC regardless of the forms of the branches C_1 and C_2 and the continuation C. The operator $\mathring{,}$ is defined by $\eta \,\mathring{,}\, C = \eta; C$, $I \,\mathring{,}\, C = I; C$ and $(C_1; C_2) \,\mathring{,}\, C = C_1; (C_2 \,\mathring{,}\, C)$. It extends the scope of bound names: any name p bound in C has its scope extended also to C'. This scope extension is capture-avoiding, as the Barendregt convention guarantees that p is not used in C'.

Rule $\lfloor C|\mathrm{Struct} \rceil$ uses structural precongruence $\preceq_{\mathscr{D}}$. The main rules defining $\preceq_{\mathscr{D}}$ are given in Fig. 2 (bottom). We write $C \equiv_{\mathscr{D}} C'$ when $C \preceq_{\mathscr{D}} C'$ and $C' \preceq_{\mathscr{D}} C$, $\mathrm{pn}(C)$ for the set of process names (free or bound) in a choreography C, and $A \# B$ when two sets A and B are disjoint. These rules formalise the notion of parallelism in PC, recalling out-of-order execution. Rule $\lfloor C|\text{Eta-Eta}\rfloor$ permutes two communications performed by processes that are all distinct, modelling that processes run independently of one another. For example, p. $*$ -> q; r. $*$ -> s $\equiv_\mathscr{D}$ r. $*$ -> s; p. $*$ -> q because these two communications are non-interfering, but p. $*$ -> q; q. $*$ -> s $\not\equiv_\mathscr{D}$ q. $*$ -> s; p. $*$ -> q: since the second communication causally depends on the first (both involve q).

This reasoning is extended to instructions in rule $\lfloor C|\text{I-I}\rfloor$; in particular, procedure calls that share no arguments can be swapped. This is sound, as a procedure can only refer to processes that are either passed as arguments or started inside its body, and the latter cannot be leaked to the original call site. Thus, any actions obtained by unfolding the first procedure call involve different processes than those obtained by unfolding the second one. As the example below shows, calls to the same procedure can be exchanged, since X and Y need not be distinct. Omitted rules include moving actions inside or outside both branches of a conditional, or switching independent nested conditionals. Rule $\lfloor C|\text{Unfold}\rfloor$ unfolds a procedure call, again using the $\mathring{,}$ operator defined above.

Example 3. In our merge sort example, structural precongruence $\preceq_\mathscr{D}$ allows the recursive calls MS<q_1> and MS<q_2> to be exchanged. Furthermore, after the calls are unfolded, their code can be interleaved in any way.

This example exhibits map-reduce behaviour: each new process receives its input, runs independently from all others, and then sends its result to its creator.

Example 4. In a more refined example of implicit parallelism, we swap communications from procedure calls that share process names. Consider the procedure

```
auth(c,a,r,l) = c.creds -> a.rCreds;
                a.chk -> r.res; a.log -> l.app
```

Client c sends its credentials to an authentication server a, which stores the result of authentication in r and appends a log of this operation at process l. In the choreography auth<c, a1, r1, l>; auth<c, a2, r2, l>, a client c authenticates at two different authentication servers a1 and a2. After unfolding the two calls, rule $\lfloor C|\text{Eta-Eta}\rfloor$ yields the following interleaving:

```
c.creds -> a1.rCreds; c.creds -> a2.rCreds;
a2.chk -> r2.res; a1.chk -> r1.res;
a1.log -> l.app; a2.log -> l.app
```

Thus, the two authentications proceed in parallel. Observe that the logging operations cannot be swapped, since they use the same logging process l.

Example 5. A more sophisticated example involves modularly composing different procedures that take multiple parameters. Here, we write a choreography where a client c downloads a collection of files from a server s. Files are downloaded in parallel via streaming, by having the client and the server each create subprocesses to handle the transfer of each file. Thus, the client can request and start downloading each file without waiting for previous downloads to finish.

```
par_download(c,s) = if c.more
  then c -> s [more]; c start c'; s start s';
       s: c <-> s'; c.top -> s'; pop<c>;
       c: c' <-> s'; download<c',s'>;
       par_download<c,s>; c'.file -> c.store
  else c -> s [end]
```

At the start of **par_download**, the client c checks whether it wants to download more files and informs the server s of the result via a label selection. In the affirmative case, the client and the server start two subprocesses, c' and s' respectively, and the server introduces c to s' (s : c <-> s'). The client c sends to s' the name of the file to download (c.top -> s') and removes it from its collection, using procedure **pop** (omitted), afterwards introducing its own subprocess c' to s'. The file download is handled by c' and s' (using procedure **download**), while c and s continue operating (**par_download**<c, s>). Finally, c' waits until c is ready to store the downloaded file.

Procedure **download** has a similar structure. It implements a stream where a file is sequentially transferred in chunks from a process s to another process c.

```
download(c,s) = if s.more
   then s -> c [more]; s.next -> c.app; pop<s>; download<c,s>
   else s -> c [end]
```

The implementation of **par_download** exploits implicit parallelism considerably. All calls to **download** are made with disjoint sets of parameters (processes), and can thus be fully parallelised: many instances of **download** run at the same time, each one implementing a (sequential) stream. Due to our semantics, we effectively end up executing many streaming behaviours in parallel.

We can even compose **par_download** with **auth**, such that we execute the parallel download only if the client can successfully authenticate with an authentication server a. Below, we use the shortcut $p \to \tilde{q}[l]$ for $p \to q_1[l]; \ldots; p \to q_n[l]$.

```
auth<c,a,r,1>; if r.ok then r -> c,s[ok]; par_download<c,s>
                       else r -> c,s[ko]
```

3   Typability and Deadlock-Freedom

We give a typing discipline for PC, to check that (a) the types of functions and processes are respected by communications and (b) processes that need to communicate are first properly introduced (or connected). Regarding (b), two processes created independently can communicate only after they receive the names of each other. For instance, in Example 5, the execution of **download**<c', s'> would get stuck if c' and s' were not properly introduced in **par_download**, since our semantics requires them to be connected.

Typing judgements have the form $\Gamma; G \vdash C \triangleright G'$, read "$C$ is well-typed according to Γ, and running C with a connection graph that contains G yields a connection graph that includes G'". Typing environments Γ are used to track

$$\frac{}{\Gamma;G \vdash \mathbf{0} \triangleright G} \ \lfloor T|End \rfloor \qquad \frac{p \xleftrightarrow{G} q \quad \Gamma;G \vdash C \triangleright G'}{\Gamma;G \vdash p \to q[l]; C \triangleright G'} \ \lfloor T|Sel \rfloor$$

$$\frac{\begin{array}{c} p \xleftrightarrow{G} q \quad \Gamma \vdash p : T_p, q : T_q \quad \Gamma;G \vdash C \triangleright G' \\ * : T_p \vdash_T e : T_1 \quad * : T_q \vdash_T f : T_1 \to T_q \end{array}}{\Gamma;G \vdash p.e \to q.f; C \triangleright G'} \ \lfloor T|Com \rfloor$$

$$\frac{p \xleftrightarrow{G} q \quad p \xleftrightarrow{G} r \quad \Gamma;G \cup \{q \leftrightarrow r\} \vdash C \triangleright G'}{\Gamma;G \vdash p: q <\text{->} r; C \triangleright G'} \ \lfloor T|Tell \rfloor$$

$$\frac{\Gamma, q : T; G \cup \{p \leftrightarrow q\} \vdash C \triangleright G'}{\Gamma;G \vdash p \, \mathsf{start} \, q^T; C \triangleright G'} \ \lfloor T|Start \rfloor \qquad \frac{\Gamma;G \vdash C \triangleright G'}{\Gamma;G \vdash 0; C \triangleright G'} \ \lfloor T|EndSeq \rfloor$$

$$\frac{\Gamma \vdash p : T \quad * : T \vdash_T e : \mathsf{bool} \quad \Gamma;G \vdash C_i \triangleright G_i \quad \Gamma;G_1 \cap G_2 \vdash C \triangleright G'}{\Gamma;G \vdash (\mathsf{if} \, p.e \, \mathsf{then} \, C_1 \, \mathsf{else} \, C_2); C \triangleright G'} \ \lfloor T|Cond \rfloor$$

$$\frac{\begin{array}{c} \Gamma \vdash X(\widetilde{q^T}) : G_X \triangleright G'_X \quad \Gamma \vdash p_i : T_i \\ G_X[\tilde{p}/\tilde{q}] \subseteq G \quad \Gamma;G \cup (G'_X[\tilde{p}/\tilde{q}]) \vdash C \triangleright G' \end{array}}{\Gamma;G \vdash X\langle \tilde{p} \rangle; C \triangleright G'} \ \lfloor T|Call \rfloor$$

Fig. 3. Procedural choreographies, typing rules.

the types of processes and procedures; they are defined as: $\Gamma ::= \emptyset \mid \Gamma, p : T \mid \Gamma, X : G \triangleright G'$. A typing $p : T$ states that process p stores values of type T, and a typing $X : G \triangleright G'$ records the effect of the body of X on graph G.

The rules for deriving typing judgements are given in Fig. 3. We assume standard typing judgements for functions and expressions, and write $* : T \vdash_T e : T$ and $* : T_1 \vdash_T f : T_2 \to T_3$ meaning, respectively "e has type T assuming that $*$ has type T" and "f has type $T_2 \to T_3$ assuming that $*$ has type T_1". Verifying that communications respect the expected types is straightforward, using the connection graph G to track which processes have been introduced to each other. In rule $\lfloor T|Start \rfloor$, we implicitly use the fact that q does not occur in G (again using the Barendregt convention). The final graph G' is only used in procedure calls (rule $\lfloor T|Call \rfloor$). Other rules leave it unchanged.

To type a procedural choreography, we need to type its set of procedure definitions $\mathcal{D}$. We write $\Gamma \vdash \mathcal{D}$ if: for each $X(\widetilde{q^T}) = C_X \in \mathcal{D}$, there is exactly one typing $X(\widetilde{q^T}) : G_X \triangleright G'_X \in \Gamma$, and this typing is such that $\Gamma, \widetilde{q : T}, G_X \vdash C_X \triangleright G'_X$. We say that $\Gamma \vdash \langle \mathcal{D}, C \rangle$ if $\Gamma, \Gamma_{\mathcal{D}}; G_C \vdash C, G'$ for some $\Gamma_{\mathcal{D}}$ such that $\Gamma_{\mathcal{D}} \vdash \mathcal{D}$ and some G', where G_C is the full graph whose nodes are the free process names in C. The choice of G_C is motivated by observing that (i) all top-level processes should know each other and (ii) eventual connections between processes not occuring in C do not affect its typability.

Well-typed choreographies either terminate or diverge.[3]

---

[3] Since we are interested in communications, we assume evaluation of functions and expressions to terminate on values with the right types (see Sect. 5, Faults).

Theorem 1 (Deadlock freedom/Subject reduction). *Let $\langle \mathcal{D}, C \rangle$ be a procedural choreography. If $\Gamma \vdash \mathcal{D}$ and $\Gamma; G_1 \vdash C \triangleright G_1'$ for some Γ, G_1 and G_1', then either: (i) $C \preceq_{\mathcal{D}} 0$; or, (ii) for every σ, there exist G_2, C' and σ' such that $G_1, C, \sigma \rightarrow_{\mathcal{D}} G_2, C', \sigma'$ and $\Gamma'; G_2 \vdash C' \triangleright G_2'$ for some $\Gamma' \supseteq \Gamma$ and G_2'.*

Checking that $\Gamma \vdash \langle \mathcal{D}, C \rangle$ is not trivial, as it requires "guessing" $\Gamma_{\mathcal{D}}$. However, this set can be computed from $\langle \mathcal{D}, C \rangle$.

Theorem 2. *Given Γ, $\mathcal{D}$ and C, $\Gamma \vdash \langle \mathcal{D}, C \rangle$ is decidable.*

The key idea behind the proof of Theorem 2 is that type-checking may require expanding recursive definitions, but their parameters only need to be instantiated with process names from a finite set. A similar idea yields type inference for PC.

Theorem 3. *There is an algorithm that, given any $\langle \mathcal{D}, C \rangle$, outputs: (i) a set Γ such that $\Gamma \vdash \langle \mathcal{D}, C \rangle$, if such a Γ exists; or (ii) NO, if no such Γ exists.*

Theorem 4. *The types of arguments in procedure definitions and the types of freshly created processes can be inferred automatically.*

Remark 3 (Inferring introductions). These results allow us to omit type annotations in choreographies, if the types of functions and expressions at processes are given (in $\vdash_T$). Thus, programmers can write choreographies as in our examples.

The same reasoning can be used to infer missing introductions (p: q <-> r) in a choreography automatically, thus lifting the programmer also from having to think about connections. However, while the types inferred for a choreography do not affect its behaviour, the placement of introductions does. In particular, when invoking procedures one is faced with the choice of adding the necessary introductions inside the procedure definition (weakening the conditions for its invocation) or in the code calling it (making the procedure body more efficient).

Example 6. Consider a procedure $X(\mathsf{p}, \mathsf{q}, \mathsf{r}) = \mathsf{p}.* \texttt{->} \mathsf{q}; \mathsf{p} \colon \mathsf{q} \texttt{<->} \mathsf{r}; \mathsf{q}.* \texttt{->} \mathsf{r}$, whose invokation requires only that p is connected to q and r. If we invoke X twice with the same parameters, as in $X\langle \mathsf{p}, \mathsf{q}, \mathsf{r} \rangle; X\langle \mathsf{p}, \mathsf{q}, \mathsf{r} \rangle$, we end up performing the same introduction p: q <-> r twice. We could avoid this duplication by rewriting X as $X(\mathsf{p}, \mathsf{q}, \mathsf{r}) = \mathsf{p}. * \texttt{->} \mathsf{q}; \mathsf{q}. * \texttt{->} \mathsf{r}$ and then performing the introduction only once before invoking the procedure – $\mathsf{p} : \mathsf{q} \texttt{<->} \mathsf{r}; X\langle \mathsf{p}, \mathsf{q}, \mathsf{r} \rangle; X\langle \mathsf{p}, \mathsf{q}, \mathsf{r} \rangle$. However, this makes invoking X more complicated, and deciding which variant is best depends heavily on the context.

4   Synthesising Process Implementations

We now present our EndPoint Projection (EPP), which compiles a choreography to a concurrent implementation represented in terms of a process calculus.

4.1   Procedural Processes (PP)

We introduce our target process model, Procedural Processes (PP).

$$B ::= \mathsf{q}!e; B \mid \mathsf{p}?f; B \mid \mathsf{q}!!r; B \mid \mathsf{p}?r; B \mid \mathsf{q} \oplus l; B \mid \mathsf{p}\&\{l_i : B_i\}_{i \in I}; B$$

$$\mid \mathbf{0} \mid \mathsf{start}\,\mathsf{q}^T \rhd B_2; B_1 \mid \mathsf{if}\ e\ \mathsf{then}\ B_1\ \mathsf{else}\ B_2; B \mid X\langle \tilde{\mathsf{p}} \rangle; B \mid \mathbf{0}; B$$

$$\mathscr{B} ::= X(\tilde{\mathsf{q}}) = B, \mathscr{B} \mid \emptyset \qquad N, M ::= \mathsf{p} \rhd_v B \mid (N \mid M) \mid \mathbf{0}$$

$$\frac{u = (f[w/*])(e[v/*])}{\mathsf{p} \rhd_v \mathsf{q}!e; B_1 \mid \mathsf{q} \rhd_w \mathsf{p}?f; B_2 \ \to_{\mathscr{B}} \ \mathsf{p} \rhd_v B_1 \mid \mathsf{q} \rhd_u B_2} \ \lfloor \mathrm{P|Com} \rfloor$$

$$\frac{j \in I}{\mathsf{p} \rhd_v \mathsf{q} \oplus l_j; B \mid \mathsf{q} \rhd_w \mathsf{p}\&\{l_i : B_i\}_{i \in I} \ \to_{\mathscr{B}} \ \mathsf{p} \rhd_v B \mid \mathsf{q} \rhd_w B_j} \ \lfloor \mathrm{P|Sel} \rfloor$$

$$\frac{\mathsf{q}'\ \mathrm{fresh}}{\mathsf{p} \rhd_v (\mathsf{start}\,\mathsf{q}^T \rhd B_2); B_1 \ \to_{\mathscr{B}} \ \mathsf{p} \rhd_v B_1[\mathsf{q}'/\mathsf{q}] \mid \mathsf{q}' \rhd_{\perp_T} B_2} \ \lfloor \mathrm{P|Start} \rfloor$$

$$\frac{}{\mathsf{p} \rhd_v \mathsf{q}!!r; B_1 \mid \mathsf{q} \rhd_w \mathsf{p}?r; B_2 \mid r \rhd_u \mathsf{p}?\mathsf{q}; B_3 \ \to_{\mathscr{B}} \ \mathsf{p} \rhd_v B_1 \mid \mathsf{q} \rhd_w B_2 \mid r \rhd_u B_3} \ \lfloor \mathrm{P|Tell} \rfloor$$

Fig. 4. Procedural processes, syntax and semantics (selected rules).

Syntax. The syntax of PP is given in Fig. 4 (top). A term $\mathsf{p} \rhd_v B$ is a process, where p is its name, v is its value, and B is its behaviour. Networks, ranged over by N, M, are parallel compositions of processes, where $\mathbf{0}$ is the inactive network. Finally, $\langle \mathscr{B}, N \rangle$ is a procedural network, where $\mathscr{B}$ defines the procedures that the processes in N may invoke. Values, expressions and functions are as in PC.

A process executing a send term $\mathsf{q}!e; B$ sends the evaluation of expression e to q, and proceeds as B. Term $\mathsf{p}?f; B$ is the dual receiving action: the process executing it receives a value from p, combines it with its value as specified by f, and then proceeds as B. Term $\mathsf{q}!!r$ sends process name r to q and process name q to r, making q and r "aware" of each other. The dual action is $\mathsf{p}?r$, which receives a process name from p that replaces the bound variable r in the continuation. Term $\mathsf{q} \oplus l; B$ sends the selection of a label l to process q. Selections are received by the branching term $\mathsf{p}\&\{l_i : B_i\}_{i \in I}$, which can receive a selection for any of the labels l_i and proceed as B_i. Branching terms must offer at least one branch. Term $\mathsf{start}\,\mathsf{q} \rhd B_2; B_1$ starts a new process (with a fresh name) executing B_2, and proceeds in parallel as B_1. Conditionals, procedure calls, and termination are standard. Term $\mathsf{start}\,\mathsf{q} \rhd B_2; B_1$ binds q in B_1, and $\mathsf{p}?r; B$ binds r in B.

Semantics. The main rules defining the reduction relation $\to_{\mathscr{B}}$ for PP are shown in Fig. 4 (bottom). As in PC, they are parameterised on the set of behavioural procedures $\mathscr{B}$. Rule $\lfloor \mathrm{P|Com} \rfloor$ models value communication: a process p executing a send action towards a process q can synchronise with a receive-from-p action at q; in the reductum, f is used to update the memory of q by combining its contents with the value sent by p. The placeholder $*$ is replaced with the current value of p in e (resp. q in f). Rule $\lfloor \mathrm{P|Sel} \rfloor$ is standard selection [15], where the sender process selects one of the branches offered by the receiver.

Rule $\lfloor \mathrm{P|Tell} \rfloor$ establishes a three-way synchronisation, allowing a process to introduce two others. Since the received names are bound at the receivers, we use α-conversion to make the receivers agree on each other's name, as in session types [15]. (Differently from PC, we do not assume the Barendregt convention here, in line with the tradition of process calculi.) Rule $\lfloor P|\text{Start}\rfloor$ requires the name of the created process to be globally fresh.

All other rules are standard. Relation $\rightarrow_{\mathscr{B}}$ is closed under a structural pre-congruence $\preceq_{\mathscr{B}}$, which supports associativity and commutativity of parallel (|), standard garbage collection of $\mathbf{0}$, and unfolding of procedure calls.

Example 7. We show a process implementation of the merge sort choreography in Example 1 from Sect. 1. All processes are annotated with type $\mathbf{List}(T)$ (omitted); id is the identity function (Example 2).

```
MS p (p) = if is_small then 0
    else start q1 ▷ (p?id; MS p <q1>; p!*);
         start q2 ▷ (p?id; MS p <q2>; p!*);
         q1!split1; q2!split2; q1?id; q2?merge
```

In the next section, we show that our EPP generates this process implementation automatically from the choreography in Example 1.

4.2   EndPoint Projection (EPP)

We now show how to compile programs in PC to processes in PP.

Behaviour Projection. We start by defining how to project the behaviour of a single process p, a partial function denoted $\llbracket C \rrbracket_\mathsf{p}$. The rules defining behaviour projection are given in Fig. 5. Each choreography term is projected to the local action of the process that we are projecting. For example, a communication term p.e -> q.f projects a send action for the sender p, a receive action for the receiver q, or skips to the continuation otherwise. The rules for projecting a selection or an introduction (name mobility) are similar.

The rule for projecting a conditional uses the partial merging operator $\sqcup$: $B \sqcup B'$ is isomorphic to B and B' up to branching, where the branches of B or B' with distinct labels are also included. The interesting rule defining merge is:

$$(\mathsf{p}\&\{l_i : B_i\}_{i\in I}; B) \sqcup (\mathsf{p}\&\{l_j : B'_j\}_{j\in J}; B') =$$
$$\mathsf{p}\&(\{l_k : (B_k \sqcup B'_k)\}_{k\in I\cap J} \cup \{l_i : B_i\}_{i\in I\setminus J} \cup \{l_j : B'_j\}_{j\in J\setminus I}); (B \sqcup B')$$

The idea of merging comes from [2]. Here, we extend it to general recursion, parametric procedures, and process starts. Merging allows the process that decides a conditional to inform other processes of its choice later on, using selections. It is found repeatedly in most choreography models [2,7,17].

Building on behaviour projection, we define how to project the set $\mathscr{D}$ of procedure definitions. We need to consider two main aspects. The first is that, at runtime, the choreography may invoke a procedure X multiple times, but potentially passing a process r at different argument positions each time. This means that r may be called to play different "roles" in the implementation of

$$[\![p.e \rightarrow q.f; C]\!]_r = \begin{cases} q!e; [\![C]\!]_r & \text{if } r = p \\ p?f; [\![C]\!]_r & \text{if } r = q \\ [\![C]\!]_r & \text{o.w.} \end{cases} \quad [\![p \rightarrow q[l]; C]\!]_r = \begin{cases} q \oplus l; [\![C]\!]_r & \text{if } r = p \\ p\&\{l : [\![C]\!]_r\} & \text{if } r = q \\ [\![C]\!]_r & \text{o.w.} \end{cases}$$

$$[\![p : q \leftrightarrow r; C]\!]_s = \begin{cases} q!!r; [\![C]\!]_s & \text{if } s = p \\ p?r; [\![C]\!]_s & \text{if } s = q \\ p?q; [\![C]\!]_s & \text{if } s = r \\ [\![C]\!]_s & \text{o.w.} \end{cases} \quad [\![X\langle\tilde{p}\rangle; C]\!]_r = \begin{cases} X_r\langle\tilde{p}\rangle; [\![C]\!]_r & \text{if } r = p_i \\ [\![C]\!]_r & \text{o.w.} \end{cases}$$

$$[\![0]\!]_r = 0 \quad [\![0; C]\!]_r = [\![C]\!]_r$$

$$[\![\text{if } p.e \text{ then } C_1 \text{ else } C_2; C]\!]_r = \begin{cases} \text{if } e \text{ then } [\![C_1]\!]_r \text{ else } [\![C_2]\!]_r; [\![C]\!]_r & \text{if } r = p \\ ([\![C_1]\!]_r \sqcup [\![C_2]\!]_r); [\![C]\!]_r & \text{o.w.} \end{cases}$$

$$[\![p \text{ start } q^T; C]\!]_r = \begin{cases} \text{start } q \triangleright [\![C]\!]_q; [\![C]\!]_r & \text{if } r = p \\ [\![C]\!]_r & \text{o.w.} \end{cases}$$

Fig. 5. Procedural choreographies, behaviour projection.

the procedure. For this reason, we project the behaviour of each possible process parameter p as the local procedure X_p. The second aspect is: depending on the role that r is called to play by the choreography, it needs to know the names of the other processes that it is supposed to communicate with in the choreographic procedure. We deal with this by simply passing all arguments (some of which may be unknown to the process invoking the procedure). This is not a problem: for typable choreographies, typing ensures that those parameters are not actually used in the projected procedure (so they act as "dummies"). We do this for clarity, since it yields a simpler formulation of EPP. In practice, we can annotate the EPP by analysing which parameters of each recursive definition are actually used in each of its projections, and instantiating only those.

We thus define $[\![\mathscr{D}]\!] = \bigcup \left\{ [\![X(\widetilde{q^T}) = C]\!] \mid X(\widetilde{q^T}) = C \in \mathscr{D} \right\}$ where, for $\widetilde{q^T} = q_1^{T_1}, \ldots, q_n^{T_n}$, we set $[\![X(\widetilde{q^T}) = C]\!] = \{X_{q_1}(\tilde{q}) = [\![C]\!]_{q_1}, \ldots, X_{q_n}(\tilde{q}) = [\![C]\!]_{q_n}\}$.

Definition 1 (EPP). *Given a procedural choreography $\langle \mathscr{D}, C \rangle$ and a state σ, the EPP $[\![\mathscr{D}, C, \sigma]\!]$ is the parallel composition of the processes in C with all definitions from $\mathscr{D}$:* $[\![\mathscr{D}, C, \sigma]\!] = \langle [\![\mathscr{D}]\!], [\![C, \sigma]\!] \rangle = \left\langle [\![\mathscr{D}]\!], \prod_{p \in pn(C)} p \triangleright_{\sigma(p)} [\![C]\!]_p \right\rangle$ *where $[\![C, \sigma]\!]$, the EPP of C wrt state σ, is independent of $\mathscr{D}$.*

Since the σs are total, if $[\![C, \sigma]\!]$ is defined for some σ, then $[\![C, \sigma']\!]$ is defined also for all other σ'. When $[\![C, \sigma]\!] = N$ is defined for any σ, we say that C is *projectable* and that N is the projection of C, σ. The same holds for $[\![\mathscr{D}, C, \sigma]\!]$.

Example 8. The EPP of the choreography in Example 1 is given in Example 7.

Example 9. For an example involving merging and introductions, we project the procedure **par_download** (Example 5) for process s, omitting type annotations.

```
par_download s (c,s) = c&{
  more: start s' ▷ (s?c; c?id; c?c'; download s <c',s'>);
        c!!s'; par_download s <c,s>
  end: 0                                            }
```

Observe that we invoke procedure download$_s$, since s' occurs in the position of download's formal argument s.

Properties. EPP guarantees correctness by construction: the code synthesised from a choreography follows it precisely.

Theorem 5 (EPP Theorem). *If* $\langle \mathscr{D}, C \rangle$ *is projectable,* $\Gamma \vdash \mathscr{D}$, *and* $\Gamma; G \vdash C \triangleright G^*$, *then, for all* σ: *if* $G, C, \sigma \rightarrow_{\mathscr{D}} G', C', \sigma'$, *then* $[\![C, \sigma]\!] \rightarrow_{[\![\mathscr{D}]\!]} \succ [\![C', \sigma']\!]$ *(completeness); and if* $[\![C, \sigma]\!] \rightarrow_{[\![\mathscr{D}]\!]} N$, *then* $G, C, \sigma \rightarrow_{\mathscr{D}} G', C', \sigma'$ *for some* G', C' *and* σ' *such that* $[\![C', \sigma']\!] \prec N$ *(soundness).*

Above, the *pruning relation* $\prec$ from [2] eliminates branches introduced by the merging operator $\sqcup$ when they are not needed anymore to follow the originating choreography ($N \succ N'$ stands for $N' \prec N$). Pruning does not alter reductions, since the eliminated branches are never selected [2]. Combining Theorem 5 with Theorem 1 we get that the projections of typable PC terms never deadlock.

Corollary 1 (Deadlock-freedom by construction). *Let* $N = [\![C, \sigma]\!]$ *for some* C *and* σ, *and assume that* $\Gamma; G \vdash C \triangleright G'$ *for some* Γ *such that* $\Gamma \vdash \mathscr{D}$ *and some* G *and* G'. *Then, either: (i)* $N \preceq_{[\![\mathscr{D}]\!]} 0$ *(N has terminated); or (ii) there exists* N' *such that* $N \rightarrow_{[\![\mathscr{D}]\!]} N'$ *(N can reduce).*

Remark 4 (Amendment). A choreography can only be unprojectable because of unmergeable subterms, and thus can be made projectable by adding label selections. This can be formalised in an amendment algorithm, similar to [10,18]. For example, the first (unprojectable) choreography in Remark 2 can be amended to the projectable choreography presented at the end of the same remark.

The same argument as in Remark 3 applies: amendment allows us to disregard label selections, but placing them manually can be useful. For example, suppose p makes a choice that affects q and r. If q has to perform a slower computation as a result, then it makes sense for p to notify q first.

5   Related Work and Discussion

Choreographic Programming. Our examples cannot be written in previous models for choreographic programming, which lack full procedural abstraction. In state-of-the-art models [2,4], procedures cannot have continuations, there can only be a limited number of protocols running at any time (modulo dangling asynchronous actions), and the process names used in a procedure are statically determined. In PC, all these limitations are lifted.

Differently from PC, name mobility in choreographies is typically done using channel delegation [4], which is less powerful: a process that introduces two other processes requires a new channel to communicate with them thenceforth.

Some choreography models include explicit parallel composition, $C \,|\, C'$. Most behaviours of $C \,|\, C'$ are already captured in PC, for example $X\langle \mathsf{p}, \mathsf{q}\rangle \,|\, Y\langle \mathsf{r}, \mathsf{s}\rangle$ is equivalent to $X\langle \mathsf{p}, \mathsf{q}\rangle; Y\langle \mathsf{r}, \mathsf{s}\rangle$ in PC (cf. Example 3) – see [4] for a deeper discussion. If a parallel operator is desired, PC can be easily extended (cf. [2]).

In [21], choreographies can be integrated with existing process code by means of a type system, which we could easily integrate in PC.

Asynchrony. Asynchronous communication in choreographic programming was addressed in [4] using an ad-hoc transition rule. Adding asynchrony to PC is straightforward (see the technical report [9]).

Multiparty Session Types (MPST). In MPST [16], global types are choreographic specifications of single protocols, used for verifying the code of manually-written implementations in process models. Global types are similar to a simplified fragment of PC, obtained (among others) by replacing expressions and functions with constants (representing types), removing process creation (the processes are fixed), and restricting recursion to parameterless tail recursion.

MPST leaves protocol composition to the implementors of processes, which can result in deadlocks, unlike in PC. We illustrate this key difference using our syntax; we view a protocol in MPST as a (simplification of a) procedure in PC. Consider the protocols $X(\mathsf{r}, \mathsf{s}) = \mathsf{r}.e \rightarrow \mathsf{s}.f$ and $Y(\mathsf{r}', \mathsf{s}') = \mathsf{r}'.e' \rightarrow \mathsf{s}'.f'$, and their instantiations $X\langle \mathsf{p}, \mathsf{q}\rangle$ and $Y\langle \mathsf{q}, \mathsf{p}\rangle$. In MPST, a valid composition (in PP) is $\mathsf{p} \rhd_v \mathsf{q}?f'; \mathsf{q}!e \,|\, \mathsf{q} \rhd_v \mathsf{p}?f; \mathsf{p}!e'$. This network is obviously deadlocked, but MPST does not detect it because the interleaving of the two protocols is not checked. In PC, we can only obtain correct implementations, because compositions are defined at the level of choreographies, e.g., $X\langle \mathsf{p}, \mathsf{q}\rangle; Y\langle \mathsf{q}, \mathsf{p}\rangle$ or $Y\langle \mathsf{q}, \mathsf{p}\rangle; X\langle \mathsf{p}, \mathsf{q}\rangle$.

Deadlock-freedom for compositions in MPST can be obtained by restricting connections among processes participating in different protocols to form a tree [3,5]. In PC, connections can form an arbitrary graph. Another technique for MPST is to use pre-orders [7], but this is also not as expressive as PC (see [9]).

MPST can be extended to protocols where the number of participants is fixed only at runtime [27], or can grow during execution [13]. These results use ad-hoc primitives and "middleware" terms in the process model, e.g., for tracking the number of participants in a session [13], which are not needed in PC. MPST can be nested [12], partially recalling our parametric procedures. Differently from PC, nested procedures in MPST are invoked by a coordinator (requiring extra communications), and compositions of such nested types can deadlock.

Sessions and Mobility. Recent theories based on session types [2,4,5,7,16] assume that all pairs of processes in a session have a private full-duplex channel to communicate. Thus, processes in a protocol must have a complete connection graph. PC can be used to reason about different kinds of network topologies.

Another important aspect of sessions is that each new protocol execution requires the creation of a new session, whereas procedure calls in PC reuse available connections – allowing for more efficient implementations. Our parallel downloader example uses this feature (Example 5).

The standard results of communication safety found in session-typed calculi can be derived from our EPP Theorem (Theorem 5), as discussed in [4].

Faults. We have abstracted from faults and divergence of internal computations: in PC, we assume that all internal computations terminate successfully. If we relax these conditions, deadlock-freedom can still be achieved simply by using timeouts and propagating faults through communications.

Acknowledgements. We thank the anonymous reviewers for their useful comments. This work was supported by the CRC project, grant no. DFF–4005-00304 from the Danish Council for Independent Research, by grant no. DFF–1323-00247 from the Danish Council for Independent Research, Natural Sciences, and by the Open Data Framework project at the University of Southern Denmark.

References

1. Business Process Model and Notation. http://www.omg.org/spec/BPMN/2.0/
2. Carbone, M., Honda, K., Yoshida, N.: Structured communication-centered programming for web services. ACM Trans. Program. Lang. Syst. **34**(2), 8 (2012)
3. Carbone, M., Lindley, S., Montesi, F., Schürmann, C., Wadler, P.: Coherence generalises duality: a logical explanation of multiparty session types. In: CONCUR. LIPIcs, vol. 59, pp. 33:1–33:15. Schloss Dagstuhl (2016)
4. Carbone, M., Montesi, F.: Deadlock-freedom-by-design: multiparty asynchronous global programming. In: POPL, pp. 263–274. ACM (2013)
5. Carbone, M., Montesi, F., Schürmann, C., Yoshida, N.: Multiparty session types as coherence proofs. Acta Inform. **54**(3), 243–269 (2017)
6. Chor: Programming Language. http://www.chor-lang.org/
7. Coppo, M., Dezani-Ciancaglini, M., Yoshida, N., Padovani, L.: Global progress for dynamically interleaved multiparty sessions. Math. Struct. Comput. Sci. **26**(2), 238–302 (2016)
8. Cruz-Filipe, L., Montesi, F.: Choreographies in practice. In: Albert, E., Lanese, I. (eds.) FORTE 2016. LNCS, vol. 9688, pp. 114–123. Springer, Cham (2016). doi:10.1007/978-3-319-39570-8_8
9. Cruz-Filipe, L., Montesi, F.: A language for the declarative composition of concurrent protocols. CoRR, abs/1602.03729 (2016)
10. Cruz-Filipe, L., Montesi, F.: A core model for choreographic programming. In: Kouchnarenko, O., Khosravi, R. (eds.) FACS 2016. LNCS, vol. 10231, pp. 17–35. Springer, Cham (2017). doi:10.1007/978-3-319-57666-4_3
11. Dalla Preda, M., Gabbrielli, M., Giallorenzo, S., Lanese, I., Mauro, J.: Dynamic choreographies. In: Holvoet, T., Viroli, M. (eds.) COORDINATION 2015. LNCS, vol. 9037, pp. 67–82. Springer, Cham (2015). doi:10.1007/978-3-319-19282-6_5
12. Demangeon, R., Honda, K.: Nested protocols in session types. In: Koutny, M., Ulidowski, I. (eds.) CONCUR 2012. LNCS, vol. 7454, pp. 272–286. Springer, Heidelberg (2012). doi:10.1007/978-3-642-32940-1_20
13. Deniélou, P.-M., Yoshida, N.: Dynamic multirole session types. In: POPL, pp. 435–446. ACM (2011)
14. Honda, K., Mukhamedov, A., Brown, G., Chen, T.-C., Yoshida, N.: Scribbling interactions with a formal foundation. In: Natarajan, R., Ojo, A. (eds.) ICDCIT 2011. LNCS, vol. 6536, pp. 55–75. Springer, Heidelberg (2011). doi:10.1007/978-3-642-19056-8_4

15. Honda, K., Vasconcelos, V.T., Kubo, M.: Language primitives and type discipline for structured communication-based programming. In: Hankin, C. (ed.) ESOP 1998. LNCS, vol. 1381, pp. 122–138. Springer, Heidelberg (1998). doi:10.1007/BFb0053567

16. Honda, K., Yoshida, N., Carbone, M.: Multiparty asynchronous session types. J. ACM **63**(1), 9 (2016)

17. Lanese, I., Guidi, C., Montesi, F., Zavattaro, G.: Bridging the gap between interaction-and process-oriented choreographies. In: SEFM, pp. 323–332 (2008)

18. Lanese, I., Montesi, F., Zavattaro, G.: Amending choreographies. In: WWV, pp. 34–48 (2013)

19. Lu, S., Park, S., Seo, E., Zhou, Y.: Learning from mistakes: a comprehensive study on real world concurrency bug characteristics. ACM SIGARCH Comput. Archit. News **36**(1), 329–339 (2008)

20. Montesi, F.: Choreographic programming. Ph.D. thesis, IT University of Copenhagen (2013). http://fabriziomontesi.com/files/choreographic_programming.pdf

21. Montesi, F., Yoshida, N.: Compositional choreographies. In: D'Argenio, P.R., Melgratti, H. (eds.) CONCUR 2013. LNCS, vol. 8052, pp. 425–439. Springer, Heidelberg (2013). doi:10.1007/978-3-642-40184-8_30

22. MPI Forum: MPI: A Message-Passing Interface Standard. High-Performance Computing Center Stuttgart, version 3.1 (2015)

23. PI4SOA (2008). http://www.pi4soa.org

24. Qiu, Z., Zhao, X., Cai, C., Yang, H.: Towards the theoretical foundation of choreography. In: WWW, pp. 973–982. ACM (2007)

25. Savara: JBoss Community. http://www.jboss.org/savara/

26. W3C WS-CDL Working Group: Web services choreography description language version 1.0 (2004). http://www.w3.org/TR/2004/WD-ws-cdl-10-20040427/

27. Yoshida, N., Deniélou, P.-M., Bejleri, A., Hu, R.: Parameterised multiparty session types. In: Ong, L. (ed.) FOSSACS 2010. LNCS, vol. 6014, pp. 128–145. Springer, Heidelberg (2010). doi:10.1007/978-3-642-12032-9_10

An Observational Approach to Defining Linearizability on Weak Memory Models

John Derrick[1(✉)] and Graeme Smith[2]

[1] Department of Computing, University of Sheffield, Sheffield, UK
`j.derrick@sheffield.ac.uk`
[2] School of Information Technology and Electrical Engineering,
The University of Queensland, Brisbane, Australia
`smith@itee.uq.edu.au`

Abstract. In this paper we present a framework for defining linearizability on weak memory models. The purpose of the framework is to be able to define the correctness of concurrent algorithms in a uniform way across a variety of memory models. To do so linearizability is defined within the framework in terms of *memory order* as opposed to *program order*. Such a generalisation of the original definition of linearizability enables it to be applied to non-sequentially consistent architectures. It also allows the definition to be given in terms of observable effects rather than being dependent on an understanding of the weak memory model architecture. We illustrate the framework on the TSO (Total Store Order) weak memory model, and show that it respects existing definitions of linearizability on TSO.

1 Introduction

The use of *weak* (or *relaxed*) memory models is standard practice in modern multiprocessor hardware [18]. There are numerous examples including the TSO (Total Store Order) memory model [16,18], and the memory models of the Power and ARM architectures [1]. TSO is implemented by the x86 architecture used by the chip manufacturers Intel and AMD. The Power architecture is used by IBM, and ARM is the most widely used architecture in mobile devices [10].

All of these architectures provide efficiency gains by reducing the number of accesses to shared memory. For example, in the TSO architecture a buffer is used to store any writes to variables until they can be *flushed* to memory at a convenient time. This time is determined by the hardware to increase efficiency, however if necessary *fences* can be used in the code to force a write to memory. Such instructions flush the entire contents of the buffer to memory.

There is a trade-off between efficiency of the underlying architecture and the use of fences. Furthermore, the presence of both a complicated underlying architecture and associated flushes and fences means there is increased subtlety of the correctness of any given algorithm. This has motivated an increasing interest in verifying the correctness of concurrent algorithms on weak memory models; for example, see [3,8,11,17,19,20] for work on TSO.

© IFIP International Federation for Information Processing 2017
Published by Springer International Publishing AG 2017. All Rights Reserved
A. Bouajjani and A. Silva (Eds.): FORTE 2017, LNCS 10321, pp. 108–123, 2017.
DOI: 10.1007/978-3-319-60225-7_8

The standard notion of correctness for concurrent objects is *linearizability* [12]. Given a specification and a concurrent implementation, the idea of linearizability is that any concurrent execution of the implementation must be consistent with some sequential execution of the specification. The sequential execution is obtained by identifying *linearization points* at which the potentially overlapping concurrent operations are deemed to take effect instantaneously.

A number of approaches have been developed for proving linearizability on *sequentially consistent* architectures, i.e., those without a weak memory model, along with associated tool support [2,4–6,9,15,21]. In particular, Derrick et al. [5,6,15] have developed a method for proving linearizability supported by the interactive theorem prover KIV [14]. The method consists of proving a number of simulation rules relating a model (a state-transition system) derived from the code and a model representing the abstract specification. This method has been proved sound and complete, the soundness and completeness proofs themselves being done in KIV.

Our recent work, [8], extends the method of Derrick et al. to TSO. To do this, it explicitly adds details of the TSO architecture, i.e., buffers, flushes and fences, into the model derived from the code. To relate this model to the abstract specification, a new set of simulation rules is required to deal with these architectural details which do not occur in the abstract specification.[1] These rules correspond to a new definition of linearizability, referred to in [8] as TSO-linearizability, for which new tool support is required. Due to the explicit modelling of the TSO architecture, we refer to this approach as an *architectural* approach. In [7], we extend this to provide a framework for developing architectural approaches to verification for other weak memory models.

In this paper, we define a new framework for correctness in terms of the *observable* behaviour of weak memory models (as opposed to their underlying architectures). This is beneficial for two reasons. Firstly, the details of many commercial architectures, including Power and ARM, are not available publicly. However, their observable behaviour can be derived via testing: a substantial effort in this direction has already been undertaken for Power and ARM [13]. Secondly, by abstracting from the details of the underlying architecture, the observational approach allows us to use the existing simulation rules and tool support for linearizability. Specifically, the framework does not include architectural details in the model derived from the code and hence, in contrast to the architectural approach, does not require new simulation rules or tool support for each memory model.

The paper is structured as follows. Section 2 introduces the notion of linearizability. Section 3 introduces the TSO memory model and the architectural approach to linearizability on TSO from [8]. Section 4 provides our observational definition of linearizability and shows it is consistent with the architectural

---

[1] The related work of Burckhardt [3] and Gotsman [11] avoid this issue by modifying the abstract specification. We are motivated, however, to allow implementations on TSO to be proved correct with respect to standard specifications of concurrent objects.

definition for TSO. Section 5 discusses the generalisation of the framework to other weak memory models including ARM and Power.

The following is used as a running example throughout the paper.

1.1   Example: seqlock

The Linux reader-writer mechanism seqlock allows the reading of shared variables without locking the global memory, thus supporting fast write access. It works as follows. A thread wishing to *write* to the shared variables, x1 and x2, say, acquires a software lock and increments a counter c. It then proceeds to write to the variables, and finally increments c again before releasing the lock. The lock ensures synchronisation between writers, and the counter c ensures the consistency of values read by other threads as follows. The two increments of c ensure that it is odd when a thread is writing to the variables, and even otherwise. Hence, when a thread wishes to *read* the shared variables, it waits in a loop until c is even before reading them. Also, before returning it checks that the value of c has not changed (i.e., another write has not begun). If it has changed, the thread starts over.

Figure 1 provides an abstract specification, in which operations are regarded as atomic. A valid behaviour[2] of seqlock on a sequentially consistent architecture is: $\langle write(t_1, 1, 2);\ read(t_1, 1, 2);\ read(t_2, 1, 2)\rangle$, where, for example, $write(t_1, 1, 2)$ denotes thread t_1 calling the *write* operation with parameters 1 and 2.

```
word x1 = 0, x2 = 0;

atomic write(in word d1,d2) {        atomic read(out word d1,d2) {
    x1 = d1;                             d1 = x1;
    x2 = d2;                             d2 = x2;
}                                    }
```

Fig. 1. seqlock specification

The assumption of atomicity is dropped in the concurrent implementation given in Fig. 2 where the statements of operations may be interleaved. Here a local variable c0 is used by the **read** operation to record the (even) value of c before the operation begins updating local variables d1 and d2.

2   Linearizability

Linearizability [12] is the standard correctness criterion for verifying concurrent implementations such as seqlock. Linearizability provides the illusion that

---

[2] We use the term *behaviour* to informally refer to a sequence of operations an object may undergo. Later we formalise this as *histories* used in the standard definition of linearizability, and as *executions* used in our observational definition of linearizability.

```
word x1 = 0, x2 = 0;
word c = 0;                             read(out word d1,d2) {
                                          word c0;
write(in word d1,d2) {                    do {
   acquire;                                  do {
   c++;                                         c0 = c;
   x1 = d1;                                  } while (c0 % 2 != 0);
   x2 = d2;                                  d1 = x1;
   c++;                                      d2 = x2;
   release;                               } while (c != c0);
}                                       }
```

Fig. 2. seqlock implementation [3]

each operation executed by a thread takes effect instantaneously at some point between its invocation and its return; this point is known as the *linearization point*. For example, in seqlock the linearization point of the write operation is the second store to c; after this the values written by the operation can be read by other threads.

Linearizability is defined on *histories*, which are sequences of *events* that can be invocations or returns of operations from a set I and performed by a particular thread from a set T. Invocations have an input from domain In and returns have an output from domain Out; both domains contain the value $\perp$ indicating no input or output. On a sequentially consistent architecture we define events and histories as follows:

$$Event \,\widehat{=}\, inv \langle\!\langle T \times I \times In \rangle\!\rangle \mid ret \langle\!\langle T \times I \times Out \rangle\!\rangle$$
$$History \,\widehat{=}\, seq\, Event$$

Following [12], each event in a history can be uniquely identified by its operation which we assume is annotated with a subscript representing the occurrence of that operation in the history, so $write_n$ is the nth write operation.

Since operations are atomic in an abstract specification, its histories are *sequential*, i.e., each operation invocation will be followed immediately by its return. The histories of a concurrent implementation, however, may have overlapping operations and hence have the invocations and returns of operations separated. However to be *legal*, a history should not have returns for which there has not been an invocation.

Example 1. The following is a possible history of the seqlock implementation:

$$\langle inv(t_1, write_1, (1,2)), inv(t_2, read_1, \perp), ret(t_1, write_1, \perp), ret(t_2, read_1, (1,2)) \rangle$$

Since $write_1$ and $read_1$ overlap, h is not sequential. It is however legal.   □

The histories of specifications are also *complete*, i.e., they have a return for each invocation. This is not necessarily the case for implementation histories.

To make an implementation history complete, it is necessary to add additional returns for those operations which have been invoked and are deemed to have occurred, and to remove the remaining invocations without matching returns.

Definition 1 (Linearizability [12]**).**   *An implementation of a concurrent object is linearizable with respect to a specification of the object iff for each history h of the implementation, (1) there is a (sequential) history hs of the specification such that the operations of a legal completion of h are identical to those of hs, and (2) the* precedence ordering *of h is preserved by that of hs, i.e., only overlapping operations of h may be reordered with respect to each other in hs.*   □

3   The TSO Memory Model

A weak memory model gives rise to additional behaviours that are not possible on a sequentially consistent architecture. As an example of a weak memory model, we consider the TSO architecture [16, 18].

In TSO, each processor core uses a *store buffer*, which is a FIFO queue that holds pending *stores* (i.e., writes) to memory. When a thread running on a processor core needs to store to a memory location, it enqueues the store to the buffer and continues computation without waiting for the store to be committed to memory. Pending stores do not become visible to threads on other cores until the buffer is *flushed*, which commits (some or all) pending stores to memory. The value of a memory location *loaded* (i.e., read) by a thread is the most recent in that processor's local buffer, and only from the memory if there is no such value in the buffer (i.e., initially or when all stores for that location have been flushed). The use of local buffers allows a load by one thread, occurring after a store by another, to return an older value as if it occurred before the store.

In general, flushes are controlled by the CPU. However, a programmer may explicitly include a *fence*, or *memory barrier*, instruction to force flushes to occur. Therefore, although TSO allows some non-sequentially consistent behaviours, it is used in many modern architectures on the basis that these can be prevented, where necessary, by programmers using fence instructions.

On TSO for example, when we run seqlock the `acquire` command of the software lock necessarily has a fence to ensure synchronization between writer threads, however a fence is not required by the `release` command, the effect of which may be delayed. This can lead to unexpected behaviour on TSO. For example, $\langle write(t_1, 1, 2); \; read(t_1, 1, 2); \; read(t_2, 0, 0)\rangle$ is a possible behaviour if t_1's local buffer is not flushed until after t_2's *read*.

The effects of weak memory models, such as TSO, can be understood in terms of potential reordering of program *commands*, i.e., atomic interactions with memory such as loads, stores and fences. The order that the commands of a program p occur in code is captured by the *program order*, which we denote by $<_p$. On a sequentially consistent architecture each thread preserves the program order. However, this is not the case on weak memory models, including TSO.

In particular, the order of a *store* occurring before a *load* in TSO is not preserved in the shared memory unless the store is flushed before the load occurs. To formalise such effects we introduce a *memory order*, which we denote by $<_{m(p)}$, and which denotes the order the commands of program p take effect in the shared memory. The effect of TSO can then be characterised by saying that *load* $<_p$ *store* $\Rightarrow$ *load* $<_{m(p)}$ *store*, etc., but that *store* $<_p$ *load* does not imply *store* $<_{m(p)}$ *load*.

These effects are summarised in the following table taken from [18]. The commands include an atomic *read-modify-write*, RMW (e.g., a compare-and-swap (CAS)), and a fence. To be atomic, the former needs to write to memory immediately and hence necessarily includes a fence on TSO (since the write will be placed at the end of the FIFO store buffer). In the table, X denotes an enforced ordering and B denotes that commands can be reordered but *bypassing* is required if the commands are to the same variable. Bypassing means that the value read is the one that was most recently written by the thread even if it is not yet in the shared memory.

TSO	Command 2			
Command 1	Load	Store	RMW	Fence
Load	X	X	X	X
Store	B	X	X	X
RMW	X	X	X	X
Fence	X	X	X	X

3.1   Linearizability on TSO

The effect of store buffers means that it is necessary to adapt the linearizability definition for TSO. This is done in [7,8] by considering how the histories of the implementation are altered, and defining a transformation which then allows concurrent histories to be compared with abstract ones.

To do this, the flush commands are recorded as special events in the TSO histories. Such an event is identified by the thread from whose buffer a value is flushed, and either an operation, if the flush is of the last value written by the operation, or $\perp$ otherwise. Events and histories on TSO are then defined as follows:

$$Event_{TSO} \cong inv \langle\!\langle T \times I \times In \rangle\!\rangle \mid ret \langle\!\langle T \times I \times Out \rangle\!\rangle \mid flush \langle\!\langle T \times (I \cup \{\perp\}) \rangle\!\rangle$$
$$History_{TSO} \cong seq\, Event_{TSO}$$

The predicate $flush?(e)$ holds for an event $e \in Event_{TSO}$ iff e is a flush event.

In a sequentially consistent architecture an operation by a thread takes effect at some point between its invocation and return. On a weak memory model, however, the effect of an operation may be delayed until some, or all, of its stores have been flushed. On TSO an operation may actually take effect at any time up to the flush of the last value written by the operation. Implementation histories are thus transformed to reflect this by extending the duration of operations which perform stores: the *effective return* of an operation in a TSO history is either the flush of the final value written by the operation or the return of the operation, whichever occurs later in the history.[3] To represent this, a transformation is defined on histories by:

- moving the return of an operation to replace the final flush for the operation when such a flush occurs after the return, and
- removing all other flushes.

This is encapsulated in the following definition, where for a sequence s, *head* s is the first element of s, *tail* s is s without the first element, $s \oplus \{n \mapsto v\}$ replaces the nth value of s with value v, $\#s$ is the length of s, $s(n)$ is the nth element of s, and $s \frown t$ is the concatention of s with a sequence t:

$$trans(h) \cong \begin{cases} \langle\,\rangle & \text{if } h = \langle\,\rangle \\ trans(tail\ h) & \text{if } flush?(head\ h) \\ trans(tail\ (h \oplus \{n \mapsto head\ h\})) & \text{if } DelayedRet(h, n), n \leq \#h \\ \langle head\ h \rangle \frown trans(tail\ h) & \text{otherwise} \end{cases}$$

where $DelayedRet(h, n) \cong ret?(head\ h) \wedge flush?(h(n)) \wedge (head\ h).i = h(n).i$.

Example 2. One history h_{TSO} of the behaviour $\langle write(t_1, 1, 2);\ read(t_1, 1, 2);\ read(t_2, 0, 0)\rangle$ is:

$$\langle inv(t_1, \mathbf{write}_1, (1, 2)), flush(t_1, \perp), ret(t_1, \mathbf{write}_1, \perp), inv(t_1, \mathbf{read}_1, \perp),$$
$$ret(t_1, \mathbf{read}_1, (1, 2)), inv(t_2, \mathbf{read}_2, \perp), ret(t_2, \mathbf{read}_2, (0, 0)),$$
$$flush(t_1, \perp), flush(t_1, \perp), flush(t_1, \perp), flush(t_1, \perp), flush(t_1, \mathbf{write}_1))\rangle$$

where t_1's local buffer is not fully flushed until after the two reads (there are 6 stores including the acquisition and release of the lock). $trans(h_{TSO})$ is then

$$\langle inv(t_1, \mathbf{write}_1, (1, 2)), inv(t_1, \mathbf{read}_1, \perp), ret(t_1, \mathbf{read}_1, (1, 2)),$$
$$inv(t_2, \mathbf{read}_2, \perp), ret(t_2, \mathbf{read}_2, (0, 0)), ret(t_1, \mathbf{write}_1, \perp)\rangle \qquad \square$$

The transformed history intuitively captures the behaviour on TSO and can be compared to histories of the abstract specification using the definition of linearizability of Sect. 2. Thus, linearizability on TSO is defined [8] by first transforming a concurrent history according to *trans*, then (as in the standard definition) comparing the result to an abstract history.

Definition 2 (TSO-linearizability). *An implementation of a concurrent object is linearizable on TSO with respect to a specification of the object if for each history h_{TSO} of the implementation, there exists a (sequential) history hs of the specification such that conditions of Definition 1 hold with $h = trans(h_{TSO})$.*

$\square$

---

[3] This principle is also used in other work on linearizability in TSO [19].

4   Observational Definition of Linearizability on Weak Memory Models

The approach to defining linearizability on TSO in Sect. 3.1 can be similarly applied to other weak memory models [7]. However, it depends on an understanding of the implementation details of the architecture which are used to derive the implementation histories. It also leads to a different relationship between concrete and abstract histories, specifically one involving a composition of a history transformation function and the standard definition of linearizability. This means existing proof techniques, and their support tools, need to be extended.

Adopting an observational, rather than architectural, definition of linearizability overcomes both of these problems. It abstracts from architectural details, being based instead on memory order, and requires the standard linearizability relationship to hold between concrete and abstract histories.

In this section, we use the memory order $<_{m(p)}$ to define our framework for linearizability. To do so we begin by formalising the notion of an execution, which allows us to define the memory order in terms of the program commands.

4.1   Executions

On any memory model, an *execution* is a sequence of commands, which interact with shared memory. Branching statements (such as `if (condition)` and `while (condition)`) are included in executions as loads of the shared variables in `condition`, and their presence in a program affects the executions of that program. For example, letting $store(x, v)$ be a command which writes value v to variable x, and $load(x)$ be a command which reads x, the executions of the program fragment

```
x = n;
if (x > 0) y = n;
```

include $\langle store(x, 1), load(x), store(y, 1)\rangle$ when $n = 1$ and $\langle store(x, 0), load(x)\rangle$ when $n = 0$, but not $\langle store(x, 0), load(x), store(y, 0)\rangle$ when $n = 0$.

We now formalise what we mean by commands. A *command* is either an *invocation* of an operation, or a *load*, a *store*, an atomic *read-modify-write*, or a memory-model specific command. For example, for TSO we add *fence* and *flush* commands. We could add *returns* of operations to commands but instead identify the return of an operation with the last command associated with that operation. Each command is identified as being executed by a thread from type T, belonging to an occurrence of an operation of type I[4]. Invocations have an associated input from domain In. Load commands have an associated variable of type Var (the variable that they read) and write and read-modify-write commands

---

[4] To distinguish identical commands such as the two stores to `c` in the `write` operation of seqlock we would add other identifying information such as program counters, but we elide that detail here.

have both an associated variable and a value of type *Val* (the value written to that variable). For example, the statement x1 = d1 in operation write of seqlock when performed by a thread $t \in T$ is represented by the command $store(t, \text{write}_n, x1, d1)$.

$$Command \,\hat{=}\, inv\langle\!\langle T \times I \times In \rangle\!\rangle \mid store\langle\!\langle T \times I \times Var \times Val \rangle\!\rangle \mid$$
$$load\langle\!\langle T \times I \times Var \rangle\!\rangle \mid RMW\langle\!\langle T \times I \times Var \times Val \rangle\!\rangle \mid \ldots$$

For a command c, we let $c.t \in T$ denote the thread that executed the command and $c.i \in I$ denote the operation it belongs to, and (where applicable) $c.var \in Var$ denote the variable of the command. We let the predicate $inv?(c)$ hold iff c is an invocation command, and $store?(c)$, $load?(c)$ and $rmw?(c)$ iff it is a store, load or read-modify-write command, respectively. For TSO, we let the predicates $fence?(c)$ and $flush?(c)$ hold iff c is a fence or flush command.

We now define the executions *exec* for a program p on a sequentially consistent architecture, and those $exec_m$ on a memory model m. These are subsets of $exec_0$ which are the executions of p that can occur on any memory model that supports bypassing. First, an *Execution* is defined as a sequence of commands.

$$Execution \,\hat{=}\, \text{seq } Command$$

We then let *Object* denote the set of all concurrent objects. Such objects are represented by the implementation model (a state transition system) in the proof method of Derrick et al. [5,6,15]. For any $o \in Object$ and program p comprising a sequence of (potentially overlapping) calls to o's operations, let $exec_0(o, p)$ denote the set of executions of p obtained by *any* reordering of the commands of p that satisfy the following properties:

(a) If a certain command occurs within a branch of the program due to, for example, an if or while statement, the command should occur in an execution precisely when that particular branch is taken in the execution. This ensures the control structure of the program is respected in the reordered executions.

(b) Whenever a load r is moved before a store w to the same variable, the resulting executions behave as if the value read by r is that written by w. This captures the notion of bypassing introduced in Sect. 3. In a state transition-system approach (like that of Derrick et al. [5,6,15]) it could be captured by an additional variable for each thread t and shared variable x capturing the latest value written to x by t.

So $exec_0(o, p)$ contains all reorderings of p's commands that satisfy (a) and (b), and thus corresponds to those that can occur on any weak memory model that supports bypassing. Since bypassing is a common feature of weak memory models, we use this set of executions as the basis of our definitions. However, (b) could be dropped for a particular memory model if necessary.

The program order $<_p \subseteq Command \times Command$ of program p captures the order that the commands occur in the code run by each thread. An invocation command $inv(t, i, in)$, although not explicitly appearing in the code, is ordered as if it appeared in the code before the first statement of i, i.e., $inv(t, i, in) <_p c$ for all commands c of operations called by p with $c.t = t$ and $c.i = i$.

Note that $<_p$ is not a total order. It does not relate commands of different threads. We assume all synchronisation between threads (e.g., acquiring and releasing locks) is done in terms of loads and stores to shared variables. We don't actually formalise $<_p$ here although one could since a program can be formalised as a sequence of invocation commands, and then $<_p$ can be formalised in terms of the order of the invocations, program counters, etc., which define the program order for each thread.

The executions of a program p on a sequentially consistent architecture are precisely those executions which respect the program order $<_p$:

$$exec(o, p) \,\widehat{=}\, \{e : exec_0(o, p) \mid \forall i, j : \operatorname{dom} e \bullet e(i) <_p e(j) \Rightarrow i < j\}$$

For a given memory model m, $<_{m(p)} \subseteq Command \times Command$ is a partial order on commands capturing the *memory order*. This order is generally weaker than the program order allowing reordering of certain commands (as in the table for TSO in Sect. 3). The executions of a program p on memory model m are those executions which respect the order $<_{m(p)}$:

$$exec_m(o, p) \,\widehat{=}\, \{e : exec_0(o, p) \mid \forall i, j : \operatorname{dom} e \bullet e(i) <_{m(p)} e(j) \Rightarrow i < j\}$$

For all $c_1, c_2 \in Command$, the memory order for TSO is defined to maintain the program order unless the first command is a store and the second a load (the condition represented in the table in Sect. 3).

$$c_1 <_{TSO(p)} c_2 \Leftrightarrow c_1 <_p c_2 \wedge (\neg\, (store?(c_1) \wedge load?(c_2)) \,\vee$$
$$(\exists f : Command \bullet c_1 <_p f \wedge f <_p c_2 \wedge fence?(f)))$$

The final predicate ensures we maintain program order if c_1 and c_2 are separated by a fence. Note that bypassing when the commands are to the same variable is covered by condition (b) above.

Example 3. Consider behaviour $\langle write(t_1, 1, 2);\ read(t_1, 1, 2);\ read(t_2, 0, 0)\rangle$ of seqlock consistent with a program p. For all commands c_1 and c_2 where $c_1.i =$ write$_1$ and $c_2.i =$ read$_1$, we have $c_1 <_{TSO(p)} c_2$. However, it is not the case that $c_1 <_{TSO(p)} c_2$ for any c_1 and c_2 where $c_1.t \neq c_2.t$. Considering just the operation $write(t_1, 1, 2)$, the second c++ statement corresponds to commands *load* (t_1, write_1, c) followed by $store(t_1, \text{write}_1, c, 2)$. These commands are preceded by the command $store(t_1, \text{write}_1, x2, 2)$ corresponding to the statement $x2 = d2$ (as $d2 = 2$). Hence, we have $store(t_1, \text{write}_1, x2, 2) <_p load(t_1, \text{write}_1, c) <_p store(t_1, \text{write}_1, c, 2)$. However, on TSO while $store(t_1, \text{write}_1, x2, 2) <_{TSO(p)} store(t_1, \text{write}_1, c, 2)$ and $load(t_1, \text{write}_1, c) <_{TSO(p)} store(t_1, \text{write}_1, c, 2)$, it is not the case that $store(t_1, \text{write}_1, x2, 2) <_{TSO(p)} load(t_1, \text{write}_1, c)$. $\square$

4.2   Relating Executions to Histories

Histories can be derived from a set of executions as follows. Let out_o be a partial function which returns the output value produced on completion of the execution e on object o[5]. The domain of out_o will be those executions which end with the final command of an operation of o. The history corresponding to an execution e is then defined by $hist(e)$, where $lasts$ is the last element of a sequence s, and $fronts$ is the sequence s without the last element:

$$hist(e) \cong \begin{cases} \langle \rangle & \text{if } e = \langle \rangle \\ hist(front e)^\frown \langle last e \rangle & \text{if } inv?(last e) \\ hist(front e)^\frown \langle ret((last e).t, (last e).i, out_o(e)) \rangle & \text{if } e \in \text{dom } out_o \\ hist(front e) & \text{otherwise} \end{cases}$$

4.3   Linearizability on a Weak Memory Model

The observational definition of linearizability generalises that of Sect. 2. Whereas the concrete histories which the existing definition refers to are elements of $\{hist(e) \mid e \in exec(o, p)\}$, those for the observational definition are elements of $\{hist(e) \mid e \in exec_m(o, p)\}$, for a given memory model m.

Definition 3 (Linearizability on memory model m). *An implementation of a concurrent object o is linearizable on memory model m with respect to a specification of the object when, for any program p representing calls to the object, for each history in $\{hist(e) \mid e \in exec_m(o, p)\}$, there exists a (sequential) history hs of the specification such that the conditions of Definition 1 hold.* ☐

Note that the relationship between abstract and concrete histories in this definition are identical to that in Definition 1. Hence, there is no need to change the proof method or tool support. The memory model would be accounted for in the derivation of the implementation model of the approach of Derrick et al. [5,6,15], rather than in the simulation rules.

Below we show that, for TSO, Definition 3 is equivalent to Definition 2. Given $o \in Object$, we let $tso(o)$ denote the corresponding object on TSO, i.e., the object extended to include store buffers and flush commands for each thread (see [8] for one approach for doing this). The function $hist$ that derives TSO histories from TSO executions is as in Sect. 4.2 with the addition of flush commands being retained.

Theorem 1. *Given $Hist(E) \cong \{hist(e) \mid e \in E\}$ and $Trans(H) \cong \{trans(h) \mid h \in H\}$, for any set of executions E and set of histories H:*

$$Trans(Hist(exec(tso(o), p))) = Hist(exec_m(o, p))$$

That is, the set of concrete histories related to abstract histories by the standard definition of linearizabilty are the same in each approach.

---

[5] Since commands are deterministic there is exactly one such value.

Proof. For each $e \in exec(o, p)$ there will be a set of executions in $exec(tso(o), p)$. Each such execution e_{tso} is derived from e by adding flush commands such that the following holds.

$$\exists \, map_{tso} : \{i : \text{dom } e_{tso} \mid store?(e_{tso}(i))\} \rightarrowtail\!\!\!\rightarrow \{i : \text{dom } e_{tso} \mid flush?(e_{tso}(i))\} \bullet$$
$$(\forall i : \text{dom } map_{tso} \bullet$$
$$i < map_{tso}(i) \, \wedge$$
$$(\nexists j : \text{dom } e_{tso} \bullet i < j < map_{tso}(i) \wedge (fence?(e_{tso}(j)) \vee rmw?(e_{tso}(j)))))) \, \wedge$$
$$(\forall i, j : \text{dom } map_{tso} \bullet i < j \wedge e_{tso}(i).t = e_{tso}(j).t \Rightarrow map_{tso}(i) < map_{tso}(j))$$

That is, there exists a bijection mapping the positions of stores in e_{tso} and flushes in e_{tso} such that the flushes occur after the matching stores but before the next fence or read-write-modify command (which includes a fence as discussed in Sect. 3), if any, and the matching flushes for stores of a given thread t are in the order of the stores. The latter is due to the store buffer for a given thread being a FIFO queue.

Furthermore, all threads other than a given thread t run as if each store of t occurs at the point where the associated flush occurs.

Similarly, for each $e \in exec(o, p)$ there will be a set of executions in $exec_m(o, p)$. Each such execution e_m is derived by reordering commands, i.e., $itemse_m = itemse$ (where $itemss$ is the bag of elements in the range of sequence s), such that the following holds.

$$\exists \, map_m : \{i : \text{dom } e \mid store?(e(i+1))\} \rightarrowtail\!\!\!\rightarrow \{i : \text{dom } e_m \mid store?(e_m(i))\} \bullet$$
$$(\forall i : \text{dom } map_m \bullet$$
$$i < map_m(i) \, \wedge$$
$$(\nexists j : \text{dom } e_m \bullet i < j < map_m(i) \wedge (fence?(e_m(j)) \vee rwm?(e_m(j)))))) \, \wedge$$
$$(\forall i, j : \text{dom } map_m \bullet i < j \wedge e_m(i).t = e_m(j).t \Rightarrow map_m(i) < map_m(j))$$

That is, there exists a bijection mapping the positions of the commands immediately preceding stores before reordering (i.e., in e) to the positions of the stores in the reordered execution e_m. The stores cannot be reordered with fences or read-modify-write commands, nor with other stores of the same thread. The latter ensures the order of the moved stores is the same as their original ordering.

In this case, all threads other than a given thread t run as if each store of t occurs at the point where the store is moved to (t runs as if the store occurs in its original position due to bypassing).

It can readily be deduced from the above that for any $e_{tso} \in exec(tso(o), p)$ there is an $e_m \in exec_m(o, p)$, and vice versa, such that the executions include the same commands (apart from flush commands) and for a given store command s, the position of s's flush with respect to other commands in e_{tso} is the position of s with respect to other commands in e_m.

Applying *hist* to e_{tso} and then *trans* to the resulting history gives us a history h_{tso} where the return of each operation is either the last command of that operation, or a flush associated with a store of the operation, whichever occurs later in e_{tso}.

```
word x=0, y=0;

OpOne(out word x1, y1) {          OpTwo(out word x1, y1) {
    x=1;                               y=1;
    x1=x;                              y1=y;
    y1=y;                              x1=x;
}                                 }
```

Fig. 3. Simple concurrent object

Applying *hist* to e_m gives us a history h_m where the return of each operation is the last command of that operation which may be a store which has been moved forward in the execution beyond the original last command of the operation.

Hence, due to the correspondence between positions of flushes in e_{tso} and the positions that stores are moved to in e_m it follows that $h_{tso} = h_m$. Therefore, $Trans(Hist(exec(tso(o), p))) = Hist(exec_m(o, p))$ as required.   □

Example 4. Consider the concurrent object in Fig. 3 and a program p on the object in which a thread t_1 calls OpOne and a thread t_2 calls OpTwo. If the values stored to x and y are not flushed until the end, then one can observe the following behaviour on TSO: $\langle OpOne(t_1, 1, 0); OpTwo(t_2, 0, 1) \rangle$. The table below captures the program order of p, and the memory order that results. (Commands are abbreviated to their essential components for readability.)

Name	Program order of p	Memory order for TSO
inv_1	$inv(t_1)$	
s_1	$store(t_1, x, 1)$	$inv_1 <_{TSO(p)} s_1$
l_1	$load(t_1, x)$	$inv_1 <_{TSO(p)} s_1, inv_1 <_{TSO(p)} l_1$
l_2	$load(t_1, y)$	$inv_1 <_{TSO(p)} s_1, inv_1 <_{TSO(p)} l_1 <_{TSO(p)} l_2$
inv_2	$inv(t_2)$	
s_2	$store(t_2, y, 1)$	$inv_2 <_{TSO(p)} s_2$
l_3	$load(t_2, y)$	$inv_2 <_{TSO(p)} s_2, inv_2 <_{TSO(p)} l_3$
l_4	$load(t_2, x)$	$inv_2 <_{TSO(p)} s_2, inv_2 <_{TSO(p)} l_3 <_{TSO(p)} l_4$

From this one can construct valid executions that respect program order, e.g., $e = \langle inv_1, s_1, l_1, l_2, inv_2, s_2, l_3, l_4 \rangle$. An associated execution on TSO which corresponds to the behaviour $\langle OpOne(t_1, 1, 0); OpTwo(t_2, 0, 1) \rangle$ is $e_{tso} = \langle inv_1, s_1, l_1, l_2, inv_2, s_2, l_3, l_4, flush(t_1, OpOne_1), flush(t_2, OpTwo_1) \rangle$. The corresponding execution respecting memory order is $e_m = \langle inv_1, l_1, l_2, inv_2, l_3, l_4, s_1, s_2 \rangle$. The histories of e_{tso} and e_m can then be calculated as follows:

$$hist(e_{tso}) = \langle\, inv(t_1, \mathtt{OpOne}_1, \perp), ret(t_1, \mathtt{OpOne}_1, (1,0)), inv(t_2, \mathtt{OpTwo}_1, \perp),$$
$$ret(t_2, \mathtt{OpTwo}_1, (0,1)), flush(t_1, \mathtt{OpOne}_1), flush(t_2, \mathtt{OpTwo}_1)\rangle$$
$$hist(e_m) = \langle\, inv(t_1, \mathtt{OpOne}_1, \perp), inv(t_2, \mathtt{OpTwo}_1, \perp), ret(t_1, \mathtt{OpOne}_1, (1,0)),$$
$$ret(t_2, \mathtt{OpTwo}_1, (0,1))\rangle$$

Then it is easy to see that $trans(hist(e_{tso}))$ is the same as $hist(e_m)$.   □

5   Generalising to Other Memory Models

The novelty of the work presented here is that it allows the definition of linearizability to be easily applied to other well understood architectures. One example that is easy to illustrate is the Partial Store Order (PSO). PSO essentially mimics TSO except with one additional relaxation, namely that PSO only guarantees stores to the same variable are in order whereas stores to different variables may be reordered. Hence, for all $c_1, c_2 : Command$, its memory order on program p is

$$c_1 <_{PSO(p)} c_2 \Leftrightarrow c_1 <_p c_2 \wedge$$
$$(\neg\, (store?(c_1) \wedge load?(c_2) \vee$$
$$store?(c1) \wedge store?(c2) \wedge c1.var \neq c2.var) \vee$$
$$(\exists f : Command \bullet c_1 <_p f \wedge f <_p c_2 \wedge fence?(f)))$$

The Power and ARM architectures are more complex. As well as allowing reordering of commands these architectures (1) are *non-multiple-copy-atomic*, meaning a write by one thread may propagate to the other threads at different times, and (2) allow *speculative execution*, where statements after a branch command may be executed before the branch condition has been determined (and executions of paths not subsequently followed discarded).

The former can be incorporated into our framework by allowing each thread to have its own copy of the global variables in the implementation model (as suggested in [13]). The latter can be incorporated by enabling the implementation model to nondeterministically decide on a branch condition at any time and then terminate when the decision is found to be incorrect. Since speculative execution does not effect the external behaviour of a concurrent object before the branch point is reached, no new behaviour is introduced when an execution is terminated at the branch point. The nondeterminism ensures all possible speculative executions are considered, including those which do not terminate at the branch point.

Like command reordering, the above behaviours of Power and ARM can be observed via systematic testing [13]; they do not require an architectural understanding of the memory model. Incorporating them into our framework is an ongoing area of work.

In addition to providing a general definition of correctness for a variety of memory models, the framework allows us to use the existing simulation rules and tool support for linearizability. Specifically, since the framework does not include architectural details in the model derived from the code we do not need new simulation rules or tool support for each memory model. All that is needed is the ability to derive implementation models from code. This is an important area of future work. In Derrick et al. [5], sequentially consistent executions are derived from a state transition system in which each transition corresponds to a command and is enabled precisely when a program counter variable pc, for a given thread, is set to the line number of that command in the program code. To allow reordering, we would need to allow certain commands to be able to occur over a range of values of pc, while respecting additional constraint on the relative order of their occurrence with other commands such as fences.

References

1. Alglave, J., Fox, A., Ishtiaq, S., Myreen, M.O., Sarkar, S., Sewell, P., Nardelli, F.Z.: The semantics of power and ARM multiprocessor machine code. In: Petersen, L., Chakravarty, M.M.T. (eds.) DAMP 2009, pp. 13–24. ACM (2008)
2. Amit, D., Rinetzky, N., Reps, T., Sagiv, M., Yahav, E.: Comparison under abstraction for verifying linearizability. In: Damm, W., Hermanns, H. (eds.) CAV 2007. LNCS, vol. 4590, pp. 477–490. Springer, Heidelberg (2007). doi:10.1007/978-3-540-73368-3_49
3. Burckhardt, S., Gotsman, A., Musuvathi, M., Yang, H.: Concurrent library correctness on the TSO memory model. In: Seidl, H. (ed.) ESOP 2012. LNCS, vol. 7211, pp. 87–107. Springer, Heidelberg (2012). doi:10.1007/978-3-642-28869-2_5
4. Calcagno, C., Parkinson, M., Vafeiadis, V.: Modular safety checking for fine-grained concurrency. In: Nielson, H.R., Filé, G. (eds.) SAS 2007. LNCS, vol. 4634, pp. 233–248. Springer, Heidelberg (2007). doi:10.1007/978-3-540-74061-2_15
5. Derrick, J., Schellhorn, G., Wehrheim, H.: Mechanically verified proof obligations for linearizability. ACM Trans. Program. Lang. Syst. **33**(1), 4:1–4:43 (2011)
6. Derrick, J., Schellhorn, G., Wehrheim, H.: Verifying linearisability with potential linearisation points. In: Butler, M., Schulte, W. (eds.) FM 2011. LNCS, vol. 6664, pp. 323–337. Springer, Heidelberg (2011). doi:10.1007/978-3-642-21437-0_25
7. Derrick, J., Smith, G.: A framework for correctness criteria on weak memory models. In: Bjørner, N., de Boer, F. (eds.) FM 2015. LNCS, vol. 9109, pp. 178–194. Springer, Cham (2015). doi:10.1007/978-3-319-19249-9_12
8. Derrick, J., Smith, G., Dongol, B.: Verifying linearizability on TSO architectures. In: Albert, E., Sekerinski, E. (eds.) IFM 2014. LNCS, vol. 8739, pp. 341–356. Springer, Cham (2014). doi:10.1007/978-3-319-10181-1_21
9. Doherty, S., Groves, L., Luchangco, V., Moir, M.: Formal verification of a practical lock-free queue algorithm. In: Frutos-Escrig, D., Núñez, M. (eds.) FORTE 2004. LNCS, vol. 3235, pp. 97–114. Springer, Heidelberg (2004). doi:10.1007/978-3-540-30232-2_7
10. Fitzpatrick, J.: An interview with Steve Furber. Commun. ACM **54**(5), 34–39 (2011)
11. Gotsman, A., Musuvathi, M., Yang, H.: Show no weakness: sequentially consistent specifications of TSO libraries. In: Aguilera, M.K. (ed.) DISC 2012. LNCS, vol. 7611, pp. 31–45. Springer, Heidelberg (2012). doi:10.1007/978-3-642-33651-5_3
12. Herlihy, M., Wing, J.M.: Linearizability: a correctness condition for concurrent objects. ACM Trans. Program. Lang. Syst. **12**(3), 463–492 (1990)

13. Maranget, L., Sarkar, S., Sewell, P.: A tutorial introduction to the ARM and POWER relaxed memory models (2012). Draft available from http://www.cl.cam. ac.uk/~pes20/ppc-supplemental/test7.pdf
14. Reif, W., Schellhorn, G., Stenzel, K., Balser, M.: Structured specifications and interactive proofs with KIV. In: Automated Deduction, pp. 13–39. Kluwer (1998)
15. Schellhorn, G., Wehrheim, H., Derrick, J.: A sound and complete proof technique for linearizability of concurrent data structures. ACM Trans. Comput. Log. **15**(4), 31:1–31:37 (2014)
16. Sewell, P., Sarkar, S., Owens, S., Nardelli, F.Z., Myreen, M.O.: x86-TSO: a rigorous and usable programmer's model for x86 multiprocessors. Commun. ACM **53**(7), 89–97 (2010)
17. Smith, G., Derrick, J., Dongol, B.: Admit your weakness: verifying correctness on TSO architectures. In: Lanese, I., Madelaine, E. (eds.) FACS 2014. LNCS, vol. 8997, pp. 364–383. Springer, Cham (2015). doi:10.1007/978-3-319-15317-9_22
18. Sorin, D.J., Hill, M.D., Wood, D.A.: A Primer on Memory Consistency and Cache Coherence. Synthesis Lectures on Computer Architecture. Morgan & Claypool Publishers, San Rafael (2011)
19. Travkin, O., Mütze, A., Wehrheim, H.: SPIN as a linearizability checker under weak memory models. In: Bertacco, V., Legay, A. (eds.) HVC 2013. LNCS, vol. 8244, pp. 311–326. Springer, Cham (2013). doi:10.1007/978-3-319-03077-7_21
20. Travkin, O., Wehrheim, H.: Handling TSO in mechanized linearizability proofs. In: Yahav, E. (ed.) HVC 2014. LNCS, vol. 8855, pp. 132–147. Springer, Cham (2014). doi:10.1007/978-3-319-13338-6_11
21. Vafeiadis, V.: Modular fine-grained concurrency verification. Ph.D. thesis, University of Cambridge (2007)

Applying a Dependency Mechanism for Voting Protocol Models Using Event-B

J. Paul Gibson[1], Souad Kherroubi[2], and Dominique Méry[2(✉)]

[1] Telecom Sud Paris, SAMOVAR UMR 5157 CNRS Research Laboratory,
METHODES Team, Évry, France
[2] Université de Lorraine, LORIA UMR 7503 CNRS Research Laboratory,
MOSEL Team, Nancy, France
dominique.mery@loria.fr

Abstract. The design of e-voting systems requires the use of techniques which guarantee that the resulting system is safe, secure and preserves privacy. We develop Event-B models of a voting system, by applying a decomposition pattern and a technique of contextualisation, using a *dependency mechanism*. Through refinement, we take into account the precise regulation and structure of a specific voting process, and reason formally about the system's resistence to common attacks and threats.

1 Introduction

In general, elections are critical processes concerned with the collection, recording and counting of votes [9]. All election processes use protocols satisfying security, safety and privacy properties, which are difficult to express and to validate. We have applied a correct-by-construction refinement technique to formally model and reason about a voting process. The formal approach helps us to validate the coherency of different types of interacting assumptions and requirements [10].

1.1 Diffferent Points of View

There are many different points of view concerning elections. Firstly, citizens are mostly not overly-concerned with the interacting tasks used in reaching the decision. They refer to abstract processes such as *voting* and *counting*, without fully understanding the subtle details. Secondly, e-voting domain experts are concerened with the complexity of modelling the election process at different levels of abstraction. From our, third, point of view, as system engineers, a voting process is managed by a system which facilitates voting, whilst satisfying the requirements of the vote with respect to the current legal position. When the system is electronic, it may also have to meet legal requirements which are

This work was supported by grant ANR-13-INSE-0001 (The IMPEX Project http://impex.gforge.inria.fr (or http://impex.loria.fr) from the Agence Nationale de la Recherche (ANR).

A. Bouajjani and A. Silva (Eds.): FORTE 2017, LNCS 10321, pp. 124–138, 2017.
DOI: 10.1007/978-3-319-60225-7_9

not relevant for the traditional manual systems. A final point of view is one of security: voting systems make use of information and communication technologies (ICT), and their dependability relies on security analysis for identification of threats in order to select countermeasures.

1.2 Contextual Reasoning

We [12] have previously shown the importance of context in proofs, where it captures the system designer's intention, as well as giving the system model a precise and unambiguous semantics. Our study demonstrates that context is always related to an activity, a focus or a situation. More precisely, the context is a *"moment universals"* that depends on an intentional concept i.e. "action". By reasoning over the structure of the Event-B, the *context of proof* is decomposed into — *(i) Constraints*: conditions having their own existence and concerned with the theory defined for Event-B, corresponding to the sets, constants and axioms defined in the Event-B contexts; *(ii) Hypotheses*: that are assumed to be true, but not always verified, and which are expressed by restrictions on the constraints, and suppositions on the corrupt behaviours in the system. *(iii) Dependencies*: this knowledge is deduced, and expressed as a combination of situations and constraints over time. The use of dependencies was inspired by the work of [2,8,17], and led us to formalize a dependency mechanism in Event-B as a proof of the coherency of the contexts in Event-B.

1.3 Refinement and Decomposition Patterns

The correct-by-construction approach [16] can be applied for integrating progressively *properties and details of the voting process*. In the case of the voting system, we decompose it into three dependent and sequential phases: the *preparation* phase, the *recording* phase and the *tallying* phase. These phases are sequential and linked in a pipeline, where the activation of the next phase depends on the termination of the previous one. One phase may use data computed during the previous phase; this data is dynamically generated in one phase but is then used to statically instantiate the configuration parameters of the next phase. We have defined this approach as a domain-independent re-usable template, using a formal *dependency pattern*, defined in a separate work [12]. Patterns [11] are applied to refinement-based processes; they help to increase productivity and improve quality by providing guarantees with respect to avoidance of security risks and attacks [14]. We use the *sequential decomposition* pattern and identify the three phases characterized by three main liveness properties: (1) *preparation* collects information for defining the persons authorized to vote and candidates/options authorized to be presented as choices in the election; (2) *recording* permits authorized voters to choose their preferred candidate(s) or option(s); and (3) *tallying* counts the votes for each candidate, or given option. Thus, our three stage pipeline is a composition of two instances of the *sequential decomposition* pattern.

1.4   Formal Reasoning About E-voting

Many properties and requirements are expressed in the literature of e-voting systems. We follow the reasoning of [7] which argues that, in the ideal case, a secure voting system should guarantee eligibility, confidentiality, anonymity and verifiability. *Verifiability* ensures that all voters can trust the proclaimed result without having to trust a particular authority or actor in the system. Furthermore, it ensures the existence of an algorithm that can exhibit the proof of the result of tallying and integrity of the authorities. In our case, the proof obligations generated show that the system has behaved correctly. *Confidentiality* guarantees knowledge of each voter is limited only to his/her vote. The *Anonymity* of a vote is guaranteed by breaking the link between the voter and theirr vote. *Eligibility* of voters determines whether or not a voter is entitled to vote. Our model expresses this property as a condition concerning the *authentication* and *authorization* of each voter before recording their vote. *Authentication* identifies voters using *credentials* and *passwords* previously provided for this purpose.

2   The Modelling Framework

Event-B is a formal language well-suited to the modelling of *reactive* systems that respond to external stimuli over time. In this set-theoretic language in first-order logic (FOL), guarded *events* provide state transition behaviour. The two syntactic units of structuring are the static *context* and the dynamic *machine*. The context comprises sets, constants, axioms, and any theorems that must be derived from those axioms. The machine comprises dynamic variables and the events that update them. Safety properties are expressed as either invariants or theorems. Every machine *sees* at least one context.

An event is observed in a model with constants c and sets s subject to *axioms* $P(s,c)$ and an *invariant* $I(s,c,v)$. Consistency proof obligations (POs) require that events are well-defined, feasible and maintain invariants. The term *refinement* is overloaded, referring both to the process of transforming models, and to the more concrete model which refines the abstract one. When model $N(w)$ refines $M(v)$, it contains a refinement relation, or "gluing invariant" $J(s,c,v,w)$. New events may be introduced in refinement to act on new variables, effectively refining stuttering steps (called "skip" in Event-B). The refinement POs enforce the standard forward simulation refinement rule [1] that every concrete step of a refining event re-establishes the gluing invariant subject to some corresponding step of the abstract refined event, or skip.

Figure 1 summarizes the two kinds of models that are used in the formal development. In this work the modelling process deals with various languages, as seen by considering the triptych of Bjoerner [5]: $\mathcal{D}, \mathcal{S} \longrightarrow \mathcal{R}$. Here, the domain $\mathcal{D}$ deals with properties, axioms, sets, constants, functions, relations, and theories. The system model $\mathcal{S}$ expresses a model or a refinement-based chain of models of the system. Finally, $\mathcal{R}$ expresses requirements for the design of the system. One must note that the Event-B modelling language is not expressing liveness properties and we follow the methodology introduced by Méry and Poppleton [18] for managing such properties. We will use a notation from TLA to express liveness

```
                                          ┌────────────────────────────────────┐
                                          │ MACHINE 𝓜                          │
                                          │ REFINES   𝒜𝓜                       │
                                          │ SEES   𝒟                           │
                                          │ VARIABLES   x                      │
                                          │ INVARIANTS                         │
 ┌─────────────────────────────────┐      │   inv₁ : I₁(x, S₁, … Sₙ, C₁, …, Cₘ) … │
 │ CONTEXT 𝒟                       │      │   invᵣ : Iᵣ(x, S₁, … Sₙ, C₁, …, Cₘ)  │
 │ EXTENDS   𝒜𝒟                    │      │ THEOREMS                           │
 │ SETS                            │      │   th₁ : SAFE₁(x, S₁, … Sₙ, C₁, …, Cₘ) … │
 │   S₁, … Sₙ                      │      │   thₛ : SAFEₛ(x, S₁, … Sₙ, C₁, …, Cₘ) │
 │ CONSTANTS                       │      │ EVENTS                             │
 │   C₁, …, Cₘ                     │      │   EVENT initialisation             │
 │ AXIOMS                          │      │     BEGIN                          │
 │   ax₁ : P₁(S₁, … Sₙ, C₁, …, Cₘ) …│      │       x : |(P(x'))                 │
 │   axₚ : Pₚ(S₁, … Sₙ, C₁, …, Cₘ)  │      │     END …                          │
 │ THEOREMS                        │      │   EVENT e                          │
 │   th₁ : Q₁(S₁, … Sₙ, C₁, …, Cₘ) …│      │     ANY  t                         │
 │   th_q : Q_q(S₁, … Sₙ, C₁, …, Cₘ)│      │     WHERE                          │
 └─────────────────────────────────┘      │       G x, t                       │
                                          │     THEN                           │
                                          │       x : |(P x, x', t))           │
                                          │     END …                          │
                                          │ END                                │
                                          └────────────────────────────────────┘
```

Fig. 1. Context and machine

properties under fairness assumptions. We have to interpret our Event-B models over traces generated from the Event-B machines and we extend the scope of the Event-B machines by using TLA as follows. Let M be an EVENT B machine and D a context seen by M. Let x be the list of variables of M, let E be the set of events of M, and let $Init(x)$ be the initialisation event in M. The temporal framework of M over D is defined by the TLA specification denoted: $Spec(M) \triangleq BA(Init)(x) \wedge \Box[Next]_x \wedge FAIR$, where $Next \equiv \exists e \in E.BA(e)(x, x')$ and FAIR defines the fairness assumptions.

Following Lamport [15] the specification $spec(M)$ is valid for the set of infinite traces simulating M with respect to the events of M. $Spec(M)$ is thus defined by the initial conditions, the next relation and fairness constraints. In practice we have to discover the weakest fairness assumptions, denoted FAIR(M), that allow us to derive the required liveness properties. These fairness assumptions emerge from the proof rules applied, and are expressed in terms of the temporal operators of TLA, namely WF and SF . FAIR(M) is thus a combination of fairness operators over events of M. Liveness properties for M are, de facto, defined in TLA as follows: M satisfies $P \rightsquigarrow Q$, when $\Gamma(M) \vdash Spec(M) \implies (P \rightsquigarrow Q)$. When deriving the proof of $Spec(M) \implies (P \rightsquigarrow Q)$, we apply the right introduction rule of the implication and then we eliminate the conjunctive connective in the left part of the $\vdash$ symbol. Thus $\Gamma(M)$ will be increased by fairness assumptions and we can use an alternative form for expressing the initial sequent: $\Gamma(M)$ is the proof context of M. In review, the refinement of Event-B models preserves the safety properties; and for preserving the liveness properties we follow the technique proposed by Mery and Poppleton [18] (see Fig. 2).

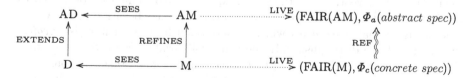

Fig. 2. Summary of the integrated formal methods refinement methodology

3   Modelling the Voting System

The 3 phases of our voting process are each developed, and verified, in a separate refinement chain. In this paper, we present only the final 2 stages of the pipeline: the vote recording and the tally (count) phases. The system description also includes the conditions over the environment that express voter behaviour and possible attacks on the system. In particular, our development disregards different roles and/or actors in the system: the only actor represented is the voter who interacts with the system interface. In particular, our refinement-based approach takes into account intruders with the following capabilities: *(1) establishing a connection*; *(2) closing an already established session*; *(3) making choices*; *(4) adding signatures*; *(5) adding ballots: ballot stuffing*; *(6) adding signatures and ballots simultaneously*; *(7) removing signatures*; *(8) removing ballots*; and *(9) accessing signatures, credentials, passwords*. These different assumptions concerning corrupt behavior correspond to the part of the world in which the system is immersed. They situate the developed system and we qualify them as *"context of assumptions"*.

3.1   Combining Refinement and Composition, Using the Dependency Pattern

Figure 3 illustrates the refinement-based approach followed in our development, and shows the use of the dependency pattern mechanism (**depends**) to compose the machines associated with sequential phases of the voting process.

3.2   Refining the Voting Phase in Seven Steps

The first phase is described by an Event-B context *C0_Recording* which defines the constraints and static elements that are seen by the 9 machines in our development. The first Event-B context introduces the necessary elements to start a recording phase of votes i.e.: sets, constants and static properties such as *Electors*, *Choices*, *Envelopes*, *PollStation*, *Representatives*, *Bulletins*, *Sig*, *electoral_roll*, *voters_hosting*, *start_time*, *end_time* etc....

Abstract model - In this first model the state of the system is characterized by two variables that represent the registered votes and the elapsed time in the system. The votes are modelled as a relationship between all signatures (*Sig*) and the electors' choices (*Choices*). The invariant in this machine simply provides a means to type these variables. The precondition for this phase, as expressed by the initialization event, is that the time is equal to the opening time of the offices fixed in the context *C0_Recording* and that no vote has been recorded. A vote modifies the variable *rec_votes* which is performed by the event *register_votes*. In this model, we distinguish only the values of variables *rec_votes* which take their values in *Sig $\leftrightarrow$ Choices* without precising the undertaken actions. The event *forwarding_time* changes the value of the variable *timer* introduced in this machine to express the progression of time in the system. The variable

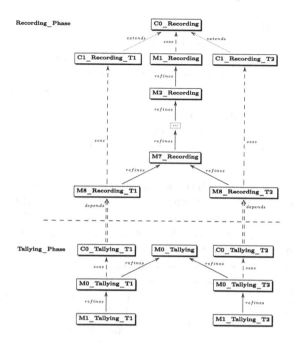

Fig. 3. Structure of the refinement-based formal development of the voting system

value is incremented by the action of thes event $forwarding\_time$ until the closing time of the offices end_time is reached. We note that this event has a convergent status under which a weak fairness assumption is made. Thus, this event ($forwarding\_time$) will not be observable when the value of the $timer$ variable has reached end_time. Note that the vote event can be observed only when the voting has begun and that the closing time has not yet been reached (see $grd1$). The convergence of these events is proved using a simple variant. Then, at the end of voting, no one can cast a vote or record a signature: the only event that will be observable is $finish$.

VARIABLES $rec\_votes, timer$
INVARIANTS
    $inv1 : rec\_votes \in Sig \nleftrightarrow Choices$
    $inv2 : timer \in start\_time .. end\_time$
VARIANT $end\_time - timer$
INITIALISATION
    $act1 : rec\_votes := \varnothing$
    $act2 : timer := start\_time$
EVENT $register\_votes$
    WHEN
        $grd1 : timer \geq start\_time \wedge timer < end\_time$
        $grd2 : \forall i, j \cdot i \mapsto j \in interrupt\_sequences \Rightarrow timer \notin i .. j$
    THEN
        $act1 : rec\_votes : |rec\_votes' \in (Sig \nleftrightarrow Choices)$
    END

EVENT $forwarding\_time$
STATUS convergent
WHEN
    $grd : timer < end\_time$
THEN
    $act : timer := timer + 1$
END
EVENT finish
    WHEN
        $grd1 : timer = end\_time$
    THEN
    $act : skip$
    END

In the following seven refinements, termination proofs are the same as those for this initial abstract machine. Since all events that will be introduced in the following will also be guarded by the guards *grd1* and *grd2* of the event *register_votes*, no event changes the time and *forwarding_time* and *finish* remain unchanged. We also recall that all variables introduced in the followed refinements are initialized with the empty set, with the exception of intruder knowledge variables.

Refinement 1 - distinguishes the votes that are either registred or deleted. The recording of votes is done by the event *register_votes* refined by itself, while tdeleting votes is done by the event *remove_votes*. Both events refine the former introduced in the abstract model *register_votes*.

Refinement 2 - introduces intrusion scenarios, where people present themselves to vote on behalf of someone else, without having permission to do so. Such a scenario is a single example of one among many forbidden scenarios that may exist. We distinguish at this level of refinement, the votes recorded correctly and those that are corrupted. Four new variables (*valid_sig*, *valid_choices*, *valid_votes*, *corrupt_votes_sig*) are introduced:

INVARIANTS
$inv1 : valid\_sig \subseteq Sig$
$inv2 : valid\_choices \subseteq Choices$
$inv3 : valid\_votes \in valid\_sig \rightarrowtail vote$
$inv4 : corrupt\_votes\_sig \in Sig \leftrightarrow Choices$
$inv5 : valid\_votes \subseteq rec\_votes$
$inv6 : corrupt\_votes\_sig \subseteq rec\_votes$
$inv7 : corrupt\_votes\_sig \cap valid\_votes = \varnothing$

The votes or choices are identified in the set of choices (*inv2*), while the signatures are a subset of the set *Sig* (*inv1*) defined in the Event-B context *C0_Recording*.

The property *inv3* associates each correct choice with one and only one signature, and each signature with one and only one correct choice. Thus, at any time the number of votes at the polls equals the number of signatures honestly recorded. Votes can be corrupt, but these are detected. The invariant property *inv7* indicates that the correct votes and the corrupt votes partition the set of all votes cast. Others variables are also introduced separately in order to identify corrupt signatures and invalid choices. The event to register the votes introduced in the first model is refined into two events that allow the storage of both types of vote. This corruption scenario is one in which corrupt choices and corrupted signatures are introduced simultaneously via the event *corrupt_choices_sig_simultaneously*. This refinement also introduces two other scenarios of corruption consisting of stuffing ballot boxes, or recording votes, without valid signatures. Two new events are introduced at this level. The event *stuffing_choices* consists of adding a corrupt choice by changing the variable *alone_corrupt_choices*, while the event *corrupt_sig_only* adds a corrupted signature by changing the variable *alone_corrupt_sig*. The variable *alone_corrupt_choices* is a subset of all choices, while the corrupted signatures are a subset of *Sig*.

Refinement 3 - introduces the main actor in the system i.e.: the voter (elector). Voters having voted correctly become registered voters in the variable *honest_voters*. Dishonest voters are registered in the variable *dishonest_voters*. Voters who voted correctly can impersonate other voters in order to vote for them (or steal their vote). The honest voters are linked to their correct signatures via the variable *honest_voters_sig*, and an honest voter can have only one signature at a time, and vice versa; thus, a correct signature is assigned to one and only one voter at a time (*inv3*). The corrupted signatures of the voters are defined in the relation between electors and the set of signatures (*Sig*) (*inv4*). Note that the domain and co-domain of these two variables have no common element (*inv5* et *inv6*).

$$inv5 : dom(corrupt\_sig\_voters) \cap dom(honest\_voters\_sig) = \varnothing$$
$$inv6 : ran(corrupt\_sig\_voters) \cap ran(honest\_voters\_sig) = \varnothing$$
$$inv7 : honest\_know \in honest\_voters \rightarrow \mathbb{P}(valid\_choices)$$
$$inv8 : \forall v, elec, sig \cdot \left(\begin{array}{l} v \in valid\_choices \wedge elec \in honest\_voters \wedge sig \in valid\_sig \\ \wedge elec \mapsto sig \in honest\_voters\_sig \wedge sig \mapsto v \notin rec\_votes \end{array} \right)$$
$$\Rightarrow elec \mapsto \{v\} \notin honest\_know)$$
$$inv12 : \forall elec1, elec2, v1, v2 \cdot \left(\begin{array}{l} elec1 \in dom(honest\_know) \wedge honest\_know(elec1) = v1 \\ \wedge elec2 \in dom(honest\_know) \\ \wedge honest\_know(elec2) = v2 \wedge elec1 \neq elec2 \end{array} \right)$$
$$\Rightarrow (\forall vx \cdot (vx \in v1 \Rightarrow vx \notin v2)))$$

Removing correct choices already made implies knowledge of the choices made by the honest voter. To ensure the secrecy of the vote, we add a variable representing voter knowledge (*inv7*). This variable is a total function of the voters who voted towards all subsets of choices. Secrecy is expressed by the invariant *inv12* which states that the knowledge of how each known voter has voted is restricted to the voter themselves. Deleting a choice correctly implies that only the voter knows his/her choice and how they have voted. In contrast, an intrusion deletion does not require any knowledge of choices or how a voter has voted.

Refinement 4 - introduces authentication, which requires that the system has some guaranteed means of identification of voters. In our model, this is ensured by the following two constants introduced in the Event-B context *C0_Recording* i.e.: *Credentials_assign* and *Passwords_assign* that are defined as:

Credentials_assign $\in$ *Electors* $\rightarrowtail$ *Credentials*, and *Passwords_assign* $\in$ *Electors* $\rightarrowtail$ *Passwords*. The model consists of an assignment of credentials and passwords to eligible voters. Thus, each voter has his own identification that gives permission for access to his account that is by definition, unique to each voter. The authentication in our system consists of verification by introducing two events for this purpose. The first event allows electors who wish to establish a connection to access to their voting account (login), while the second allows the disconnection of a voter having already established a connection. An authentication modifies the variable *electors_session* introduced for this purpose. We note that this authentication allows access to the account for voting purposes, recording voting, etc. .... The identification is expressed as follows:

$$inv6 : \forall s, v \cdot (s \mapsto v \in valid\_votes)$$
$$\Rightarrow \exists elec, mdp, cred \cdot \left(\begin{array}{l} (elec \mapsto s) \in dom(voters\_hosting) \wedge elec \mapsto mdp \in Passwords\_assign \\ \wedge elec \mapsto cred \in Credentials\_assign \end{array} \right)$$

Authorization to vote requires that the elector entitled to vote has not yet voted. This check is performed by refinements 5 and 6. This stage distinguishs also intruders that try to establish a connection with stolen credentials and passwords. We thus introduce all variables that correspond to intruders' knowledge, and events for misused identity credentials, passwords, signatures and possibly removing choices already made by honest voters. Introducing these details means that the invariants $inv8$ and $inv12$ introduced in the previous refinement are not sufficient. We need to express the requirement that knowledge of honest valid voters is not known by intruders. The following property expresses for instance the fact that honest choices are not known by the dishonest intruders.

$$inv14 : \forall elec1, v1 \cdot (\, elec1 \in dom(honest\_know) \land honest\_know(elec1) = v1\,)$$
$$\Rightarrow \forall elec2 \cdot \; elec2 \in dom(dishonest\_know\_choice)$$
$$\Rightarrow \forall vx \cdot (\, vx \in v1 \Rightarrow elec2 \mapsto \{vx\} \notin dishonest\_know\_choice\,)$$

Refinement 5 - considers location. In traditional systems, voting is done in a physical location or polling station, whilst in e-voting we replace the concrete locations with an abstract/virtual concept. Thus, we introduce in this refinement a new variable $regis\_votes\_offices$, which assigns each vote cast correctly to one and only one polling station.

$$inv1 : regis\_votes\_offices \in PollStation \leftrightarrow (rec\_votes)$$
$$inv2 : \forall ve \cdot (ve \in rec\_votes \Rightarrow (\exists h \cdot (h \mapsto ve \in regis\_votes\_offices)))$$
$$inv3 : \;\forall v1, b1, b2 \cdot (b1 \mapsto v1 \in regis\_votes\_offices \land b2 \mapsto v1 \in regis\_votes\_offices \Rightarrow b1 = b2)$$

The recording of the vote is thus restricted by location; in other words, a restriction of authorizations for voters to cast a vote in the offices to which they were assigned. A list is established beforehand to assign eligible offices to voters; this being defined by the constant $voters\_hosting$ in the Event-B context $C0\_Recording$ ($voters\_hosting \in electoral\_roll \rightarrow PollStation$). Thus, the events to record votes are reinforced by the guards:

$$grd8 : \exists sig \cdot (sig \in Sig \land heberg \in PollStation \land ((votant\_x \mapsto sig) \mapsto heberg) \in voters\_hosting)$$
$$grd9 : \; heberg \mapsto (s \mapsto v) \notin regis\_votes\_offices \land (s \mapsto v) \notin ran(regis\_votes\_offices)$$

and the next action is added to update the variable $regis\_votes\_offices$: $act7$: $regis\_votes\_offices := regis\_votes\_offices \cup \{heberg \mapsto (s \mapsto v)\}$. Thus, eligibility for honest voters is expressed as follows:

$$inv4 : (\forall s, v, h \cdot (s \mapsto v \in valid\_votes \land h \mapsto (s \mapsto v) \in regis\_votes\_offices$$
$$\Rightarrow \exists elec \cdot (elec \in votant \land elec \mapsto s \in honest\_voters\_sig \land (elec \mapsto s) \mapsto h \in voters\_hosting)))$$

which expresses that for all correctly recorded choices ($valid\_votes$) in polling stations ($regis\_votes\_offices$), there exists an eligible voter having a valid signature ($honest\_voters\_sig$ introduced in the third refinement), with an identical signature, previously registered in the system, that casts this said choice.

Refinement 6 - models the depedency between the choice offerred to, and taken by, the voters and the specific type of election/referendum being run; and the anonymity of this choice. The recording of a vote is preceded by the choice that can be made by an eligible elector. The choice of bulletins must be anonymous, which can be guaranteed by the use of envelopes, as is the case in classic voting. We introduce in this refinement several new variables that facilitate the modelling of envelopes during the vote recording process. The variable *valid_envelopes* corresponds to the envelopes chosen by voters. A voter who took an envelope is added to the variable *voters_envelopes*. Each valid choice is assigned to a single valid envelope. The choice of voter is made concrete by the event *choose*. To make a choice, a voter must have authorization for this action. The actions enabled by this event are guarded by the existence of the person who wishes to initiate a process of voting in the list previously established *electoral_roll* and that no signature is yet registered to his vote.

Refinement 7 - Different elections have different modes/types of voting. For example, a *majoritarian voting* where a presidential candidate must be elected is represented by paper ballot where every candidate is the option to vote and each paper corresponds to one candidate (vote or poll). This constraint is shown in Event-B by the following constant: $axmt1 : bulletins\_representatives \in Representatives \rightarrowtail Bulletins$ where *Representatives* corresponds to the set of all representatives needed for a specific election including designations that may be chosen by a voter. For instance, this set can contain: $candidat_1, candidat_2, \ldots, candidat_n, None\_of\_the\_above$, in the case of a presidential election. It may also contain *favorable, unfavorable*, if the choice in a referendum is an adherence to any law.

In the case of a *preferential voting* or *cumulative voting*, voters should make their choice on paper ballot, where all candidates are listed on all these papers. This choice corresponds to a preference order mentioned next to each candidate on the same paper ballot. This constraint corresponds to a Cartesian product presented as follows in the Event-B method: $axmt2 : bulletins\_representatives = Representatives \times Bulletins$. These constraints situate our development and thus contextualize the proofs. We have shown that constraints rely on the static part in the system, and we qualify this as a **context of constraints**. Each type of voting is defined in a different Event-B context. These two Event-B contexts extend the first one introduced in the beginning of this section ($C0\_Recording$) and are noted by $C1\_Recording\_T1$ et $C1\_Recording\_T2$. At this stage of refinement, the machine introduced in the previous refinement is refined into two different machines. This decomposition allows each machine to see a different Event-B context. Thus, the machine $M8\_Recording\_T1$, (respectively the machine $M8\_Recording\_T2$) sees the Event-B context $C1\_Recording\_T1$ (respectively the context $C1\_Recording\_T2$). In the following, we report on the development of the first type of voting.

Each voter who has selected a paper ballot is added in the variable *bulletins_voters* with their own bulletin. This action is observed in the event *choose*. The selected paper ballot and the voter are added to the variable *bulletins_voters*. This choice represents a ballot stored in the variable *ballots*. The voter puts one and only one name or paper (or candidate) in the ballot box. Therefore, one and only one ballot is sleeved in an envelope. The recorded bulletins are a subset of the set of *Bulletins*. This variable will serve us in the Event-B context corresponding to tallying. The variable *ballots_offices* allows us to record the ballots per polling station. The casting of votes in the ballot boxes is made concrete by modifying the variable *rec_votes* associated to a specific polling station in the recording event. It is based on the representatives indicated on the collected papers through the variable *collected_bulletins_representatives* that the affectation of voices to these representatives will be made.

Once this phase is finished, i.e.: the counter to express time comes to the end, the tallying phase can begin using the results obtained. In the following section we explain the formal dependency mechanism used to model the transfer of results.

4   Dependency Relationship Between Voting Phases

The data provided for the B contexts of this phase are deduced from the first phase corresponding to a validation of both B contexts by machines from the first phase. We detail in the following the tallying of the first type of voting that corresponds to the machine *M8_Recording_T1*.

This Event-B context includes all elements defined in the first phase, namely, *C1_Recording_T1*. The context *C0_Tallying_T1* extends *C1_Recording_T1* and contains, in addition to elements defined in *C1_Recording_T1*, some of the variables defined in the machine *M8_Recording_T1* which are defined as constants in the present context listed in twenty two axioms. For instance, *collected_bulletins_representatives,rec_votes, valid_sig* . . . .

Abstract Model: Phase of Tallying - The desired termination property for this phase of any voting protocol is identical for all types of voting, thus, the first abstract model *M0_Tallying* is common to both types of voting that we introduce in this phase. This model describes the counting via three events *tally*, *finish* and *maintain*. The only variable introduced at this level is a boolean which verifies whether counting is complete. The event *tally* is observing the value of this variable which is "false" in its guard, and does not perform any action in this machine.

Refinement 1: Phase of Tallying - In this machine which refines the *M0_Tallying* machine, the tally is done at the specific polling station. The variable *correct_result_office* characterizes the representative's scores per polling station $(inv1 : correct\_result\_office \subseteq PollStation \times (Representatives \times \mathbb{N}))$. In each polling station, the scores of each representative are unique:

$$inv2 : \forall h, r, x1, x2 \cdot \left(\begin{array}{c} h \in PollStation \land r \in Representatives \\ \land h \mapsto (r \mapsto x1) \in correct\_result\_office \\ \land h \mapsto (r \mapsto x2) \in correct\_result\_office \end{array} \right) \Rightarrow x1 = x2$$

At initialization, no representative has received any votes. The counting of the voters' choices requires representatives who are registered in the envelopes (*destroyed_envelopes_representatives*), and the ballots recorded per polling station (*destroyed_ballots_office*). In addition, one must know the representatives of registered ballots (*destroyed_bulletins_representatives*). These variables can be seen as **"copies"** of constants defined in the Event-B context seen by the present machine. To verify that all registered bulletins were correctly counted, after the end of tallying, we must ensure that all voters who have signed have a bulletin that has been counted, and vice versa, all counted bulletins correspond to choices of voters who indeed signed. We introduce a new variable *counted_bulletins_representatives* that contains the bulletins, effectively counted. As all bulletins contain at most one representation ($bulletins\_representatives \in Representatives \rightarrowtail recorded\_bulletins$), this guarantees verifiability of the dynamic behaviour of the system.

$$inv3 : destroyed\_envelopes\_representatives \subseteq envelopes\_representatives$$
$$inv4 : destroyed\_bulletins\_representatives$$
$$\subseteq (collected\_bulletins\_representatives \rhd (ran(valid\_envelopes \lhd ballots)))$$
$$inv5 : destroyed\_ballots\_office \subseteq ballots\_offices$$
$$inv6 : counted\_bulletins\_representatives$$
$$\subseteq (collected\_bulletins\_representatives \rhd (ran(valid\_envelopes \lhd ballots)))$$
$$inv7 : counted\_bulletins\_representatives \cap destroyed\_bulletins\_representatives = \varnothing$$

This property is true only if the votes were recorded correctly without being corrupted. Verifiability is also expressed in the context seen by the present machine[1]. Other properties are also expressed to say, for instance, that if there exists a corrupt paper ballot, then these are not counted. At initialization, all variables are initialized with the values of the corresponding constants, with the exception of the variable *counted_bulletins_representatives* which is initialized to the empty set. The variable *checked* introduced in the abstract model of the same phase will be maintained in this machine, and its refinement. The tally counts all correctly recorded choices in polls (*destroyed_bulletins_representatives* that is a copy of the collected choices in *collected_bulletins_representatives*). The variable *checked* is a boolean initialized to false, that asserts that the tally can continue as long as there exist ballots not yet counted. This property is expressed by the variant of this machine, and guarantees convergence of the tallying process.

Refinement 2: Phase of Tallying - Finally, the tally for each representative corresponds to the number of total votes (sum of voices by office). This refinement introduces the total computation of voices of each representative saved in the variable *global_result*: $inv1 : global\_result \in Representatives \rightarrow \mathbb{N}$. Each representative has zero votes/voices at the initialization, and the action incrementing the total voices of each representative is added to the same event for counting.

Condition for Dependencies - We recall that the dependencies between two parties (two models) $\mathcal{M}_1$ and $\mathcal{M}_2$ are defined by: *(i)* the B contexts seen by the first machines are also seen by the machines defined for the second component; *(ii)* a transformation of a some variables of the first model $\mathcal{M}_1$ into constants in the target model $\mathcal{M}_2$; *(iii)* the predicate characterizing the termination property of the first model satisfies the constraints defined in the B context of the target model.

---

[1] Note that in the real development this property is more complicated than the one presented in this document. The full, more complex model, can be obtained from the authors on request.

The stability in the first model is defined over traces generated from the machine in this model. This modelling reflects the fact that at the end of the first phase, no changes can be made on these elements as variables, because these variables in the phase of registration maintain their values at the termination. Therefore, we can define them as constants in this Event-B context. A vote is validated only when all the constraints defined in this Event-B context are valid. The validation of such constraints is based on facts or data generated during the recording phase. This implies the existence of states in the model $M8\_Recording\_T1$ satisfying these constraints that we call **context deduced or combination of situations and constraints**. The satisfaction of axioms thus defined, particularly the axioms **dep_axm23** and **dep_axm24**, expresses the *"initial configuration"* of this phase of the vote: $C0\_Tallying\_T1(s2, c2) \wedge Init_2$, where s_2 and c_2 are respectively, sets and constants of the B context $C0\_Tallying\_T1$.

This relationship expresses a dependency between these two components. In particular, the two axioms **dep_axm23** and **dep_axm24** should be validated by properties over values of state variables of the previous phase.

To express the validation of these constraints, we introduce the constant *valide*. This constant also depends on the state the machine 8 of the registration phase. The states that validate these constraints are the states which, in addition to satisfying the axioms **axm1** ... **axm22**, must also fulfill the conditions defined in the axiom **dep_axm24** which expresses constraints, such as: (1) the closing time of polls has arrived: $timer = end\_time$; (2) no corrupt signature has been recorded: $alone\_corrupt\_sig = \varnothing$; (3) no corrupt choices assigned to an envelope have been recorded: $corrupt\_choices\_envelopes = \varnothing$; (4) choices and signatures are registered in the polls provided the voters who made these choices have signed at offices where they were registered to vote: $\forall s, v, h \cdot (s \mapsto v \in rec\_votes \wedge h \mapsto (s \mapsto v) \in regis\_votes\_offices \Rightarrow \exists elec \cdot ((elec \mapsto s) \mapsto h \in voters\_hosting))$; (5) the number of correct votes is the same as the number of recorded envelopes: $correct\_choices\_envelopes \in valid\_choices \rightarrowtail valid\_envelopes$; and (6) a recorded vote (with valid choices and signatures) can not belong to two different offices: $(\forall v1, b1, b2 \cdot (b1 \mapsto v1 \in regis\_votes\_offices \wedge b2 \mapsto v1 \in regis\_votes\_offices \Rightarrow b1 = b2))$.

The designed patterns have generated 1317 proof obligations, among which 757 are discharged in an non-automatic manner. Non-automatic proof obligations are related to properties using universal quantification. The instantiation of the patterns consists in specifying values of sets in B contexts, which does not give rise to additional proof obligations and in introducing other refinements for specific needs of designers.

5 Conclusion and Future Work

5.1 Contributions: Contexts, Refinements and Dependency

Our overall contribution is to illustrate a formal method for combining contexts, refinements and dependency composition in a coherent and reusable manner. Two main voting families appear in our development. However, the specific family remains implicit. It follows that the interpretation of the results is not taken into account in our modelling. The certification of models needs to describe the voting method in order to make a decision. Such an interpretation thus depends on the context in which the proofs are made. Contexts are formal objects [17] based on McCarthy's principle that contexts are constructed incrementally from previous ones, which corresponds to *"context lifting"*. The situation appears as a new parameter in the predicates and thus, predicates depend on a situation. A lifting involves situations or times. In the Event-B formalism, situations are states and constraints are static properties defined in Event-B contexts. Thus, the dependency relationship in this formalism is defined as a combination of states and constraints. The dependency is a measurable relationship taking values from situations facts and giving rise to new proof obligations. Such a principle represents a duality to the principle of invariance in Event-B machines, claiming that states are constrained by invariants in order to establish safety in a proof system.

5.2   Future Work: Security Issues

Security is an important issue for ensuring reliable operation and protecting the integrity of stored information to guarantee a trustworthy e-voting system [6]. These are based on a systematic engineering approach achieved by the identification, detection and correcting security risks and threats, requirements and recovery strategies [13]. Thus, validation of the assumptions made by designers is performed on threat modelling attached to their contextual information to safeguard the system against unauthorized modification of data, or disclosure of information. Deeper analysis of the security in an e-voting system relies also on identifying *assets* to determine answers to questions about what the system is designed to protect, and from whom [19]. Our modelling deals only with voters. To target a particular system, it would therefore be necessary to integrate the different assets. This can be achieved by defining a set *Assets* in the Event-B context of the recording phase, and all these actors will be constants included in this set.

Our development can be combined with the already realized models of Benaïssa [3,4] that deal with the key establishment properties for the preparation phase. His works deal with the authentication properties, as well as the key establishment goals combined with the attacker's knowledge. The authentication models can be reused as input provided from the preparation phase of the vote to the voting phase in our development as a result via the dependency mechanism. We can also consider the probabilistic approaches such as blind signatures, mix nets or encryption schemes.

References

1. Abrial, J.-R.: Modeling in Event-B: System and Software Engineering. Cambridge University Press, Cambridge (2010)
2. Jon Barwise, K.: Conditionals and conditional information. In: Traugott, E., ter Meulen, A., Reilly, J., Ferguson, C. (eds.) On Conditionals, pp. 21–54. Cambridge University Press, Cambridge (1986)

3. Benaissa, N.: Modelling attacker's knowledge for cascade cryptographic protocols. In: Börger, E., Butler, M., Bowen, J.P., Boca, P. (eds.) ABZ 2008. LNCS, vol. 5238, pp. 251–264. Springer, Heidelberg (2008). doi:10.1007/978-3-540-87603-8_20

4. Benaissa, N., Méry, D.: Proof-based design of security protocols. In: Ablayev, F., Mayr, E.W. (eds.) CSR 2010. LNCS, vol. 6072, pp. 25–36. Springer, Heidelberg (2010). doi:10.1007/978-3-642-13182-0_3

5. Bjorner, D.: Software Engineering 3 Domains, Requirements, and Software Design. Texts in Theoretical Computer Science. An EATCS Series. Springer, Heidelberg (2006)

6. Chiang, L.: Trust and security in the e-voting system. Electron. Gov. Int. J. **6**(4), 343–360 (2009)

7. Cortier, V., Galindo, D., Glondu, S., Izabachene, M., et al.: A generic construction for voting correctness at minimum cost-application to helios. IACR Cryptology ePrint Arch. **2013**, 177 (2013)

8. Dapoigny, R., Barlatier, P.: Modeling contexts with dependent types. Fundam. Inform. **104**(4), 293–327 (2010)

9. Paul Gibson, J., Krimmer, R., Teague, V., Pomares, J.: A review of e-voting: the past, present and future. Ann. Telecommun. **71**(7), 279–286 (2016)

10. Paul Gibson, J., Lallet, E., Raffy, J.-L.: Feature interactions in a software product line for e-voting. In: Nakamura, M., Reiff-Marganiec, S. (eds.) Feature Interactions in Software and Communication Systems X, pp. 91–106. IOS Press, Lisbon (2009)

11. Hoang, T.S., Furst, A., Abrial, J,-R.: Event-b patterns and their tool support. In: International Conference on Software Engineering and Formal Methods, pp. 210–219 (2009)

12. Kherroubi, S., Méry, D.: Contextualisation et dépendance en event-B. In: Idani, A., Kosmatov, N. (eds.) Approches Formelles dans l'Assistance au D'éveloppement de Logiciels, AFADL 2017 (2017)

13. Kotonya, G., Sommerville, I., Engineering, R.: Processes and Techniques, 1st edn. Wiley Publishing, Hoboken (1998)

14. Kremer, S., Ryan, M.: Analysis of an electronic voting protocol in the applied pi calculus. In: Sagiv, M. (ed.) ESOP 2005. LNCS, vol. 3444, pp. 186–200. Springer, Heidelberg (2005). doi:10.1007/978-3-540-31987-0_14

15. Lamport, L.: The temporal logic of actions. ACM Trans. Program. Lang. Syst. **16**(3), 872–923 (1994)

16. Leavens, G.T., Abrial, J.-R., Batory, D.S., Butler, M.J., Coglio, A., Fisler, K., Hehner, E.C.R., Jones, C.B., Miller, D., Peyton Jones, S.L., Sitaraman, M., Smith, D.R., Stump, A.: Roadmap for enhanced languages and methods to aid verification. In: GPCE, pp. 221–236 (2006)

17. McCarthy, J.: Notes on formalizing context. In: Proceedings of the 13th International Joint Conference on Artifical Intelligence - IJCAI 1993, pp. 555–560, Morgan Kaufmann Publishers Inc, San Francisco (1993)

18. Méry, D., Poppleton, M.: Towards an integrated formal method for verification of liveness properties in distributed systems. Softw. Syst. Model. (SoSyM) (2015)

19. Myagmar, S., Lee, A.J., Yurcik, W.: Threat modeling as a basis for security requirements. In: Symposium on Requirements Engineering for Information Security (SREIS). IEEE, August 2005

Weak Simulation Quasimetric
in a Gossip Scenario

Ruggero Lanotte[1], Massimo Merro[2], and Simone Tini[1(✉)]

[1] Dipartimento di Scienza e Alta Tecnologia, Università dell'Insubria, Como, Italy
simone.tini@uninsubria.it
[2] Dipartimento di Informatica, Università degli Studi di Verona, Verona, Italy

Abstract. We propose the notion of weak simulation quasimetric as the quantitative counterpart of weak simulation for probabilistic processes. This is an asymmetric variant of the weak bisimulation metric of Desharnais et al. which maintains most of the properties of the original definition. However, our asymmetric version is particularly suitable to reason on protocols where the systems under consideration are not approximately equivalent. As a main application, we adopt our simulation theory in a simple probabilistic timed process calculus to derive an algebraic theory to evaluate the performances of gossip protocols.

1   Introduction

Behavioural semantics, such as *preorders* and *equivalences*, provide formal instruments to compare the behaviour of *probabilistic systems* [16]. Preorders allow us to determine whether a system can mimic the stepwise behaviour of another system; whereas equivalences require a sort of mutual simulation between two systems. The most prominent examples are the *simulation preorder* and the *bisimulation equivalence* [22,25]. Since probability values usually originate from observations (statistical sampling) or from requirements (probabilistic specification), both preorders and equivalences are only partially satisfactory as they can only say whether a system can mimic another one. Any tiny variation of the probabilistic behaviour of a system will break the preorder (resp. equivalence) without any further information. In practice, many system implementations can only approximate the system specification; thus, the verification of such implementations requires appropriate instruments to measure the quality of the approximation. To this end, *metric semantics* [4,6,9] have been successfully employed to formalise the *behavioural distance* between two systems.

Since metric semantics are inherently symmetric, they can be applied only when dealing with systems which are approximately equivalent. In this paper, we propose the notion of *weak simulation quasimetric* which is the asymmetric counterpart of the *weak bisimulation metric* [10], and the quantitative analogous of the *weak simulation preorder* [1,2]. We use the definition of weak simulation quasimetric to derive a definition of *weak simulation with tolerance* $p \in [0,1]$

© IFIP International Federation for Information Processing 2017
Published by Springer International Publishing AG 2017. All Rights Reserved
A. Bouajjani and A. Silva (Eds.): FORTE 2017, LNCS 10321, pp. 139–155, 2017.
DOI: 10.1007/978-3-319-60225-7_10

between two probabilistic systems; being 0 and 1 the minimum and the maximum tolerance, respectively. Thus, we will write $S \sqsubseteq_p S'$ if the system S' is able to simulate the stepwise behaviour of the system S with a tolerance (or distance) p: for $p = 0$ the two systems are weakly similar in standard manner, while for $p = 1$ they are potentially unrelated.

Our weak simulation with tolerance is suitable for compositional reasonings. The compositionality of a behavioural semantics with respect to the parallel operator is fundamental when reasoning on large-scale systems. Several quantitative analogous of the well-known notions of precongruence (and congruence) have been proposed [10,12] to ensure that systems are *approximately inter-substitutable*. We prove that weak simulation with tolerance matches one of the strongest one, namely *non-expansiveness*:

$$S_1 \sqsubseteq_{p_1} S_1' \text{ and } S_2 \sqsubseteq_{p_2} S_2' \text{ entails } S_1 \mid S_2 \sqsubseteq_{p_1+p_2} S_1' \mid S_2' \ .$$

As (non-trivial) case study, we apply our simulation theory to study and estimate the performance of *gossip networks* for Wireless Sensor Networks (WSNs).

Gossip protocols [17] rely on algorithms to deliver data packets in a network from a source to a destination. They address some critical problems of *flooding*, where each node that receives a message propagates it to all its neighbours by broadcast. The goal of gossip protocols is to reduce the number of retransmissions by making some of the nodes discard the message instead of forwarding it. Gossip protocols exhibit both *nondeterministic* and *probabilistic* behaviour. Nondeterminism arises as they deal with distributed networks in which the activities of individual nodes occur nondeterministically. As to the probabilistic behaviour, nodes are required to forward packets with a pre-specified gossip probability p_{gsp}. When a node receives a message, rather than immediately retransmitting it as in flooding, it relies on the probability p_{gsp} to determine whether or not to retransmit. The main benefit is that when p_{gsp} is sufficiently large, the entire network receives the broadcast message with very high probability, even though only a nondeterministic subset of nodes has forwarded the message.

In this paper, we rely on our simulation with tolerance to develop an *algebraic theory* for a simple probabilistic distributed timed calculus [5,19,23,24] which is particularly suitable to represent gossip networks. Our algebraic theory is also compositional as it allows us to join, and sometime merge, the tolerances of different sub-networks with different behaviours. Last but not least, our algebraic theory can be easily *mechanised*. In this extended abstract proofs are omitted.

2   A Probabilistic Timed Process Calculus

In Table 1 we define the syntax of the *Probabilistic Timed Calculus for Wireless Systems* [19], pTCWS, in a two-level structure, a lower one for *processes*, ranged over by letters P, Q and R, and an upper one for *networks*, ranged over by letters M, N, and O. We use letters $m, n, \ldots$ for logical names; greek symbols $\mu, \nu, \nu_1, \ldots$ for *sets of names*; x, y, z for *variables*; u for *values*, and v and w

Table 1. Syntax

Networks:

$$M, N ::= \mathbf{0}$$

$M, N ::= \mathbf{0}$	empty network
$\mid M_1 \mid M_2$	parallel composition
$\mid n[P]^{\nu}$	node
$\mid \mathsf{Dead}$	stucking network

Processes:

$P, Q ::= \mathsf{nil}$	termination
$\mid !\langle u \rangle.C$	broadcast
$\mid \lfloor ?(x).C \rfloor D$	receiver with timeout
$\mid \tau.C$	internal
$\mid \sigma.C$	sleep
$\mid X$	process variable
$\mid \mathsf{fix}\, X.P$	recursion

Probabilistic Choice:

$$C, D ::= \bigoplus_{i \in I} p_i{:}P_i$$

for *closed values*, i.e. values that do not contain variables. Then, we use p_i for probability weights, hence $p_i \in [0, 1]$.

A network in pTCWS is a (possibly empty) collection of nodes (which represent devices) running in parallel and using a common radio channel to communicate with each other. Nodes are unique; i.e. a node n can occur in a network only once. All nodes are assumed to have the same transmission range. The communication paradigm is *local broadcast*; only nodes located in the range of the transmitter may receive data. We write $n[P]^{\nu}$ for a node named n (the device network address) executing the sequential process P. The set ν contains (the names of) the neighbours of n. Said in other words, ν contains all nodes laying in the transmission cell of n (except n). In this manner, we model the network topology. Our wireless networks have a fixed topology. Moreover, nodes cannot be created or destroyed. Finally, we write Dead to denote a deadlocked network which prevents the execution of parallel components. This is a fictitious network which is introduced for technical convenience (see Definition 9) and not for specifying gossip protocols.

Processes are sequential and live inside the nodes. The symbol nil denotes terminated processes. The sender process $!\langle v \rangle.C$ broadcasts the value v, the continuation being C. The process $\lfloor ?(x)C \rfloor D$ denotes a receiver with timeout. Intuitively, this process either receives a value v, in the current time interval, and then continues as C where the variable x is instantiated with v, or it idles for one time unit, and then continues as D. The process $\tau.C$ performs an internal action and then continues as C. The process $\sigma.C$ models sleeping for one time unit. In processes of the form $\sigma.D$ and $\lfloor ?(x)C \rfloor D$ the occurrence of D is said to be *time-guarded*. The process $\mathsf{fix}\, X.P$ denotes *time-guarded recursion*, as all occurrences of the process variable X may only occur time-guarded in P. With an abuse of notation, we will write $?(x).C$ as an abbreviation for $\text{fix}\,X.\lfloor?(x)C\rfloor(1{:}X)$, where the process variable X does not occur in C.

The construct $\bigoplus_{i\in I}p_i{:}P_i$ denotes *probabilistic choice*, where I is a *finite*, *non-empty* set of indexes, and $p_i \in (0,1]$ denotes the probability to execute the process P_i, with $\sum_{i\in I}p_i = 1$. Notice that, as in [8], in order to simplify the operational semantics, probabilistic choices occur always underneath prefixing.

In processes of the form $\lfloor?(x)C\rfloor D$ the variable x is bound in C. Similarly, in process $\text{fix}\,X.P$ the process variable X is bound in P. This gives rise to the standard notions of *free (process) variables* and *bound (process) variables* and *α-conversion*. We identify processes and networks up to α-conversion. A process (resp. probabilistic choice) is said to be *closed* if it does not contain free (process) variables. We always work with closed processes (resp. probabilistic choices): the absence of free variables is trivially maintained at run-time. We write $\{^v/_x\}P$ (resp. $\{^v/_x\}C$) for the substitution of the variable x with the value v in the process P (resp. probabilistic choice C). Similarly, we write $\{^P/_X\}Q$ for the substitution of the process variable X with the process P in Q.

We report some *notational conventions*. $\prod_{i\in I}M_i$ denotes the parallel composition of all M_i, for $i \in I$. We write $P_1 \oplus_p P_2$ for the probabilistic process $p{:}P_1 \oplus (1-p){:}P_2$. We identify $1{:}P$ with P. We write $!\langle v\rangle$ as an abbreviation for $!\langle v\rangle.1{:}\text{nil}$. For $k > 0$ we write $\sigma^k.P$ as an abbreviation for $\sigma.\ldots.\sigma.P$, where prefix σ appears k times. Given a network M, $\text{nds}(M)$ returns the names of M. If $m \in \text{nds}(M)$, the function $\text{ngh}(m,M)$ returns the set of the neighbours of m in M. Thus, for $M = M_1|m[P]^\nu|M_2$ it holds that $\text{ngh}(m,M) = \nu$. We write $\text{ngh}(M)$ for $\bigcup_{m\in\text{nds}(M)}\text{ngh}(m,M)$.

Definition 1. The *structural congruence* over *pTCWS*, written $\equiv$, is defined as the smallest equivalence relation over networks, preserved by parallel composition, which is a commutative monoid with respect to parallel composition with neutral element **0**, and for which $n[\text{fix}\,X.P]^\nu \equiv n[\{^{\text{fix}\,X.P}/_X\}P]^\nu$.

The syntax presented in Table 1 allows us to derive networks which are somehow ill-formed. With the following definition we rule out networks: (i) where nodes can be neighbours of themselves; (ii) with two different nodes with the same name; (iii) with non-symmetric neighbouring relations. Finally, in order to guarantee clock synchronisation among nodes, we require network connectivity.

Definition 2 (Well-formedness). A network M is said to be *well-formed* if (i) whenever $M \equiv M_1 \mid m[P_1]^\nu$ it holds that $m \notin \nu$; (ii) whenever $M \equiv M_1 \mid m_1[P_1]^{\nu_1} \mid m_2[P_2]^{\nu_2}$ it holds that $m_1 \neq m_2$; (iii) whenever $M \equiv N \mid m_1[P_1]^{\nu_1} \mid m_2[P_2]^{\nu_2}$ we have $m_1 \in \nu_2$ iff $m_2 \in \nu_1$; (iv) for all $m,n \in \text{nds}(M)$ there are $m_1,\ldots,m_k \in \text{nds}(M)$, s.t. $m=m_1$, $n=m_k$, and $m_i \in \text{ngh}(m_{i+1},M)$ for $1\leq i\leq k-1$.

Henceforth, we will always work with well-formed networks.

2.1   Probabilistic Labelled Transition Semantics

Along the lines of [8], we propose an *operational semantics* for *pTCWS* associating with each network a graph-like structure representing its possible evolutions: we use a generalisation of labelled transition systems that includes probabilities. Below, we report the mathematical machinery for doing that.

Definition 3. A (discrete) *probability sub-distribution* over a *finite* set S is a function $\Delta \colon S \to [0,1]$ with $\sum_{s \in S} \Delta(s) \in (0,1]$. We denote $\sum_{s \in S} \Delta(s)$ by $|\Delta|$. The *support* of a probability sub-distribution Δ is given by $\lceil \Delta \rceil = \{s \in S : \Delta(s) > 0\}$. We write $\mathcal{D}_{\mathrm{sub}}(S)$, ranged over Δ, Θ, Φ, for the set of all probability sub-distributions over S with finite support. A probability sub-distribution $\Delta \in \mathcal{D}_{\mathrm{sub}}(S)$ is said to be a *probability distribution* if $\sum_{s \in S} \Delta(s) = 1$. With $\mathcal{D}(S)$ we denote the set of all probability distributions over S with finite support. For any $s \in S$, the *point (Dirac) distribution at s*, denoted $\overline{s}$, assigns probability 1 to s and 0 to all others elements of S, so that $\lceil \overline{s} \rceil = \{s\}$.

Let I be a finite index such that (i) Δ_i is a sub-distribution in $\mathcal{D}_{\mathrm{sub}}(S)$ for each $i \in I$, and (ii) $p_i \geq 0$ are probabilities such that $\sum_{i \in I} p_i \in (0,1]$. Then, the probability sub-distribution $\sum_{i \in I} p_i \cdot \Delta_i \in \mathcal{D}_{\mathrm{sub}}(S)$ is defined as:

$$\left(\sum_{i \in I} p_i \cdot \Delta_i\right)(s) \overset{\mathrm{def}}{=} \sum_{i \in I} p_i \cdot \Delta_i(s)$$

for all $s \in S$. We write a sub-distribution as $p_1 \cdot \Delta_1 + \ldots + p_n \cdot \Delta_n$ when the index set I is $\{1, \ldots, n\}$. Sometimes, with an abuse of notation, in the previous decomposition we admit that the terms Δ_i are not necessarily distinct (for instance $1 \cdot \Delta$ may be rewritten as $p \cdot \Delta + (1-p) \cdot \Delta$, for any $p \in [0,1]$). In the following, we will often write $\sum_{i \in I} p_i \Delta_i$ instead of $\sum_{i \in I} p_i \cdot \Delta_i$.

Definitions 1 and 2 generalise to sub-distributions in $\mathcal{D}_{\mathrm{sub}}(\mathtt{pTCWS})$. Given two sub-distributions Δ and Θ, we write $\Delta \equiv \Theta$ if $\Delta([M]_\equiv) = \Theta([M]_\equiv)$ for all equivalence classes $[M]_\equiv \subseteq \mathtt{pTCWS}$. A sub-distribution $\Delta \in \mathcal{D}_{\mathrm{sub}}(\mathtt{pTCWS})$ is said to be well-formed if its support contains only well-formed networks.

We now give the probabilistic generalisation of labelled transition systems.

Definition 4 (Probabilistic LTS). A *probabilistic labelled transition system* (pLTS) is a triple $\langle S, \mathcal{L}, \to \rangle$ where (i) S is a set of states; (ii) $\mathcal{L}$ is a set of transition labels; (iii) $\to$ is a labelled transition relation contained in $S \times \mathcal{L} \times \mathcal{D}(S)$.

The operational semantics of $\mathtt{pTCWS}$ is given by a particular pLTS $\langle \mathtt{pTCWS}, \mathcal{L}, \to \rangle$, where $\mathcal{L} = \{m!v{\triangleright}\mu, m?v, \tau, \sigma\}$ contains the labels denoting broadcasting, reception, internal actions and time passing, respectively. The definition of the relations $\overset{\lambda}{\to}$, for $\lambda \in \mathcal{L}$, is given by the SOS rules in Table 2. Some of these rules use an obvious notation for distributing parallel composition over a sub-distribution: $(\Delta \mid \Theta)(M) = \Delta(M_1) \cdot \Theta(M_2)$ if $M = M_1 | M_2$; $(\Delta \mid \Theta)(M) = 0$ otherwise.

Furthermore, the definition of the labelled transition relation relies on a semantic interpretation of (nodes containing) probabilistic processes in terms of probability distributions over networks.

Definition 5. For any probabilistic choice $\bigoplus_{i \in I} p_i{:}P_i$ over a finite index set I, we write $[\![n[\bigoplus_{i \in I} p_i{:}P_i]^\mu]\!]$ to denote the probability distribution $\sum_{i \in I} p_i \cdot \overline{n[P_i]^\mu}$.

Table 2. Probabilistic labelled transition system

$$(\text{Snd}) \ \frac{-}{m[!\langle v\rangle.C]^{\nu} \xrightarrow{m!v\triangleright\nu} [\![m[C]^{\nu}]\!]} \qquad (\text{Rcv}) \ \frac{m\in\nu}{n[\lfloor?(x).C\rfloor D]^{\nu} \xrightarrow{m?v} [\![n[\{^v/_x\}C]^{\nu}]\!]}$$

$$(\text{Rcv-0}) \ \frac{-}{0 \xrightarrow{m?v} \overline{0}} \qquad (\text{RcvEnb}) \ \frac{\neg(m\in\nu \wedge \mathsf{rcv}(P)) \wedge m\neq n}{n[P]^{\nu} \xrightarrow{m?v} \overline{n[P]^{\nu}}}$$

$$(\text{RcvPar}) \ \frac{M \xrightarrow{m?v} \Delta \quad N \xrightarrow{m?v} \Theta}{M\mid N \xrightarrow{m?v} \Delta\mid\Theta} \qquad (\text{Bcast}) \ \frac{M \xrightarrow{m!v\triangleright\nu} \Delta \quad N \xrightarrow{m?v} \Theta}{M\mid N \xrightarrow{m!v\triangleright\mu} \Delta\mid\Theta} \ \mu:=\nu\backslash\mathsf{nds}(N)$$

$$(\text{Tau}) \ \frac{-}{m[\tau.C]^{\nu} \xrightarrow{\tau} [\![m[C]^{\nu}]\!]} \qquad (\text{TauPar}) \ \frac{M \xrightarrow{\tau} \Delta \quad N\neq\mathsf{Dead}}{M\mid N \xrightarrow{\tau} \Delta\mid\overline{N}}$$

$$(\sigma\text{-0}) \ \frac{-}{0 \xrightarrow{\sigma} \overline{0}} \qquad (\text{Timeout}) \ \frac{-}{n[\lfloor?(x).C\rfloor D]^{\nu} \xrightarrow{\sigma} [\![n[D]^{\nu}]\!]}$$

$$(\sigma\text{-nil}) \ \frac{-}{n[\mathsf{nil}]^{\nu} \xrightarrow{\sigma} \overline{n[\mathsf{nil}]^{\nu}}} \qquad (\text{Sleep}) \ \frac{-}{n[\sigma.C]^{\nu} \xrightarrow{\sigma} [\![n[C]^{\nu}]\!]}$$

$$(\sigma\text{-Par}) \ \frac{M \xrightarrow{\sigma} \Delta \quad N \xrightarrow{\sigma} \Theta}{M\mid N \xrightarrow{\sigma} \Delta\mid\Theta} \qquad (\text{Rec}) \ \frac{n[\{^{\mathsf{fix}\,X.P}/x\}P]^{\nu} \xrightarrow{\lambda} \Delta}{n[\mathsf{fix}\,X.P]^{\nu} \xrightarrow{\lambda} \Delta}$$

Let us comment on the most significant rules of Table 2. In rule (Snd) a node m broadcasts a message v to its neighbours ν, the continuation being the probability distribution associated to C. In the label $m!v\triangleright\nu$ the set ν denotes the neighbours of m. In rule (Rcv) a node n gets a message v from a neighbour node m, the continuation being the distribution associated to $\{^v/_x\}C$. If no message is received in the current time interval then the node n will continue according to D, as specified in rule (Timeout). Rules (Rcv-0) and (RcvEnb) serve to model reception enabling for synchronisation purposes. For instance, rule (RcvEnb) regards nodes n which are not involved in transmissions originating from m. This may happen either because the two nodes are out of range (i.e. $m\notin\nu$) or because n is not willing to receive ($\mathsf{rcv}(P)$ is a boolean predicate that returns true if $n[P]^{\nu} \equiv n[\lfloor?(x)C\rfloor D]^{\nu}$, for some x, C, D). In both cases, node n is not affected by the transmission. Rule (Bcast) models broadcast of messages. Note that we loose track of those transmitter's neighbours that are in N. Rule (Sleep) models sleeping for one time unit. Rule (σ-Par) models time synchronisation between parallel components. Rules (Bcast) and (TauPar) have their symmetric counterparts which are not reported in the table. Finally, note that the semantics of the network Dead is different from that of $\mathbf{0}$: the network Dead does not perform any action and does prevent the evolution of any parallel component.

Extensional Labelled Transition Semantics. Our focus is on weak similarities, which abstract away non-observable actions, i.e. those actions that cannot be detected by a parallel network. The adjective *extensional* is used to stress that those activities require a contribution of the environment. To this end, we extend Table 2 by the following two rules:

$$(\text{ShhSnd}) \quad \frac{M \xrightarrow{m!v\triangleright\emptyset} \Delta}{M \xrightarrow{\tau} \Delta} \qquad\qquad (\text{ObsSnd}) \quad \frac{M \xrightarrow{m!v\triangleright\nu} \Delta \quad \nu \neq \emptyset}{M \xrightarrow{!v\triangleright\nu} \Delta}$$

Rule (ShhSnd) models transmissions that cannot be observed because there is no potential receiver outside the network M. Rule (ObsSnd) models transmissions that can be observed by those nodes of the environment contained in ν. Notice that the name of the transmitter is removed from the label. This is motivated by the fact that receiver nodes do not have a direct manner to observe the identity of the transmitter. On the other hand, a network M performing the action $m?v$ can be observed by an external node m which transmits the value v to an appropriate set of nodes in M. Notice that the action $!v\triangleright\nu$ does not propagate over parallel components (there is no rule for that). As a consequence, the Rule (ObsSnd) can only be applied to the whole network, never in a sub-network.

In the rest of the paper, the metavariable α will range over the following four kinds of actions: $!v\triangleright\nu$, $m?v$, σ, τ. They denote anonymous broadcast to specific nodes, message reception, time passing, and internal activities, respectively.

3   Weak Simulation Up to Tolerance

In this section, we introduce *weak simulation quasimetrics* as an instrument to derive a notion of approximate simulation between networks. Our goal is to define a family of relations $\sqsubseteq_p$ over networks, with $p \in [0,1]$, to formalise the concept of *simulation with a tolerance p*. Intuitively, we will write $M \sqsubseteq_p N$ if N can simulate M with a tolerance p. Thus, $\sqsubseteq_0$ will coincide with the standard weak probabilistic simulation [1,2], whereas $\sqsubseteq_1$ should be equal to pTCWS × pTCWS.

In a probabilistic setting, the definition of weak transition is somewhat complicated by the fact that (strong) transitions take processes (in our case networks) to distributions; consequently if we are to use weak transitions $\xRightarrow{\alpha}$, which abstract away from non-observable actions, then we need to generalise transitions, so that they take (sub-)distributions to (sub-)distributions.

For a network M and a distribution Δ, we write $M \xrightarrow{\hat{\tau}} \Delta$ if either $M \xrightarrow{\tau} \Delta$ or $\Delta = \overline{M}$. Then, for $\alpha \neq \tau$, we write $M \xrightarrow{\hat{\alpha}} \Delta$ if $M \xrightarrow{\alpha} \Delta$. Relation $\xrightarrow{\hat{\alpha}}$ is extended to model transitions from sub-distributions to sub-distributions. For a sub-distribution $\Delta = \sum_{i\in I} p_i \overline{M_i}$, we write $\Delta \xrightarrow{\hat{\alpha}} \Theta$ if there is a set $J \subseteq I$ such that $M_j \xrightarrow{\hat{\alpha}} \Theta_j$ for all $j \in J$, $M_i \xcancel{\xrightarrow{\hat{\alpha}}}$, for all $i \in I \setminus J$, and $\Theta = \sum_{j\in J} p_j \Theta_j$. Note that if $\alpha \neq \tau$ then this definition admits that only some networks in the support of Δ make the $\xrightarrow{\hat{\alpha}}$ transition. Then, we define $\xRightarrow{\hat{\tau}} = (\xrightarrow{\hat{\tau}})^*$, while for $\alpha \neq \tau$ we let $\xRightarrow{\hat{\alpha}}$ denote $\xRightarrow{\hat{\tau}}\xrightarrow{\hat{\alpha}}\xRightarrow{\hat{\tau}}$.

In order to define our notion of simulation with tolerance, we adapt the concept of *weak bisimulation metric* of Desharnais et al.'s [10]. In [10], the behavioural distance between systems is measured by means of suitable *pseudometrics*, namely symmetric functions assigning a numeric value to any pair of systems. Here, we define asymmetric variants, called *pseudoquasimetrics*, measuring the tolerance of the simulation between networks. Both approaches require the lifting of these functions to distributions. In [10], this is realised by means of linear programs, relying on the symmetry of pseudometrics. Since pseudoquasimetrics are not symmetric, we need a different technique. Thus, to this end, we adopt the notions of matching [26] and Kantorovich lifting [7].

Definition 6 (Pseudoquasimetric). A function d: pTCWS × pTCWS → $[0,1]$ is a *1-bounded pseudoquasimetric* over pTCWS if (i)$d(M,M) = 0$ for all $M \in$ pTCWS, and (ii) $d(M,N) \leq d(M,O) + d(O,N)$ for all $M,N,O \in$ pTCWS.

Definition 7 (Matching). Given a pair of distributions $(\Delta, \Theta) \in \mathcal{D}(\text{pTCWS}) \times \mathcal{D}(\text{pTCWS})$, a *matching* of (Δ, Θ) is a distribution $\omega \in \mathcal{D}(\text{pTCWS} \times \text{pTCWS})$ s.t.: (i) $\sum_{N \in \text{pTCWS}} \omega(M,N) = \Delta(M)$, for all $M \in$pTCWS, and (ii) $\sum_{M \in \text{pTCWS}} \omega(M,N) = \Theta(N)$, for all $N \in$ pTCWS. $\Omega(\Delta, \Theta)$ denotes the set of all matchings for (Δ, Θ).

A matching for (Δ, Θ) may be understood as a transportation schedule for the shipment of probability mass from Δ to Θ [26].

Definition 8 (Kantorovich lifting). Let d: pTCWS × pTCWS → $[0,1]$ be a pseudoquasimetric. The *Kantorovich lifting* of d is the function $\mathbf{K}(d)$: $\mathcal{D}(\text{pTCWS}) \times \mathcal{D}(\text{pTCWS}) \to [0,1]$ defined as:

$$\mathbf{K}(d)(\Delta, \Theta) \stackrel{\text{def}}{=} \min_{\omega \in \Omega(\Delta, \Theta)} \sum_{M,N \in \text{pTCWS}} \omega(M,N) \cdot d(M,N).$$

Note that since we are considering only distributions with finite support, the minimum over the set of matchings $\Omega(\Delta, \Theta)$ is well defined.

Definition 9 (Weak simulation quasimetric). We say that a pseudoquasimetric d: pTCWS × pTCWS → $[0,1]$ is a *weak simulation quasimetric* if for all networks $M, N \in$ pTCWS, with $d(M,N) < 1$, whenever $M \stackrel{\alpha}{\longrightarrow} \Delta$ there is a sub-distribution Θ such that $N \stackrel{\hat{\alpha}}{\Longrightarrow} \Theta$ and $\mathbf{K}(d)(\Delta, \Theta + (1- |\Theta|)\mathsf{Dead}) \leq d(M,N)$.

In the previous definition, if $|\Theta| < 1$ then, with probability $1- |\Theta|$, there is no way to simulate the behaviour of any network in the support of Δ (the special network Dead does not perform any action).

As expected, the kernel of a weak simulation quasimetric is a weak probabilistic simulation [1,2].

Proposition 1. Let d be a weak simulation quasimetric. The binary relation $\{(M,N) : d(M,N) = 0\} \subseteq$ pTCWS × pTCWS is a weak probabilistic simulation.

A crucial result in our construction process is the existence of the minimal weak simulation quasimetric, which can be viewed as the asymmetric counterpart of the minimal weak bisimulation metric [10].

Theorem 1. There is a weak simulation quasimetric $\mathbf{d}$ s.t. $\mathbf{d}(M,N) \leq d(M,N)$ for all weak simulation quasimetrics d and all networks $M, N \in$ pTCWS.

Now, we have all ingredients to define our simulation with tolerance p.

Definition 10 (Weak simulation with tolerance). Let $p \in [0, 1]$, we say that N *simulates* M *with tolerance* p, written $M \sqsubseteq_p N$, iff $\mathbf{d}(M, N) = q$, for some $q \le p$. We write $M \simeq_p N$ if both $M \sqsubseteq_p N$ and $N \sqsubseteq_p M$.

Since the minimum weak simulation quasimetric $\mathbf{d}$ satisfies the triangle inequality, our simulation relation is trivially transitive in an additive sense:

Proposition 2 (Transitivity). $M \sqsubseteq_p N$ and $N \sqsubseteq_q O$ imply $M \sqsubseteq_{p+q} O$.

As expected, if $M \stackrel{\hat{\tau}}{\Longrightarrow} \Delta$ then M can simulate all networks in $\lceil \Delta \rceil$.

Proposition 3. If $M \stackrel{\hat{\tau}}{\Longrightarrow} (1-q)\overline{N} + q\Delta$, for some $\Delta \in \mathcal{D}(\texttt{pTCWS})$, then $N \sqsubseteq_q M$.

Clearly the transitivity property is quite useful when doing algebraic reasoning. However, we can derive a better tolerance when concatenating two simulations, if one of them is derived by an application of Proposition 3.

Proposition 4. If $M \sqsubseteq_p N$ and $O \stackrel{\hat{\tau}}{\Longrightarrow} (1-q)\overline{N} + q\Delta$, for some $\Delta \in \mathcal{D}(\texttt{pTCWS})$, then $M \sqsubseteq_{p(1-q)+q} O$.

Intuitively, in the simulation between M and N the tolerance p must be weighted by taking into consideration that O may evolve into N with a probability $(1-q)$.

In order to understand the intuition behind our weak simulation with tolerance, we report here a few simple *algebraic laws* (we recall that $1{:}P = P$).

Proposition 5 (Simple algebraic laws).

1. $n[P]^\mu \sqsubseteq_{1-p} n[\tau.(P \oplus_p Q)]^\mu$
2. $n[Q]^\mu \sqsubseteq_r n[\tau.(\tau.(P \oplus_q Q) \oplus_p R)]^\mu$, with $r = (1-p) + pq$
3. $n[!\langle v \rangle.(\tau.(P \oplus_q \tau.P) \oplus_p Q)]^\mu \simeq_0 n[!\langle v \rangle.(P \oplus_p \tau.Q)]^\mu$
4. $n[!\langle v \rangle.!\langle w \rangle]^\mu \sqsubseteq_r n[\tau.(!\langle v \rangle.\tau.(!\langle w \rangle \oplus_q P) \oplus_p Q)]^\mu$, with $r = 1 - pq$.

The first law is straightforward. The second law is a generalisation of the first one where the right-hand side must resolve two probabilistic choices in order to simulate the left-hand side. The third law is an adaptation of the CCS tau-law $\tau.P = P$ in a distributed and probabilistic setting. Similarly, the fourth law reminds a probabilistic and distributed variant of the tau-law $a.(\tau.(P + \tau.Q)) + a.Q = a.(P + \tau.Q)$. This law gives an example of a probabilistic simulation involving sequences of actions.

A crucial property of our simulation is the possibility to reason on parallel networks in a *compositional* manner. Thus, if $M_1 \sqsubseteq_{p_1} N_1$ and $M_2 \sqsubseteq_{p_2} N_2$ then $M_1 \mid M_2 \sqsubseteq_p N_1 \mid N_2$ for some p depending on p_1 and p_2; the intuition being that if one fixes the maximal tolerance p between $M_1 \mid M_2$ and $N_1 \mid N_2$, then there are tolerances p_i between M_i and N_i ensuring that the tolerance p is respected. Following this intuition, several compositional criteria for bisimulation metrics can be found in the literature [10, 12–15]. Here, we show that our weak simulation with tolerance complies with *non-expansiveness*: one of the strongest criteria, requiring $p \le p_1 + p_2$.

Theorem 2 (Non-expansiveness law). $M_1 \sqsubseteq_{p_1} N_1$ and $M_2 \sqsubseteq_{p_2} N_2$ entails $M_1 \mid M_2 \sqsubseteq_{p_1+p_2} N_1 \mid N_2$.

Another useful property is that a network is simulated by a probabilistic choice whenever it is simulated by all components.

Proposition 6 (Additive law). Let $M \sqsubseteq_{s_i} n[P_i]^\mu | N$, for all $i \in I$, with I a finite index set. Then, $M \sqsubseteq_r n[\tau. \bigoplus_{i \in I} p_i{:}P_i]^\mu \mid N$, for $r = \sum_{i \in I} p_i s_i$.

Finally, we report a number of algebraic laws that will be useful in the next section when analysing gossip protocols.

Proposition 7 (Further algebraic laws).

1. $n[\sigma^k.\mathsf{nil}]^\mu \simeq_0 n[\mathsf{nil}]^\mu$
2. $\prod_{i \in I} m_i[P_i]^{\mu_i} \simeq_r \prod_{j \in J} n_j[Q_j]^{\nu_j}$ entails $\prod_{i \in I} m_i[\sigma.P_i]^{\mu_i} \simeq_r \prod_{j \in J} n_j[\sigma.Q_j]^{\nu_j}$
3. $n[?(x).C]^\mu \simeq_0 n[\sigma.?(x).C]^\mu$, if nodes in μ do not send in the current round
4. $m[\mathsf{nil}]^\mu | \prod_{i \in I} n_i[P_i]^{\mu_i} \sqsubseteq_0 m[\tau.(!\langle v \rangle \oplus_p \mathsf{nil})]^\mu | \prod_{i \in I} n_i[P_i]^{\mu_i}$ if $\mu \subseteq \bigcup_{i \in I} n_i$, and for all $n_i \in \mu$ it holds that $P_i \neq \lfloor ?(x)C \rfloor D$.

Intuitively: (1) nil does not prevent time passing; (2) equalities are preserved underneath σ prefixes; (3) receptions will timeout if there are not senders around; (4) broascast has no effect if there are not receivers around.

4 A Case Study: Reasoning on Gossip Protocols

The baseline model for our case study is gossiping without communication collisions, where all nodes are perfectly synchronised. For the sake of clarity, communication proceeds in synchronous rounds: a node can transmit or receive only one message per round. In our implementation, rounds are separated by σ-actions.

The processes involved in the protocol are the following:

$$\mathsf{snd}\langle u \rangle_{p_g} \overset{\text{def}}{=} \tau.(!\langle u \rangle \oplus_{p_g} \mathsf{nil}) \quad \mathsf{fwd}_{p_g} \overset{\text{def}}{=} ?(x).\mathsf{resnd}\langle x \rangle_{p_g} \quad \mathsf{resnd}\langle u \rangle_{p_g} \overset{\text{def}}{=} \sigma.\mathsf{snd}\langle u \rangle_{p_g}.$$

A sender broadcasts with a gossip probability p_g, whereas a forwarder rebroadcasts the received value, in the subsequent round, with the same probability.

We apply our simulation theory to develop algebraic reasonings on *message propagation*. As an introductory example, let us consider a fragment of a network with two sender nodes, m_1 and m_2, and two forwarder nodes, n_1 and n_2 which are both neighbours of m_1 and m_2. Then, the following holds:

$$
m_1[\mathsf{snd}\langle u \rangle_{p_1}]^\nu \mid m_2[\mathsf{snd}\langle u \rangle_{p_2}]^\nu \mid n_1[\mathsf{fwd}_q]^{\nu_1} \mid n_2[\mathsf{fwd}_r]^{\nu_2} \quad {}_s\sqsupseteq
$$
$$
m_1[\mathsf{nil}]^\nu \mid m_2[\mathsf{nil}]^\nu \mid n_1[\mathsf{resnd}\langle u \rangle_q]^{\nu_1} \mid n_2[\mathsf{resnd}\langle u \rangle_r]^{\nu_2}
$$

with tolerance $s = (1 - p_1)(1 - p_2)$. Here, the network on the left-hand-side evolves by performing two τ-actions (via rule (ShhSnd)). Thus, the algebraic law follows by an application of Proposition 3 being $1 - s$ the probability that the message u is broadcast to both forwarders.

This simple law can be generalised to an arbitrary number of senders and forwarders, under the hypothesis that parallel contexts are unable to receive messages in the current round. The following theorem relies on Proposition 3.

Theorem 3 (Message propagation). Let I and J be pairwise disjoint subsets of $\mathbb{N}$. Let M be a well-formed network defined as

$$M \equiv N \mid \prod_{i \in I} m_i[\mathsf{snd}\langle v \rangle_{p_i}]^{\nu_{m_i}} \mid \prod_{j \in J} n_j[\mathsf{fwd}_{q_j}]^{\nu_{n_j}}$$

such that, for all $i \in I$:

- $\{n_j : j \in J\} \subseteq \nu_{m_i} \subseteq \mathsf{nds}(M)$, and
- the nodes in $\nu_{m_i} \cap \mathsf{nds}(N)$ cannot receive in the current round.

Then, $M \;_r\sqsupseteq\; N \mid \prod_{i \in I} m_i[\mathsf{nil}]^{\nu_{m_i}} \mid \prod_{j \in J} n_j[\mathsf{resnd}\langle v \rangle_{q_j}]^{\nu_{n_j}}$, with $r = \prod_{i \in I}(1 - p_i)$.

Theorem 3 represents an effective tool to deal with message propagation in gossip networks. However, it requires that all forwarders n_j should be in the neighbouring of all senders m_i (constraint $\{n_j : j \in J\} \subseteq \nu_{m_i}$), which may represent a limitation in many cases. Consider, for example, a simple gossiping network GSP, with gossip probability p, composed by two source nodes s_1 and s_2, a destination node d, and three intermediate nodes n_1, n_2 and n_3:

$$\mathrm{GSP} \stackrel{\mathrm{def}}{=} \prod_{i=1}^{2} s_i[\mathsf{snd}\langle v \rangle_p]^{\nu_{s_i}} \mid \prod_{i=1}^{3} n_i[\mathsf{fwd}_p]^{\nu_{n_i}} \mid d[\mathsf{fwd}_1]^{\nu_d} \qquad (1)$$

with topology $\nu_{s_1} = \{n_1\}$, $\nu_{s_2} = \{n_1, n_2\}$, $\nu_{n_1} = \{s_1, s_2, n_3\}$, $\nu_{n_2} = \{s_2, n_3\}$, $\nu_{n_3} = \{n_1, n_2, d\}$ and $n_3 \in \nu_d$.

Here, we would like to estimate the distance between GSP, and a network DONE, in which the message v has been delivered to the destination node d.

$$\mathrm{DONE} \stackrel{\mathrm{def}}{=} \prod_{i=1}^{2} s_i[\mathsf{nil}]^{\nu_{s_i}} \mid \prod_{i=1}^{3} n_i[\mathsf{nil}]^{\nu_{n_i}} \mid d[\sigma^3.\,\mathsf{snd}\langle v \rangle_1]^{\nu_d} \qquad (2)$$

Unfortunately, we cannot directly apply Theorem 3 to capture this message propagation because node s_2, unlike s_1, can transmit to both n_1 and n_2. In this case, before applying Theorem 3, we would need a result to *compose estimates* of partial networks. More precisely, a result which would allow us to take into account, in the calculation of the tolerance, both the probability that a sender transmits and the probability that the same sender does not transmit. The following result follows from Proposition 6.

Theorem 4 (Composing networks). If $M \stackrel{\sigma}{\nrightarrow}$ then

$$N \mid m[\mathsf{snd}\langle v \rangle_p]^{\nu_m} \mid \prod_{j \in J} n_j[\lfloor ?(x_j)P_j \rfloor Q_j]^{\nu_{n_j}} \;_r\sqsupseteq\; M$$

with tolerance $r = ps_1 + (1-p)s_2$, whenever

- $N \mid m[\mathsf{nil}]^{\nu_m} \mid \prod_{j \in J} n_j[\{v/x_j\}P_j]^{\nu_{n_j}} \;_{s_1}\sqsupseteq\; M$
- $N \mid m[\mathsf{nil}]^{\nu_m} \mid \prod_{j \in J} n_j[\lfloor ?(x_j)P_j \rfloor Q_j]^{\nu_{n_j}} \;_{s_2}\sqsupseteq\; M$
- $\{n_j : j \in J\} \subseteq \nu_m \subseteq \{n_j : j \in J\} \cup \mathsf{nds}(N)$
- nodes in $\nu_m \cap \mathsf{nds}(N)$ cannot receive in the current round.[1]

---

[1] We could generalise the result to take into account more senders at the same time. This would not add expressiveness, it would just speed up the reduction process.

Intuitively: (i) in the network $N \mid m[\mathsf{snd}\langle v\rangle_p]^{\nu_m} \mid \prod_{j\in J} n_j[\lfloor?(x_j)P_j\rfloor Q_j]^{\nu_{n_j}}$ node m has not performed yet the τ-action that resolves the probabilistic choice between broadcasting v or not; (ii) in $N \mid m[\mathsf{nil}]^{\nu_m} \mid \prod_{j\in J} n_j[\{^v/_{x_j}\}P_j]^{\nu_{n_j}}$ node m has resolved the probabilistic choice deciding to broadcast v; (iii) finally, in the network $N \mid m[\mathsf{nil}]^{\nu_m} \mid \prod_{j\in J} n_j[\lfloor?(x_j)P_j\rfloor Q_j]^{\nu_{n_j}}$ node m has has resolved the probabilistic choice deciding not to broadcast v.

Now, we have all algebraic tools to compute an estimation of the tolerance r, such that GSP $_r\sqsupseteq$ DONE. In practise, we will compute the tolerance for two partial networks and then will use Theorem 4 to compose the two tolerances.

For verification reasons we assume that the environment contains a node $test$, close to the destination node, i.e. $\nu_d = \{n_3, test\}$, to test successful gossiping. For simplicity, the $test$ node can receive messages but it cannot transmit.

As a first step, we compute an estimation for the network GSP in which the sender s_2 *has already broadcast* the message v to its neighbours n_1 and n_2. To this end, we derive the following chain of similarities by applying, in sequence, (i) Proposition 7(4), (ii) Proposition 7(3), (iii) Theorem 3 and Proposition 7(2), (iv) Proposition 7(1) and Proposition 7(3), (v) Theorem 3 and Proposition 7(2), and (iv) Proposition 7(1). In all steps, we have reasoned in a compositional manner, up to common parallel components (Theorem 2).

$$
\begin{array}{l}
s_1[\mathsf{snd}\langle v\rangle_p]^{\nu_{s_1}} \mid s_2[\mathsf{nil}]^{\nu_{s_2}} \mid \prod_{i=1}^{2} n_i[\mathsf{resnd}\langle v\rangle_p]^{\nu_{n_i}} \mid n_3[\mathsf{fwd}_p]^{\nu_{n_3}} \mid d[\mathsf{fwd}_1]^{\nu_d} \\
{}_0\sqsupseteq \prod_{i=1}^{2} s_i[\mathsf{nil}]^{\nu_{s_i}} \quad \prod_{i=1}^{2} n_i[\mathsf{resnd}\langle v\rangle_p]^{\nu_{n_i}} \quad n_3[\mathsf{fwd}_p]^{\nu_{n_3}} \mid d[\mathsf{fwd}_1]^{\nu_d} \\
{}_0\sqsupseteq \prod_{i=1}^{2} s_i[\mathsf{nil}]^{\nu_{s_i}} \quad \prod_{i=1}^{2} n_i[\sigma.\mathsf{snd}\langle v\rangle_p]^{\nu_{n_i}} \quad n_3[\sigma.\mathsf{fwd}_p]^{\nu_{n_3}} \mid d[\sigma.\mathsf{fwd}_1]^{\nu_d} \\
{}_{(1-p)^2}\sqsupseteq \prod_{i=1}^{2} s_i[\mathsf{nil}]^{\nu_{s_i}} \quad \prod_{i=1}^{2} n_i[\sigma.\mathsf{nil}]^{\nu_{n_i}} \quad n_3[\sigma.\mathsf{resnd}\langle v\rangle_p]^{\nu_{n_3}} \mid d[\sigma.\mathsf{fwd}_1]^{\nu_d} \\
{}_0\sqsupseteq \prod_{i=1}^{2} s_i[\mathsf{nil}]^{\nu_{s_i}} \quad \prod_{i=1}^{2} n_i[\mathsf{nil}]^{\nu_{n_i}} \quad n_3[\sigma^2.\,\mathsf{snd}\langle v\rangle_p]^{\nu_{n_3}} \mid d[\sigma^2.\,\mathsf{fwd}_1]^{\nu_d} \\
{}_{1-p}\sqsupseteq \prod_{i=1}^{2} s_i[\mathsf{nil}]^{\nu_{s_i}} \quad \prod_{i=1}^{2} n_i[\mathsf{nil}]^{\nu_{n_i}} \quad n_3[\sigma^2.\,\mathsf{nil}]^{\nu_{n_3}} \mid d[\sigma^2.\,\mathsf{resnd}\langle v\rangle_1]^{\nu_d} \\
{}_0\sqsupseteq \prod_{i=1}^{2} s_i[\mathsf{nil}]^{\nu_{s_i}} \quad \prod_{i=1}^{3} n_i[\mathsf{nil}]^{\nu_{n_i}} \quad d[\sigma^3.\,\mathsf{snd}\langle v\rangle_1]^{\nu_d} \\
{} = \text{DONE} .
\end{array}
$$

Then, by more applications of Propositions 2 and 7(1), one application of Proposition 4, and one application of Proposition 7(2) we derive:

$$
s_1[\mathsf{snd}\langle v\rangle_p]^{\nu_{s_1}} \mid s_2[\mathsf{nil}]^{\nu_{s_2}} \mid \prod_{i=1}^{2} n_i[\mathsf{resnd}\langle v\rangle_p]^{\nu_{n_i}} \mid n_3[\mathsf{fwd}_p]^{\nu_{n_3}} \mid d[\mathsf{fwd}_1]^{\nu_d} \tag{3}
$$
$$
{}_{1-2p^2+p^3}\sqsupseteq \text{DONE}
$$

with tolerance $1 - 2p^2 + p^3$, obtained by solving the expression $(1-p)(1-(1-p)^2) + (1-p)^2$.

Similarly, we compute an estimation of the tolerance which allows the network GSP, in which the sender s_2 *did not broadcast* the message v to its neighbours, to simulate the network DONE. To this end, we derive the following chain of similarities by applying, in sequence, (i) Theorem 3 and Proposition 7(3), (ii) Proposition 7(3), (iii) Theorem 3 and Proposition 7(2), (iv) Proposition 7(1) and (3), (v) Theorem 3 and Proposition 7(2), and (vi) Propositions 7(1) and (4). In all steps, we have reasoned up to common parallel components (Theorem 2).

$$s_1[\mathsf{snd}\langle v\rangle_p]^{\nu_{s_1}} \mid s_2[\mathsf{nil}]^{\nu_{s_2}} \mid \prod_{i=1}^{3} n_i[\mathsf{fwd}_p]^{\nu_{n_i}} \mid d[\mathsf{fwd}_1]^{\nu_d}$$

$$\begin{aligned}
{}_{1-p}\sqsupseteq\ &\prod_{i=1}^{2} s_i[\mathsf{nil}]^{\nu_{s_i}} \mid n_1[\mathsf{resnd}\langle v\rangle_p]^{\nu_{n_1}} \mid \prod_{i=2}^{3} n_i[\mathsf{fwd}_p]^{\nu_{n_i}} \mid d[\mathsf{fwd}_1]^{\nu_d} \\
{}_{0}\sqsupseteq\ &\prod_{i=1}^{2} s_i[\mathsf{nil}]^{\nu_{s_i}} \mid n_1[\sigma.\mathsf{snd}\langle v\rangle_p]^{\nu_{n_1}} \mid \prod_{i=2}^{3} n_i[\sigma.\mathsf{fwd}_p]^{\nu_{n_i}} \mid d[\sigma.\mathsf{fwd}_1]^{\nu_d} \\
{}_{1-p}\sqsupseteq\ &\prod_{i=1}^{2} s_i[\mathsf{nil}]^{\nu_{s_i}} \mid n_1[\sigma.\mathsf{nil}]^{\nu_{n_1}} \mid n_2[\sigma.\mathsf{fwd}_p]^{\nu_{n_2}} \mid n_3[\sigma.\mathsf{resnd}\langle v\rangle_p]^{\nu_{n_3}} \mid d[\sigma.\mathsf{fwd}_1]^{\nu_d} \\
{}_{0}\sqsupseteq\ &\prod_{i=1}^{2} s_i[\mathsf{nil}]^{\nu_{s_i}} \mid n_1[\mathsf{nil}]^{\nu_{n_1}} \mid n_2[\sigma^2.\,\mathsf{fwd}_p]^{\nu_{n_2}} \mid n_3[\sigma^2.\,\mathsf{snd}\langle v\rangle_p]^{\nu_{n_3}} \mid d[\sigma^2.\,\mathsf{fwd}_1]^{\nu_d} \\
{}_{1-p}\sqsupseteq\ &\prod_{i=1}^{2} s_i[\mathsf{nil}]^{\nu_{s_i}} \mid n_1[\mathsf{nil}]^{\nu_{n_1}} \mid n_2[\sigma^2.\,\mathsf{resnd}\langle v\rangle_p]^{\nu_{n_2}} \mid n_3[\sigma^2.]^{\nu_{n_3}} \mid d[\sigma^2.\,\mathsf{resnd}\langle v\rangle_1]^{\nu_d} \\
{}_{0}\sqsupseteq\ &\prod_{i=1}^{2} s_i[\mathsf{nil}]^{\nu_{s_i}} \mid \prod_{i=1}^{3} n_i[\mathsf{nil}]^{\nu_{n_i}} \mid d[\sigma^3.\mathsf{snd}\langle v\rangle_1]^{\nu_d} \\
=\ &\mathrm{DONE}\ .
\end{aligned}$$

Then, by more applications of Propositions 2 and 7(1), one application of Proposition 4, and one application of Proposition 7(2) we derive:

$$s_1[\mathsf{snd}\langle v\rangle_p]^{\nu_{s_1}} \mid s_2[\mathsf{nil}]^{\nu_{s_2}} \mid \prod_{i=1}^{3} n_i[\mathsf{fwd}_p]^{\nu_{n_i}} \mid d[\mathsf{fwd}_1]^{\nu_d} \quad {}_{1-p^3}\sqsupseteq\ \mathrm{DONE}\ . \quad (4)$$

Finally, we can apply Theorem 4 to (3) and (4) to derive the following estimation for the tolerance:

$$\mathrm{GSP} \quad {}_{1-(3p^3-2p^4)}\sqsupseteq\ \mathrm{DONE}$$

Since the tolerance is $1-(3p^3-2p^4)$, it follows that the gossip network GSP will succeed in propagating the messages to the destination d, with probability at least $3p^3-2p^4$. Thus, for instance, for a gossip probability $p = 0.8$ the destination will receive the message with probability 0.716, with a margin of 10%. For $p = 0.85$ the probability at the destination increases to 0.798, with a margin of 6%; while for $p = 0.9$ the probability at destination rises to 0.88, with a difference of only 2%. So, $p = 0.9$ can be considered the threshold of our small network.[2]

Note that in the previous example both messages may reach the destination node in exactly three rounds. However, more generally, we could have different message propagation paths in the same network which might take a different amount of time to be traversed. The algebraic tools we develop up to now do not allow us to deal with paths of different lengths.

As an example, we would like to estimate the distance between the network

$$\mathrm{GSP}_2 \overset{\mathrm{def}}{=} s_1[\mathsf{snd}\langle v\rangle_1]^{\nu_{s_1}} \mid s_2[\mathsf{snd}\langle v\rangle_p]^{\nu_{s_2}} \mid n[\mathsf{fwd}_p]^{\nu_n} \mid d[\mathsf{fwd}_1]^{\nu_d}$$

with topology $\nu_{s_1} = \{d\}$, $\nu_{s_2} = \{n\}$, $\nu_n=\{s_2,d\}$ and $\nu_d = \{s_1,n,test\}$, and the networks defined as follows:

$$\mathrm{DONE}_2 \overset{\mathrm{def}}{=} s_1[\mathsf{nil}]^{\nu_{s_1}} \mid s_2[\mathsf{nil}]^{\nu_{s_2}} \mid n[\mathsf{nil}]^{\nu_n} \mid d[\tau.(\sigma.\mathsf{snd}\langle v\rangle_1 \oplus_p \sigma^2.\mathsf{snd}\langle v\rangle_1)]^{\nu_d}$$

in which the message v propagated up to the destination node d following two different paths. Thus, d will probabilistically choose between broadcasting v after one or two rounds.

The following result provide the missing instrument.

---

[2] Had we had more senders we would have estimated a better threshold.

Theorem 5 (Composing paths). Let M be a well-formed network. Then,

$$M \mid m[\tau.\bigoplus_{i\in I} p_i{:}Q_i]^{\nu_m} \; _r\sqsupseteq \; \prod_{j\in J} n_j[\text{nil}]^{\nu_{n_j}} \mid d[\tau.\bigoplus_{i\in I} p_i{:}P_i]^{\nu_d}$$

with $r = \sum_{i\in I} p_i s_i$, whenever:

- $M \mid m[Q_i]^{\nu_m} \; _{s_i}\sqsupseteq \; \prod_{j\in J} n_j[\text{nil}]^{\nu_{n_j}} \mid d[P_i]^{\nu_d}$, for any $i \in I$;
- $\nu_m \subseteq \text{nds}(M)$.

As a first step, we compute an estimation of the tolerance which allows GSP$_2$ to simulate the first probabilistic behaviour of DONE$_2$. To this end, we derive the following chain of similarities by applying, in sequence, (i) Theorem 3, (ii) again Theorem 3, (iii) Propositions 7(2) and (4). In all steps, we reason up to parallel components (Theorem 2).

$$s_1[\text{snd}\langle v\rangle_1]^{\nu_{s_1}} \mid s_2[\text{snd}\langle v\rangle_p]^{\nu_{s_2}} \mid n[\text{fwd}_p]^{\nu_n} \mid d[\text{fwd}_1]^{\nu_d}$$
$$_0\sqsupseteq s_1[\text{nil}]^{\nu_{s_1}} \mid s_2[\text{snd}\langle v\rangle_1]^{\nu_{s_2}} \mid n[\text{fwd}_p]^{\nu_n} \mid d[\text{resnd}\langle v\rangle_1]^{\nu_d}$$
$$_{1-p}\sqsupseteq s_1[\text{nil}]^{\nu_{s_1}} \mid s_2[\text{nil}]^{\nu_{s_2}} \mid n[\text{resnd}\langle v\rangle_p]^{\nu_n} \mid d[\text{resnd}\langle v\rangle_1]^{\nu_d}$$
$$_0\sqsupseteq s_1[\text{nil}]^{\nu_{s_1}} \mid s_2[\text{nil}]^{\nu_{s_2}} \mid n[\text{nil}]^{\nu_n} \mid d[\sigma.\text{snd}\langle v\rangle_1]^{\nu_d}.$$

By an application of Proposition 2 we derive:

$$s_1[\text{snd}\langle v\rangle_1]^{\nu_{s_1}} \mid s_2[\text{snd}\langle v\rangle_p]^{\nu_{s_2}} \mid n[\text{fwd}_p]^{\nu_n} \mid d[\text{fwd}_1]^{\nu_d}$$
$$_{1-p}\sqsupseteq s_1[\text{nil}]^{\nu_{s_1}} \mid s_2[\text{nil}]^{\nu_{s_2}} \mid n[\text{nil}]^{\nu_n} \mid d[\sigma.\text{snd}\langle v\rangle_1]^{\nu_d}. \tag{5}$$

Then, we compute an estimation of the tolerance which allows the network GSP$_2$ to simulate the second probabilistic behaviour of DONE$_2$. To this end, we derive the following chain of similarities by applying, in sequence, (i) Theorem 3, (ii) Theorem 3 again, Proposition 7(1), (2) and (3). Again, in all steps, we have reasoned up to parallel components (Theorem 2).

$$s_1[\text{nil}]^{\nu_{s_1}} \mid s_2[\text{snd}\langle v\rangle_p]^{\nu_{s_2}} \mid n[\text{fwd}_p]^{\nu_n} \mid d[\text{fwd}_1]^{\nu_d}$$
$$_{1-p}\sqsupseteq s_1[\text{nil}]^{\nu_{s_1}} \mid s_2[\text{nil}]^{\nu_{s_2}} \mid n[\text{resnd}\langle v\rangle_p]^{\nu_n} \mid d[\text{fwd}_1]^{\nu_d}$$
$$_{1-p}\sqsupseteq s_1[\text{nil}]^{\nu_{s_1}} \mid s_2[\text{nil}]^{\nu_{s_2}} \mid n[\text{nil}]^{\nu_n} \mid d[\sigma^2.\text{snd}\langle v\rangle_1]^{\nu_d}.$$

Then, by more applications of Proposition 2 and one application of Proposition 4 we derive:

$$s_1[\text{nil}]^{\nu_{s_1}} \mid s_2[\text{snd}\langle v\rangle_p]^{\nu_{s_2}} \mid n[\text{fwd}_p]^{\nu_n} \mid d[\text{fwd}_1]^{\nu_d}$$
$$_{1-p^2}\sqsupseteq s_1[\text{nil}]^{\nu_{s_1}} \mid s_2[\text{nil}]^{\nu_{s_2}} \mid n[\text{nil}]^{\nu_n} \mid d[\sigma^2.\text{snd}\langle v\rangle_1]^{\nu_d}. \tag{6}$$

Finally, we can apply Theorem 5 to (5) and (6) to derive

$$\text{GSP}_2 \; _r\sqsupseteq \; \text{DONE}_2$$

with $r = p(1-p) + (1-p)(1-p^2)$. Thus, the network GSP$_2$ will succeed in transmitting both messages v to the destination d, with probability at least $1-r$.

We conclude by observing that, in order to deal with paths of different length, one should apply Theorem 5 for all possible paths.

5   Conclusions, Related and Future Work

We have introduced the notion of *weak simulation quasimetric* as a means to define *weak simulation with tolerance*, i.e. a *compositional* simulation theory to express that a probabilistic system may be simulated by another one with a given tolerance measuring the distance between the two systems. Basically, weak simulation quasimetric is the asymmetric counterpart of *weak bisimulation metric* [10], and the quantitative analogous of *weak simulation preorder* [1,2].

We applied our proposal to develop an *algebraic theory* to estimate the performance of gossip networks in terms of the probability to successfully propagate messages up to the desired destination. The algebraic theory is compositional as it allows us to estimate the performance of gossip networks in terms of the behavioural distance of its sub-networks.

Our work has been inspired by [4,6,9,10], where the notion of behavioural distance between two probabilistic systems is formalised in terms of the notion of bisimulation metric. Bisimulation metric works fine for systems being approximately equivalent. However, when the simulation game works only in one direction, as in the gossip protocols analysed in the current paper, an asymmetric notion of simulation pseudometric is required.

The current paper is the ideal continuation of [19]. In that paper, the authors developed a notion of *simulation up to probability* to measure the closeness rather than the distance between two probabilistic systems. Then, as in here, simulation up to probability has been used to provide an algebraic theory to evaluate the performance of gossip networks. Despite the similarity of the two simulation theories, the simulation up to probability has a number of limitations that have motivated the current work: (i) the simulation up to probability is not transitive, while simulation quasimetrics are transitive by definition; (ii) in order to work with a transitive relation, paper [19] introduces an auxiliary rooted simulation which is much stronger than the main definition; (iii) that rooted simulation (and hence the simulation up to probability) is not suitable to compose estimates originating from paths with different lengths (as we do here by means of Theorem 5), and, more generally, to deal with more transmissions.

A nice survey of formal verification techniques for the analysis of gossip protocols appears in [3]. Probabilistic model-checking has been used in [11] to study the influence of different modelling choices on message propagation in flooding and gossip protocols, and in [18] to investigate the expected rounds of gossiping required to form a connected network and how the expected path length between nodes evolves over the execution of the protocol.

As future work, we intend to study gossip protocols with communication collisions, random delays and lossy channels. We then plan to apply our metric-based simulation theory to investigate the behaviour of IoT systems and cyber-physical systems [20,21]. In the context of probabilistic process calculi, we want to investigate which of the compositionality properties proposed in [13] hold for the operators that are usually offered by probabilistic process calculi.

Acknowledgements. We thank the anonymous reviewers for valuable comments.

References

1. Baier, C., Hermanns, H., Katoen, J.P.: Probabilistic weak simulation is decidable in polynomial time. Inf. Process. Lett. **89**(3), 123–130 (2004)
2. Baier, C., Katoen, J.-P., Hermanns, H., Haverkort, B.: Simulation for continuous-time Markov chains. In: Brim, L., Křetínský, M., Kučera, A., Jančar, P. (eds.) CONCUR 2002. LNCS, vol. 2421, pp. 338–354. Springer, Heidelberg (2002). doi:10. 1007/3-540-45694-5_23
3. Bakhshi, R., Bonnet, F., Fokkink, W., Haverkort, B.: Formal analysis techniques for gossiping protocols. Oper. Syst. Rev. **41**(5), 28–36 (2007)
4. van Breugel, F., Worrell, J.: A behavioural pseudometric for probabilistic transition systems. Theoret. Comput. Sci. **331**(1), 115–142 (2005)
5. Cerone, A., Hennessy, M., Merro, M.: Modelling MAC-layer communications in wireless systems. Log. Methods Comput. Sci. **11**(1:18) (2015)
6. Deng, Y., Chothia, T., Palamidessi, C., Pang, J.: Metrics for action-labelled quantitative transition systems. ENTCS **153**(2), 79–96 (2006)
7. Deng, Y., Du, W.: The Kantorovich metric in computer science: a brief survey. ENTCS **253**(3), 73–82 (2009)
8. Deng, Y., van Glabbeek, R.J., Hennessy, M., Morgan, C.: Characterising testing preorders for finite probabilistic processes. Log. Meth. Comput. Sci. **4**(4) (2008)
9. Desharnais, J., Gupta, J., Jagadeesan, R., Panangaden, P.: Metrics for labelled Markov processes. Theoret. Comput. Sci. **318**(3), 323–354 (2004)
10. Desharnais, J., Jagadeesan, R., Gupta, V., Panangaden, P.: The metric analogue of weak bisimulation for probabilistic processes. In: LICS 2002, pp. 413–422 (2002)
11. Fehnker, A., Gao, P.: Formal verification and simulation for performance analysis for probabilistic broadcast protocols. In: Kunz, T., Ravi, S.S. (eds.) ADHOC-NOW 2006. LNCS, vol. 4104, pp. 128–141. Springer, Heidelberg (2006). doi:10.1007/ 11814764_12
12. Gebler, D., Larsen, K.G., Tini, S.: Compositional metric reasoning with probabilistic process calculi. In: Pitts, A. (ed.) FoSSaCS 2015. LNCS, vol. 9034, pp. 230–245. Springer, Heidelberg (2015). doi:10.1007/978-3-662-46678-0_15
13. Gebler, D., Larsen, K.G., Tini, S.: Compositional bisimulation metric reasoning with probabilistic process calculi. Log. Meth. Comput. Sci. **12**(4) (2016)
14. Gebler, D., Tini, S.: Fixed-point characterization of compositionality properties of probabilistic processes combinators. In: Borgström, J., Crafa, S. (eds.) EXPRESS/SOS 2014, EPTCS, vol. 160, pp. 63–78 (2014)
15. Gebler, D., Tini, S.: SOS specifications of probabilistic systems by uniformly continuous operators. In: Aceto, L., Frutos-Escrig, D. (eds.) CONCUR 2015, LIPIcs, vol. 42, pp. 155–168. Schloss Dagstuhl - Leibniz-Zentrum fuer Informatik (2015)
16. Jonsson, B., Larsen, K.G., Yi, W.: Probabilistic extensions of process algebras. In: Handbook of Process Algebra, pp. 685–710. Elsevier (2001)
17. Kermarrec, A.M., van Steen, M.: Gossiping in distributed systems. Oper. Syst. Rev. **41**(5), 2–7 (2007)
18. Kwiatkowska, M., Norman, G., Parker, D.: Analysis of a gossip protocol in PRISM. SIGMETRICS Perform. Eval. Rev. **36**(3), 17–22 (2008)
19. Lanotte, R., Merro, M.: Semantic analysis of gossip protocols for wireless sensor networks. In: Katoen, J.-P., König, B. (eds.) CONCUR 2011. LNCS, vol. 6901, pp. 156–170. Springer, Heidelberg (2011). doi:10.1007/978-3-642-23217-6_11
20. Lanotte, R., Merro, M.: A semantic theory of the internet of things. In: Lluch Lafuente, A., Proença, J. (eds.) COORDINATION 2016. LNCS, vol. 9686, pp. 157–174. Springer, Cham (2016). doi:10.1007/978-3-319-39519-7_10

21. Lanotte, R., Merro, M.: A calculus of cyber-physical systems. In: Drewes, F., Martín-Vide, C., Truthe, B. (eds.) LATA 2017. LNCS, vol. 10168, pp. 115–127. Springer, Cham (2017). doi:10.1007/978-3-319-53733-7_8
22. Larsen, K.G., Skou, A.: Bisimulation through probabilistic testing. Inf. Comput. **94**(1), 1–28 (1991)
23. Macedonio, D., Merro, M.: A semantic analysis of key management protocols for wireless sensor networks. Sci. Comput. Program. **81**, 53–78 (2014)
24. Merro, M., Ballardin, F., Sibilio, E.: A timed calculus for wireless systems. Theoret. Comput. Sci. **412**(47), 6585–6611 (2011)
25. Segala, R., Lynch, N.: Probabilistic simulations for probabilistic processes. Nord. J. Comput. **2**, 250–273 (1995)
26. Villani, C.: Optimal Transport. Old and New. Springer, Heidelberg (2008)

Reasoning About Distributed Secrets

Nicolás Bordenabe[1], Annabelle McIver[1]([✉]), Carroll Morgan[2],
and Tahiry Rabehaja[1]

[1] Department of Computing, Macquarie University, Sydney, Australia
{nicolas.bordenabe,annabelle.mciver,tahiry.rabehaja}@mq.edu.au
[2] DATA61 and University of New South Wales, Sydney, Australia
carroll.morgan@unsw.edu.au

Abstract. In 1977 Tore Dalenius described how partial disclosure about one secret can impact the confidentiality of other correlated secrets, and indeed this phenomenon is well-known in privacy of databases. The aim here is to study this issue in a context of programs with distributed secrets. Moreover, we do not assume that secrets never change, in fact we investigate what happens when they do: we explore how updates to some (but not all) secrets can affect confidentiality elsewhere in the system.

We provide methods to compute robust upper bounds on the impact of such information leakages with respect to all distributed secrets. Finally we illustrate our results on a defence against side channels.

Keywords: Quantitative information flow · Foundations of security · Program semantics · Secure refinement

1 Introduction

This paper concerns information flow when secrets are distributed amongst several agents. For example, let X, Y and Z represent three agents with respective secrets x, y and z, where $z = f(x, y)$ for some function f. In this basic scenario, each secret is correlated via a known function (f), so that if something is leaked about one of the secrets, then something is also leaked about the others.

Partial disclosure about one secret leading to collateral disclosure about another is well documented in privacy of statistical databases, and was first addressed by Dalenius [9] who argued that ideal designs for privacy should prevent it: "Nothing about an individual should be learnable from the database that cannot be learned without access to the database". Later he argued the infeasibility of such a strict goal, and more recently Dwork [11] addressed the same concern demonstrating that whenever there is a (known) *correlation* between two pieces of information, anything learned about one piece implies that something might also be learned about the other.

In secure programming generally, i.e. not just read-only databases, this corresponds to leaking information about a secret "high-level" variable x, which then consequentially leaks information about a different high-level variable z that *does*

A. Bouajjani and A. Silva (Eds.): FORTE 2017, LNCS 10321, pp. 156–170, 2017.
DOI: 10.1007/978-3-319-60225-7_11

not appear in the program at all, but is known only via "auxiliary information" to be correlated with the initial value of x (as in z = f(x, y) mentioned above). Because of the generality of this programming-language perspective, we call this effect *collateral leakage*.

Our approach is information theoretic where we model secrets as probability distributions $\mathbb{D}\mathcal{X}$ over some secret space $\mathcal{X}$, and we assume that programs are mechanisms which can both update secrets and leak some information about them. Within this setting we study the broader phenomenon of collateral leakage where secrets might be distributed between several non-colluding agents, and where those secrets could be correlated.

We extend our recent work by using Hidden Markov Models (*HMM*'s) in a new way to handle collateral leakage. In particular we study how to analyse the system-wide impact of information leaks caused by program execution on some, but not all, of the secrets. These issues have been addressed partially in other work, but here we bring all these results together and take them further. In summary, we do the following:

- We review standard *HMM*'s and show how to view *HMM* matrices as mappings from correlations expressed as distributions in $\mathbb{D}\mathcal{X}^2$ to correlations $\mathbb{D}\mathcal{X}^2$, when the *HMM* is only able to update the second component in the product $\mathcal{X}^2$ (Sect. 3.2).
- We show how this unusual view of *HMM*'s –as mechanisms that update correlations– can be used to study the impact of information flow on correlated secrets, even when those secrets are not mentioned in particular program fragments (Sect. 4), and we provide methods to calculate exact and approximate leakages. Full proofs of these results can be found at [3].
- We illustrate some of our results on the analysis of a defence against side channels in cryptography (Sect. 5).

A particular novelty of this approach is "security refinement" which determines a partial order on *HMM*'s extending previous work [20] to *HMM*'s as correlation transformers. Refinement allows programs to be compared in a compositional manner: this does not seem possible with less general notions of leakage [21].

2   Motivation: Correlated Passwords

2.1   Changing a Password: Is it Only "Fresh", or Actually "Different"?

The example of Fig. 1 contrasts two users' approaches to updating their passwords; for simplicity each password is just one letter, chosen from {A, B, C}. User Lax may update to any of the three, uniformly at random, including his current one; but User Strict must *change* his password, again uniformly, now choosing from only two of course. Because the original password X was uniformly distributed (which we assume for simplicity), in both cases the distribution of its final value is uniform as well; but an important difference, as we will see, is that for Lax the final X is independent of the initial X, while for Strict it is correlated.

// Password X is initially uniformly distributed over $\mathcal{X} = \{A, B, C\}$.

"Lax" user		"Strict" user	
X:∈ [A,B,C]	*	X:∈ [X$^+$,X$^-$]	$
leak [X$^+$,X$^-$]	†	leak [X$^+$,X$^-$]	†

* [...] *is a uniform distribution over* {...}*; and* X:∈ *chooses* X *from it.*

$ X$^+$ *is the letter following* X *in* $\mathcal{X}$ *(wrapping around), and* X$^-$ *the preceding.*

† leak [...] *chooses a value from the distribution* [...] *and passes it to the adversary: she does not know however whether that value was* X$^+$ *or* X$^-$.

Fig. 1. Updating a password

In the second statement, at †, we confront (hostile) information flow: both users suffer an "over the shoulder" attack while logging in with their new password. We imagine that an observer hears a key-click and sees a key that is *not* being pressed: she thus learns one value that the new password definitely isn't.

Figure 1 illustrates our concerns in a very simple way: the secret (password) is updated, and it is its *final* value the adversary wants to capture (indeed she will not be using its *old* value to hack this account). And yet –as we will see– third party agents can be affected.

One reason that in Fig. 1 it's natural to focus on the final state is that our aim (in program semantics) is to integrate security "correctness" with (ordinary) functional correctness of programs, i.e. to treat the two within the same framework [20]; and since functional correctness (and correctness comparisons, i.e. refinement [22]) is determined wrt. the final values a program produces, we should do the same for security correctness. Indeed it is in both cases the concentration on final values that allows small state-modifying programs, whether secure or not, to be sequentially composed to make larger ones [18–20].

Now the example above was constructed so that the two programs have the same final distribution and the adversary has the same knowledge of it — in both cases she knows exactly one value that the password is not. So are these programs equivalent in terms of their functional- and information-flow behaviour?

Here is where we encounter our criterion. As closed systems with a single secret, the password stored in variable X, Lax/Strict are indeed equivalent programs when the initial distribution is uniform. But they are *not* equivalent if we consider correlations between X and some *other* variable not mentioned in either, but present in a larger system with secrets distributed amongst other users. For example, suppose our young user selected his password X to be "the same as Dad's" that is stored in variable Z. And suppose Mum knows he did so.

So Dad says "You'd better change your password, son. Making it the same as someone else's is not safe." But as luck would have it Mum is in the bedroom, later, when Son changes it, and sees one of the two values that it has not become. In that case son Lax would leak no information about Dad's password; but with Strict, Dad's password is twice as likely (1/2) to be what Mum saw as it is to be one of the other two values (1/4 each). (See (8) below for details.)

Can this simple, almost fanciful example be dismissed? We don't think so: the facts are indisputable, that in the Strict case Mum learns something about Dad's password but in the Lax case she does not: we return to this in Sect. 3.2; and we give a more elaborate example in Sect. 5. Have we invented this problem? No: it was recognised by Dalenius [9] and formalised by Dwork [11]. But (we believe) its impact has not been studied in respect of program refinement.

We stress the point that this phenomenon is truly remarkable if placed in the context of rigorous reasoning about programs generally. We have

$$(\text{var } X; \text{ Lax}) \text{ and } (\text{var } X; \text{ Strict}) \quad \text{are the same over uniform initial } X \quad (1)$$

but $(\text{var } Z; \text{ var } X := Z; \text{ Lax}) \qquad \text{are different over uniform initial } Z \quad (2)$
and $(\text{var } Z; \text{ var } X := Z; \text{ Strict})$

What kind of familiar program algebra would invalidate an equality (1) because of variables added (2) that are not referred to by either program? The semantics of Lax and of Strict *must* differ in (1) as well.

In our extended *HMM* model described next, we show how Lax and of Strict are indeed modelled differently by keeping track of how programs change the *correlation* between initial and final program state. (In this case Son's initial and final passwords.)

3   *HMM*'s: Generalising Channels for Secure Refinement

3.1   Systems with Distributed Secrets

In a system of distributed secrets different secrets are handled by different system commands, possibly by different system components. Our aim here is to study the impact those commands have on all system secrets, whether or not they are part of any particular command. There are two reasons why this is important. The first is related to the issue raised by Dalenius, that a rigorous analysis of security must consider the prospect of the mechanism being executed in an environment where other secrets can be impacted. The second is related to compositionality in program semantics — the semantics must include enough detail so that conclusions drawn from local analysis of program fragments in isolation will be consistent with any emergent behaviours when those fragments are executed in larger contexts.

In our use of *HMM*'s detailed below we concentrate on showing how to use an analysis of an *HMM* in a compositional way — i.e. the analysis not only informs us about the leaks and updates to the variables described in a particular *HMM* matrix, but allows us as well to draw conclusions about leaks of other correlated variables if we consider the *HMM* to be executed as part of a larger system.

Review of the Channel Model for Quantitative Information Flow. Traditional models of information flow use "channels" to model flows in so-called "mechanisms", i.e. stochastic matrices which describe the relationship between secrets of type $\mathcal{X}$ and observations of type $\mathcal{Y}$. We recall first the standard notions of information flow in this setting, which we then extend to *HMM*'s.

Given channel matrix C, the entry C_{xy} is the probability that y is observed given that the secret is x. Channel matrices are *stochastic* meaning that for each x, $\sum_{y:\mathcal{Y}} C_{xy} = 1$. We write $\alpha \rightarrow \beta$ for the type of stochastic matrices over $\alpha \times \beta$, thus C is of type $\mathcal{X} \rightarrow \mathcal{Y}$. A fundamental assumption is that the secret x, once set, never changes and the measurements of information flow that the channel model supports thus involve comparisons between the attacker's prior knowledge of the secret, and how that changes to posterior knowledge when observations $\mathcal{Y}$ are taken into account. The prior knowledge is captured by a probability distribution $\pi : \mathbb{D}\mathcal{X}$ which assigns a probability π_x to each possible value $x : \mathcal{X}$; posterior distributions emerge when π is combined with C and are calculated using Bayesian reasoning. For observation y and prior π, the posterior probability that the secret is x given observation y is $C_{xy} \times \pi_x / (\sum_{x':\mathcal{X}} C_{x'y} \times \pi_{x'})$. The *vulnerability* of a secret wrt. leaks can be assessed by measuring the extent to which the attacker can use the information leaked.

Notions of Vulnerability of Secrets and Leakage of Channels. Vulnerability is a generalisation of entropy (of distributions), no longer necessarily e.g. Shannon but now others more adapted for secure programming, and whose great variety allows fine-grained control of the significance of the information that might be leaked [2].

Given a state-space $\mathcal{X}$, vulnerability is induced by a *gain function* over that space, typically g of type $\mathbb{G}_w\mathcal{X} = \mathcal{W} \rightarrow \mathcal{X} \rightarrow \mathbb{R}$, for some space of *actions* $w : \mathcal{W}$. When $\mathcal{W}$ is obvious from context, or unimportant, we will omit it and write just $g : \mathbb{G}\mathcal{X}$. Given g and w (but not yet x) the function[1] $g.w$ is of type $\mathcal{X} \rightarrow \mathbb{R}$ and can thus be regarded as a random variable on $\mathcal{X}$. The range of $\mathcal{W}$ models a set of *actions* available to the attacker and the value $g.w.x$ represents his gain if he picks w and the secret's value turns out to be x. His optimal average gain, or *g-vulnerability* is then $V_g[\pi] = \max_{w \in \mathcal{W}} \sum_{x:\mathcal{X}} g.w.x \times \pi_x$.

A particularly simple example is $\mathcal{W} = \mathcal{X}$ with $g.w.x = (1$ if $w = x$ else $0)$ so that the adversary gains 1 if he guesses correctly and 0 otherwise: we call this particular gain-function g_{id}. A benefit of the more general $\mathcal{W}$'s is that they allow representation of many conventional entropy functions (including even Shannon), thus bringing them all within the same framework [21]. Given a g, prior π and a channel C we can model the *expected conditional g-vulnerability* as the maximal gain wrt. the channel C, or the average of the vulnerabilities of the posteriors:

$$V_g[\pi, C] := \sum_{y:\mathcal{Y}} \max_{w:\mathcal{W}} C_{xy} \times \pi_x \times g.w.x. \tag{3}$$

Inspired by mutual information, we can define more general notions of leakage by comparing the g-vulnerability of a prior with the expected conditional

---

[1] We write dot for function application, left associative, so that function g applied to argument w is $g.w$ and then $g.w.x$ is $(g.w)$ applied to x, that is using the Currying technique of functional programming.

vulnerability. The *multiplicative g-leakage* of C wrt prior π and gain function g is the ratio between the posterior and prior g-vulnerabilities:

$$\mathcal{L}_g(\pi, C) := \quad \log_2 V_g[\pi, C]/V_g[\pi]. \tag{4}$$

The *capacity* of a channel is the supremum of that leakage (4), but varying in its definition depending on whether the supremum is over either gain functions, or priors or both:

$$\mathcal{L}_\forall(\pi, C) := \sup_g \mathcal{L}_g(\pi, C), \quad \mathcal{L}_g(\forall, C) := \sup_\pi \mathcal{L}_g(\pi, C), \quad \mathcal{L}_\forall(\forall, C) := \sup_{\pi, g} \mathcal{L}_g(\pi, C).$$

Remarkably, it can be shown that $\mathcal{L}_\forall(\forall, C)$ equals $\mathcal{L}_{g_{id}}(\forall, C)$ ("min-capacity"): it is the most robust estimation of leakage, and can always be achieved for the uniform prior [1], making it straightforward to calculate. Moreover $\mathcal{L}_{g_{id}}(\forall, C)$ (also called $\mathcal{ML}(C)$) provides an upper bound for information leakage computed from the traditional Shannon entropy. Thus if $\mathcal{ML}(C)$ is no more than k then this means that no more than k bits are leaked by C for any prior. Capacities are useful because if they can be computed for a given channel C we are able to argue that the channel's leaks are insignificant if its calculated capacity is small.

3.2   *HMM's* Leak Information About Secrets *and* Update Them

The original model for *HMM*'s describes a two stage process acting on a secret in $\mathbb{D}\mathcal{X}$: first information about the secret is leaked, and then the value of the secret is updated. The first stage is equivalent to the action of a channel as described above, and the second stage is effected by a Markov transition. A Markov transition is also described by a matrix M (say) so that $M_{xx'}$ is the probability that initial state x will result in final state x'. An *HMM-step* then comprises a channel and a transition together, but acting independently on the initial state: we call C its channel and M its *markov* (lower case), and write $(C{:}M)$ of type $\mathcal{X} \twoheadrightarrow \mathcal{Y} {\times} \mathcal{X}$. Defined $(C{:}M)_{xyx'} = C_{xy} {\times} M_{xx'}$, it is a stochastic matrix with rows $\mathcal{X}$ and columns $\mathcal{Y} {\times} \mathcal{X}$. In this way *HMM*'s generalise both Markov processes and channels, and can therefore model a program that both leaks secrets and updates them. We shall, in particular, study how to use *HMM*'s when there are distributed secrets.

We begin by generalising *HMM* steps in order to model behaviour of programs consisting of multiple leak and assignment steps. We define sequential composition for *HMM*'s which summarises the overall information flow: in fact sequential composition is a natural operator if we are using them to model programs. Let $H^{1,2}$ of the same type $\mathcal{X} \twoheadrightarrow \mathcal{Y} {\times} \mathcal{X}$ be *HMM*'s. The composed type is the $\mathcal{X} \twoheadrightarrow \mathcal{Y}^2 {\times} \mathcal{X}$ that takes initial state x to final state x' via some intermediate state x'', leaking information (y^1, y^2) –as it goes– gradually into the set $\mathcal{Y}^2$. We define

$$(H^1; H^2)_{x(y^1 y^2)x'} = \sum_{x''} H^1_{xy^1 x''} {\times} H^2_{x'' y^2 x'}, \tag{5}$$

and note that it is again stochastic. Sequential compositions are strictly more general than the HMM-steps built directly from $(C{:}M)$ — that is, for some arbitrary composition (5) it does not necessarily correspond to a single step $(C{:}M)$ for some C and M. By keeping track of sequences of observations compositions of HMM-steps allow observers to accumulate multiple leaks over time and to draw conclusions based on their amalgamated knowledge.

Returning now to our example at Fig. 1 we illustrate how a program can be modelled as an HMM, by composing individual HMM steps. Recall the program snippet $\mathtt{X}{:}\in [\mathtt{X^+},\mathtt{X^-}]$; leak $[\mathtt{X^+},\mathtt{X^-}]$ where first $\mathtt{X}$ is updated and then something is leaked. The first statement $\mathtt{X}{:}\in [\mathtt{X^+},\mathtt{X^-}]$ corresponds this Markov matrix $\mathcal{X}{\rightarrow}\mathcal{X}$:

$$
M^{S1}: \quad
\begin{array}{c}
\\ A \\ B \\ C
\end{array}
\begin{array}{c}
A\ \ B\ \ C \\
\left(\begin{array}{ccc}
0 & 1/2 & 1/2 \\
1/2 & 0 & 1/2 \\
1/2 & 1/2 & 0
\end{array}\right)
\end{array}
$$

For Strict the output for each initial state is a uniform choice over anything *but* the input. As an HMM we write it $(I^c{:}M^{S1})$, where I^c is the identity channel that leaks nothing.

The second statement leak $[\mathtt{X^+},\mathtt{X^-}]$ corresponds to a channel matrix in $\mathcal{X}{\rightarrow}\mathcal{Y}$, where in fact $\mathcal{Y}{=}\mathcal{X}$ because the observables are of the same type as the state:[2]

$$
C^2: \quad
\begin{array}{c}
\\ A \\ B \\ C
\end{array}
\begin{array}{c}
\circ A\ \ \ \circ B\ \ \ \circ C \\
\left(\begin{array}{ccc}
0 & 1/2 & 1/2 \\
1/2 & 0 & 1/2 \\
1/2 & 1/2 & 0
\end{array}\right)
\end{array}
$$

This leaks uniformly any value not equal to the current state, and $\circ A$, $\circ B$, $\circ C$ denote the observations. We write it as $(C^2{:}I^m)$, where I^m is the identity Markov process that leaves all states unchanged.

For Strict the result is this HMM using (5) to form the composition $(I^c{:}M^{S1}); (C^2{:}I^m)$, we can write it as a single matrix $\mathcal{X}{\rightarrow}\mathcal{Y}{\times}\mathcal{X}$:

	$\circ A$			$\circ B$			$\circ C$		
	A	B	C	A	B	C	A	B	C
A	0	1/4	1/4	0	0	1/4	0	1/4	0
B	0	0	1/4	1/4	0	1/4	1/4	0	0
C	0	1/4	0	1/4	0	0	1/4	1/4	0

The labels $\circ A$, $\circ B$, $\circ C$ denote the observations corresponding to those from C^2. Notice that the rows are *not* identical, because the first HMM-step updates the state in a way dependent on its incoming value.

Observe that there is a great deal of information concerning the current and former values of $\mathtt{X}$: for example, if the secret was originally uniformly distributed over the three values, and if $\circ A$ is observed, then the probability that the initial state was A but is now B is $1/4$. Preserving this information about initial and final correlations in the semantics is precisely how we can analyse the effect that leaks about $\mathtt{X}$ has on other variables (such as $\mathtt{Z}$ in Fig. 1). We therefore consider HMM's to be transformers not of individual secrets, but rather of secret correlations in

---

[2] Although the matrices C^2 and M^{S1} look the same, they are describing different aspects of the system.

$\mathbb{D}\mathcal{X}^2$. When an *HMM* transforms a correlation, the first component remains unchanged, but the second is updated, as before, according to the *HMM*. Thus given a correlation between X of type $\mathcal{X}$ and some other secret X' (of the same type) the *HMM* now produces a joint distribution $\mathcal{X} \times \mathcal{Y} \times \mathcal{X}$ which describes the correlation between the (unchanged) X', the observations, *and* the updated X.

Definition 1. *Given an HMM H of type $\mathcal{X} \rightarrow \mathcal{Y} \times \mathcal{X}$, and a distribution $\Pi \in \mathbb{D}\mathcal{X}^2$, we write $\Pi\rangle H : \mathbb{D}\mathcal{X} \times \mathcal{Y} \times \mathcal{X}$ for the joint distribution defined:*

$$(\Pi\rangle H)_{x_0 y x} \quad := \quad \sum_{x':\mathcal{X}} \Pi_{x_0 x'} \times H_{x' y x}. \tag{6}$$

The probability that y is observed is $p_y := \sum_{x_0, x}(\Pi\rangle H)_{x_0 y x}$. Given that y is observed, the (posterior) probability that the correlation is now (x_0, x) is defined by: $(\Pi\rangle H)_{x_0 y x}/p_y$.

When Π^* is the correlation $\Pi^*_{(x_0, x)} = 1/3$ if and only if $x_0 = x$, then $(\Pi^*\rangle \mathsf{Strict})$ allows us to compute the chance that the correlation between initial and final values, given that A is observed: in that case the chance that initial state was A and the final is now B is $1/4$, but the chance that the final state is the same as the initial is 0.

Next, we extend the definition of refinement of abstract *HMM*'s in closed systems [18, 20] to take correlations into account.

Definition 2. *Let $H^1 : \mathcal{X} \rightarrow \mathcal{Y}^1 \times \mathcal{X}$ and $H^2 : \mathcal{X} \rightarrow \mathcal{Y}^2 \times \mathcal{X}$ be HMM's over base type $\mathcal{X}$ with observation types $\mathcal{Y}^1, \mathcal{Y}^2$ respectively. We say that $H^1 \sqsubseteq H^2$ if and only if there is a refinement matrix $R : \mathcal{Y}^1 \rightarrow \mathcal{Y}^2$ such that $H^1 \cdot R = H^2$, where $H^1 \cdot R := \sum_{y:\mathcal{Y}^1} H^1_{xy} \times R_y$.*[3]

A special case of a refinement matrix R is given by $y \mapsto y^*$ for fixed observation y^* — this removes all information flow in H so that $H \cdot R$ is maximal in the refinement order and therefore only records state updates. We write mkv.H for this maximal refinement of H.[4,5]

Definition 2 has an equivalent formulation in terms of gain functions: $H^1 \sqsubseteq H^2$ means that the gain for an attacker of H^1 will always be at least as high as a gain for an attacker observing H^2, because he can use the extra observations to improve his strategy. Note however that the attacker's gains are related to guessing the *correlation*. Given an *HMM* H and gain function g, we define

$$V_g[\Pi, H] \quad := \quad \sum_{y:\mathcal{Y}} \max_{w:\mathcal{W}} \sum_{x,x',x''} \Pi_{xx'} \times H_{x'yx''} \times g.w.(x, x''). \tag{7}$$

---

[3] We have overloaded matrix multiplication, to mean that the summation is always over the shared state in $M^1 \cdot M^2$.

[4] Notice that the exact value y^* is not important for refinement comparisons.

[5] Definition 2 defines a pre-order on *HMM*'s, but it can be made into a partial order on "abstract *HMM*'s", introduced elsewhere [21].

Theorem 1. *Let H^1, H^2 be HMM's. We have $H^1 \sqsubseteq H^2$ if and only if $V_g[\Pi, H^1] \geq V_g[\Pi, H^2]$, for all $g: \mathcal{W} \to \mathcal{X}^2 \to \mathbb{R}$, and $\Pi: \mathbb{D}\mathcal{X}^2$.*

If we use an initial correlation $\Pi_{(x,x')} = 1/3$ if and only if $x = x'$, we see that Lax $\not\sqsubseteq$ Strict since $V_{gcid}[\Pi, \text{Lax}] = 1/6$ whereas $V_{gcid}[\Pi, \text{Strict}] = 1/4$. Here *gcid* corresponds to *gid*, but where $\mathcal{W} = \mathcal{X}^2$. Similarly Strict $\not\sqsubseteq$ Lax since $V_{[AA]}[\Pi, \text{Lax}] = 1/9$ but $V_{[AA]}[\Pi, \text{Strict}] = 0$, where $[AA]$ is the gain function which gives 1 only for secret (correlation) (A, A), and 0 for everything else.

Crucially, refinement is compositional for sequential composition.

Lemma 1. *Let $H^1 \sqsubseteq H^2$, then $H^1; H \sqsubseteq H^2; H$ and $H; H^1 \sqsubseteq H; H^2$ for any HMM $H: \mathcal{X} \to \mathcal{Y} \times \mathcal{X}$.*

4   Reasoning About Distributed, Correlated Secrets

We return now to a system of distributed secrets described by $\mathcal{X}$ and $\mathcal{Z}$, and we study how to model information flow about $\mathcal{Z}$ when only $\mathcal{X}$ is updated by a program fragment. Given an *HMM* $H : \mathcal{X} \to \mathcal{Y} \times \mathcal{X}$ representing such a fragment, we can describe the effect that H has on some initial correlation $\Pi : \mathbb{D}(\mathcal{X} \times \mathcal{Z})$ between $\mathcal{X}$ and $\mathcal{Z}$ by computing the joint distribution $J: \mathbb{D}(\mathcal{Z} \times \mathcal{Y} \times \mathcal{X})$: $J_{zyx} := \sum_{x': \mathcal{X}} \Pi_{zx'} \times H_{x'yx}$. Moreover Theorem 1 implies that if $H \sqsubseteq H'$ then $V_g[\Pi, H^1] \geq V_g[\Pi, H^2]$, for $g: \mathcal{W} \times \mathcal{Z} \times \mathcal{X} \to \mathbb{R}$.

We show next that robust upper bounds for leakage $\mathcal{Z}$ follows from leakage about the initial state of $\mathcal{X}$.

Define $\overleftarrow{\Pi}$ to be the $\mathcal{Z}$-marginal of Π, i.e. $\overleftarrow{\Pi} = \sum_{x: \mathcal{X}} \Pi_{xz}$ and let matrix $\overrightarrow{\overleftarrow{\Pi}}$ in $\mathcal{Z} \to \mathcal{X}$ be given by $\overrightarrow{\overleftarrow{\Pi}}_{zx} = \Pi_{xz}/\overleftarrow{\Pi}_z$ if $\overleftarrow{\Pi}_z > 0$ and 0 otherwise. This factors Π into its marginal and a conditional, and indeed $\Pi_{xz} = \overleftarrow{\Pi}_z \times \overrightarrow{\overleftarrow{\Pi}}_{zx}$. Now the matrix multiplication $\overrightarrow{\overleftarrow{\Pi}} \cdot H$ gives an *HMM* of type $\mathcal{Z} \to \mathcal{Y} \times \mathcal{X}$. Since we are interested in the leakage about $\mathcal{Z}$ only we can define a channel on $\mathcal{Z}$ alone by forgetting the final value of $\mathcal{X}$. This gives us the "effective collateral channel".

Definition 3. *The* effective collateral channel *of H, written chn.H, is a stochastic matrix of type $\mathcal{X} \to \mathcal{Y}$ and defined simply by ignoring the final state: thus $(\text{chn}.H)_{xy} := \sum_{x'} H_{xyx'}$.*

Definition 4. *The* collateral leakage *resp.* capacity *of H wrt a prior $\Pi: \mathbb{D}(\mathcal{Z} \times \mathcal{X})$ is the collateral leakage resp. capacity of $\overrightarrow{\overleftarrow{\Pi}} \cdot \text{chn}.H$.*

Refinement of collateral channels and their corresponding *HMM*'s is consistent.

Lemma 2. *If $H^1 \sqsubseteq H^2$ then $V_g[\pi, \text{chn}.H^1] \geq V_g[\pi, \text{chn}.H^2]$ for $g: \mathcal{W} \times \mathcal{X} \to \mathbb{R}$ and $\pi: \mathbb{D}\mathcal{X}$.*

Proof. Define $\Pi^*_{xx'} := \pi_x$ if and only if $x = x'$. Observe now that $V_g[\pi, \text{chn}.H^1] = V_{g^*}[\Pi^*, H]$, where $g^*.w.x.x' = g.w.x.x$. The result now follows by Theorem 1.

Using Definition 3 on the HMM $(I^c{:}M^{S1}); (C^2{:}I^m)$ described above, we can calculate the effective collateral channel for the program Strict. It describes the information leak about the initial state of Son's password only.

$$\text{chn.Strict}: \quad \begin{array}{c} \circ A \ \circ B \ \circ C \\ \begin{array}{c} A \\ B \\ C \end{array} \begin{pmatrix} 1/2 & 1/4 & 1/4 \\ 1/4 & 1/2 & 1/4 \\ 1/4 & 1/4 & 1/2 \end{pmatrix} \end{array}$$

We see now clearly that Mum's best guess for Son's initial setting of his password is to guess the value she observes; she has now learned something about Dad's *current* password. (8)

The simplicity of Definitions 3, 4 conceals that it can be difficult in practice to calculate the collateral leakage of an HMM. One reason is that a model for initial state only is *not compositional* i.e. chn.$(H^1; H^2)$ cannot be calculated from just chn.H^1 and chn.H^2 alone. This implies that if H is expressed as a sequential composition of many smaller ones, e.g. if we have $H = H^1; H^2; \cdots ; H^N$, still the final states of the *intermediate* H's must be retained, not only to form the composition, but because the overall y observation from H comprises all the smaller observations $y^1 \cdots y^N$ with each y^{n+1} being determined by the final state $(x')^n$ of the H^n just before — we can abstract only at the very end.

In the special case however where each H is an HMM-step $(C^n{:}M^n)$, the calculation of the effective channel can be somewhat decomposed.

Lemma 3. *Let H be an HMM and $(C{:}M)$ an HMM-step. Then*

$$\begin{aligned} \text{chn.}\,(C{:}M) &= C \\ \text{chn.}\,((C{:}M); H) &= C \parallel (M{\cdot}\text{chn.}H) \end{aligned}$$

where in general $(C^1\Vert C^2)_{x,(y^1 y^2)} = C^1_{xy^1} \times C^2_{xy^2}$ is parallel composition of channels. The M cannot be discarded, since it affects the prior of the "tail" H of the sequential composition.

We see in the example above that we do not have to construct the full HMM, and then reduce it as we did at (8) but instead just perform the matrix multiplication of its components, so that chn.Strict $= M^{S1}{\cdot}C^2$. Even with Lemma 3, in general chn.H can be challenging to compute because its size (given by the number of columns in the stochastic matrix representation) grows exponentially with the number of single-step HMM's, in the definition of H, that have non-trivial channel portions. We give an example of such a calculation in Sect. 5 (fast exponentiation for cryptography).

On the other hand, if we want to compute only the collateral *capacity*, we can obtain at least an upper bound at considerably less cost, without the need to compute chn.H exactly. The following provides an upper bound for $\mathcal{L}_\forall(\forall, \text{chn.}H)$, and requires only linear resources.

Lemma 4. *For any H let CCap.H be defined*

$$\begin{aligned} \text{CCap.}\,(C{:}M) &= \mathcal{L}_\forall(\forall, C) && \text{if } H = (C{:}M) \\ \text{CCap.}\,((C{:}M); H') &= \mathcal{L}_\forall(\forall, C) + \min(\mathcal{L}_\forall(\forall, M), \text{CCap.}H') && \text{if } H = (C{:}M); H' \end{aligned}$$

Then $\mathcal{L}_\forall(\forall, \text{chn.}H) \le \text{CCap.}H$ with the stochastic matrix M treated as a channel.

In fact Lemma 4 provides a very robust estimate of the collateral capacity of an *HMM*, since it does not mention $\mathcal{Z}$ or the correlating Π. And it is the best possible general bound, achieving equality for some examples, e.g. Fig. 1: CCap for Strict is $\log(3/2)$, and for Lax it is $\log 1 = 0$, confirming that Strict leaks some information about correlated secrets whereas Lax leaks nothing. Both these values are equal to the calculated leakages in their given scenarios. It is also easy to calculate since for any channel we have from [1] that $\mathcal{L}_\forall(\forall, C) = \mathcal{L}_{g_{id}}(\Upsilon_\mathcal{X}, C)$, where $\Upsilon_\mathcal{X}$ is the uniform prior on $\mathcal{X}$.

Lemma 5. *Let $H, H': \mathcal{X} \rightarrow \mathcal{Y} \times \mathcal{X}$ be HMMs. CCap.$H = 0 \Rightarrow$ CCap.$(H'; H) =$ CCap.H'.*

Proof. From Theorem 4 the unfolding of the recursive definition for CCap.$(H'; H)$ will eventually yield a minimum between non-negative terms which include CCap.H. The result now follows, because this allows a simplification to CCap.H'.

In cases where we know the correlation Π (and thus $\mathcal{Z}$), we can compute the collateral capacity by identifying the optimising gain function in Definition 4.

Theorem 2. *Given H and $\Pi: \mathbb{D}(\mathcal{Z} \times \mathcal{X})$ with $\overleftarrow{\Pi}, \overrightarrow{\Pi}$ resp. the marginals of Π on $\mathcal{Z}, \mathcal{X}$; define conditional $\overrightarrow{\overrightarrow{\Pi}}$ as above. There exists $\hat{g}: \mathbb{G}_z\mathcal{Z}$ and $\hat{g}^\Pi: \mathbb{G}_z\mathcal{X}$ such that*

$$\mathcal{L}_\forall(\overleftarrow{\Pi}, \overrightarrow{\overrightarrow{\Pi}} \cdot chn.H) \quad = \quad \mathcal{L}_{\hat{g}}(\overleftarrow{\Pi}, \overrightarrow{\overrightarrow{\Pi}} \cdot chn.H) \quad = \quad \mathcal{L}_{\hat{g}^\Pi}(\overrightarrow{\Pi}, chn.H).$$

This shows that it is possible to construct the gain-function that maximizes the collateral capacity, and even allows its exact calculation. Moreover, it also shows that the collateral capacity of H wrt. $\mathcal{Z}$ can be understood as regular g-leakage of H wrt. the *initial* state of $\mathcal{X}$.

The next theorem is more general, and gives an upper bound over all possible correlations: it is determined by the extremal leakage of the initial prior $\pi: \mathbb{D}\mathcal{X}$, thus easy to calculate [1].

Theorem 3. *Given H and Π as above, $\Upsilon_\mathcal{X}$ is uniform on $\mathcal{X}$, then*

$$\mathcal{L}_\forall(\overleftarrow{\pi}, \overrightarrow{\overrightarrow{\Pi}} \cdot chn.H) \quad \leq \quad \mathcal{L}_{g_{id}}(\Upsilon_\mathcal{X}, chn.H), \qquad \text{where } \overleftarrow{\pi}, \overrightarrow{\overrightarrow{\Pi}} \text{ are as defined in Theorem 2.}$$

Note that when X,Z are completely correlated, i.e. when $\overrightarrow{\overrightarrow{\Pi}}$ and $\overleftarrow{\overleftarrow{\Pi}}$ are both the identity, the inequality in Theorem 3 becomes equality. Finally we note that the separation of information flow from state updates sometimes does simplify sequences of *HMM* steps, when either the chn.H or mkv.H contains no probabilistic updates, then the channel can be approximated by (chn.H : mkv.H). We provide details at [3].

5   Case Study: Side Channel Analysis

Keys for public-key cryptography are best if independent, but that is not to say that they necessarily are: recently [16] discovered an unexpected sharing of the prime numbers used to generate them. Although that discovery concerned public keys (and hence also the private keys), it makes the point that we cannot assume not-yet-discovered correlations do not exist between private keys alone. That motivates our example here, the collateral leakage from a fast-exponentiation algorithm that might compromise *someone else's* private key.

```
// B for base, the cleartext; E for exponent, the key: precondition is B,E >= 0,0 .
// P for power, the ciphertext.
P:= 1
while E!=0  // Invariant is P*(B^E) = b^e, where b,e are initial values of B,E .
    D:∈ [2,3,5]              // D for divisor; uniform choice from {2,3,5}.
    R:= E mod D;            // R for remainder.
    if R!=0 then P:= P*B^R fi // | Side-channel |: is E divisible exactly by D ?
    B:= B^D                 // D is small: assume no side-channel here.
    E:= E div D             // State update of E here. (No side-channel.)
end
// Now P=b^e and E=0: but what has an adversary learned about the initial e ?
```

Although our state comprises B,E,P,D,R we concentrate only on the secrecy of E. In particular, we are not trying to discover B or P in this case; and D,R are of no external significance afterwards anyway.

Fig. 2. Defence against side channel analysis in exponentiation, Exp(B,E)

Figure 2 implements fast exponentiation, with a random choice of divisor to defend against a side channel that leaks program flow (of a conditional) [24]. Since the program code is public, that leak is effectively of whether divisor D exactly divides the current value of E, which value is steadily decreased by the update at the end of each iteration: thus additional information is leaked every time. In the standard (and fastest) algorithm the divisor D is always 2, but that ultimately leaks E's initial value exactly, one bit (literally) on each iteration. The final value of E is always zero, of no significance; but its initial value represents collateral leakage about subsequent use of this same key (obviously), but also the use of other apparently unrelated keys elsewhere [16]. The obfuscating defence is to vary the choice of D unpredictably from one iteration to the next, choosing it secretly from some set $\mathcal{D}$, here $\{2, 3, 5\}$ although other options are possible. The divisor D itself is not leaked.

Since the output of Exp(B, E) of Fig. 2 is a function of its inputs, and as mentioned above its behaviour can be summarised by a single-step *HMM*, of the form (chn.Exp(B, E): "Output B^E"). Thus our task is to compute chn.Exp(B, E). We modelled the loop as a sequential composition of *HMM*-steps for a fixed number of iterations and used Lemma 3 to construct a channel that captures the leakage of information about the initial state of the program. We assumed that all variables are secret, and that every iteration leaks some information at the if statement "if R!= 0", revealing whether the (hidden) R at that point is 0 or not, and therefore possibly information about the other variables too. Interesting however, is that although this leak appears to be standard, the obfuscation provided by the choice of R means that overall the calculation of chn.Exp(B, E) shows that the information leak is highly probabilistic, the more randomness provided by $\mathcal{D}$. We provide detailed calculations in [3] of the construction of the *HMM*'s. Although our calculation is wrt. the uniform prior on E, and even though we do not know the extent of any correlation between this key E and others used elsewhere, by using the multiplicative capacity [1, Sect. VI.C], we can bound the maximum leakage about the initial value of E with the min-capacity of such a channel. Furthermore, by relying on Theorem 3 we can see that this min-capacity can also be used as a bound on the collateral leakage *with respect to any other secret that might be correlated to* E. For example, if E has 8 bits then a maximum of 3.51 of those bits of E's initial state will be leaked; moreover no more than of 3.51 of bits of *any other secret* Z in the system, that could be correlated to E will be leaked. This is therefore a very robust upper bound on the impact of system-wide leakage.

Size of E	$\mathcal{D}=\{2\}$	$\mathcal{D}=\{2,3\}$	$\mathcal{D}=\{2,3,5\}$
4 bits	4	2.80	2.22
5 bits	5	3.32	2.61
6 bits	6	3.83	2.92
7 bits	7	4.34	3.21
8 bits	8	4.88	3.51

Note that in the case $\mathcal{D}=\{2\}$ the whole secret E is leaked. As explained at end §??, that $\mathcal{L}_{g_{id}}$ gives the upper bound $\mathcal{L}_\forall$ for all vulnerabilities.

Fig. 3. Collateral leakage in bits wrt E for different $\mathcal{D}$'s, for *Prog* given at Fig. 2.

Our table Fig. 3 confirms that the larger the divisor set $\mathcal{D}$, the less effective is the side channel; and the protection is increased with more bits for E.

6   Related Work, Conclusions and Prospects

In this paper we have studied information leakage in systems where several secrets are distributed across a system. We have demonstrated how to use an *HMM* model to analyse *collateral leakage* in programs where some, but not all, secrets can change. We have shown that when correlations are present across the system, the impact of collateral leakages can still be predicted by local reasoning on program statements that process particular subsets of secrets. Our model represents the first step towards a general method for analysing leakages in distributed contexts.

Our work extends classical analyses of quantitative information flow which assume that secrets do not change. Early approaches to measuring leakage are based on determining a "change in uncertainty" of some "prior" value of the secret — although how to measure the uncertainty differs in each approach. For example Clark et al. [6] use Shannon entropy to estimate the number of bits being leaked; and Clarkson et al. [8] model a change in belief. The role of capacity when the prior is not known was stressed by Chatzikokolakis et al. [5]. Smith [23] demonstrated the importance of using measures which have some operational significance, and this idea was developed further by introducing the notion of g-leakage to express such significance in a very general way. The partial order used here on *HMM*'s is the same as the g-leakage order explored in by Alvim et al. [1], but it appeared also in even earlier work [18]. Unlike information flows that e.g. only use Shannon entropy, our $\sqsubseteq$ based on gain functions respects composition of programs, making it suitable for equality reasoning in algebras [20].

More recently Marzdiel et al. [17] analysed information flow of dynamic secrets, using a model based on probabilistic automata. This reflects a view that in general systems secrets are not necessarily static. In other work [20] we have explored a model based on the analysis of final states only, but it cannot be used to explore general correlations with fresh variables, as we do here.

Clark et al. [7] give techniques for static analysis of quantitative information flow based on Shannon entropy for a small while-language. Extended *HMM*'s for modelling side channels have been explored by Karlof and Wagner [14] and Green et al. [13] for e.g. key recovery. We note that in Sect. 5 our quantitative capacity bounds on side channels are valid even for collateral leakage, when the program is executed as a procedure call. In Sect. 5 we observe that there is a relationship between reducing the impact of a side channel and the performance of the algorithm. Others [10] have explored this trade-off between confidentiality and performance using a game theory setting.

Bordenabe and Smith [4] explore collateral leakage in the context of a static secrets, and our work can be seen as a generalisation of their approach when secrets can be updated. Kawamoto et al. [15] also study gain function leakage for complex systems made from components. Their focus is different to ours in that they consider how to decompose a channel in order to compute the leakage more easily; they do not deal with the general problem of collateral leakage.

References

1. Alvim, M.S., Chatzikokolakis, K., McIver, A., Morgan, C., Palamidessi, C., Smith, G.: Additive and multiplicative notions of leakage, and their capacities. In: CSF, pp. 308–322. IEEE (2014)
2. Alvim, M.S., Scedrov, A., Schneider, F.B.: When not all bits are equal: worth-based information flow. In: Abadi, M., Kremer, S. (eds.) POST 2014. LNCS, vol. 8414, pp. 120–139. Springer, Heidelberg (2014). doi:10.1007/978-3-642-54792-8_7
3. Bordenabe, N., McIver, A., Morgan, C., Rabehaja, T.: Compositional security and collateral leakage (2016). arXiv:1604.04983
4. Bordenabe, N.E., Smith, G.: Correlated secrets in quantitative information flow. In: IEEE 29th Computer Security Foundations Symposium, CSF 2016, Lisbon, Portugal, 27 June - 1 July 2016, pp. 93–104 (2016)
5. Chatzikokolakis, K., Palamidessi, C., Panangaden, P.: Anonymity protocols as noisy channels. Inf. Comput. **206**(2–4), 378–401 (2008)
6. Clark, D., Hunt, S., Malacaria, P.: Quantitative analysis of the leakage of confidential data. Electron. Notes Theoret. Comput. Sci. **59**(3), 238–251 (2001)
7. Clark, D., Hunt, S., Malacaria, P.: Quantified interference for a while language. Electron. Notes Theoret. Comput. Sci. **112**, 149–166 (2005)

8. Clarkson, M.R., Myers, A.C., Schneider, F.B.: Belief in information flow. In: 18th IEEE Computer Security Foundations Workshop, (CSFW-18 2005), 20–22 June 2005, Aix-en-Provence, France, pp. 31–45 (2005)

9. Dalenius, T.: Towards a methodology for statistical disclosure control. Statistik Tidskrift **15**, 429–444 (1977)

10. Doychev, G., Köpf, B.: Rational protection against timing attacks. In: IEEE 28th Computer Security Foundations Symposium, CSF 2015, Verona, Italy, 13–17 July 2015, pp. 526–536 (2015)

11. Dwork, C.: Differential privacy. In: Bugliesi, M., Preneel, B., Sassone, V., Wegener, I. (eds.) ICALP 2006. LNCS, vol. 4052, pp. 1–12. Springer, Heidelberg (2006). doi:10.1007/11787006_1

12. Espinoza, B., Smith, G.: Min-entropy as a resource. Inf. Comput. **226**, 57–75 (2013)

13. Green, P.J., Noad, R., Smart, N.P.: Further hidden Markov model cryptanalysis. In: Rao, J.R., Sunar, B. (eds.) CHES 2005. LNCS, vol. 3659, pp. 61–74. Springer, Heidelberg (2005). doi:10.1007/11545262_5

14. Karlof, C., Wagner, D.: Hidden Markov model cryptanalysis. In: Walter, C.D., Koç, Ç.K., Paar, C. (eds.) CHES 2003. LNCS, vol. 2779, pp. 17–34. Springer, Heidelberg (2003). doi:10.1007/978-3-540-45238-6_3

15. Kawamoto, Y., Chatzikokolakis, K., Palamidessi, C.: Compositionality results for quantitative information flow. In: Norman, G., Sanders, W. (eds.) QEST 2014. LNCS, vol. 8657, pp. 368–383. Springer, Cham (2014). doi:10.1007/978-3-319-10696-0_28

16. Lenstra, A.K., Hughes, J.P., Augier, M., Kleinjung, T., Wachter, C.: Ron was wrong, Whit is right. Technical report, EPFL IC LACAL, Station 14, CH-1015 Lausanne, Switzerland (2012)

17. Mardziel, P., Alvim, M.S., Hicks, M.W., Clarkson, M.R.: Quantifying information flow for dynamic secrets. In: 2014 IEEE Symposium on Security and Privacy, SP 2014, Berkeley, CA, USA, 18–21 May 2014, pp. 540–555 (2014)

18. McIver, A., Meinicke, L., Morgan, C.: Compositional closure for bayes risk in probabilistic noninterference. In: Abramsky, S., Gavoille, C., Kirchner, C., Meyer auf der Heide, F., Spirakis, P.G. (eds.) ICALP 2010. LNCS, vol. 6199, pp. 223–235. Springer, Heidelberg (2010). doi:10.1007/978-3-642-14162-1_19

19. McIver, A., Meinicke, L., Morgan, C.: Hidden-Markov program algebra with iteration. Math. Struct. Comput. Sci. **25**, 320–360 (2014)

20. McIver, A., Morgan, C., Rabehaja, T.: Abstract Hidden Markov Models: a monadic account of quantitative information flow. In: Proceedings of LICS 2015 (2015)

21. McIver, A., Morgan, C., Smith, G., Espinoza, B., Meinicke, L.: Abstract channels and their robust information-leakage ordering. In: Abadi, M., Kremer, S. (eds.) POST 2014. LNCS, vol. 8414, pp. 83–102. Springer, Heidelberg (2014). doi:10.1007/978-3-642-54792-8_5

22. Morgan, C.C.: Programming from Specifications, 2nd edn. Prentice-Hall, Upper Saddle River (1994). http://www.cs.ox.ac.uk/publications/books/PfS/

23. Smith, G.: On the foundations of quantitative information flow. In: Alfaro, L. (ed.) FoSSaCS 2009. LNCS, vol. 5504, pp. 288–302. Springer, Heidelberg (2009). doi:10.1007/978-3-642-00596-1_21

24. Walter, C.D.: MIST: an efficient, randomized exponentiation algorithm for resisting power analysis. In: Preneel, B. (ed.) CT-RSA 2002. LNCS, vol. 2271, pp. 53–66. Springer, Heidelberg (2002). doi:10.1007/3-540-45760-7_5

Classical Higher-Order Processes
(Short Paper)

Fabrizio Montesi[✉]

University of Southern Denmark, Odense, Denmark
fmontesi@imada.sdu.dk

Abstract. Classical Processes (CP) is a calculus where the proof theory of classical linear logic types processes à la π-calculus, building on a Curry-Howard correspondence between session types and linear propositions. We contribute to this research line by extending CP with process mobility, inspired by the Higher-Order π-calculus. The key to our calculus is that sequents are asymmetric: one side types sessions as in CP and the other types process variables, which can be instantiated with process values. The controlled interaction between the two sides ensures that process variables can be used at will, but always respecting the linear usage of sessions expected by the environment.

1 Introduction

Session types define protocols that discipline how concurrent processes may interact [10]. The type theory of sessions for (a variant of) the π-calculus [11] was found to be in a Curry-Howard correspondence with intuitionistic linear logic, where processes correspond to proofs, session types to propositions, and communication to cut elimination [4]. Properties that are normally obtained through additional machinery on top of session types, like deadlock-freedom, come for free from the properties of linear logic, like cut elimination. The correspondence was later revisited for classical linear logic, yielding the calculus of Classical Processes (CP) [19]. The design of CP is guided by the logic, making the correspondence stricter at the cost of deviating some more from the standard π-calculus.

The solidity of the correspondence between session types and linear logic propositions has been confirmed repeatedly. From the initial seminal idea, different extensions have been proposed in order to capture, among others, multiparty sessions [6,8], the paradigm of choreographic programming [7,12], behavioural polymorphism [2,3,6,19], and integrations with functional programming [17].

In this paper, we begin extending this research line towards a key generalisation of the π-calculus: the Higher-Order π-calculus (HOπ) [15]. HOπ supports process mobility: communicated values can be processes, which can then be run or re-transmitted by the receiver – by using *process variables* to refer to the received processes in its program. Our main contribution is the development of CHOP (Classical Higher-Order Processes), which extends CP to process mobility

A. Bouajjani and A. Silva (Eds.): FORTE 2017, LNCS 10321, pp. 171–178, 2017.
DOI: 10.1007/978-3-319-60225-7_12

in the same fashion as in HOπ. In CP, typing judgements are of the form $P \vdash \Delta$, read "process P uses its sessions according to Δ". If we ignore the P, this is the standard one-sided sequent form of classical linear logic. The key aspect of CHOP is that it extends the one-sided sequents used in CP to two-sided sequents, which are manipulated by combining the typing of linear channels of CP (on the right) with a new discipline that types process variables (on the left). So our typing judgements are now of the form $\Theta \vdash P :: \Delta$, read "process P uses its session endpoints according to Δ, possibly using some process variables according to Θ". Why the "possibly" for the usage of process variables? In HOπ, a process variable can be used by the receiving process at will (zero or more times). This expressivity is carried over to CHOP by interpreting process variables as non-linear resources. As a result, we get a hybrid type system that consists of two fragments. The first is inherited directly from CP, used to manipulate linear resources (session communications), while the second disciplines the usage of process variables.

2   Classical Higher-Order Processes (CHOP)

We introduce the calculus of Classical Higher-Order Processes (CHOP), which extends the latest version of the calculus of Classical Processes (CP) [6].

Types. There are two kinds of types in CHOP: session types, ranged over by A, B, C, D, and process types, ranged over by T. Session types are inherited directly from CP, and correspond to linear logic propositions. We range over atomic propositions in session types with X, Y. Process types are used to type the communication of processes and the use of process variables.

We start by giving the syntax of session types, in the following, along with a short explanation of their meanings.

$$
\begin{array}{llll}
A, B, C, D ::= & A \otimes B & \textit{(send A, proceed as B)} \quad | & A \,\bindnasrepma\, B & \textit{(receive A, proceed as B)} \\
| & A \oplus B & \textit{(select A or B)} \quad | & A \,\&\, B & \textit{(offer A or B)} \\
| & 0 & \textit{(unit for } \oplus) \quad | & \top & \textit{(unit for } \&) \\
| & 1 & \textit{(unit for } \otimes) \quad | & \bot & \textit{(unit for } \bindnasrepma) \\
| & ?A & \textit{(client request)} \quad | & !A & \textit{(server accept)} \\
| & \exists X.A & \textit{(existential)} \quad | & \forall X.A & \textit{(universal)} \\
| & X & \textit{(atomic propositions)} \quad | & X^{\bot} & \textit{(dual of atomic proposition)}
\end{array}
$$

CP uses the standard notion of duality from linear logic to check that types are compatible. Above, each type constructor on the left-hand side is dual to that used on the right-hand side. We write $A^{\bot}$ for the type dual to A, defined inductively in the standard way (cf. [19] for details). For example, $(A \otimes B)^{\bot} = A^{\bot} \bindnasrepma B^{\bot}$.

Each session in CP has two endpoints (one for each process in the session). Endpoints are ranged over by x, y, z. Session environments, ranged over by Γ, Δ, associate endpoints to session types: $\Gamma = \{x_1 : A_1, \ldots, x_n : A_n\}$. We make the standard assumption that Γ and Δ have distinct endpoints when writing Γ, Δ.

In CHOP, we can refer to processes that we receive at runtime (via process mobility) by using process variables, ranged over by p, q, r. A process environment Θ maps process variables to process types: $\Theta = \{p_1 : T_1, \ldots, p_n : T_n\}$. There is only one form for process types: $T :: = \Theta \to \Delta$. A process type assignment $p : \Theta \to \Delta$ reads "p implements Δ provided that the process variables in Θ are available". Note that Θ may be empty, meaning that p does not need to invoke other process variables to implement its session behaviour as specified in Δ.

Processes and Typing. Let P, Q, R range over processes, the program terms of CHOP. We explain terms together with their respective typing rules. A typing judgement $\Theta \vdash P::\Delta$ states that P implements the communication behaviour specified in Δ, possibly using the process variables specified in Θ.

We first briefly recap the terms and typing rules that we inherit from CP, displayed in Fig. 1. (We omit the rules for exponentials and quantifiers, for space reasons. Θ is carried in the same way as for the other rules.) The process terms in Fig. 1 are the same as in [6]. We adopt the same convention of having sent objects always in square brackets $[\ldots]$, and, dually, in an input operation the received variable is always bound in round parentheses $(\ldots)$. The endpoint name that we output in a send $x[y].(P \mid Q)$ and in a client request $?x[y].P$ is bound, as in the internal π-calculus [16]. (This will not be the case for process variables, as we are going to see shortly.) A forwarder term $x \to y^B$ forwards communications from x to y. The restriction term $(\boldsymbol{\nu} x^A y)(P \mid Q)$ connects two endpoints x and y to form a session, thus x and y are now able to communicate.

$$\frac{}{\Theta \vdash x \to y^A :: x : A^\perp, y : A} \text{ Axiom} \qquad \frac{\Theta \vdash P :: \Gamma, x : A \quad \Theta \vdash Q :: \Delta, y : A^\perp}{\Theta \vdash (\boldsymbol{\nu} x^A y)(P \mid Q) :: \Gamma, \Delta} \text{ Cut}$$

$$\frac{\Theta \vdash P :: \Gamma, y : A \quad \Theta \vdash Q :: \Delta, x : B}{\Theta \vdash x[y].(P \mid Q) :: \Gamma, \Delta, x : A \otimes B} \otimes \qquad \frac{\Theta \vdash P :: \Gamma, y : A, x : B}{\Theta \vdash x(y).P :: \Gamma, x : A \,\mathbin{\rotatebox[origin=c]{180}{\&}}\, B} \,\rotatebox[origin=c]{180}{\&}$$

$$\frac{\Theta \vdash P :: \Gamma, x : A}{\Theta \vdash x[\mathsf{inl}].P :: \Gamma, x : A \oplus B} \oplus_1 \qquad \frac{\Theta \vdash P :: \Gamma, x : B}{\Theta \vdash x[\mathsf{inr}].P :: \Gamma, x : A \oplus B} \oplus_2$$

$$\frac{\Theta \vdash P :: \Gamma, x : A \quad \Theta \vdash Q :: \Gamma, x : B}{\Theta \vdash x.\mathsf{case}(P, Q) :: \Gamma, x : A \,\&\, B} \,\&$$

$$\frac{}{\Theta \vdash x[] :: x : \mathbf{1}} \mathbf{1} \qquad \frac{\Theta \vdash P :: \Gamma}{\Theta \vdash x().P :: \Gamma, x : \perp} \perp \qquad \frac{}{\Theta \vdash x.\mathsf{case}() :: \Gamma, x : \top} \top$$

Fig. 1. CHOP, selected typing rules (Part 1, sessions).

We now move to the new terms and typing rules introduced in this work for the communication of process terms, given in Fig. 2.

Rule MP allows us to use process variables. It states that if we invoke a process variable p, typed with $\Theta \to \Delta$, and the process environment provides all

$$\frac{}{\Theta',\Theta,p:\Theta \to \Delta \vdash p :: \Delta} \text{ MP} \qquad \frac{\Theta' \vdash Q :: \Delta' \quad \Theta,q:\Theta' \to \Delta' \vdash P :: \Delta}{\Theta \vdash P[q\!:=\!Q] :: \Delta} \text{ CHOP}$$

$$\frac{\Theta \vdash P :: \Delta}{\Theta \vdash x[P] :: x:\Theta \to \Delta} \to\text{R} \qquad \frac{\Theta,p:T \vdash R :: \Delta}{\Theta \vdash x(p).R :: \Delta, x:T^{\perp}} \perp\text{R}$$

Fig. 2. CHOP, typing rules (Part 2, higher-order processes).

the process variables that p may in turn use according to Θ, then we obtain an implementation of the session behaviour specified by Δ.

There are two ways of instantiating a process variable. One is receiving a process – $x(p).R$ – which allows us to use p later on (Rule $^\perp$R). The other is by defining the body of a variable explicitly. We denote this as an *explicit substitution* (inspired by the $\lambda\sigma$-calculus [1]) $P[q\!:=\!Q]$, read "let q be Q in P". We formalise how substitutions are propagated and applied later on, in our semantics for CHOP. Rule CHOP allows us to substitute Q for q in P, provided that Q and q have compatible typing. If you think in terms of processes, CHOP stands for "Cut for Higher-Order Processes". If you think in terms of logic, CHOP stands for "Cut for Higher-Order Proofs". The idea is that a variable p stands for a "hole" in a proof, which has to be filled as expected by the type for p. This idea is also the reason for which Modus Ponens (MP), which is usually admissible, is given as an axiom. Since p represents a missing part of our proof, we do not know that its type is valid (i.e., that there exists a proof for some P such that $\Theta \vdash P::\Delta$). We delegate this responsibility to the term that instantiates p with a process.

Lastly, a term $x[P]$ sends P along x (recalling a weakened version of the right rule for implication, $\to R$).

As an example, consider the following cloud server implementation. It provides a choice between two options. In the first case, we expect the client to send us an application p to run, which requires a connection with an internally-provided database (DB). In the second case, we expect to receive both the application p and the database q that it needs to use, putting them in parallel. (Thus, we may decide to use DB or not.) We omit the types for restrictions.

$$\big(x.\text{case}(x(p).(\boldsymbol{\nu}zw)\,(p \mid d),\ x(y).x(p).y(q).(\boldsymbol{\nu}zw)\,(p \mid q))\big)[d\!:=\!DB]$$

Semantics. To give a semantics to CHOP, we follow the same approach as in [7,19]: we derive term reductions and equivalences from sound proof transformations.

Communications in CHOP are still defined by cut reductions over linear propositions, as in CP. The key insight that underlies our semantics for process mobility is that we interpret process types as atomic propositions in linear logic. That is, in the eyes of linear logic, a process type T is an atomic proposition (X). This twist allows us to integrate the expressivity of CP with our new rules: the dual of T is just $T^\perp$. (Different typing systems are often integrated this way.) A consequence is that we can cut a process output with a process input, as below.

$$\cfrac{\cfrac{\Theta \vdash P::\Delta}{\Theta \vdash x[P]::x : \Theta \to \Delta} \to\!\mathrm{R} \qquad \cfrac{\Theta, p : \Theta \to \Delta \vdash Q::\Gamma}{\Theta \vdash y(p).Q::\Gamma, y : (\Theta \to \Delta)^\perp} \perp \mathrm{R}}{\Theta \vdash (\nu x^{\Theta \to \Delta} y)\,(x[P] \mid y(p).Q)::\Gamma} \text{ Cut}$$

The above cut can always be eliminated by rewriting it into a (smaller) chop:

$$\cfrac{\Theta \vdash P::\Delta \qquad \Theta, p : \Theta \to \Delta \vdash Q::\Gamma}{\Theta \vdash Q[p\!:\!=\!P]::\Gamma} \text{ Chop}$$

By following this idea we can derive the key β-reductions ($\longrightarrow$) for process mobility in CHOP, given in the following. We also give some examples of equivalences ($\equiv$) that define how explicit substitutions are propagated.

$$(\nu x^{\Theta \to \Delta} y)\,(x[P] \mid y(p).Q) \longrightarrow Q[p\!:\!=\!P]$$

$$p[p\!:\!=\!P] \longrightarrow P$$

$$(x[y].(Q \mid R))[p\!:\!=\!P] \equiv x[y].(Q[p\!:\!=\!P] \mid R[p\!:\!=\!P]))$$

$$(x(y).Q)[p\!:\!=\!P] \equiv x(y).(Q[p\!:\!=\!P])$$

For space reasons, we do not include all reductions and conversions. Note that we inherit all the original ones from CP (cf. [6]), for example those given below.

$$(\nu x^A y)\,(w \to x^A \mid Q) \longrightarrow Q\{w/y\}$$

$$(\nu x^{A \otimes B} y)\,(x[u].(P \mid Q) \mid y(v).R) \longrightarrow (\nu u^A v)\,(P \mid (\nu x^B y)\,(Q \mid R))$$

$$(\nu x^1 y)\,(x[] \mid y().P) \longrightarrow P$$

$$(\nu x^{A \oplus B} y)\,(x[\mathsf{inl}].P \mid y.\mathsf{case}(Q, R)) \longrightarrow (\nu x^A y)\,(P \mid Q)$$

$$(\nu x^{A \oplus B} y)\,(x[\mathsf{inr}].P \mid y.\mathsf{case}(Q, R)) \longrightarrow (\nu x^B y)\,(P \mid R)$$

$$(\nu x^{\exists X.B} y)\,(x[A].P \mid y(X).Q) \longrightarrow (\nu x^{B\{A/X\}} y)\,(P \mid Q\{A/X\})$$

3   Related Work

Other session calculi include primitives for moving processes by relying on a functional layer [14,17]. Differently, CHOP is nearer to the original Higher-Order π-calculus (HOπ) [15], where the communicated values are processes, instead of functions (or values as intended in λ-calculus). A consequence is that the theory of CHOP is simpler. For example, our language of session types remains separate from process types, which are opaque atomic propositions in the session types of CHOP. As such, we do not require the additional asymmetric connectives in session types used in [17] for communicating processes ($\supset$ and $\wedge$). The "send a process and continue over channel x" primitive of [17] can be encoded in CHOP as $x[y].(y[P] \mid Q)$ (similarly for receive). However, the functional layer in [17] allows for a remarkably elegant integration of recursive types, which is missing in CHOP. A possible direction to recover this feature is the work presented in [18].

In previous works, the process values that can be sent usually have the form $\lambda \tilde{x}.P$, to enable reuse in contexts that use different channel names. In CHOP, this is not necessary since we can get the same result with the forwarder term inherited from CP, which the receiver of a process can use to manipulate its names. For example, suppose that p has a free session endpoint x that we want to rename to w. We can just write $(\boldsymbol{\nu} y^A x)\,(w \to y^A \mid p)$ to obtain the desired effect: whichever process will replace p will communicate over w instead of x. (It is straightforward to generalise this construction to arbitrarily many names, and to offer it through syntactic sugar, e.g., let $\tilde{x} = \tilde{w}$ in P.) This is often done in practice, e.g., in the setting of microservices [9]; for example, in the Jolie programming language, the constructs of aggregation and embedding are used to implement this pattern [13], but without any type safety guarantees on the usage of sessions as in CHOP.

In [6,8], the notion of duality found in linear logic is replaced with coherence, which allows many processes to participate in a same session. We leave an extension of CHOP to such multiparty sessions to future work.

The calculus of Linear Compositional Choreographies (LCC) [7] gives a propositions-as-types correspondence for Choreographic Programming [12] based on linear logic. CHOP may provide the basis for extending LCC with process mobility, potentially yielding the first higher-order choreography calculus.

4   Conclusions

We presented CHOP, an attempt at extending CP to higher-order process communication. This paper is meant as a first attempt at formulating its theory. The reductions supported by CHOP, derived by sound proof transformations, are promising in the sense that: they realise communication as expected; they preserve typing; and they point out how process substitutions may be implemented efficiently (applied only where they are needed), recalling explicit substitutions for the λ-calculus [1].

We have deliberately postponed presenting the metatheory for CHOP. The reason is that its main results require careful formulation, since differently from CP it makes sense for processes to get stuck (in CP, well-typed processes always progress). For example, the process $(\boldsymbol{\nu} x^{\perp \mathscr{8} 1} y)\,(x(y).y().x[] \mid p)$ cannot reduce because of the free process variable p. We conjecture that a progress result can be formulated by appropriately instantiating free process variables whenever they are needed, similarly to how catalyser processes can be used in standard session types to provide all missing communication endpoints [5].

We end this work with an open question on expressivity. One of the reasons for which the standard π-calculus does not include process mobility is that it can be simulated through channel mobility. Now that we have an extension of CP to process mobility, can we prove the same result for CHOP? This would provide additional confidence on the fact that the propositions-as-types correspondence between linear logic propositions and session types is on the right track.

Acknowledgements. The author thanks Luís Cruz-Filipe and the anonymous reviewers for their useful comments. This work was supported by the CRC project, grant no. DFF–4005-00304 from the Danish Council for Independent Research, and by the Open Data Framework project at the University of Southern Denmark.

References

1. Abadi, M., Cardelli, L., Curien, P.-L., Lévy, J.-J.: Explicit substitutions. J. Funct. Program. **1**(4), 375–416 (1991)
2. Caires, L., Pérez, J.A.: Multiparty session types within a canonical binary theory, and beyond. In: Albert, E., Lanese, I. (eds.) FORTE 2016. LNCS, vol. 9688, pp. 74–95. Springer, Cham (2016). doi:10.1007/978-3-319-39570-8_6
3. Caires, L., Pérez, J.A., Pfenning, F., Toninho, B.: Behavioral polymorphism and parametricity in session-based communication. In: Felleisen, M., Gardner, P. (eds.) ESOP 2013. LNCS, vol. 7792, pp. 330–349. Springer, Heidelberg (2013). doi:10.1007/978-3-642-37036-6_19
4. Caires, L., Pfenning, F., Toninho, B.: Linear logic propositions as session types. MSCS **26**(3), 367–423 (2016). Also: Caires and Pfenning, CONCUR, pages 222–236, 2010
5. Carbone, M., Dardha, O., Montesi, F.: Progress as compositional lock-freedom. In: Kühn, E., Pugliese, R. (eds.) COORDINATION 2014. LNCS, vol. 8459, pp. 49–64. Springer, Heidelberg (2014). doi:10.1007/978-3-662-43376-8_4
6. Carbone, M., Lindley, S., Montesi, F., Schürmann, C., Wadler, P.: Coherence generalises duality: a logical explanation of multiparty session types. In: CONCUR, LIPIcs, vol. 59, pp. 33:1–33:15 (2016)
7. Carbone, M., Montesi, F., Schürmann, C.: Choreographies, logically. Distributed Computing, pp. 1–17 (2017). Also: CONCUR, pages 47–62, 2014
8. Carbone, M., Montesi, F., Schürmann, C., Yoshida, N.: Multiparty session types as coherence proofs. Acta Inf. **54**(3), 243–269 (2017). Also: CONCUR, pp. 412–426, 2015
9. Dragoni, N., Giallorenzo, S., Lluch-Lafuente, A., Mazzara, M., Montesi, F., Mustafin, R., Safina, L.: Microservices: yesterday, today, and tomorrow. In: Present And Ulterior Software Engineering (PAUSE). Springer (2017, to appear). https://arxiv.org/abs/1606.04036
10. Honda, K., Vasconcelos, V., Kubo, M.: Language primitives and type disciplines for structured communication-based programming. In: ESOP, pp. 22–138 (1998)
11. Milner, R., Parrow, J., Walker, D.: A calculus of mobile processes, I. Inf. Comput. **100**(1), 1–40 (1992)
12. Montesi, F.: Choreographic programming. Ph.D. thesis, IT University of Copenhagen (2013). http://www.fabriziomontesi.com/files/choreographic_programming.pdf

13. Montesi, F., Guidi, C., Zavattaro, G.: Service-oriented programming with Jolie. In: Bouguettaya, A., Sheng, Q.Z., Daniel, F. (eds.) Web Services Foundations, pp. 81–107. Springer, Heidelberg (2014)
14. Mostrous, D., Yoshida, N.: Session typing and asynchronous subtyping for the higher-order π-calculus. Inf. Comput. **241**, 227–263 (2015)
15. Sangiorgi, D.: From π-calculus to higher-order π-calculus — and back. In: Gaudel, M.-C., Jouannaud, J.-P. (eds.) CAAP 1993. LNCS, vol. 668, pp. 151–166. Springer, Heidelberg (1993). doi:10.1007/3-540-56610-4_62
16. Sangiorgi, D.: Pi-calculus, internal mobility, and agent-passing calculi. TCS **167**(1&2), 235–274 (1996)
17. Toninho, B., Caires, L., Pfenning, F.: Higher-order processes, functions, and sessions: a monadic integration. In: Felleisen, M., Gardner, P. (eds.) ESOP 2013. LNCS, vol. 7792, pp. 350–369. Springer, Heidelberg (2013). doi:10.1007/978-3-642-37036-6_20
18. Toninho, B., Caires, L., Pfenning, F.: Corecursion and non-divergence in session-typed processes. In: Maffei, M., Tuosto, E. (eds.) TGC 2014. LNCS, vol. 8902, pp. 159–175. Springer, Heidelberg (2014). doi:10.1007/978-3-662-45917-1_11
19. Wadler, P.: Propositions as sessions. JFP **24**(2–3), 384–418 (2014). Also: ICFP, pp. 273–286 (2012)

Weak Nominal Modal Logic

Joachim Parrow[✉], Tjark Weber, Johannes Borgström,
and Lars-Henrik Eriksson

Department of Information Technology, Uppsala University, Uppsala, Sweden
joachim.parrow@it.uu.se

Abstract. Previous work on nominal transition systems explores strong
bisimulation and a general kind of Hennessy-Milner logic with infinite but
finitely supported conjunction, showing that it is remarkably expressive.
In the present paper we treat weak bisimulation and the corresponding
weak Hennessy-Milner logic, where there is a special unobservable action.
We prove that logical equivalence coincides with bisimilarity and explore
a few variants of the logic. In this way we get a general framework for
weak bisimulation and logic in which formalisms such as the pi-calculus
and its many variants can be uniformly represented.

1 Introduction

In many models of concurrent computation there is a fundamental distinction
between two kinds of actions: on one hand, those that are strictly internal
to a process, and thus cannot be observed by its environment; on the other
hand, those that represent an interaction with the environment and thus are
observable. The discriminatory power of the model must then be weak enough,
roughly speaking, that unobservables do not count. This idea emerged in the
early 1980s in a variety of concurrency models, for example in Milner's observation equivalence, Lamport's notion of stuttering, and the denotational models
of Hoare [6,19,20]. A good example is weak bisimulation in numerous process
calculi. Here the special action τ represents anything unobservable, and the
bisimulation game requires a simulating process to mimic actions with the same
observable content, i.e., it is allowed to have more or fewer τs. Similarly, the
so called weak modal logics cannot express formulas to test for the presence or
absence of τs.

In our earlier work [23] we develop a theory of nominal transition systems,
bisimulation, and modal logic, with the goal to be as general as possible and
subsume many models in the literature. The states of the transition systems
may be tested by state predicates from an arbitrary logic. Transitions between
states can take arbitrarily structured labels and also bind names (like in the
scope extrusions of the pi-calculus). Thus we can uniformly represent not only
the pi-calculus but also many of its high-level extensions. Our results include a
treatment of bisimulation and an adequate Hennessy-Milner logic (HML) where
logical equivalence coincides with bisimilarity. We make ample comparisons to

© IFIP International Federation for Information Processing 2017
Published by Springer International Publishing AG 2017. All Rights Reserved
A. Bouajjani and A. Silva (Eds.): FORTE 2017, LNCS 10321, pp. 179–193, 2017.
DOI: 10.1007/978-3-319-60225-7_13

other work to support our claim that their primitives can be encoded in our general framework. Main technical points include the use of nominal sets to represent how states, actions and predicates depend on names, and the use of finitely supported infinite conjunctions in the logic to represent a variety of quantifiers and fixpoints. Section 2 below recapitulates the necessary background. All of that work is of the so-called strong variety: all actions are counted as observable.

In this paper we extend our investigation to nominal transition systems where there is a special unobservable action τ. In Sect. 3 we define and explore the notion of weak bisimulation. In comparison to existing work in process algebra there are subtleties in the interplay of unobservable actions and state predicates. In Sect. 4 we introduce a weak HML and prove that its induced logical equivalence coincides with weak bisimulation. The logic is formulated as a sublogic of our earlier logic [23] and contains only formulas that do not distinguish between weakly bisimilar states. Again the main subtlety is in the interplay between state predicates and action modalities. The logic does not admit disjunctions of state predicates, and in Sect. 5 we prove that this does not affect the expressive power. In Sect. 6 we demonstrate that state predicates can be encoded as additional transitions: self loops labelled with the predicate. Section 7 describes how our results can apply to existing models of computation, Sect. 8 relates to existing work on weak modal logics, and in Sect. 9 we conclude with a summary of the main insights gained and prospects for further work.

Our main results in Sects. 3 and 4, including the adequacy of the weak logic, have been formalised in the interactive theorem prover Isabelle/HOL using the nominal datatype package. Our Isabelle theories, comprising approximately 1,300 lines of machine-readable definitions and proofs, are available from the Archive of Formal Proofs.[1] They extend an earlier formalisation [25] of nominal transition systems and our logic for strong bisimilarity, from which they re-use the definition of (strong) formulas.

2   Background

In this section we recapitulate the relevant definitions from our earlier work [23], to which we refer for more extensive explanations, examples, and relation to previous work on transition systems and Hennessy-Milner logics.

2.1   Nominal Sets

Nominal sets [24] is a general theory of objects that contain names, and in particular formulates the notion of alpha-equivalence when names can be bound. The reader need not know nominal set theory to follow this paper, but some key definitions will make it easier to appreciate our work, and we recapitulate them here.

---

[1] https://devel.isa-afp.org/entries/Modal_Logics_for_NTS.shtml.

We assume a countably infinite multi-sorted set of atomic identifiers or *names* $\mathcal{N}$ ranged over by $a, b, \ldots$. A *permutation* is a bijection on names that leaves all but finitely many names invariant. The singleton permutation that swaps names a and b and has no other effect is written $(a\,b)$, and the identity permutation, which swaps nothing, is written id. Permutations are ranged over by π, π'. The effect of applying a permutation π to an object X is written $\pi \cdot X$. Formally, the permutation action $\cdot$ can be any operation that satisfies id $\cdot X = X$ and $\pi \cdot (\pi' \cdot X) = (\pi \circ \pi') \cdot X$, but a reader may comfortably think of $\pi \cdot X$ as the object obtained by permuting all names in X according to π.

A set of names N *supports* an object X if for all π that leave all elements of N invariant it holds $\pi \cdot X = X$. In other words, if N supports X then names outside N do not matter to X. If a finite set supports X then there is a unique minimal set supporting X, called the *support* of X, written $\mathrm{supp}(X)$, intuitively consisting of exactly the names that matter to X. In general, the support of a set is not the same as the union of the support of its members. An example is the set of all names; the support of each element a is the set $\{a\}$, but the whole set has empty support since $\pi \cdot \mathcal{N} = \mathcal{N}$ for any permutation π.

We write $a\#X$, pronounced "a is fresh for X," for $a \notin \mathrm{supp}(X)$. The intuition is that if $a\#X$ then X does not depend on a in the sense that a can be replaced with any fresh name without affecting X. If A is a set of names we write $A\#X$ for $\forall a \in A\,.\,a\#X$.

A *nominal set* S is a set with a permutation action such that $X \in S$ implies $\pi \cdot X \in S$, and where each member $X \in S$ has finite support. A main point is that then each member has infinitely many fresh names available for alpha-conversion.

A set of names N supports a function f on a nominal set if for all π that leave all elements of N invariant it holds $\pi \cdot f(X) = f(\pi \cdot X)$, and similarly for relations and functions of higher arity. Thus we extend the notion of support to finitely supported functions and relations as the minimal finite support, and can derive general theorems such as $\mathrm{supp}(f(X)) \subseteq \mathrm{supp}(f) \cup \mathrm{supp}(X)$.

An object that has empty support is called *equivariant*. For instance, a unary function f is equivariant if $\pi \cdot f(X) = f(\pi \cdot X)$ for all π, X. The intuition is that an equivariant object does not treat any name special.

2.2   Nominal Transition Systems

Definition 1. *A nominal transition system is characterised by the following*

- STATES: *A nominal set of states ranged over by P, Q.*
- PRED: *A nominal set of state predicates ranged over by φ.*
- *An equivariant binary relation $\vdash$ on STATES and PRED. We write $P \vdash \varphi$ to mean that in state P the state predicate φ holds.*
- ACT: *A nominal set of actions ranged over by α.*
- *An equivariant function bn from ACT to finite sets of names, which for each α returns a subset of $\mathrm{supp}(\alpha)$, called the binding names.*

- *An equivariant transition relation* $\rightarrow$ *on states and residuals. A residual is a pair of action and state. For* $\rightarrow (P, (\alpha, P'))$ *we write* $P \xrightarrow{\alpha} P'$. *The transition relation must satisfy alpha-conversion of residuals: If* $a \in \mathrm{bn}(\alpha), b \# \alpha, P'$ *and* $P \xrightarrow{\alpha} P'$ *then also* $P \xrightarrow{(a\,b)\cdot\alpha} (a\,b) \cdot P'$.

In [23] we motivate and demonstrate many examples of nominal transition systems, including the pi-calculus and several extensions of it. Here states, actions and transitions are familiar, and the binding names correspond to the names in scope extrusions. State predicates represent what the environment can perceive of a state, for example equality tests of expressions, or connectivity between communication channels.

Definition 2. *A* bisimulation R *is a symmetric binary relation on states in a nominal transition system satisfying the following two criteria:* $R(P, Q)$ *implies*

1. Static implication: $P \vdash \varphi$ *implies* $Q \vdash \varphi$.
2. Simulation: *For all* α, P' *such that* $\mathrm{bn}(\alpha) \# Q$ *there exist* Q' *such that if* $P \xrightarrow{\alpha} P'$ *then* $Q \xrightarrow{\alpha} Q'$ *and* $R(P', Q')$.

We write $P \mathrel{\dot\sim} Q$ *to mean that there exists a bisimulation* R *such that* $R(P, Q)$.

Static implication and symmetry means that bisimilar states must satisfy the same state predicates. The simulation requirement is familiar from the pi-calculus.

2.3   Hennessy-Milner Logic

We define a Hennessy-Milner logic including infinitary conjunctions; as demonstrated in [23] this results in high expressiveness using a very compact formal definition. In order to avoid set-theoretic paradoxes we begin by fixing some infinite cardinal κ to bound the cardinality of conjunctions. We define the formulas, ranged over by $A, B, \ldots$, and the validity of a formula A in a state P, written $P \models A$, by induction as

Definition 3.

$$P \models \bigwedge_{i \in I} A_i \quad \text{if for all } i \in I \text{ it holds that } P \models A_i$$
$$P \models \neg A \qquad \text{if not } P \models A$$
$$P \models \varphi \qquad \text{if } P \vdash \varphi$$
$$P \models \langle \alpha \rangle A \quad \text{if there exists } P' \text{ such that } P \xrightarrow{\alpha} P' \text{ and } P' \models A$$

Support and name permutation are defined as usual (permutation distributes over all formula constructors). In $\bigwedge_{i \in I} A_i$ it is required that the indexing set I has bounded cardinality, by which we mean that $|I| < \kappa$. We assume that κ is sufficiently large; specifically, we require $\kappa > \aleph_0$ (so that we may form countable conjunctions) and $\kappa > |\mathrm{STATES}|$. It is also required that the set of conjuncts $\{A_i \mid i \in I\}$ has finite support; this is then the support of the conjunction. This is strictly weaker than requiring the set to be uniformly bounded, i.e., that there is a finite set of names supporting all members. Alpha-equivalent formulas are identified; the only binding construct is in $\langle\alpha\rangle A$ where $bn(\alpha)$ binds into A. In the last clause we assume that $\langle\alpha\rangle A$ is a representative of its alpha-equivalence class such that $bn(\alpha)\#P$.

We write $\top$ for the empty conjunction and $A_0 \wedge A_1$ for the binary conjunction $\bigwedge_{i\in\{0,1\}} A_i$. Bounded and finitely supported disjunction $\bigvee$ is defined in the usual way as the dual of conjunction. Universal and existential quantifiers are defined as conjunction and disjunction over the set of instances. In [23] we expand on the expressive power and relate to existing logics.

Definition 4. *Two states P and Q are* logically equivalent, *written $P \doteq Q$, if for all A it holds that $P \models A$ iff $Q \models A$.*

Theorem 1. *(Theorems 6 and 9 in [23])* $P \sim Q$ iff $P \doteq Q$.

The implication from left to right is by induction over formulas. The other direction is by contraposition: if not $P \sim Q$ then there is a distinguishing formula A such that $P \models A$ and not $Q \models A$.

3   Weak Bisimulation

The logics and bisimulations considered in [23] are of the strong variety, in the sense that all transitions are regarded as equally significant. In many models of concurrent computation there is a special action that is *unobservable* in the sense that in a bisimulation, and also in the definition of the action modalities, the presence of extra such transitions does not matter. This leads to notions of *weak* bisimulation and accompanying weak modal logics. For example, a process that has no transitions is weakly bisimilar to any process that has only unobservable transitions, and these satisfy the same weak modal logic formulas. We shall here introduce these ideas into the nominal transition systems, where the presence of state predicates requires some care in the definitions.

To cater for unobservable transitions assume a special action τ with empty support. The following definitions are standard:

Definition 5.

1. $P \Rightarrow P'$ *is defined by induction to mean $P = P'$ or $P \xrightarrow{\tau} \circ \Rightarrow P'$.*
2. $P \overset{\alpha}{\Rightarrow} P'$ *means $P \Rightarrow \circ \xrightarrow{\alpha} \circ \Rightarrow P'$.*
3. $P \overset{\hat{\alpha}}{\Rightarrow} P'$ *means $P \Rightarrow P'$ if $\alpha = \tau$ and $P \overset{\alpha}{\Rightarrow} P'$ otherwise.*

Intuitively $P \overset{\hat{\alpha}}{\Rightarrow} P'$ means that P can evolve to P' through transitions with the only observable content α. We call this a weak action α and it will be the basis for the semantics in this section.

The normal way to define weak bisimilarity is to weaken $Q \xrightarrow{\alpha} Q'$ to $Q \overset{\hat{\alpha}}{\Rightarrow} Q'$ in the simulation requirement. This results in the weak simulation criterion:

Definition 6. *A binary relation R on* STATES *is a* weak simulation *if $R(P,Q)$ implies that for all α, P' with $bn(\alpha)\#Q$ there exists Q' such that*

$$\text{if } P \xrightarrow{\alpha} P' \text{ then } Q \overset{\hat{\alpha}}{\Rightarrow} Q' \text{ and } R(P',Q')$$

However, just replacing the simulation requirement with weak simulation in Definition 2 will not suffice. The reason is that through the static implication criterion in Definition 2, an observer can still observe the state predicates directly, and thus distinguish between a state that satisfies φ and a state that does not but can silently evolve to another state that satisfies φ:

Example 1.

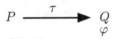

Certainly $\{(P,Q),(Q,Q)\}$ is a weak simulation according to Definition 6. But $P \nvdash \varphi$ and $Q \vdash \varphi$, thus they are in no static implication. We argue that if φ is the *only* state predicate (in particular, there is no predicate $\neg\varphi$), then the only test that an observer can apply is "if φ then ...," and here P and Q will behave the same; P can pass the test after an unobservable delay. Thus P and Q should be deemed weakly bisimilar, and static implication as in Definition 2 is not appropriate.

Therefore we need a weak counterpart of static implication where τ transitions are admitted before checking predicates, that is, if $P \vdash \varphi$ then $Q \Rightarrow Q' \vdash \varphi$. In other words, Q can unobservably evolve to a state that satisfies φ. However, this is not quite enough by itself. Consider the following example where $P \vdash \varphi_0, P \vdash \varphi_1, R \vdash \varphi_1$ and $Q \vdash \varphi_0$, with transitions $P \xrightarrow{\tau} R$ and $Q \xrightarrow{\tau} R$:

Example 2.

Here we do not want to regard P and Q as weakly bisimilar. They do have the same transitions and can satisfy the same predicates, possibly after a τ transition. But an observer of P can first determine that φ_1 holds, and then determine that φ_0 holds. This is not possible for Q: an observer who concludes φ_1 must already have evolved to R.

Similarly, consider the following example where the only difference between P and Q is that $P \vdash \varphi$ but not $Q \vdash \varphi$:

Example 3.

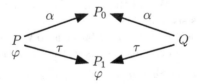

Again we do not want to regard P and Q as weakly bisimilar. Intuitively, an observer of Q that determines that φ holds must already be at P_1 and thus have preempted the possibility to do α, whereas for P, the predicate φ holds while retaining the possibility to do α. For instance, P in parallel with a process of kind "if φ then γ" can perform γ followed by α, but Q in parallel with the same cannot do that sequence.

In conclusion, the weak counterpart of static implication should allow the simulating state to proceed through unobservable actions to a state that *both* satisfies the same predicate *and* continues to bisimulate. This leads to the following:

Definition 7. *A binary relation R on states is a* weak static implication *if $R(P,Q)$ implies that for all φ there exists Q' such that*

$$\text{if } P \vdash \varphi \text{ then } Q \Rightarrow Q' \text{ and } Q' \vdash \varphi \text{ and } R(P,Q')$$

Definition 8. *A* weak bisimulation *is a symmetric binary relation on states satisfying both weak simulation and weak static implication. We write $P \approx Q$ to mean that there exists a weak bisimulation R such that $R(P,Q)$.*

In Example 1, $\{(P,Q),(Q,P),(Q,Q)\}$ is a weak bisimulation. In Examples 2 and 3, P and Q are not weakly bisimilar.

It is interesting to compare this with weak bisimilarities defined for psi-calculi [16]. A psi-calculus contains a construct of kind "if φ then ..." to test if a state predicate is true. These constructs may be nested; for instance, "if φ_0 then if φ_1 then ..." effectively tests if both φ_o and φ_1 are true simultaneously. If state predicates are closed under conjunction, Definition 8 coincides with the definition of simple weak bisimulation in [16]. In general, however, Definition 8 is less discriminating. Consider $P_0 \xrightarrow{\tau} P_1 \xrightarrow{\tau} P_0$ where for $i = 0, 1$: $P_i \vdash \varphi_i$. Compare it to Q with no transitions where both $Q \vdash \varphi_0$ and $Q \vdash \varphi_1$:

Example 4.

Here all of P_0, P_1 and Q are weakly bisimilar, unless the predicates are closed under conjunction, in which case the predicate $\varphi_0 \wedge \varphi_1$ distinguishes between them. In psi-calculi Q would not be simply weakly bisimilar to P_0 or P_1 for the same reason.

We proceed to establish some expected properties of weak bisimilarity.

Lemma 1. *If $P \approx Q$ and $P \xrightarrow{\hat{\alpha}} P'$ with $\mathrm{bn}(\alpha)\#Q$ then for some Q' it holds $P' \approx Q'$ and $Q \xrightarrow{\hat{\alpha}} Q'$.*

Proof. The proof has been formalised in Isabelle; it is by induction and case analysis according to Definition 5.

Lemma 2. $\approx$ *is an equivariant equivalence relation.*

Proof. The proofs of equivariance, reflexivity, symmetry, and transitivity have been formalised in Isabelle.

4   Weak Logic

We here define a Hennessy-Milner logic adequate for weak bisimilarity. Since weak bisimilarity identifies more states than strong bisimilarity, the logic needs to be correspondingly less expressive: it must not contain formulas that distinguish between weakly bisimilar states. Our approach is to keep the definition of formulas (Definition 3) and identify an adequate sublogic.

One main idea is to restrict the action modalities $\langle \alpha \rangle$ to occur only in accordance with the requirement of a weak bisimulation, thus checking for $\overset{\hat{\alpha}}{\Rightarrow}$ rather than for $\overset{\alpha}{\rightarrow}$. We therefore define the derived *weak action* modal operator $\langle\!\langle \alpha \rangle\!\rangle$ in the following way, where $\langle \tau \rangle^i A$ is defined to mean A if $i = 0$ and $\langle \tau \rangle \langle \tau \rangle^{i-1} A$ otherwise.

Definition 9 (Weak action modality).

$$\langle\!\langle \tau \rangle\!\rangle A = \bigvee_{i \in \omega} \langle \tau \rangle^i A \qquad\qquad \langle\!\langle \alpha \rangle\!\rangle A = \langle\!\langle \tau \rangle\!\rangle \langle \alpha \rangle \langle\!\langle \tau \rangle\!\rangle A \quad \text{for } \alpha \neq \tau$$

Note that in $\langle\!\langle \alpha \rangle\!\rangle A$ the names in $\mathrm{bn}(\alpha)$ bind into A. As usual we consider formulas up to alpha-conversion in the standard sense, i.e., to prove a property of a formula it is enough to prove a property of an alpha-variant. It is then straightforward to show (and formalise in Isabelle) that $\langle\!\langle \alpha \rangle\!\rangle A$ corresponds to the weak transitions used in the definition of weak bisimilarity:

Proposition 1. *Assume* $\mathrm{bn}(\alpha) \# P$. *Then*

$$P \models \langle\!\langle \alpha \rangle\!\rangle A \quad \textit{iff} \quad \exists P'. P \overset{\hat{\alpha}}{\Rightarrow} P' \textit{ and } P' \models A$$

In particular, for $\alpha = \tau$, we have that $\langle\!\langle \tau \rangle\!\rangle A$ holds iff A holds after zero or more τ transitions.

Thus a first step towards a weak sublogic is to replace $\langle \alpha \rangle$ by $\langle\!\langle \alpha \rangle\!\rangle$ in Definition 3. By itself this is not enough; that sublogic is still too expressive. For instance, the formula φ asserts that φ holds in a state; this holds for Q but not for P in Example 1, even though they are weakly bisimilar.

To disallow φ as a weak formula we require that state predicates only occur guarded by a weak action $\langle\!\langle \tau \rangle\!\rangle$. This solves part of the problem. In Example 1 we can no longer use φ as a formula, and the formula $\langle\!\langle \tau \rangle\!\rangle \varphi$ holds of both P and Q. Still, in Example 1 there would be the formula $\langle\!\langle \tau \rangle\!\rangle \neg \varphi$ which holds for P but not for Q, and in Example 4 the formula $\langle\!\langle \tau \rangle\!\rangle (\varphi_0 \wedge \varphi_1)$ holds for Q but not for P_0. Clearly a logic adequate for weak bisimulation cannot have such formulas. The more draconian restriction that state predicates occur *immediately* under $\langle\!\langle \tau \rangle\!\rangle$ would indeed disallow both $\langle\!\langle \tau \rangle\!\rangle \neg \varphi$ and $\langle\!\langle \tau \rangle\!\rangle (\varphi_0 \wedge \varphi_1)$ but would also disallow any formula distinguishing between P and Q in Examples 2 and 3.

A solution is to allow state predicates under $\langle\!\langle \tau \rangle\!\rangle$, and never directly under negation or in conjunction with another state predicate. The logic is:

Definition 10 (Weak formulas). *The set of* weak formulas *is the sublogic of Definition 3 given by*

$$A \quad ::= \quad \bigwedge_{i \in I} A_i \quad | \quad \neg A \quad | \quad \langle\!\langle \alpha \rangle\!\rangle A \quad | \quad \langle\!\langle \tau \rangle\!\rangle (A \wedge \varphi)$$

Note that since $P \overset{\hat{\alpha}}{\Rightarrow} \circ \Rightarrow P'$ holds iff $P \overset{\hat{\alpha}}{\Rightarrow} P'$ we have that $\langle\!\langle \alpha \rangle\!\rangle \langle\!\langle \tau \rangle\!\rangle A$ is logically equivalent to $\langle\!\langle \alpha \rangle\!\rangle A$. We thus abbreviate $\langle\!\langle \alpha \rangle\!\rangle \langle\!\langle \tau \rangle\!\rangle (A \wedge \varphi)$ to $\langle\!\langle \alpha \rangle\!\rangle (A \wedge \varphi)$. We also abbreviate $\langle\!\langle \alpha \rangle\!\rangle (\top \wedge \varphi)$ to $\langle\!\langle \alpha \rangle\!\rangle \varphi$.

Compared to Definition 3, the state predicates can now only occur in formulas of the form $\langle\!\langle \tau \rangle\!\rangle (A \wedge \varphi)$, i.e., under a weak action, and not under negation or conjunction with another predicate. For instance, in Example 1 above, neither φ nor $\langle\!\langle \tau \rangle\!\rangle \neg \varphi$ are weak formulas, and in fact there is no weak formula to distinguish between P and Q. Similarly, in Example 4 $\langle\!\langle \tau \rangle\!\rangle (\varphi_0 \wedge \varphi_1)$ is not a weak formula, and no weak formula distinguishes between Q and P_i.

To argue that the logic still is expressive enough to provide distinguishing formulas for states that are not weakly bisimilar, consider Example 2 and the formula $\langle\!\langle \tau \rangle\!\rangle ((\langle\!\langle \tau \rangle\!\rangle \varphi_0) \wedge \varphi_1)$ which holds for P but not for Q. Similarly, in Example 3 $\langle\!\langle \tau \rangle\!\rangle ((\langle\!\langle \alpha \rangle\!\rangle \top) \wedge \varphi)$ holds for P but not for Q.

Definition 11. *Two states P and Q are* weakly logically equivalent, *written $P \equiv Q$, if for all weak formulas A it holds that $P \models A$ iff $Q \models A$.*

Theorem 2. *If $P \approx Q$ then $P \equiv Q$.*

Proof. The proof has been formalised in Isabelle. It is by induction over weak formulas.

Theorem 3. *If $P \equiv Q$ then $P \approx Q$.*

Proof. The proof has been formalised in Isabelle. The idea is to prove that $\equiv$ is a bisimulation by contraposition: for any non-bisimilar pair of states there exists a distinguishing weak formula.

5   Disjunction Elimination

As defined in Sect. 2, disjunction is a derived logical operator, expressed through conjunction and negation. This is still true in the weak modal logic, but there is a twist in that neither general conjunctions nor negations may be applied to unguarded state predicates. The examples in Sect. 3 demonstrate why this restriction is necessary: negated or conjoined state predicates in formulas would mean that adequacy no longer holds. Interestingly, we can allow disjunctions of unguarded predicates while maintaining adequacy; in fact, adding disjunction would not increase the expressive power of the logic. In this section we demonstrate this.

The *extended* weak logic is as follows, where a simultaneous induction defines both extended weak formulas (ranged over by E) and preformulas (ranged over by B) corresponding to subformulas with unguarded state predicates.

Definition 12 (Extended weak formulas E and preformulas B).

$$E ::= \bigwedge_{i \in I} E_i \quad | \quad \neg E \quad | \quad \langle\!\langle \alpha \rangle\!\rangle E \quad | \quad \langle\!\langle \tau \rangle\!\rangle B$$

$$B ::= E \wedge B \quad | \quad \varphi \quad | \quad \bigvee_{i \in I} B_i$$

The last clause in the definition of preformulas is what distinguishes this logic from the logic in Definition 10. (Thus an extended weak formula is also an ordinary weak formula if it does not contain a disjunction of unguarded state predicates.) For instance, $\langle\!\langle \tau \rangle\!\rangle (\varphi_0 \vee \varphi_1)$ is an extended weak formula, as is

$$\langle\!\langle \tau \rangle\!\rangle (((\langle\!\langle \beta \rangle\!\rangle \top) \wedge \varphi_0) \vee ((\langle\!\langle \gamma \rangle\!\rangle \top) \wedge \varphi_1))$$

saying that it is possible to do a sequence of unobservable actions such that either continuing with β and satisfying φ_0 hold, or continuing with γ and satisfying φ_1 hold.

Theorem 4. *For any extended weak formula E there is an (ordinary) weak formula $\Delta(E)$ such that $E \doteq \Delta(E)$.*

Proof. The idea is to push disjunctions in preformulas to top level using the fact that (finite) conjunction distributes over disjunction, and then use the fact that the action modality distributes over disjunction to transform disjunctions of preformulas into disjunctions of weak formulas.

6   State Predicates as Actions

We shall here demonstrate that omitting state predicates does not really entail a loss of expressiveness: for any transition system $\mathbf{T}$ there is another transition system $\mathcal{S}(\mathbf{T})$ where state predicates are replaced by self-loops. In this section we formally define this transformation $\mathcal{S}$ and derive some of its properties. To formulate this idea we introduce the notation $\text{STATES}_\mathbf{T}$ to mean the states in the transition system $\mathbf{T}$, and similarly for actions, bn, transitions, bisimilarity, etc.

Definition 13. *The function $\mathcal{S}$ from transition systems to transition systems is defined as follows:*

- $\text{STATES}_{\mathcal{S}(\mathbf{T})} = \text{STATES}_\mathbf{T}$
- $\text{ACT}_{\mathcal{S}(\mathbf{T})} = \text{ACT}_\mathbf{T} \uplus \text{PRED}_\mathbf{T}$
- $\text{bn}_{\mathcal{S}(\mathbf{T})}(\alpha) = \text{bn}_\mathbf{T}(\alpha)$ *if* $\alpha \in \text{ACT}_\mathbf{T}$*;* $\text{bn}_{\mathcal{S}(\mathbf{T})}(\varphi) = \emptyset$ *if* $\varphi \in \text{PRED}_\mathbf{T}$
- $\text{PRED}_{\mathcal{S}(\mathbf{T})} = \vdash_{\mathcal{S}(\mathbf{T})} = \emptyset$
- $P \xrightarrow{\alpha}_{\mathcal{S}(\mathbf{T})} P'$ *if* $P \xrightarrow{\alpha}_\mathbf{T} P'$ *(for* $\alpha \in \text{ACT}_\mathbf{T}$*);* $P \xrightarrow{\varphi}_{\mathcal{S}(\mathbf{T})} P$ *if* $P \vdash_\mathbf{T} \varphi$ *(for* $\varphi \in \text{PRED}_\mathbf{T}$*)*

It is easy to see that if $\mathbf{T}$ is a transition system then so is $\mathcal{S}(\mathbf{T})$. In particular equivariance of $\rightarrow_{\mathcal{S}(\mathbf{T})}$ follows from equivariance of $\rightarrow_\mathbf{T}$ and $\vdash_\mathbf{T}$ and the fact that the union of equivariant relations is equivariant.

Theorem 5. *If $P \approx_{\mathbf{T}} Q$ then $P \approx_{\mathcal{S}(\mathbf{T})} Q$.*

Proof. We prove that $\approx_{\mathbf{T}}$ is a weak $\mathcal{S}(\mathbf{T})$-bisimulation.

Theorem 6. *If $P \approx_{\mathcal{S}(\mathbf{T})} Q$ then $P \approx_{\mathbf{T}} Q$.*

Proof. We prove that $\approx_{\mathcal{S}(\mathbf{T})}$ is a weak $\mathbf{T}$-bisimulation. It needs a lemma that if $P \Rightarrow Q \Rightarrow R$ and $P \approx R$ then $Q \approx R$.

A corresponding transformation of weak formulas turns state predicates into actions in the following way.

Definition 14. *The partial function $\mathcal{S}$ from weak formulas on the transition system $\mathbf{T}$ to weak formulas on the transition system $\mathcal{S}(\mathbf{T})$ is defined by*

$$\mathcal{S}(\langle\!\langle \tau \rangle\!\rangle ((\langle\!\langle \tau \rangle\!\rangle A) \wedge \varphi)) = \langle\!\langle \varphi \rangle\!\rangle \mathcal{S}(A)$$

and is homomorphic on the first three cases in Definition 10.

$\mathcal{S}$ is not total since a formula $\langle\!\langle \tau \rangle\!\rangle (A \wedge \varphi)$ is in its domain only when $A = \langle\!\langle \tau \rangle\!\rangle A'$ for some A'. It is easy to see that $\mathcal{S}$ is injective and surjective, i.e., every weak formula A on $\mathcal{S}(\mathbf{T})$ has a unique formula B on $\mathbf{T}$ such that $\mathcal{S}(B) = A$. We write $\mathcal{S}^{-1}$ for the inverse of $\mathcal{S}$. Thus

$$\mathcal{S}^{-1}(\langle\!\langle \varphi \rangle\!\rangle A) = \langle\!\langle \tau \rangle\!\rangle ((\langle\!\langle \tau \rangle\!\rangle \mathcal{S}^{-1}(A)) \wedge \varphi)$$

and $\mathcal{S}^{-1}$ is homomorphic on all other operators.

Theorem 7. $P \models_{\mathcal{S}(\mathbf{T})} A$ *iff* $P \models_{\mathbf{T}} \mathcal{S}^{-1}(A)$.

Proof. By induction over weak formulas on $\mathcal{S}(\mathbf{T})$.

An interesting consequence is that to express the distinguishing formulas guaranteed by Theorem 3, it is enough to consider formulas in $\mathrm{dom}(\mathcal{S})$, i.e., in the last clause of Definition 10, it is enough to consider $A = \langle\!\langle \tau \rangle\!\rangle A'$. The reason is that if $P \not\approx_{\mathbf{T}} Q$ then by Theorem 6 also $P \not\approx_{\mathcal{S}(\mathbf{T})} Q$, which by Theorem 3 means there is a distinguishing formula B for P and Q in $\mathcal{S}(\mathbf{T})$, which by Theorem 7 means that $\mathcal{S}^{-1}(B)$ is a distinguishing formula in $\mathbf{T}$.

Finally, consider the apparently more appealing definition of $\mathcal{S}$ by

$$\mathcal{S}(\langle\!\langle \tau \rangle\!\rangle (A \wedge \varphi)) = \langle\!\langle \varphi \rangle\!\rangle \mathcal{S}(A)$$

Here $\mathcal{S}$ is total and a bijection, but with this definition, Theorem 7 fails. A counterexample is $A = \neg \langle\!\langle \alpha \rangle\!\rangle \top$, $P \vdash_{\mathbf{T}} \varphi$ with $P \xrightarrow{\tau}_{\mathbf{T}} Q$ and $P \xrightarrow{\alpha}_{\mathbf{T}} Q$ for some $\alpha \neq \tau$, where Q has no outgoing transitions, cf. the diagrams below:

Since $P \xRightarrow{\varphi}_{\mathcal{S}(\mathbf{T})} Q$ and Q has no $\langle\!\langle \alpha \rangle\!\rangle$ action, we have that

$$P \models_{\mathcal{S}(\mathbf{T})} \langle\!\langle \varphi \rangle\!\rangle \neg \langle\!\langle \alpha \rangle\!\rangle \top$$

The only state that satisfies φ also has an $\langle\!\langle \alpha \rangle\!\rangle$ action, thus it does *not* hold that

$$P \models_{\mathbf{T}} \langle\!\langle \tau \rangle\!\rangle ((\neg \langle\!\langle \alpha \rangle\!\rangle \top) \wedge \varphi)$$

7 Applications

In our earlier work [23] we outlined how several advanced process algebras can be given a semantics in terms of nominal transition systems. For all of these the present paper thus defines weak bisimulation, a weak HML, and an adequacy theorem. We here comment briefly on some of them.

The pi-calculus already has several notions of weak bisimulation, and Definition 8 corresponds to the early weak bisimulation. In the pi-calculus there are no state predicates, thus the weak static implication is unimportant. There is an HML adequate for strong bisimulation [22] but we are not aware of a weak HML. Our result here contributes a weak HML adequate for early weak bisimulation.

The applied pi-calculus [1] comes equipped with a labelled transition system and a notion of weak labelled bisimulation. States contain a record of emitted messages; this record has a domain and can be used to equate open terms M and N modulo some rewrite system. The definition of bisimulation requires bisimilar processes to have the same domain and equate the same open terms, i.e., to be strongly statically equivalent. In order to model this strong static equivalence in our weak logic, we add state predicates "$x \in$ dom" and "$M \equiv N$" to the labelled transition system. Since these are invariant under silent transitions, weak and strong static implication coincide, and our weak HML is adequate for Abadi and Fournet's early weak labelled bisimilarity.

The spi-calculus [2] has a formulation as an environment-sensitive labelled transition system [4] equipped with state formulae ϕ. As above, adding state predicates "$x \in$ dom" to this labelled transition system makes our weak HML adequate with respect to Boreale's weak bisimilarity.

Our earlier work also describes how to make nominal transition systems of multiple-labelled transition systems [11], the explicit fusion calculus [26], the concurrent constraint pi-calculus [7], and psi-calculi [16]. These calculi can become interesting applications of our ideas since they have actions with binders and non-trivial state predicates. Each of them has a special unobservable action, but until now only psi-calculi have a notion of weak labelled bisimulation (as remarked in Sect. 3), and none have a weak HML. Through this paper they all gain both bisimulation and logic, although more work is needed to establish how compatible the bisimulation equivalence is with their respective syntactic constructs. A complication with all but the multiple-labelled systems is that the natural formulation of bisimulation makes use of substitutive effects (or in psi-calculi, the similar assertion extensions) which are bisimulation requirements on neither predicates nor actions. In order to map them into our framework these would need to be cast as actions. This could be an interesting area of further research.

8 Related Work

The first published HML is by Hennessy and Milner (1980–1985) [13,14,21]. They work with image-finite CCS processes, where finite (binary) conjunction suffices for adequacy, and define both strong and weak versions of the logic. Milner et al. (1993) [22] give a strong HML for the pi-calculus.

Kozen's modal μ-calculus (1983) [18] subsumes several other weak temporal logics including CTL* (Cranen et al. 2011) [9], and can encode weak transitions using least fixed points. Dam (1996) [10] gives a modal μ-calculus for the pi-calculus, treating bound names using abstractions and concretions, and provides a model checking algorithm. Bradford and Stevens (1999) [5] give a generic framework for parameterising the μ-calculus on data environments, state predicates, and action expressions. The logic defined in the present paper can encode the weakest fixpoint operator of μ-calculi by a disjunction of its finite unrollings, in the same way as the strong version of our logic [23].

There are several weak HMLs for variants of the pi-calculus. Hüttel and Pedersen (2007) [15] define a weak HML for an applied pi-calculus with a subterm-convergent rewrite system augmented with test rules. Koutavas and Hennessey (2012) [17] give a weak HML for a higher-order pi-calculus with both higher-order and first-order communication using an environment-sensitive LTS. The conjunction operator of the logic is infinite, without an explicit bound on its cardinality. Without such a bound the set of formulas is not well-defined: let $\mathcal{F}$ be the set of all formulas, and consider the subset of formulas $\mathcal{S} := \{\bigwedge_{A \in I} A \mid I \subseteq \mathcal{F}\}$. By Cantor's Theorem $|\mathcal{S}| > |\mathcal{F}|$, which is a contradiction. Xu and Long (2015) [27] define a weak HML with countable conjunction for a purely higher-order pi-calculus. The adequacy proof uses stratification.

There are several extensions of HML with spatial modalities. The one most closely related to our logic is by Berger et al. (2008) [3]. They define an HML with both strong and weak action modalities, fixpoints, spatial conjunction and adjunction, and a scope extrusion modality, to study a typed value-passing pi-calculus with selection and recursion. The logic has three (may, must, and mixed) proof systems that are sound and relatively complete.

9   Conclusion

Nominal transition systems include both labelled transitions and state predicates, and can therefore accommodate a wide variety of formalisms. We have defined weak bisimulation and a corresponding weak modal logic on nominal transition systems, and proved the adequacy result: logical equivalence coincides with weak bisimilarity. The use of finitely supported infinite conjunctions is critical for this result.

A key insight is the notion of weak static implication: to bisimulate a state satisfying a state predicate it must be possible to take zero or more unobservable transitions to reach a state that *both* satisfies the predicate *and* continues to bisimulate. Another important conclusion is that in the logic, state predicates must be guarded by a weak action and cannot directly be combined conjunctively or negated. They may be combined disjunctively, but doing so does not increase expressiveness, since the action modality distributes over disjunction.

Many formalisms, among them most process algebras, feature labelled transitions but no state predicates. It is a folklore fact that this entails no loss of expressiveness. Here we formulate this as a theorem, showing that checking a predicate corresponds to executing a transition leading back to the same state. Formally this is done through a transformation that replaces predicates with loops, and showing that weak bisimilarity is precisely preserved. We also show how the so obtained weak modal logic correlates with the original one.

Nominal transition systems constitute a possible semantics for many formalisms, and an interesting idea for further work is to explore operators on them. For instance, a parallel composition operator would enable closer relations to existing process algebras. There are many different ways to approach this, and to gain general results it would be interesting to define classes of operators, for example through general formats, and explore their properties. There is a huge literature on operator formats for process algebras, of which a few are on nominal process algebras [8,12], but as we understand it none yet treat nominal transition systems in their full generality.

References

1. Abadi, M., Fournet, C.: Mobile values, new names, and secure communication. In: Proceedings of POPL 2001, pp. 104–115. ACM (2001)
2. Abadi, M., Gordon, A.D.: A calculus for cryptographic protocols: the spi calculus. Inf. Comput. **148**(1), 1–70 (1999)
3. Berger, M., Honda, K., Yoshida, N.: Completeness and logical full abstraction in modal logics for typed mobile processes. In: Aceto, L., Damgård, I., Goldberg, L.A., Halldórsson, M.M., Ingólfsdóttir, A., Walukiewicz, I. (eds.) ICALP 2008. LNCS, vol. 5126, pp. 99–111. Springer, Heidelberg (2008). doi:10.1007/978-3-540-70583-3_9
4. Boreale, M., De Nicola, R., Pugliese, R.: Proof techniques for cryptographic processes. SIAM J. Comput. **31**(3), 947–986 (2001)
5. Bradfield, J.C., Stevens, P.: Observational mu-calculus. Technical report RS-99-5, BRICS (1999)
6. Brookes, S.D., Hoare, C.A.R., Roscoe, A.W.: A theory of communicating sequential processes. J. ACM **31**(3), 560–599 (1984)
7. Buscemi, M.G., Montanari, U.: CC-Pi: a constraint-based language for specifying service level agreements. In: Nicola, R. (ed.) ESOP 2007. LNCS, vol. 4421, pp. 18–32. Springer, Heidelberg (2007). doi:10.1007/978-3-540-71316-6_3
8. Cimini, M., Mousavi, M.R., Reniers, M.A., Gabbay, M.J.: Nominal SOS. ENTCS **286**, 103–116 (2012)
9. Cranen, S., Groote, J.F., Reniers, M.: A linear translation from CTL* to the first-order modal μ-calculus. Theoret. Comput. Sci. **412**(28), 3129–3139 (2011)
10. Dam, M.: Model checking mobile processes. Inf. Comput. **129**(1), 35–51 (1996)
11. De Nicola, R., Loreti, M.: Multiple-labelled transition systems for nominal calculi and their logics. Math. Struct. Comput. Sci. **18**(1), 107–143 (2008)
12. Fiore, M., Staton, S.: A congruence rule format for name-passing process calculi. Inf. Comput. **207**(2), 209–236 (2009)
13. Hennessy, M., Milner, R.: On observing nondeterminism and concurrency. In: Bakker, J., Leeuwen, J. (eds.) ICALP 1980. LNCS, vol. 85, pp. 299–309. Springer, Heidelberg (1980). doi:10.1007/3-540-10003-2_79
14. Hennessy, M., Milner, R.: Algebraic laws for nondeterminism and concurrency. J. ACM **32**(1), 137–161 (1985)

15. Hüttel, H., Pedersen, M.D.: A logical characterisation of static equivalence. ENTCS **173**, 139–157 (2007). Proceedings of MFPS XXIII
16. Johansson, M., Bengtson, J., Parrow, J., Victor, B.: Weak equivalences in psi-calculi. In: Proceedings of LICS 2010, pp. 322–331 (2010)
17. Koutavas, V., Hennessy, M.: First-order reasoning for higher-order concurrency. Comput. Lang. Syst. Struct. **38**(3), 242–277 (2012)
18. Kozen, D.: Results on the propositional μ-calculus. Theoret. Comput. Sci. **27**(3), 333–354 (1983)
19. Lamport, L.: What good is temporal logic? In: IFIP Congress, pp. 657–668 (1983)
20. Milner, R.: A Calculus of Communicating Systems. LNCS, vol. 92. Springer, Heidelberg (1980). doi:10.1007/3-540-10235-3
21. Milner, R.: A modal characterisation of observable machine-behaviour. In: Astesiano, E., Böhm, C. (eds.) CAAP 1981. LNCS, vol. 112, pp. 25–34. Springer, Heidelberg (1981). doi:10.1007/3-540-10828-9_52
22. Milner, R., Parrow, J., Walker, D.: Modal logics for mobile processes. Theoret. Comput. Sci. **114**(1), 149–171 (1993)
23. Parrow, J., Borgström, J., Eriksson, L.-H., Gutkovas, R., Weber, T.: Modal logics for nominal transition systems. In: Proceedings of CONCUR 2015. LIPIcs, vol. 42, pp. 198–211. Schloss Dagstuhl - Leibniz-Zentrum für Informatik (2015)
24. Pitts, A.M.: Nominal Sets. Cambridge University Press, Cambridge (2013)
25. Weber, T., Eriksson, L.-H., Parrow, J., Borgström, J., Gutkovas, R.: Modal logics for nominal transition systems. Archive of Formal Proofs, October 2016. http://isa-afp.org/entries/Modal_Logics_for_NTS.shtml. Formal proof development
26. Wischik, L., Gardner, P.: Explicit fusions. Theoret. Comput. Sci. **340**(3), 606–630 (2005)
27. Xian, X., Long, H.: A logical characterization for linear higher-order processes. J. Shanghai Jiaotong Univ. (Sci.) **20**(2), 185–194 (2015)

Type Inference of Simulink Hierarchical Block Diagrams in Isabelle

Viorel Preoteasa[1][(✉)], Iulia Dragomir[2], and Stavros Tripakis[1,3]

[1] Aalto University, Espoo, Finland
viorel.preoteasa@gmail.com
[2] Verimag, Saint-Martin-d'Héres, France
[3] University of California, Berkeley, USA

Abstract. Simulink is a de-facto industrial standard for embedded system design. In previous work, we developed a compositional analysis framework for Simulink, the Refinement Calculus of Reactive Systems (RCRS), which allows checking compatibility and substitutability of components. However, standard type checking was not considered in that work. In this paper we present a method for the type inference of Simulink models using the Isabelle theorem prover. A Simulink diagram is translated into an (RCRS) Isabelle theory. Then Isabelle's powerful type inference mechanism is used to infer the types of the diagram based on the types of the basic blocks. One of the aims is to handle formally as many diagrams as possible. In particular, we want to be able to handle even those diagrams that may have typing ambiguities, provided that they are accepted by Simulink. This method is implemented in our toolset that translates Simulink diagrams into Isabelle theories and simplifies them. We evaluate our technique on several case studies, most notably, an automotive fuel control system benchmark provided by Toyota.

1 Introduction

Simulink is a widespread tool from Mathworks for modeling and simulating embedded control systems. A plethora of formal verification tools exist for Simulink, both from academia and industry, including Mathwork's own Design Verifier. Formal verification is extremely important, particularly for safety critical systems. Formal verification techniques make steady progress and are increasingly gaining acceptance in the industry.

At the same time, we should not ignore more "lightweight" methods, which can also be very beneficial. In this paper, we are interested in particular in type checking and type inference. Type checking is regularly used in many programming languages, as part of compilation, and helps to catch many programming mistakes and sometimes also serious design errors. Type inference is a more

This work has been partially supported by the Academy of Finland and the U.S. National Science Foundation (awards #1329759 and #1139138).

A. Bouajjani and A. Silva (Eds.): FORTE 2017, LNCS 10321, pp. 194–209, 2017.
DOI: 10.1007/978-3-319-60225-7_14

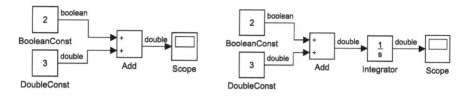

Fig. 1. Two Simulink diagrams. Both are accepted (i.e., simulated) by Simulink.

advanced technique which usually includes type checking but in addition permits types to be inferred when those are not given by the user, thus automatically extracting valuable information about the design. Importantly, both type checking and type inference are typically much less expensive than formal verification. We therefore view both of them as complementary to formal verification for the rigorous design of safety-critical systems.

Simulink already provides some kind of type checking and inference as part of its basic functionality. In the version R2016b that we used while writing this article, the user has to open a diagram and then click on *Display → Signals & Ports → Port Data Types*, upon which Simulink (computes and) displays the typing information, for example, as shown in Fig. 1. Unfortunately, Simulink analyses are proprietary, and as such it is difficult to know what type checking and inference algorithms are used. Moreover, the way Simulink uses the typing information is often strange, as illustrated by the examples that follow.

Consider first the two diagrams shown in Fig. 1. Both these examples capture implicit type conversions performed by Simulink. In both diagrams, there are two *Constant* blocks, with values 2 and 3 respectively. In the first block, we manually set the output type to be *Boolean*. In the second block we manually set the output type to *double*. The outputs of the two constants are fed into an *Add* block which performs addition. In the rightmost diagram, the result is fed into an *Integrator*. The block *Scope* plots and displays the output over time.

Both diagrams of Fig. 1 are *accepted* by Simulink, meaning that they can be simulated. Although Simulink issues a warning that says "Parameter precision loss occurred ... A small quantization error has occurred." the results of the simulation appear as expected: a constant value 4 in the case of the leftmost diagram, and a straight slope from values 0 to 40 for the rightmost diagram, when simulated from 0 to 10 time units. Simulink performs an implicit conversion of 2 to the Boolean value *true*, and then another implicit conversion of *true* to the real value 1, in order for the addition to be performed. These implicit conversions are stipulated in the Simulink documentation (when the source block allows them). Therefore, the result is $3 + 1 = 4$.

Although these examples seem unusual, they are designed to be minimal and expose possible problems, similar to those detected in a Fuel Control System (FCS) benchmark provided by Toyota [9]. It is common practice to mix, in languages that allow it, Boolean and numeric values in a way exposed by these examples. We have tested this behavior extensively and we have observed that other languages that perform automatic conversions between Boolean and numeric values behave consistently with Simulink (e.g., C: (double)3 + (bool)2 = 4.0, Python: float(3) + bool(2) = 4.0).

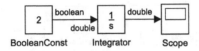

Fig. 2. A diagram rejected by Simulink.

Now, consider the diagram shown in Fig. 2, where the output of the same Boolean constant block as the one used in the previous diagrams is fed directly into the integrator. In this case, Simulink *rejects* this diagram (meaning it refuses to simulate it). It issues an error message saying: "Data type mismatch. Input of Integrator expects a signal of data type 'double'. However, it is driven by a signal of data type 'boolean'." The Integrator, as well as other block types, accepts only inputs of type double and implicit conversions (from Boolean to double or vice-versa) are not allowed and performed. We remark that Simulink does not treat diagrams in a consistent way with respect to typing. One of the goals of this paper is to present a formal type checking and inference framework for Simulink, where such examples are treated consistently (and meaningfully).

The contribution of this work is a type inference mechanism for Simulink diagrams, on top of the type inference mechanism of the Isabelle theorem prover [12]. One important feature of this approach is handling Simulink basic blocks locally, without knowledge of their environment. The challenge of this work is embedding the more relaxed type system of Simulink into the formal type system of Isabelle, while preserving the semantics, and as much typing information as possible. We apply this technique to several case studies, including the FCS benchmark.

This work is part of a larger project on translating Simulink diagrams into Isabelle theories suitable for analysis and verification [6,15,16]. Because Isabelle's language is formal and precise, we can directly obtain concise and correct code in other languages that can be used for processing Simulink models. For example, from the Isabelle model we easily obtain Python code for simulations, and Z3 SMT solver [4] model for automatically checking properties.

Our techniques apply to the entire Simulink language, provided we know how to translate basic blocks. Simulink contains many basic blocks but all of them fall into some of the categories discussed in this paper.

2   Related Work

The verification of Simulink diagrams has been extensively studied in the literature, by proposing model transformations of Simulink diagrams to a formal framework. Formal frameworks include Hybrid Automata [1], BIP [19], NuSMV [10], Boogie [17], Timed Interval Calculus [2], Function Blocks [24], I/O Extended Finite Automata [25], Hybrid CSP [26], and SpaceEx [11]. Many of the target formalisms define a typing feature, and the proposed model translations make use of it: a basic block is mapped to some "expression" on inputs and outputs, where the types of inputs and outputs are dependent of the block type.

The static type checking is then delegated to the target framework, if such functionality is available. However, these studies mostly aim for formal verification of Simulink diagrams and do not report about type checking.

The most relevant work with respect to type checking Simulink diagrams is described in [18,23]. [23] presents a translation from discrete-time Simulink to Lustre, where the type system of Simulink is formalized as a simple polymorphic type system and unification is used to infer types. It is unclear how the above type system handles the subtleties studied in this paper. [18] presents the SimCheck framework, which among other functions allows the user to annotate ports and wires with types and also units (e.g., cm). A translation to Yices [7] supports the automated static and behavioral type checking. In contrast to SimCheck, we automatically infer the types and dimensions of signals from the Simulink diagrams, but we do not infer or check for physical units.

In previous work, we have presented the *Refinement Calculus of Reactive Systems* (RCRS) [6,15], a compositional framework for static analysis of hierarchical block diagrams in general, and Simulink models in particular. In the RCRS framework blocks are specified syntactically by general formulas (*contracts*) on input, output, and state variables. These contracts are then composed using serial, parallel and feedback composition operators. Such contracts can be seen as richer types, and the compatibility and contract synthesis methods developed in RCRS can be seen as type checking and type inference techniques. However, the contracts considered in RCRS are much more powerful than the types considered in this paper, and the compatibility and synthesis algorithms of RCRS are much more expensive (requiring in general quantifier elimination and satisfiability checking in expressive logics). Therefore, the framework proposed in this paper is much more lightweight.

In this work we use the Isabelle theorem prover which has a standard type inference mechanism [3], briefly discussed in Sect. 3.1. Our goal is to give an embedding of Simulink into a language and framework suitable for further processing (simplifications, checking of properties, and even simulation). Other systems for logical reasoning (e.g., PVS [13], Z3 [4], Coq [20]) could also be used for this purpose. As we use type inference, our work cannot be directly transferred to systems that do not have it (PVS, Z3). Translations of Simulink diagrams into systems with proper subtyping (PVS, Coq) need also different treatment since in these systems typing of a term is not always decidable.

We do not use type coercions (implicit type conversions) in our approach. We encode possible coercions explicitly in the representations of basic blocks.

3 Preliminaries

3.1 Isabelle

Isabelle/HOL is an interactive theorem prover based on higher order logic. Isabelle provides an environment which consists of a powerful specification and proving language and it has a rich theory library of formally verified mathematics. Notable features of Isabelle include a type system with type inference, polymorphism and overloading, and axiomatic type classes.

Isabelle's type system includes the basic types bool, real, int, nat, type variables $'a$, $'b$, etc., and predefined type constructors $'a \to 'b$ (functions from $'a$ to $'b$) and $'a \times 'b$ (Cartesian product of $'a$ and $'b$). *Type expressions* are build from basic types and type variables using the type constructors. For term $f(x, g(y))$ we can specify that it has a type t by using $:t$ after the term $f(x, g(y)) : t$.

Definitions in Isabelle are introduced using declarations of the form

$$\text{definition } f(x)(y)(g) = g(x)(y).$$

This definition introduces a function $f : 'a \to 'b \to ('a \to 'b \to 'c) \to 'c$, and Isabelle uses the *type inference* mechanism to deduce its type. The type of f is the *most general type* such that the expression $f(x)(y)(g) = g(x)(y)$ is *well typed*. A type t is *more general* than a type t' if t' can be obtained from t by instantiating the type variables in t with some type expressions [12].

We can also use specific types in definitions:

$$\text{definition } h(x : \text{real})(y)(g) = g(x)(y)$$

In our translation of Simulink to Isabelle we use the type inference mechanism.

Another important feature of Isabelle that we use is the type classes [8]. This is a mechanism that can be used, for example, to overload a polymorphic function $+ : 'a \to 'a \to 'a$ on different types for $'a$.

class plus =
   fixes $+ : 'a \to 'a \to 'a$
instantiation nat : plus
   definition $0 + x = x \mid \text{Suc}(x) + y = \text{Suc}(x + y)$

instantiation real : plus
   definition $x + y = \ldots$

We define the type class plus with the constant $+$ of polymorphic type $'a \to 'a \to 'a$, and two instantiations to natural and real numbers. In a term $x + y$, the type of x and y is not just a type variable $'a$, but a type variable $'a$ of class plus. This is represented syntactically as $x : 'a : \text{plus}$. The terms $(x : \text{nat}) + y$ and $(x : \text{real}) + y$ are well typed because the types nat and real are defined as instances of plus. Moreover, in the term $(x : \text{nat}) + y$, the plus operator is the one defined in the instance of nat : plus, while $x + y$ does not in general have a definition. The term $(x : \text{bool}) + y$ is not well typed because bool is not defined as an instance of plus.

3.2 Representation of Simulink Diagrams as Predicate Transformers

A (fragment of a) Simulink diagram is modeled intuitively as a discrete symbolic transition system with input, output, current and next state. The intuition behind this representation is the following. Initially, the current state has a default value. The system representation works in discrete steps, and, at each step, it updates the output and the next state based on the input and the current state.

For example, an integrator block like the one from Fig. 1 is discretized as a system parameterized by $dt > 0$, with input x and current state s, and output $y := s$ and next state $s' := s + x \cdot dt$.

Formally, we model these systems in Isabelle as *monotonic predicate transformers* [5], mapping predicates (sets) over the output and next state into predicates (sets) over the input and current state. A monotonic predicate transformer S with input x, current state s, output y and next state s', for a set q of pairs (y, s'), $S(q)$ returns the set of all pairs (x, s) such that if the execution of S starts in (x, s) then S does not fail and results in a pair $(y, s') \in q$. A detailed discussion of the choice for this semantics is outside the scope of this paper, and is extensively presented in [6,15,21].

In Isabelle, the integrator block is represented as the predicate transformer

$$\mathsf{Integrator}(dt)(q)(x, s) = q(s, s + x \cdot dt)$$

and it has the type $'a \to ('a : \mathsf{plus} \times 'a \to \mathsf{bool}) \to ('a \times 'a \to \mathsf{bool})$. In what follows we do not make a distinction between the input and current state, and output and next state, respectively. In general, a Simulink diagram is modeled as a predicate transformer with input (and current state) of a type variable $'a$, and output (and next state) of a type variable $'b$. The type of this predicate transformer is $('b \to \mathsf{bool}) \to ('a \to \mathsf{bool})$ and we use the notation $'a \xrightarrow{\circ} 'b$ for it (this may appear reversed, but is correct and in accordance with the discussion on predicate transformers above). Often $'a$ and $'b$ will be Cartesian products, including the empty product (unit). We denote by $()$: unit the *empty tuple*.

For a predicate transformer mapping, for example, inputs (x, y, z) into output expressions $(x + y, x \cdot z)$, we use the notation $[x, y, z \rightsquigarrow x + y, x \cdot z]$ where

$$[x, y, z \rightsquigarrow x + y, x \cdot z](q)(x, y, z) = q(x + y, x \cdot z)$$

Using this notation, the constant and the integrator blocks become

$$\mathsf{Const}(a) = [() \rightsquigarrow a], \quad \mathsf{Integrator}(dt) = [x, s \rightsquigarrow s, s + x \cdot dt].$$

We denote by Id the identity predicate transformer ($[x \rightsquigarrow x]$).

A block diagram is modeled in Isabelle as an expression of predicate transformers corresponding to the basic blocks, using three composition operators: serial ($\circ$), parallel ($\|$), and feedback (fb). The serial composition of predicate transformers is exactly the composition of functions. The parallel and feedback compositions are described in [6,16]. For this presentation, the typing of these operations is important. The typing of the serial composition is standard. The parallel and feedback compositions have the types:

$$\| : ('a \xrightarrow{\circ} 'b) \to ('c \xrightarrow{\circ} 'd) \to ('a \times 'c \xrightarrow{\circ} 'b \times 'd),$$
$$\mathsf{fb} : ('a \times 'b \xrightarrow{\circ} 'a \times 'c) \to ('b \xrightarrow{\circ} 'c)$$

Using these notations, the predicate transformer for the rightmost diagram from Fig. 1 is given by

$$((((\mathsf{Const}(s\_bool(2))) \| \mathsf{Const}(3)) \circ [x, y \rightsquigarrow x + y]) \| \mathsf{Id}) \circ \mathsf{Integrator}(dt)$$

We use here the Id predicate transformer to model and connect the current state of the integrator. We also use the polymorphic function s_bool which for 2 returns True if the type of the result is Boolean, and 1 if the type of the result is real. The type of the result in this case is real as it is inferred from the addition block (following the constant blocks).

4   Constant Blocks

Simulink diagrams may contain constant blocks, parameterized by numeric constants. These are blocks without input and with one single output which is always equal to the constant's parameter. By default, Simulink constants do not have associated types. In order to have the possibility to instantiate these types later for reals, integers, Booleans, or other types, we use uninterpreted constants. By default, numeric constants in Isabelle are polymorphic. If no type is explicitly set to a constant in a term $t = 12$, then Isabelle associates a type variable $'a :$ numeral to this constant. If the term is used in a context where the type is more specific $(t = 12 \land \mathsf{Suc}(t) = t')$ then Isabelle uses the type class instantiation to the specific type (in this case natural because of the successor function).

Due to this polymorphic treatment of constants, in some contexts the problem arises that the types of these constants are not part of the type of the resulting predicate transformer. Consider for example the diagram from Fig. 3a. The Isabelle definition for this diagram is

$$\mathsf{Compare} = (\mathsf{Const}(1 : {'a} : \mathsf{numeral}) \,\|\, \mathsf{Const}(2)) \circ [x, y \rightsquigarrow x \neq y] \; (= [() \rightsquigarrow 1 \neq 2])$$

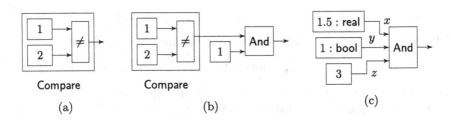

Fig. 3. (a) Comparison on constants, (b) Comparison into conjunction, (c) And on typed constants

In this definition $'a$ is the inferred type of constants 1 and 2. The problem with this definition is that the type $'a$ is not part of the type of Compare : unit $\overset{\circ}{\rightarrow}$ bool. If this definition was allowed, then we would have an unsound system, because for example if $'a$ is instantiated by real, then (1 : real) $\neq$ 2 is true and Compare $= [() \rightsquigarrow \mathsf{True}]$, but if $'a$ is instantiated by unit, then (1 : unit) $\neq$ 2 is false (unit contains only one element) and Compare $= [() \rightsquigarrow \mathsf{False}]$, and we can derive $[() \rightsquigarrow \mathsf{False}] = [() \rightsquigarrow \mathsf{True}]$ which is false. In order to instantiate unit for $'a$, the type unit must be of class numeral. Although by default this is not the case in Isabelle, we can easily add an instantiation of unit as numeral and obtain this contradiction.

Isabelle allows this kind of definition, but it gives a warning message ("Additional type variable(s) in specification of Compare : $'a$: numeral"), and it defines the function Compare to depend on an additional type variable:

$$\mathsf{Compare}('a : \mathsf{numeral}) = (\mathsf{Const}(2 : {}'a) \,\|\, \mathsf{Const}(1)) \circ [x, y \rightsquigarrow x \neq y]$$

Now Compare(real) and Compare(unit) are different terms, so they are not equal anymore and we cannot derive $[() \rightsquigarrow \mathsf{False}] = [() \rightsquigarrow \mathsf{True}]$. Assume now that we compose the Compare block with a conjunction block as in Fig. 3b.

$$A = (\mathsf{Compare} \,\|\, \mathsf{Const}(1)) \circ \mathsf{And}$$

However, this definition is now incorrect because Compare has an additional type parameter. The correct definition would be:

$$A('a : \mathsf{numeral}) = (\mathsf{Compare}('a) \,\|\, \mathsf{Const}(1)) \circ \mathsf{And}$$

When we generate the definition for the diagram from Fig. 3b we do not know that Compare needs the additional type parameter. To have control over the type parameters we add them systematically for all constants occurring in the diagram. Moreover, we define the constants with a variable parameter. Due to the lack of space, the rationale for these definitions is discussed in [14].

With this method the constant blocks from Fig. 3b are defined by

$$\mathsf{ConstA}(x : {}'a) = \mathsf{Const}(1 : {}'a) \; \text{ and } \; \mathsf{ConstB}(y : {}'b) = \mathsf{Const}(2 : {}'b) \; \text{ and } \atop \mathsf{ConstC}(z : {}'c) = \mathsf{Const}(1 : {}'c) \tag{1}$$

and the diagram is defined by

$$A(x, y, z) = (((\mathsf{ConstA}(x) \,\|\, \mathsf{ConstB}(y)) \circ [x, y \rightsquigarrow x \neq y]) \,\|\, \mathsf{ConstC}(z)) \circ \mathsf{And} \tag{2}$$

In this approach, variables x, y, z are used only to control the types of the constants. In this definition, because outputs of ConstA and ConstB are entering the comparison block, the types of x and y are unified. If we need an instance of A for type real for constants ConstA and ConstB and type Boolean for ConstC, then we can specify it using the term $A(x : \mathsf{real}, y : \mathsf{real}, z : \mathsf{bool})$.

This definition mechanism is implemented in our Simulink to Isabelle model translator under the $-\mathsf{const}$ option. When the option is set, then the constants are defined as in (1), and the diagrams using these constants are defined as in (2). When the option is not given, then the constants are defined as in:

$$\mathsf{ConstA} = \mathsf{Const}(1) \; \text{ and } \; \mathsf{ConstB} = \mathsf{Const}(2) \; \text{ and } \; \mathsf{ConstC} = \mathsf{Const}(1)$$

and they are used as in: $A = (((\mathsf{ConstA} \,\|\, \mathsf{ConstB}) \circ [x, y \rightsquigarrow x \neq y]) \,\|\, \mathsf{ConstC}) \circ \mathsf{And}$. When the constant blocks in a Simulink diagram define an output type, we simply use them as in $\mathsf{Const}(1.5 : \mathsf{real})$ (Fig. 3c).

5 Conversion Blocks

Simulink diagrams may also contain conversion blocks. The type of the input of
a conversion is inherited and the type of the output is usually specified (Boolean,
real, ...). However we can have also situations when the output is not specified,
and it is inherited from the type of the inputs of the block that follows a conversion. In Fig. 4a we illustrate an explicit conversion to real, while Fig. 4b presents
an unspecified conversion.

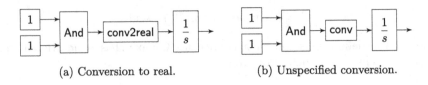

(a) Conversion to real.   (b) Unspecified conversion.

Fig. 4. Conversions examples.

As with the other blocks we want to define these conversions locally, without
knowing the types of the inputs and outputs, when the output type is unspecified.
In doing so, we use the overloading mechanism of Isabelle. Overloading is a
feature that allows using the same constant name with different types. For the
conversion blocks we introduce the following definitions.

$$\textsf{consts conv} : {}'a \rightarrow {}'b$$
$$\textsf{overloading}$$
$$\textsf{conv}(x : {}'a) := x$$
$$\textsf{conv}(x : \textsf{bool}) := \textsf{if } x \textsf{ then } (1 : \textsf{real}) \textsf{ else } 0$$
$$\textsf{conv}(x : \textsf{real}) := (x \neq 0)$$

This definition introduces an arbitrary function conv from a type variable $'a$ to
a type variable $'b$, and it also defines three overloadings for this function. The
term conv(x) in general is of type $'b$ and x is of type $'a$. If we restrict the type
$'a$ and $'b$ to real and bool, then we have

$$(\textsf{conv}(x : \textsf{real}) : \textsf{bool}) = (x \neq 0)$$

When we translate a conversion block, if we know the output type, then we use
the conversion restricted to this output type, otherwise we use the unrestricted
conversion. For example the conversion from Fig. 4a is translated into $[x \rightsquigarrow (\textsf{conv}(x) : \textsf{real})]$. The entire diagram from Fig. 4a is translated into

$$((((\textsf{Const}(1) \parallel \textsf{Const}(1)) \circ \textsf{And} \circ [x \rightsquigarrow (\textsf{conv}(x) : \textsf{real})]) \parallel \textsf{Id}) \circ [x, s \rightsquigarrow s, s + x \cdot dt] \quad (3)$$

The identity block (Id) is used here for the current state input of the integral
block. The conversion from Fig. 4b is translated into $[x \rightsquigarrow \textsf{conv}(x)]$. This diagram
becomes

$$((((\textsf{Const}(1) \parallel \textsf{Const}(1)) \circ \textsf{And} \circ [x \rightsquigarrow \textsf{conv}(x)]) \parallel \textsf{Id}) \circ [(x : \textsf{real}), s \rightsquigarrow s, s + x \cdot dt]$$

and compared with (3) the only difference is that in the later case, the type of the output of the conversion is not specified. However, in both cases, the inputs of the conversions must be Boolean because of the And block, and the outputs must be real because of the integral block. In both cases the translations are equivalent to $[(s : \text{real}) \rightsquigarrow s, s + dt]$.

6   Boolean Blocks

Simulink Boolean blocks are also challenging to implement due to the fact that, for example, the inputs to a conjunction block could have different types (real, Boolean, unspecified), as illustrated in Fig. 3c. In languages that allow it (e.g., C, Python), it is common practice to use numerical values in Boolean expressions, with the meaning that non-zero is true. Similarly, it is common practice to use Boolean values in numeric expressions. Simulink also allows these cases, but Isabelle does not. We show in this and next section how to solve these problems.

Consider the example from Fig. 3c. If we would simply take the conjunction of all inputs

$$(\text{Const}(1.5 : \text{real}) \,\|\, \text{Const}(1 : \text{bool}) \,\|\, \text{Const}(3)) \circ [x, y, z \rightsquigarrow x \wedge y \wedge z]$$

we will obtain in Isabelle a type error, because x has type real, y has type bool and z has type $'a : \text{numeral}$, and their conjunction is not well typed.

To fix this typing problem, we implement the conjunction block in the following way: $\text{And} = [x, y, z \rightsquigarrow (x \neq 0) \wedge (y \neq 0) \wedge (z \neq 0)]$. In this expression the types of variables x, y, and z are independent of each other, and also of the Boolean output, and they can match the types of the blocks that are input to And. There are still some details to consider. If input x is real, then $x \neq 0$ is true if and only if x is not zero, and this coincides with the semantics of And in Simulink. However, if the input y is Boolean, then the expression $y \neq 0$ is not well typed, unless we add additional class instantiation in Isabelle:

$$\text{instantiation bool} : \text{zero} =$$
$$(0 : \text{bool}) := \text{False}$$

Intuitively this instantiation provides the interpretation of constant 0 as False, when 0 is used as a Boolean value. With this the expression $(y : \text{bool}) \neq 0$ is equivalent to $y \neq \text{False}$ and it is equivalent to y. The same holds for the expression $1 : \text{bool}$ which is not well typed unless we provide an instantiation of bool as numeral, where every (non-zero) numeral constant is True. These definitions formalize the behavior described by Simulink in its documentation.

Using this approach, the translation of the diagram from Fig. 3c is:

$$(\text{Const}(1.5 : \text{real}) \,\|\, \text{Const}(1 : \text{bool}) \,\|\, \text{Const}(3)) \circ [x, y, z \rightsquigarrow x \neq 0 \wedge y \neq 0 \wedge z \neq 0]$$

and it is equal to

$$(\text{Const}(1.5 : \text{real}) \,\|\, \text{Const}(\text{True}) \,\|\, \text{Const}(3)) \circ [x, y, z \rightsquigarrow x \neq 0 \wedge y \wedge z \neq 0]$$

because y is of type bool and $(y \neq 0) = y$. If we expand the serial composition and simplify the term, we obtain $[() \rightsquigarrow (3 : 'a : \{\text{numeral, zero}\}) \neq 0]$. The equality $(3 : 'a : \{\text{numeral, zero}\}) \neq 0$ cannot be simplified. This is because the type $'a : \{\text{numeral, zero}\}$ has all numeric constants $1, 2, \ldots$ (numeral) and the constant 0 (zero), but no relationship between these constants is known. If we know that we only use the type $'a$ with instances where the numeric constants $1, 2, \ldots$ are always different from 0, then we can create a new class based on numeral and zero that has also the property that $n \neq 0$ for all $n \in \{1, 2, \ldots\}$. Formally we can introduce this class in Isabelle by

$$\text{class numeral\_nzero} = \text{zero} + \text{numeral} +$$
$$\text{assume numeral\_nzero[simp]} : (\forall a.\text{numeral}(a) \neq 0)$$

The new class numeral_nzero contains the numeric constants $\{0, 1, \ldots\}$ but also it has the property that all numbers $1, 2, \ldots$ are different from 0 ($\forall a.\text{numeral}(a) \neq 0$). In this property a ranges over the binary representations of the numbers $1, 2, \ldots$. This property is called numeral_nzero, and the [simp] declaration tells Isabelle to use it automatically as simplification rule. Now the equality $(3 : 'a : \text{numeral\_nzero}) \neq 0$ is also automatically simplified to True.

We provide the following class instantiation:

$$\text{instantiation bool : numeral\_nzero} =$$
$$(0 : \text{bool}) := \text{False} \mid (\text{numeral}(a) : \text{bool}) := \text{True}$$

Because in this class we have also the assumption ($\forall a.\text{numeral}(a) \neq 0$), we need to prove it, and it trivially holds because False $\neq$ True. Similarly we need to introduce instantiations of numeral_nzero to real, integer, and natural numbers. In these cases, since real, integer, and natural are already instances of numeral and zero, we do not need to define 0 and numeral(a), but we only need to prove the property ($\forall a.\text{numeral}(a) \neq 0$).

With this new class, the translation of diagram from Fig. 3c becomes:

$$(\text{Const}(1.5 : \text{real}) \parallel \text{Const}(1 : \text{bool}) \parallel \text{Const}(3 : 'a : \text{numeral\_nzero})) \circ$$
$$[x, y, z \rightsquigarrow x \neq 0 \wedge y \neq 0 \wedge z \neq 0]$$

Because of the properties of types real, bool, and $'a : \text{numeral\_nzero}$, it is equal to

$$(\text{Const}(1.5 : \text{real}) \parallel \text{Const}(\text{True}) \parallel \text{Const}(3 : 'a : \text{numeral\_nzero})) \circ$$
$$[x, y, z \rightsquigarrow x \neq 0 \wedge y \wedge z \neq 0]$$

and, after expanding the serial composition and symplifying the term, we obtain $[() \rightsquigarrow \text{True}]$.

Although the translation of Boolean blocks is rather involved, the result obtained especially after basic Isabelle simplifications is simple and intuitive, as shown above. Moreover, for the translation of a Boolean block we do not need to consider its context, and the correctness of the translation can be assessed locally. Basically an element e in a conjunction $(e \wedge \ldots)$ is replaced by $((e \neq 0) \wedge \ldots)$. By creating the class numeral_nzero and the instantiations to bool and real, the typing of e ($e : \text{bool}$ or $e : \text{real}, \ldots$) defines the semantics of the expression $e \neq 0$.

7   Generic Translations

The approach described so far works well for diagrams that do not mix values of different types (Boolean, real) in operations. However, there are some diagrams that are accepted by Simulink and cannot be translated with the approach described above due to type mismatch. Figures 1 and 2 give three examples of this kind of diagrams.

Figure 1 illustrates diagrams accepted by Simulink, while the diagram represented in Fig. 2 is not accepted by Simulink. The simulation of leftmost diagram from Fig. 1 gives 4 (2 : bool results in True, and then converted to real is 1). The rightmost diagram from Fig. 1 is equivalent to a diagram where constant 4 is input for an integral block. However none of these diagrams result in correct translations when using the method presented so far. This is due to type mismatches:

$$(\mathsf{Const}(2 : \mathsf{bool}) \parallel \mathsf{Const}(3 : \mathsf{real})) \circ \mathsf{Add}$$
$$(((\mathsf{Const}(2 : \mathsf{bool}) \parallel \mathsf{Const}(3 : \mathsf{real})) \circ \mathsf{Add}) \parallel \mathsf{Id}) \circ [(x : \mathsf{real}), s \rightsquigarrow s, s + x \cdot dt]$$
$$(\mathsf{Const}(2 : \mathsf{bool}) \parallel \mathsf{Id}) \circ [(x : \mathsf{real}), s \rightsquigarrow s, s + x \cdot dt]$$

In the first case, we try to add a Boolean to a real. The second example contains the first example as a sub-diagram, and it has the same type incompatibility. In the third example the output of $\mathsf{Const}(2 : \mathsf{bool})$ of type bool is used as the input for the first component of $[(x : \mathsf{real}), s \rightsquigarrow s, s + x \cdot dt]$ which expects a real.

To be able to translate these diagrams, we use type variables instead of the concrete types bool, real, ... Because we work with expressions containing arithmetic and Boolean operations, we need to use type variables of appropriate classes. For example, to translate the leftmost diagram from Fig. 1, we cannot just use an arbitrary type $'a$ because $'a$ must be of class numeral for the constants 2 and 3, and of class plus. In fact only class numeral is required here because plus is a subclass of numeral. The generic translation of this diagram is:

$$\mathsf{ConstA}(x : \; 'a : \mathsf{numeral}) = \mathsf{Const}(2 : \; 'a), \quad \mathsf{ConstB}(y : \; 'a : \mathsf{numeral}) = \mathsf{Const}(3 : \; 'a)$$
$$A(x, y) = (\mathsf{ConstA}(x) \parallel \mathsf{ConstB}(y)) \circ [a, b \rightsquigarrow a + b]$$

In this translation, we only need to specify the types for the constants as discussed in Sect. 4. However, when we use the type variable $'a$ for numeric constants $1, 2, \ldots$, then we must specify it using the class numeral. If the expression involving the elements of type $'a$ contains some other operators, then we must include also the classes defining these operators. For example we need to have: $\mathsf{ConstA}(x : \; 'a : \{\mathsf{numeral}, \mathsf{mult}\}) = \mathsf{Const}((2 : \; 'a) \cdot 3)$. To simplify this we introduce a new class simulink that contains all mathematical and Boolean operators as well as all real functions that can occur in Simulink diagrams.

$$\mathsf{class \; simulink} = \mathsf{zero} + \mathsf{numeral} + \mathsf{minus} + \mathsf{uminus} + \mathsf{power} + \mathsf{ord} +$$
$$\mathsf{fixes \; s\_exp}, \; \mathsf{s\_sin} : \; 'a \rightarrow 'a \; \mid \; \mathsf{fixes \; s\_and} : \; 'a \rightarrow 'a \rightarrow 'a$$
$$\ldots$$
$$\mathsf{assume \; numeral\_nzero[simp]} : (\forall a.\mathsf{numeral}(a) \neq 0)$$

Class zero contains the symbol 0, class numeral contains the numbers $1, 2, \ldots$, classes minus and uminus contains the binary and unary minus operators, class power contains the power and multiplication operators, and class ord contains the order operators. Because the real functions exp, sin, ... and the Boolean functions are defined just for reals and Boolean types respectively, and they do not have generic type classes, we introduce the generic versions of these functions and operators in the class simulink (s_exp, s_sin, $\ldots$, s_and, $\ldots$). Additionally we assume that constant 0 is different from all numeric constants $1, 2, \ldots$.

Using this new class the translation of the rightmost diagram from Fig. 1 is given by

$$\text{ConstA}(x : 'a : \text{simulink}) = \text{Const}(\text{s\_bool}(2 : 'a))$$
$$\text{ConstB}(y : 'a : \text{simulink}) = \text{Const}(3 : 'a)$$
$$\text{Integral}(dt : 'a : \text{simulink}) = [s, x \rightsquigarrow s, s + x \cdot dt]$$
$$\text{Add} = [(x : 'a : \text{simulink}), y \rightsquigarrow x + y]$$
$$A(x, y, dt) = (((\text{ConstA}(x) \parallel \text{ConstB}(y)) \circ \text{Add}) \parallel \text{Id}) \circ \text{Integral}(dt)$$

The inferred type of A is $A(x : 'a : \text{simulink}, y : 'a, dt : 'a) : 'a \xrightarrow{\circ} 'a \times 'a$

In this generic translation there are some details to consider when translating a constant block of type Boolean like the ones from Fig. 1 (2 : bool). In order to use $A(x, y, dt)$ in the end, we still need to instantiate the type variable $'a$. In this case, it would be appropriate to instantiate $'a$ with type real. If we simply use $\text{Const}(2 : 'a)$ in definition of ConstA, then when instantiating $'a$, we will obtain the constant 2 and we will add it to 3 resulting in 5, and this is not the result obtained when simulating the diagram in Simulink. To preserve the Simulink semantics in the generic case, we translate Boolean constants using a function s_bool which for a parameter x returns 1 if x is different from 0 and 0 otherwise:

$$\text{definition s\_bool}(x) := \text{if } x \neq 0 \text{ then 1 else } 0$$

The typing of $x : 'a$ and of $\text{s\_bool}(x) : 'b$ defines again a more precise semantics for $\text{s\_bool}(x)$. For example if both $'a$ and $'b$ are bool, then $\text{s\_bool}(x) = x$. Similarly, we define instantiations for bool and real for all the generic functions defined in the simulink class. These instantiations are detailed in [14].

We implemented this strategy in our Simulink to Isabelle model translator under the $-$generic option. When this option is missing, then all blocks are defined using their specific types. If this option is given, then only type variables of class simulink are used.

Additionally, we implemented the option $-$type *isabelle_type* with an Isabelle type parameter, which adds a new definition where it instantiates all type variables to the type parameter.

For example, if we apply the translation using the options $-$const, $-$generic, and $-$type real to the rightmost diagram from Fig. 1, we obtain:

$\mathsf{ConstA}(x : \ 'a : \mathsf{simulink}) := \mathsf{Const}(\mathsf{s\_bool}(2 : \ 'a))$
$\mathsf{ConstB}(y : \ 'a : \mathsf{simulink}) := \mathsf{Const}(3 : \ 'a)$
$\mathsf{Integral}(dt : \ 'a : \mathsf{simulink}) := [s, x \rightsquigarrow s, s + x \cdot dt]$
$\mathsf{Add} := [(x : \ 'a : \mathsf{simulink}), y \rightsquigarrow x + y]$
$\mathsf{A}(x, y, dt) := (((\mathsf{ConstA}(x) \ \| \ \mathsf{ConstB}(y)) \circ \mathsf{Add}) \ \| \ \mathsf{Id}) \circ \mathsf{Integral}(dt)$
$\mathsf{A\_type}(dt) := \mathsf{A}(0 : \mathsf{real}, 0 : \mathsf{real}, dt : \mathsf{real})$

and also the simplified versions A and A_type:

$$\mathsf{A}(x, y, dt) = [s \rightsquigarrow s, s + (1 + 3) \cdot dt] \quad \text{and} \quad \mathsf{A\_type}(dt) = [s \rightsquigarrow s, s + 4 \cdot dt]$$

In the generic version s_bool(2) is automatically simplified to 1 using the definition of s_bool and the assumption numeral_nzero, and in A_type the expression $1+3$ is further simplified to 4. In A_type we can eliminate the variables providing types for constants because these types are now instantiated to real.

8   Implementation and Validation

The mechanism presented above for translating Simulink diagrams is implemented in the Refinement Calculus of Reactive Systems framework, available from http://rcrs.cs.aalto.fi. In this framework, Simulink diagrams are translated into Isabelle theories, where diagrams are modeled using predicate transformers. The framework allows the user to perform various analyses on the formal model such as simplification, compatibility checking, safety property verification and simulation.

In order to handle a large set of diagrams, we introduced three translation options: −const, −generic, and −type isabelle_type, where each solves different possible corner cases. These options allow some control over the translation process. More details about these options are available in the extended version of this work [14].

We have extensively tested all combinations of interactions of numeric and Boolean blocks, and we carefully implemented the observed behavior. We have also tested our technique on several examples, including an industrial case study: the Fuel Control System (FCS) benchmark from Toyota [9]. All examples presented in this paper are excerpts from the FCS model. The latter contains 1 constant-related problem as described in Sect. 4, 5 implicit conversions, and 5 explicit conversions from which 1 has the inherited output type. Our approach allowed to detect and correct the implicit bool to real conversion present in the FCS model.

Simulink's type system is not formalized, thus it is difficult to make formal claims about its relation to our work. Our experience shows that in most cases our translation results in types that are more general than those in the original diagram.[1] Therefore, instantiating the remaining type variables can be done such that the types of the translation match the types inferred by Simulink.

---

[1] The only exception is when Boolean values are used in numeric expressions, as discussed in Sect. 7, in which case *true* and *false* are modeled as the numbers 1 and 0.

9   Conclusions and Future Work

We presented a type inference technique for Simulink diagrams which relies on Isabelle's type inference. The main advantage of our technique is that it treats the basic blocks of the diagram *compositionally*, i.e., locally and without knowledge of their context.

Our work is not necessarily restricted to Simulink and could also be used to translate from other weakly typed languages and/or other hierarchical block diagram notations. It could in principle be also applicable to similar in style dataflow languages, with synchronous or asynchronous semantics, which are standard in modeling and reasoning about distributed systems (e.g., see [22]). Our work could also help in implementing translations *into* other systems than Isabelle (e.g., PVS, Z3, Coq), although several challenges need to be overcome as mentioned in Sect. 2. The investigation of all these possibilities is part of future work.

References

1. Agrawal, A., Simon, G., Karsai, G.: Semantic translation of Simulink/stateflow models to hybrid automata using graph transformations. Electron. Notes Theoret. Comput. Sci. **109**, 43–56 (2004)
2. Chen, C., Dong, J.S., Sun, J.: A formal framework for modeling and validating Simulink diagrams. Formal Aspects Comput. **21**(5), 451–483 (2009)
3. Damas, L., Milner, R.: Principal type-schemes for functional programs. In: POPL 1982, pp. 207–212. ACM (1982)
4. De Moura, L., Bjørner, N.: Z3: an efficient SMT solver. In: Ramakrishnan, C.R., Rehof, J. (eds.) TACAS 2008. LNCS, vol. 4963, pp. 337–340. Springer, Heidelberg (2008). doi:10.1007/978-3-540-78800-3_24
5. Dijkstra, E.: Guarded commands, nondeterminacy and formal derivation of programs. Comm. ACM **18**(8), 453–457 (1975)
6. Dragomir, I., Preoteasa, V., Tripakis, S.: Compositional semantics and analysis of hierarchical block diagrams. In: Bošnački, D., Wijs, A. (eds.) SPIN 2016. LNCS, vol. 9641, pp. 38–56. Springer, Cham (2016). doi:10.1007/978-3-319-32582-8_3
7. Dutertre, B., de Moura, L.: The Yices SMT solver. Technical report, SRI International (2006)
8. Haftmann, F., Wenzel, M.: Constructive type classes in Isabelle. In: Altenkirch, T., McBride, C. (eds.) TYPES 2006. LNCS, vol. 4502, pp. 160–174. Springer, Heidelberg (2007). doi:10.1007/978-3-540-74464-1_11
9. Jin, X., Deshmukh, J.V., Kapinski, J., Ueda, K., Butts, K.: Powertrain control verification benchmark. In: HSCC, pp. 253–262. ACM (2014)
10. Meenakshi, B., Bhatnagar, A., Roy, S.: Tool for translating Simulink models into input language of a model checker. In: Liu, Z., He, J. (eds.) ICFEM 2006. LNCS, vol. 4260, pp. 606–620. Springer, Heidelberg (2006). doi:10.1007/11901433_33
11. Minopoli, S., Frehse, G.: SL2SX translator: from Simulink to SpaceEx models. In: HSCC, pp. 93–98. ACM (2016)
12. Nipkow, T., Wenzel, M., Paulson, L.C.: Isabelle/HOL: A Proof Assistant for Higher-Order Logic. Springer, Heidelberg (2002)

13. Owre, S., Rushby, J.M., Shankar, N.: PVS: a prototype verification system. In: Kapur, D. (ed.) CADE 1992. LNCS, vol. 607, pp. 748–752. Springer, Heidelberg (1992). doi:10.1007/3-540-55602-8_217

14. Preoteasa, V., Dragomir, I., Tripakis, S.: Type inference of Simulink hierarchical block diagrams in Isabelle. CoRR, abs/1612.05494 (2016)

15. Preoteasa, V., Tripakis, S.: Refinement calculus of reactive systems. In: EMSOFT, pp. 2:1–2:10. ACM (2014)

16. Preoteasa, V., Tripakis, S.: Towards compositional feedback in non-deterministic and non-input-receptive systems. In: LICS. ACM (2016)

17. Reicherdt, R., Glesner, S.: Formal verification of discrete-time MATLAB/Simulink models using boogie. In: Giannakopoulou, D., Salaün, G. (eds.) SEFM 2014. LNCS, vol. 8702, pp. 190–204. Springer, Cham (2014). doi:10.1007/978-3-319-10431-7_14

18. Roy, P., Shankar, N.: SimCheck: a contract type system for Simulink. Innov. Syst. Softw. Eng. 7(2), 73–83 (2011)

19. Sfyrla, V., Tsiligiannis, G., Safaka, I., Bozga, M., Sifakis, J.: Compositional translation of Simulink models into synchronous BIP. In: SIES, pp. 217–220. IEEE (2010)

20. The Coq Development Team. The Coq Proof Assistant Reference Manual – Version V8.6, December 2016

21. Tripakis, S., Lickly, B., Henzinger, T.A., Lee, E.A.: A theory of synchronous relational interfaces. ACM Trans. Program. Lang. Syst. 33(4), 14:1–14:41 (2011)

22. Tripakis, S., Pinello, C., Benveniste, A., Sangiovanni-Vincentelli, A., Caspi, P., Natale, M.D.: Implementing synchronous models on loosely time-triggered architectures. IEEE Trans. Comput. 57(10), 1300–1314 (2008)

23. Tripakis, S., Sofronis, C., Caspi, P., Curic, A.: Translating discrete-time Simulink to Lustre. ACM Trans. Embed. Comput. Syst. 4(4), 779–818 (2005)

24. Yang, C., Vyatkin, V.: Transformation of Simulink models to IEC 61499 Function Blocks for verification of distributed control systems. Control Eng. Pract. 20(12), 1259–1269 (2012)

25. Zhou, C., Kumar, R.: Semantic translation of Simulink diagrams to input/output extended finite automata. Discret. Event Dyn. Syst. 22(2), 223–247 (2012)

26. Zou, L., Zhany, N., Wang, S., Franzle, M., Qin, S.: Verifying Simulink diagrams via a Hybrid Hoare Logic Prover. In: EMSOFT, pp. 9:1–9:10 (2013)

Creating Büchi Automata for Multi-valued Model Checking

Stefan J.J. Vijzelaar$^{(\boxtimes)}$ and Wan J. Fokkink

VU University Amsterdam, Amsterdam, The Netherlands
{s.j.j.vijzelaar,w.j.fokkink}@vu.nl

Abstract. In explicit state model checking of linear temporal logic properties, a Büchi automaton encodes a temporal property. It interleaves with a Kripke model to form a state space, which is searched for counterexamples. Multi-valued model checking considers additional truth values beyond the Boolean *true* and *false*; these values add extra information to the model, e.g. for the purpose of abstraction or execution steering. This paper presents a method to create Büchi automata for multi-valued model checking using quasi-Boolean logics. It allows for multi-valued propositions as well as multi-valued transitions. A logic for the purpose of execution steering and abstraction is presented as an application.

1 Introduction

Model checking is a technique used to automatically verify whether a system adheres to a given specification; or more specifically for this paper, that a property is never violated during the execution of a system. This can be implemented as a search through a product state space of two interleaved automata: the Kripke model that describes the system under verification; and the Büchi automaton that describes the property under verification. The Kripke model is generally an abstraction of a concrete system; it can be created by hand or is derived with the help of automation from a more detailed model. The Büchi automaton encodes the negation of the property being verified, which is usually expressed in linear temporal logic (LTL). The resulting product state space can then be searched for executions of the system that violate the property.

Algorithms to generate Büchi automata generally assume that the Kripke model and LTL property are based on Boolean logic. We are interested in verification based on multi-valued logics. These logics extend the set of Boolean truth values *true* and *false* with new truth values. Thus additional information can be encoded, such as uncertainty caused by a loss of information during abstraction, or the ability of certain transitions to be enabled or disabled at will during execution. We need multi-valued versions of Kripke models, Büchi automata and LTL to support these applications.

Multi-valued definitions of Kripke models and Büchi automata follow naturally from their Boolean definitions. Creating a multi-valued Büchi automaton,

© IFIP International Federation for Information Processing 2017
Published by Springer International Publishing AG 2017. All Rights Reserved
A. Bouajjani and A. Silva (Eds.): FORTE 2017, LNCS 10321, pp. 210–224, 2017.
DOI: 10.1007/978-3-319-60225-7_15

that correctly encodes a temporal property for multi-valued model checking, however, requires more care. When model checking LTL properties using Boolean logic, it is customary to assume all executions of the Kripke model are infinite.

This assumption can be guaranteed using stutter extension: the ability to extend any finite execution to an infinite one without influencing the validity of certain LTL properties. In the multi-valued setting this is not possible.

In this paper we show how to create multi-valued Büchi automata for LTL properties. We present definitions of the LTL operators that are compatible with multi-valued logics and do not require stutter extension. To ensure correct results for the weak next operator, we introduce the notion of maximality: a progress condition that considers to what degree of truth executions can halt when competing executions can to some degree continue. Based on these revised LTL definitions we describe an algorithm for constructing Büchi automata for multi-valued Kripke models, supporting both multi-valued atomic propositions and transitions.

To give an example of multi-valued LTL model checking we look at the application of execution steering. Our nine-valued steering logic indicates which transitions in a Kripke model can be enabled or disabled during execution. This shows the necessity of maximality to get correct multi-valued results.

Although there is a considerable amount of work on model checking with multi-valued logics (see e.g. [4,9]), to our knowledge there are no algorithms for explicit state multi-valued LTL model checking supporting multi-valued propositions and transitions. Chechik et al. use Büchi automata for verification of multi-valued computations, but with Boolean transitions [5]; Andrade et al. use a SAT solver for multi-valued LTL model checking over quasi-Boolean logics [1].

2 Preliminaries

Models and temporal logics typically use Boolean logic: transitions between states either exist or do not exist; atomic propositions either hold for a state or do not hold; and by extension temporal properties over a model can be verified or falsified. They are either *true* or *false*. It is customary to only draw *true* transitions in a graph: missing transitions are assumed to be *false*.

Additional truth values in the logic can increase its expressiveness and lead to more informative answers when verifying a property. Such multi-valued logics, which are logics with more than two truth values, can be defined using lattices.

2.1 Lattices

A lattice $\mathcal{L} = \langle L, \sqsubseteq \rangle$ is a partially ordered ($\sqsubseteq$) set of elements L, in which any two elements have a least upper bound (join or $\sqcup$) and a greatest lower bound (meet or $\sqcap$). A lattice has a join and meet for each non-empty finite subset of elements. Therefore, a non-empty finite lattice is bounded, and has a least element (bottom or $\bot$) and greatest element (top or $\top$). In a distributive lattice meet and join distribute over each other.

A Boolean logic can be described as a lattice consisting of only two elements, with *false* being the bottom and *true* being the top; see Fig. 1a. The Boolean conjunction ($\wedge$) and disjunction ($\vee$) operations map respectively to the meet ($\sqcap$) and join ($\sqcup$) of the lattice. To create a multi-valued logic we can use lattices that have additional elements beyond *true* and *false*.

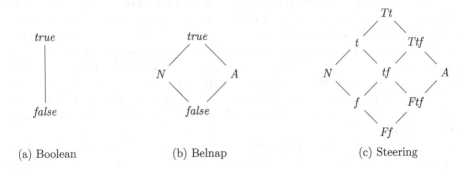

(a) Boolean   (b) Belnap   (c) Steering

Fig. 1. Distributive lattices

2.2   Quasi-Boolean Logics

The multi-valued logics we are interested in are quasi-Boolean logics, also called De Morgan logics. Without the requirements of excluded middle ($x \vee \neg x = true$) and noncontradiction ($x \wedge \neg x = false$), they generalise Boolean logics.

The lattice of a quasi-Boolean logic $\mathcal{L} = \langle L, \leq, \neg \rangle$ is bounded and distributive: the bottom element is *false*, the top element is *true*, meet is used as a conjunction ($\wedge$), and join is used as a disjunction ($\vee$). Negation ($\neg$) requires an appropriate involution which, in addition to being its own inverse, should adhere to De Morgan's laws. It follows by definition that disjunction and conjunction are distributive, and the law of double negation applies.

A typical example of a distributive lattice is the one used for Belnap logic, as depicted in Fig. 1b. This logic can be used to encode may and must transitions resulting from abstraction, using respectively N or *true* for may transitions, and A or *true* for must transitions. The steering logic shown in Fig. 1c can encode steering information and will be explained in more detail later. Per definition its element Tt is equal *true* and its element Ff is equal to *false*; and one could define the elements N and A as respectively the empty string and $TFtf$ for reasons of consistency, but this is deemed impractical.

Note that the lattices in Fig. 1 are depicted as Hasse diagrams in which only the transitive reduction of the partial ordering is represented by lines between elements: an element is smaller in $\leq$ than any directly connected element that is further up. (The transitive closure relates any indirectly connected elements.)

2.3   Multi-valued Kripke Models

Multi-valued Kripke models are a generalisation of Kripke models and can use values of any quasi-Boolean logic for transitions and atomic propositions, instead of being limited to the usual Boolean values *true* and *false*. Similarly temporal properties are evaluated over the Kripke model by using the operators as defined by the quasi-Boolean logic. We follow the definition presented in [10].

Definition 1. *A multi-valued Kripke model is a tuple* $M = \langle \mathcal{L}, AP, S, s_0, R, \Theta \rangle$, *where* $\mathcal{L} = \langle L, \leq, \neg \rangle$ *is a quasi-Boolean logic, AP a set of atomic propositions, S a finite set of states, s_0 the initial state, $R : S \times S \to L$ a transition relation mapping to truth values of $\mathcal{L}$, and $\Theta : AP \to (S \to L)$ a labelling function assigning truth values to states for each atomic proposition.*

Definition 2. *A path $\pi = s_1, s_2, \ldots$ is an infinite sequence of states in a multivalued Kripke model $M = \langle \mathcal{L}, AP, S, s_0, R, \Theta \rangle$ with $s_n \in S$ for all $n \geq 1$. The path is called finite iff $R(s_k, s_{k+1}) = false$ for some $k \geq 1$, and infinite otherwise.*

2.4   Linear Temporal Logic

Linear temporal logic (LTL) is used to describe properties of paths through a Kripke model. We use LTL in release positive normal form to aid in our construction of Büchi automata. This is without loss of generality, since any LTL formula can be written in release positive normal form [3]. We also distinguish between a weak and a strong next operator to allow for transitions with truth values different than *true*, for example, when considering finite paths.

Definition 3. *An LTL formula φ over a set of atomic propositions AP is in release positive normal form if:*

$$\varphi = l \mid p \mid \neg p \mid \varphi_1 \wedge \varphi_2 \mid \varphi_1 \vee \varphi_2 \mid \mathsf{X}_s\, \varphi \mid \mathsf{X}_w\, \varphi \mid \varphi_1 \,\mathsf{U}\, \varphi_2 \mid \varphi_1 \,\mathsf{R}\, \varphi_2$$

With $l \in L$ a truth value; $p \in AP$ a proposition; X_s and X_w the strong and weak next operators; U and R the until and release operators; and $\neg, \wedge, \vee$ the Boolean connectives.

The strong next operator $\mathsf{X}_s\, \varphi$ requires that the next state on a path is reachable and that φ holds in this next state. The weak next operator $\mathsf{X}_w\, \varphi$ requires that φ holds in the next state on a path or that this next state is unreachable. Note that these definitions coincide when the next state is reachable. The until operator $\varphi \,\mathsf{U}\, \psi$ verifies whether φ holds in all states up to, but not necessarily including, a state where ψ holds. The release operator $\varphi \,\mathsf{R}\, \psi$ verifies whether ψ holds in all states up to, and including, a state where φ holds. For the until operator to hold it is required for ψ to hold eventually; for the release operator it is sufficient when ψ holds indefinitely. Precise semantics of these operators will be presented in the next section when we look at multi-valued LTL.

LTL formulas apply to paths in the Kripke model using its labelling function Θ; but the formulas do not state whether they apply to all paths or a single path.

An LTL property can either be universally quantified, when we want to verify the property, or existentially quantified, when we want to find a counterexample. A property that needs to be verified for all paths can be put in its negated form to look for counterexamples; a step often taken by model checkers.

2.5   Multi-valued Büchi Automata

Multi-valued Büchi automata as used in this paper are a generalisation of Boolean non-deterministic Büchi automata by using a multi-valued transition relation.

Definition 4. *A multi-valued non-deterministic Büchi automaton is a tuple $A = \langle \mathcal{L}, \Sigma, Q, q_0, \delta, F \rangle$, where $\mathcal{L} = \langle L, \leq, \neg \rangle$ is a quasi-Boolean logic, Σ an alphabet, Q a finite set of states, q_0 the initial state, $\delta : Q \times \Sigma \times Q \rightarrow L$ a transition relation to truth values of $\mathcal{L}$, and $F \subseteq Q$ a set of accepting states.*

The quasi-Boolean logic of the Büchi automata is chosen to match the logic of the Kripke model. The alphabet Σ is defined as $\Sigma = L^{AP}$ with AP the set of atomic propositions of the Kripke model; the transition relation δ can then be defined using the operators of the quasi-Boolean logic.

2.6   Bilattices

Bilattices [7] contain two orderings over the same set of elements. A bilattice is distributive if the meet and join operators of both its orderings are distributive with respect to each other, resulting in twelve distributive laws.

Definition 5. *A bilattice is a tuple $\mathcal{B} = \langle L, \leq_1, \leq_2 \rangle$, with L a set of elements, and $\leq_1$, $\leq_2$ partial orderings on L. Both $\langle L, \leq_1 \rangle$ and $\langle L, \leq_2 \rangle$ form a lattice.*

In the context of logics and abstractions, one ordering is generally called the truth ordering $\leq_t$ and the other the information ordering $\leq_i$ (see e.g. [10]). The truth ordering, with a suitable definition for negation, defines a quasi-Boolean logic; the information ordering models information loss due to abstraction.

The lattices in Fig. 1b and c are also bilattices: an element is smaller in $\leq_t$ than any directly connected element that is further up, and an element is smaller in $\leq_i$ than any directly connected element that is more to the right. To distinguish between lattice operations of the two orderings, we use $\wedge$ or $\vee$ to indicate a meet or join over $\leq_t$, and $\otimes$ or $\oplus$ to indicate a meet or join over $\leq_i$. For more details on using the information order for abstraction of a Kripke model see [11].

3   Multi-valued LTL

The Boolean definitions of LTL operators can be carried over to a multi-valued logic by using the multi-valued definitions of the Boolean connectives. Some simplifications made to the definitions in Boolean logics, however, do not apply to the multi-valued setting, and can cause problems if not correctly dealt with.

3.1   Stutter Extension of Kripke Models

In Boolean LTL model checking it is customary to assume that all transitions on paths through the Kripke model are *true*, and that all paths are infinite [3]. This can be ensured by using the stutter invariance of LTL properties without a next operator: the truth of such properties does not change if a state already on a path is finitely repeated. For example the path $\pi_1 = s_1, s_2, s_3, \ldots$ cannot be distinguished from $\pi_2 = s_1, s_2, s_2, s_2, s_3, \ldots$ by stutter invariant properties.

The requirement that stuttering is limited to a finite number of repetitions prevents paths from diverging; a path that diverges gets stuck in the repeated state, and never continues on the original path. This however does not apply to deadlock states, since there is no path to continue on; therefore, in Boolean LTL model checking, self loops can be placed on deadlock states, such that finite paths ending in a deadlock state change into infinite paths diverging on the deadlock state. This is called a stutter extension and when applied to a Boolean Kripke model ensures that all its paths are infinite.

3.2   Strong and Weak Next Operators

In Boolean model checking with stutter extensions there is no difference between strong and weak next, since all transitions in a path are *true* and there is always a next state. In multi-valued model checking this is no longer the case, since besides *true* and *false* there can be truth values for which stutter extension is not a solution. Adding a self loop in those cases would cause unwanted divergence, and it would suggest that an execution can simultaneously halt and continue.

Without stutter extensions, even Boolean model checking needs to make a distinction between a strong and weak next operator, but at least the requirement of stutter invariance can be safely dropped.

Definition 6. *Given a single path $\pi = s_1, s_2, \ldots$ in a multi-valued Kripke model $M = \langle \mathcal{L}, AP, S, s_0, R, \Theta \rangle$. The strong and weak next operators of LTL have the following definitions respectively:*

$$[\mathsf{X}_s \, \varphi]_1 = R(s_1, s_2) \wedge [\varphi]_2 \qquad\qquad [\mathsf{X}_w \, \varphi]_1 = \neg R(s_1, s_2) \vee [\varphi]_2$$

Evaluation of a property ψ over the path $\pi' = s_n, s_{n+1}, \ldots$ is indicated by $[\psi]_n$.

These definitions only consider a single path in isolation, ignoring all other transitions in the Kripke model that are not a part of it. We will remove this restriction in the following sections when we introduce the notion of maximality; and we will see that it is necessary to consider the truth values of all outgoing transitions for each state in a path.

For Boolean logic, due to the law of excluded middle, an alternative definition of X_w is $\neg R(s_1, s_2) \vee (R(s_1, s_2) \wedge [\varphi]_2)$. This can be rewritten as $(\neg R(s_1, s_2) \vee [\varphi]_2) \wedge (R(s_1, s_2) \vee \neg R(s_1, s_2))$, in which the second disjunct is *true*. In quasi-Boolean logics we lack the law of excluded middle, but the linear-time semantics of LTL still require that transitions are either taken or not: it makes no sense to evaluate a property over an execution that neither halts nor continues. We assume this requirement holds for each transitions of the Kripke model by taking $R(s_1, s_2) \vee \neg R(s_1, s_2) = true$, resulting in the definition for X_w as given above. This does not introduce any requirements on the Kripke model or make any assumptions on the value of $R(s_1, s_2)$.

3.3 Until and Release Operators

Using the definitions for strong and weak next, we can define the until and release operators for a single multi-valued path. The next operators, which would otherwise break stutter invariance, will preserve this invariance when used in the context of the until and release operators. Note that the duality $\neg(\varphi \cup \psi) = \neg\varphi \, R \, \neg\psi$ between until and release is preserved, since we have $\neg X_s \varphi = X_w \neg\varphi$.

Definition 7. *Using the weak and strong next operator, the until and release operators have the following expansion laws:*

$$\varphi \cup \psi \equiv \psi \vee (\varphi \wedge X_s(\varphi \cup \psi)) \qquad \varphi \, R \, \psi \equiv \psi \wedge (\varphi \vee X_w(\varphi \, R \, \psi))$$

By definition $\varphi \cup \psi$ is the least solution of its expansion law and requires that ψ is evaluated at some point, while $\varphi \, R \, \psi$ is the greatest solution of its expansion law and does not require that φ is evaluated at some point.

Due to the additional requirement on $\varphi \cup \psi$, its expansion can not ignore ψ indefinitely. In disjunctive normal form, only the clauses of finite length are considered: the infinite clause $c = \varphi \wedge X_s(c)$ is not included in the evaluation.

In Boolean Kripke models, these expansions work as expected. In a path where $\varphi \cup \psi$ encounters a *false* transition, the strong next operator ensures that the property becomes *false* if ψ has not been *true* yet. The strong next requires ψ to hold at some point. Similarly when $\varphi \, R \, \psi$ encounters a *false* transition, the weak next operator ensures that the property becomes *true* even when φ has not been *true* yet. The weak next allows φ to never hold.

3.4 Paths with False Transitions

The definitions of the LTL operators given in the previous sections are correct for a single Boolean or quasi-Boolean path, but can give incorrect results when universally or existentially quantifying over all paths in a Kripke model. This becomes apparent when we consider paths with *false* transitions.

In principle, paths with *false* transitions can be safely ignored if their first *false* transition originates from a non-deadlock state. However, quasi-Boolean logics allow for transitions that are only partially *false* and states that are only partially deadlocked. In the following we investigate paths with *false* transitions to exemplify the issue and reach a more general solution.

In Fig. 2a we see a Kripke model with each state labelled by the propositions that are *true* in that state, while propositions that are not part of the label are *false*. All transitions drawn in the figure have the transition value *true*, while

(a) Single path   (b) Steering

Fig. 2. Example Kripke models

omitted transitions have the transition value *false*. The small incoming arrow indicates the initial state of the model.

If we only consider paths without *false* transitions, then $\varphi \cup \psi$ holds universally, but $\psi R \varphi$ does not hold existentially. This follows from the only path $\pi_1 = \varphi, \psi, \psi, \ldots$ without *false* transitions. (States are uniquely identified by their propositions in this example.) If we allow paths to include *false* transitions, then we should also consider the path $\pi_2 = \varphi, \varphi, \ldots$ among others.

Quantifying over all paths, irrespective of transition values, would give incorrect results. The property $\psi R \varphi$ would hold existentially, since it holds for π_2. (The execution effectively halts after the first φ in the path by taking a *false* transition, and φ is never released.) The property $\varphi \cup \psi$ would not hold universally, since it does not hold for π_2. (The execution halts, and ψ will never hold.) We need to adapt the definitions of the LTL operators if we want to use them on a multi-valued Kripke model.

3.5 Maximality

Paths with *false* transitions can give incorrect results. The same problem applies to multi-valued transitions that are only partially *true*. To get correct results we need to consider to what extent a transition is allowed to stop the execution; this is done by taking into account the other transitions from the same state. For the specific case of a *false* transition this means that we only halt the execution to the extent we can not make progress through any of the other transitions. This requirement is formalised using the notion of maximality.

Definition 8. *Given a multi-valued Kripke model* $M = \langle \mathcal{L}, AP, S, s_0, R, \Theta \rangle$, *for the transition from state* $s_1 \in S$ *to* $s_2 \in S$, *the predicate* other, *the predicate* halt, *and the maximality* max *are defined as:*

$$\mathrm{other}(s_1, s_2) = \bigvee_{o \in S \setminus \{s_2\}} R(s_1, o)$$
$$\mathrm{halt}(s_1, s_2) = \neg \mathrm{other}(s_1, s_2) \wedge \neg R(s_1, s_2)$$
$$\mathrm{max}(s_1, s_2) = \neg \mathrm{other}(s_1, s_2) \vee \ R(s_1, s_2)$$

Maximality of a transition is defined by its own value, and the values of other transitions from the same state. Looking at the border cases, a *true* transition is always maximal, but the maximality of a *false* transition depends on the other transitions. This ensures that halting the execution, by taking a *false* transition from the current state, depends on the degree to which the current state is a deadlock state. In addition, maximality is equal to the transition value if any other transition is *true*, or equal to *true* if all other transitions are *false*.

Including the value s_2 in the disjunction over $o \in S \backslash \{s_2\}$ in the definition of other results in an alternative definition for maximality: $\max'(s_1, s_2) = \max(s_1, s_2) \wedge (R(s_1, s_2) \vee \neg R(s_1, s_2))$. The definitions coincide for Boolean logic, but not for multi-valued logics without excluded middle. We assume $R(s_1, s_2) \vee \neg R(s_1, s_2) = true$ for each transitions of the Kripke model by using the original definition for maximality; otherwise, we would incorrectly test for excluded middle and fail for any transition value other than *true* or *false*.

We revise the definitions of our LTL operators to require maximality; this is comparable to requiring fair paths under a fairness condition. A property under fairness in the universal case requires a path to be not fair or uphold the property, while the existential case requires a path to be fair and uphold the property. We can similarly change our definitions to require maximality of transitions in addition to the original requirements.

In a multi-valued setting, maximality can not be evaluated separately from the LTL property for the path as a whole, but needs to be evaluated simultaneously with the LTL property for each individual transition. This is necessary, since a violation of a property at state s_n of a path, should only be influenced by the maximality of the path up to s_n. This requires us to choose between existential or universal quantification of our LTL formulas and modify our definitions accordingly to include maximality. In the following we assume existential quantification, since Büchi automata are used to search for counterexamples. Imposing maximality on top of Definition 7 gives us the following existential definitions:

Definition 9. *Given a path* $\pi = s_1, s_2, \ldots$ *in a multi-valued Kripke model* $M = \langle \mathcal{L}, AP, S, s_0, R, \Theta \rangle$ *such that* $s_1, s_2, \ldots \in S$. *The strong next and weak next have the following existential definitions:*

$$[X_s \, \varphi]_1 = R(s_1, s_2) \wedge [\varphi]_2 \qquad [X_w \, \varphi]_1 = \max(s_1, s_2) \wedge (\mathrm{halt}(s_1, s_2) \vee [\varphi]_2)$$

We can define the strong next operator analogous to weak next as $\max(s_1, s_2) \wedge (R(s_1, s_2) \wedge [\varphi]_2)$, but this reduces to the definition given above since $\max(s_1, s_2) \wedge R(s_1, s_2) = R(s_1, s_2)$. The strong next operator already works correctly in the existential case for *false* transitions. In the definition of the weak next operator, $\mathrm{halt}(s_1, s_2)$ replaces the $\neg R(s_1, s_2)$ of the original definition to prevent introducing a test for noncontradiction: $\max(s_1, s_2) \wedge \neg R(s_1, s_2) = \mathrm{halt}(s_1, s_2) \vee (R(s_1, s_2) \wedge \neg R(s_1, s_2))$. We assume noncontradiction for each transition of the Kripke model by taking $R(s_1, s_2) \wedge \neg R(s_1, s_2) = false$. Note that indeed $\max(s_1, s_2) \wedge \mathrm{halt}(s_1, s_2) = \mathrm{halt}(s_1, s_2)$.

4   Steering Logic

We take a closer look at the nine-valued lattice of Fig. 1c. Our motivation for developing this logic and the theory of this paper is to investigate multi-valued abstraction in the context of steerability: guiding the execution of a program to avoid bugs. This can for example be done by the scheduler of the operation system or by instrumenting the original program. Values of the nine-valued lattice should be interpreted as values indicating the steerability of transitions. They can be attached to transitions using quasi-Boolean guards in the modelling language: a quasi-Boolean expression that determines the transition value.

4.1   Semantics

The lattice of Fig. 1c can be used to encode steerability information in a model. Values of the lattice are effectively subsets of $\{t, f, T, F\}$ with N being the empty set, and A being the complete set. We use the convention that lowercase letters indicate truth under steering and uppercase letters indicate truth by default. Negation is defined as exchanging T with F and t with f in the subset. Keep in mind that while the subset construction is helpful to understand the semantics behind the truth values, the subsets are indivisible as truth values of the logic.

The intuition of the individual values is that T indicates a transition that is enabled by default: during execution it can be non-deterministically chosen to further the execution. A value t indicates a transition that can be enabled when controlling the execution: if we want this transition to be considered, we will have to influence the execution. Similarly F is a transition that is disabled by default, while f can be disabled when controlling the execution.

We could use all possible subsets of these base values to form a lattice, but we can reduce the number of values by adding a restriction: if a subset contains an uppercase value, then it also needs to contain the corresponding lowercase value. For example, we do not allow the value T, but do allow the value Tt. The reason for this restriction is that a transition that is enabled by default can be trivially enabled when controlled, simply by not exerting any influence.

To indicate a steerable transition we can also use the values tf, Ttf, and Ftf. They respectively indicate a transition that: can be enabled or disabled when controlled (tf); is enabled by default, but can be disabled when controlled (Ttf); and is disabled by default, but can be enabled when controlled (Ftf). Using these values in a multi-valued Kripke model enables us to detect how a property is influenced by the ability to steer an execution. For example, a property with the value tf can be enforced or broken using steering, while a value Ttf holds by default, but can be broken using steering.

4.2   Example

To demonstrate the necessity of maximality, we give an example using steering logic. In Fig. 2b we have a state space with multi-valued transitions: labeled transitions have the value as depicted, unlabelled transitions have the value *true*, and omitted transitions have the value *false*. The t transition can be enabled by steering, while the f transition can be disabled.

If we evaluate the existential property $\varphi \mathrel{R} \psi$ in the initial state, then we have two infinite paths without *false* transitions: one taking the t transition and the other taking the f transition. Paths with *false* transitions are ignored a priori: without maximality they lead to incorrect results and with maximality they have no influence. For the remaining two paths, with or without maximality, $\varphi \, R \, \psi$ is *false* after the t transition and *true* after the f transition.

To calculate $\varphi \, R \, \psi$ without maximality we use Definition 6. The path over the t transition gives $[\varphi \, R \, \psi]_1 = true \wedge (false \vee (\neg t \vee false)) = f$. The path over the f transition gives $[\varphi \, R \, \psi]_1 = true \wedge (false \vee (\neg f \vee true)) = true$. The *true* result of the second path suggests that $\varphi \, R \, \psi$ holds, irrespective of how we steer; but it forgoes that, with the f transition disabled, it is ignored in favour of any other transition, such as the t transition. The initial state is never a deadlock state: we are not allowed to halt the execution by disabling the f transition.

In comparison, to calculate $\varphi \, R \, \psi$ with maximality we use Definition 9. The path over the t transition gives $[\varphi \, R \, \psi]_1 = true \wedge (false \vee ((\neg f \vee t) \wedge ((\neg t \wedge \neg f) \vee false))) = f$. The path over the f transition gives $[\varphi R \psi]_1 = true \wedge (false \vee ((\neg t \vee f) \wedge ((\neg t \wedge \neg f) \vee true))) = f$. The f result of the second path correctly models that by disabling the f transition we can steer to ignore this path in favour of others. The maximality in the path over the f transition correctly models the influence of the other transitions on our ability to halt the execution.

5   Creating Büchi Automata

Explicit state LTL model checking verifies a property by searching for counterexamples in a state space: the product of a Kripke model describing the program, and a Büchi automaton encoding the negation of the property. Counterexamples are paths ending in an accepting cycle of the state space: cycles containing states that have been marked as accepting in the Büchi automaton.

The truth of a counterexample is the conjunction of its transition values, while multiple counterexamples can be combined using disjunction. The negation of this disjunction is the truth of the property. If no accepting cycles with truth larger than *false* are found, then the property is *true* for the model.

5.1   The Algorithm

Our algorithm for generating multi-valued Büchi automata is an adaptation of the algorithm presented in [8]. It starts with a graph consisting of a single node containing a single proof obligation: the LTL formula under verification. Nodes in the graph are then iteratively expanded by creating new transitions to new nodes. The transitions contain requirements on atomic propositions of the current state, while the new nodes contain proof obligations for the next state.

Our algorithm differs from [8] in that we cannot use all of the transitions in the multi-valued Kripke model in their positive form: we also require support for calculating $\neg R(s_1, s_2)$ and $\neg other(s_1, s_2)$. In addition we use the more conventional method of evaluating atomic propositions of the Kripke model using the transitions of the Büchi automaton, instead of its states.

The Kripke model is modified to include the atomic propositions r and o. After each transition from a state $s_1 \in S$ to a state $s_2 \in S$, the model ensures that $r = R(s_1, s_2)$ and $o = \mathrm{other}(s_1, s_2)$. These propositions are then used to calculate $\max(s_1, s_2)$ and $\mathrm{halt}(s_1, s_2)$. This can require duplication of the original state if there are multiple incoming transitions for which r and o do not agree. When interleaved with the Büchi automaton all transitions of the Kripke model are *true*; only r will be equal to $R(s_1, s_2)$.

Given a multi-valued Kripke model with atomic propositions AP and quasi-Boolean logic $\mathcal{L} = \langle L, \leq, \neg \rangle$, we want to create a Büchi automaton to verify whether a temporal property $\neg\varphi$ holds universally for the complete state space of the model. The algorithm creates a proof graph on the basis of which we can construct the Büchi automaton.

Definition 10. *A proof graph is a tuple $\mathcal{G} = \langle N, n_0, T, R \rangle$ with $N : \mathcal{P}(\mathcal{P}(LTL))$ a set of proof nodes, n_0 the initial node, $T : \mathcal{P}(\mathcal{P}(LTL))$ a set of proof transitions and $R : N \times N \to T$ a transition relation.*

Each node and transition is a set of proof obligations: a set of LTL formulas that need to be verified. Initially proof nodes are related using $\{false\}$ transitions. We can assume without loss of generality that all LTL formulas are in release positive normal form.

The algorithm starts by creating a single initial node $\{\varphi\}$ in the proof graph, with φ the counterexample we are searching for. This initial node will be made the current node, making it the first node up for expansion. (In the following t and f are variables and should not be considered as truth values.)

(a) Expand O_1 (b) Match f

Fig. 3. Preliminaries

A node $n = O_1$ is expanded by creating an initial transition $t = O_1$ from n to a destination $d = \emptyset$, as shown in Fig. 3a. Starting with this initial transition, a transition t from a node n to a destination d is processed by removing an obligation $f \in t$ from t and executing the following rules by matching on the formula f. When this results in a split, a copy t' of t is created to a corresponding copy d' of d. Processing continues on t, or in case of a split on both t and t', until only literals (p or $\neg p$, with $p \in AP$) and truth values ($l \in L$) remain.

$\varphi \wedge \psi$	Add φ and ψ to t.
$\varphi \vee \psi$	Split t, add φ to t, add ψ to t'.
$\mathsf{X}_s\, \varphi$	Add r and φ to d.
$\mathsf{X}_w\, \varphi$	Split t, add $\neg r$ and $\neg o$ to d, add $r \vee \neg o$ and φ to d'.
$\varphi\, \mathsf{U}\, \psi$	Split t, add φ and $\mathsf{X}_s(\varphi\, \mathsf{U}\, \psi)$ to t, add ψ to t'.
$\varphi\, \mathsf{R}\, \psi$	Split t, add ψ and $\mathsf{X}_w(\varphi\, \mathsf{R}\, \psi)$ to t, add φ and ψ t'.

Applying the rules on an obligation f of transition t from O_1 to O_2, as depicted in Fig. 3b, will result in the transitions of Fig. 4. With regard to the temporal operators we effectively follow Definitions 7 and 9 when put in disjunctive normal form.

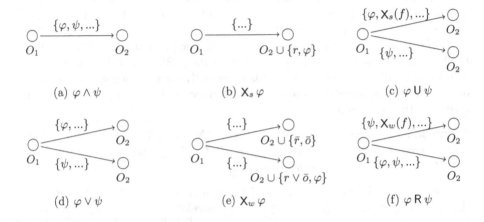

(a) $\varphi \wedge \psi$ (b) $X_s\, \varphi$ (c) $\varphi\, U\, \psi$

(d) $\varphi \vee \psi$ (e) $X_w\, \varphi$ (f) $\varphi\, R\, \psi$

Fig. 4. Splitting transitions

After processing the current node, the algorithm checks for optimisations. Transitions that are inconsistent in their proof obligations, such that their conjunction results in *false*, are removed. Truth values in a transition are combined into a single value using conjunction. Nodes with identical proof obligations are combined; and multiple transitions $t_1, \ldots, t_n$ between the same two nodes are replaced by a single transition $\{\bigwedge(t_1) \vee \ldots \vee \bigwedge(t_n)\}$.

Expansion continues in a depth-first manner by following one of the transitions to a new current node. Only nodes that have not been visited before are considered. The algorithm stops when all nodes have been visited.

5.2   The Multi-valued Büchi Automaton

Having constructed a proof graph, we can create the multi-valued Büchi automaton $\langle \mathcal{L}, \Sigma, Q, q_0, \delta, F \rangle$ required for interleaving with the multi-valued Kripke model $\langle \mathcal{L}, AP, S, s_0, R, \Theta \rangle$. We create a state q_k for each node n_k of the proof graph; the initial node n_0 corresponds to the initial Büchi state q_0.

Transitions between Büchi states correspond to transitions between proof states. The transition relation $\delta : Q \times \Sigma \times Q \to L$ of the Büchi automaton returns a conjunction of the proof obligations contained in the corresponding transition between proof nodes. In the case of multi-valued Kripke models we use $\Sigma = L^{AP}$, such that $\delta : Q \times L^{AP} \times Q \to L$. We can therefore define the transition relation as $\delta(q_s, \sigma, q_t) = \sigma\,(\bigwedge(R(n_s, n_t)))$ with $\sigma : L^{AP}$ being used as a mapping from atomic propositions to truth values. (When applied to an expression, each occurrence of an atomic proposition is replaced by its corresponding truth value.)

The construction of the proof graph for an LTL property φ might suggest that any infinite path in the graph corresponds to a proof of φ. This is however not the case for the until operator, and the reason why accepting states of the Büchi automaton are significant. When evaluating $\varphi \cup \psi$ in the Boolean setting, its definition requires that ψ becomes *true* at some point during the execution. For the multi-valued setting this means that in the disjunctive normal form of the until operator we do not consider the conjunct that is the infinite conjunction of φ. This is enforced in the Büchi automaton by creating an acceptance set F for each sub-formula of the form $\varphi \cup \psi$, such that $q_k \in F$ iff $\varphi \cup \psi \notin n_k$ or $\psi \in n_k$. An accepting run of the Büchi automaton should pass infinitely often through at least one member of each acceptance set.

Our definition of multi-valued Büchi automata only allows for one acceptance set. This limitation simplifies the requirements on the model checker looking for accepting loops in the combined state space. It is straightforward to convert a Büchi automaton with multiple acceptance sets to one with a single acceptance set, by putting multiple copies of the original Büchi automaton in sequence: make one copy for each acceptance set, and have transitions move from one copy to the next after reaching an accepting state for the current acceptance set. For further details see [3], where generalised non-deterministic Büchi automata (GNBA) are transformed into non-deterministic Büchi automata (NBA).

Theorem 1. *The product state space of a modified Kripke model and a multi-valued Büchi automaton as described in Sect. 5 encodes the given LTL property $\neg\varphi$ such that the disjunction of all counterexamples is the truth of φ.*

Proof (Sketch). This follows directly from Definitions 7 and 9. The algorithm ensures that each accepting path through the Büchi automaton corresponds to a conjunct of φ in disjunctive normal form. Finite conjuncts correspond to paths diverging on an accepting state $\emptyset$ with a *true* self-loop. Only paths of conjuncts that require a $\gamma \cup \psi$ but do not consider ψ at some point, are not accepting. $\square$

The resulting multi-valued Büchi automaton can be used to verify the property φ over the multi-valued Kripke model when the transitions of the Kripke model in the interleaved state space are all valued as *true*. The actual transition value is derived from atomic propositions in the target Kripke state by the Büchi automaton. (Transitions of the Büchi automaton can be described as a conjunction of this transition value and an additional truth value derived from the original atomic propositions of the Kripke model.) These additional atomic propositions can however increase the size of the Kripke model.

We can opt for an implementation that slightly deviates from the normal definition of a Büchi automaton. Instead of encoding the transition values with atomic propositions in the target Kripke state, we can use atomic propositions of the Büchi automaton to signal the Kripke model what value we require for its next transition. The Kripke model can then directly calculate these values from its state, without having to resort to additional bookkeeping. Changes to the size of the Büchi automaton are negligible, since the additional state of the atomic propositions is directly related to the original destination Büchi state.

This alternate implementation might even result in a reduced size for the Büchi automaton when there are original states that only differ in their calculation of the transition value.

6 Future Work

We are implementing the presented algorithm to facilitate multi-valued model checking in the (distributed) SpinJa model checker [6,12]. Together with the steering logic that was considered in Sect. 4, this will allow us to investigate execution steering based on abstract models [11], building on our previous implementation of multi-valued model checking [2,13].

References

1. Andrade, J.O., Kameyama, Y.: Efficient multi-valued bounded model checking for LTL over quasi-Boolean algebras. IEICE Trans. **95**–**D**(5), 1355–1364 (2012)
2. Augustijn, R.: Multivalued logics and hyper transitions in SpinJa. Master's thesis. Vrije Universiteit Amsterdam (2015)
3. Baier, C., Katoen, J.P.: Principles of Model Checking. MIT Press, Cambridge (2008)
4. Bruns, G., Godefroid, P.: Model checking with multi-valued logics. In: Díaz, J., Karhumäki, J., Lepistö, A., Sannella, D. (eds.) ICALP 2004. LNCS, vol. 3142, pp. 281–293. Springer, Heidelberg (2004). doi:10.1007/978-3-540-27836-8_26
5. Chechik, M., Devereux, B., Gurfinkel, A.: Model-checking in finite state-space systems with fine-grained abstractions using SPIN. In: Dwyer, M. (ed.) SPIN 2001. LNCS, vol. 2057, pp. 16–36. Springer, Heidelberg (2001). doi:10.1007/3-540-45139-0_3
6. de Jonge, M., Ruys, T.C.: The SpinJa model checker. In: Pol, J., Weber, M. (eds.) SPIN 2010. LNCS, vol. 6349, pp. 124–128. Springer, Heidelberg (2010). doi:10.1007/978-3-642-16164-3_9
7. Fitting, M.: Bilattices and the theory of truth. J. Philos. Logic **18**, 225–256 (1989)
8. Gerth, R., Peled, D.A., Vardi, M.Y., Wolper, P.: Simple on-the-fly automatic verification of linear temporal logic. In: Dembiński, P., Średniawa, M. (eds.) PSTV. IFIP, vol. 38, pp. 3–18. Springer, Heidelberg (1995). Chapman & Hall
9. Kupferman, O., Lustig, Y.: Lattice automata. In: Cook, B., Podelski, A. (eds.) VMCAI 2007. LNCS, vol. 4349, pp. 199–213. Springer, Heidelberg (2007). doi:10.1007/978-3-540-69738-1_14
10. Meller, Y., Grumberg, O., Shoham, S.: A Framework for compositional verification of multi-valued systems via abstraction-refinement. In: Liu, Z., Ravn, A.P. (eds.) ATVA 2009. LNCS, vol. 5799, pp. 271–288. Springer, Heidelberg (2009). doi:10.1007/978-3-642-04761-9_21
11. Vijzelaar, S.J.J., Fokkink, W.J.: Multi-valued simulation and abstraction using lattice operations. ACM Trans. Embedded Comput. Syst. **16**(2), 42:1–42:26 (2017)
12. Vijzelaar, S.J.J., Verstoep, C., Fokkink, W.J., Bal, H.E.: Distributed MAP in the SpinJa model checker. In: PDMC, EPTCS, vol. 72, pp. 84–90 (2011)
13. Vijzelaar, S.J.J., Verstoep, C., Fokkink, W.J., Bal, H.E.: Bonsai: cutting models down to size. In: Voronkov, A., Virbitskaite, I. (eds.) PSI 2014. LNCS, vol. 8974, pp. 361–375. Springer, Heidelberg (2015). doi:10.1007/978-3-662-46823-4_29

Privacy Assessment Using Static Taint Analysis (Tool Paper)

Marcel von Maltitz$^{(\boxtimes)}$, Cornelius Diekmann, and Georg Carle

Technische Universität München, Munich, Germany
{vonmaltitz,diekmann,carle}@net.in.tum.de

Abstract. When developing and maintaining distributed systems, auditing privacy properties gains more and more relevance. Nevertheless, this task is lacking support of automated tools and, hence, is mostly carried out manually. We present a formal approach which enables auditors to model the flow of critical data in order to shed new light on a system and to automatically verify given privacy constraints. The formalization is incorporated into a larger policy analysis and verification framework and overall soundness is proven with Isabelle/HOL. Using this solution, it becomes possible to automatically compute architectures which follow specified privacy conditions or to input an existing architecture for verification. Our tool is evaluated in two real-world case studies, where we uncover and fix previously unknown violations of privacy.

1 Introduction

Privacy enhancing technologies provide measures to improve the privacy properties of systems, when applied correctly. But they are not necessarily sufficient, as privacy must also be incorporated on the level of the system *architectures* and already be considered during the design of a newly developed system [4]. There exist multiple approaches [1–4,7,17] which aim for developing a high-level concept of privacy in order to enable privacy assessment and auditing of IT systems and their designs. Nevertheless, detailed, often manual, examination is necessary, making audits a complex and time-consuming task. Driven empirically and by running code, *dynamic taint analysis* has been recently used successfully in the Android world to enhance user privacy [12,18] by tracking the flow of critical information at runtime. However measures from the formal world still offer unleveraged potential for assessing privacy conformance of architectures. We aim for connecting the best of both worlds by making privacy-relevant aspects more explicit and easier to verify.

The abstract concept of 'security' has been made more tangible and verifiable by deriving protection goals, in particular *confidentiality, integrity,* and *availability.* The same method has been applied to the abstract concept of 'privacy' and

This work has been supported by the German Federal Ministry of Education and Research, project DecADe, grant 16KIS0538.

Published by Springer International Publishing AG 2017. All Rights Reserved
A. Bouajjani and A. Silva (Eds.): FORTE 2017, LNCS 10321, pp. 225–235, 2017.
DOI: 10.1007/978-3-319-60225-7_16

another triad of protection goals was derived: *Unlinkability, Transparency,* and *Intervenability* [2,17].

In distributed systems, privacy aspects can be examined by focusing on the flow of data between system components. Borrowing ideas from dynamic taint analysis and their success in the Android world, we demonstrate that coarse-grained taint analysis is applicable to auditing of *distributed* architectures regarding the aforementioned privacy goals, can be done completely *static* (preventing runtime failures), while providing strong *formal guarantees.*

We motivate this concept by a simple, fictional example: A house, equipped with a smart meter to measure its energy consumption. In addition, the owner provides location information via her smartphone to allow the system to turn off the lights when she leaves the home. Once every month, the aggregated energy consumption is sent over the internet to the energy provider for billing.

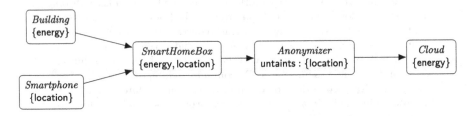

Fig. 1. Example: privacy concerns and information flow in a smart home

We are interested in the privacy implications of this setup and perform a taint tracking analysis. The software architecture is visualized in Fig. 1. The *Building* produces information about its energy consumption, hence we label it as taint source and assign it the energy label. Likewise, the *Smartphone* tracks the location of its owner. Both data is sent to the *SmartHomeBox*. Since the *SmartHomeBox* aggregates all data, it is assigned the set {energy, location} of taint labels. The user wants to transmit only the energy information, not her location to the energy provider's *Cloud*. Therefore, the *Anonymizer* filters the information and removes all location information. We call this process *untainting*. With the *Anonymizer* operating correctly, only energy-related information ends up in the energy provider's *Cloud*, since {energy, location}\{location} = {energy}.

Even for clearly specified privacy requirements, the confidence in a software evaluation may vary vastly. For example, the Common Criteria [6] define several Evaluation Assurance Levels (EAL). For the highest assurance level, formal verification is required, e.g. using the theorem prover Isabelle/HOL [16]. One remarkable work in the field of formal verification with Isabelle/HOL is the verification of information-flow enforcement for the C implementation of the seL4 microkernel [15]. Similarly, to provide high confidence in our results, we have carried out this research completely in Isabelle/HOL. For brevity, we skip all proofs in this paper. Further details can be found in the full version of this paper and the proofs are provided in the accompanying theory files (cf. Section Availability).

Our proposed solution is a small—yet, fully formal and real-world applicable—step towards modeling (privacy-critical) data flows in distributed systems using taint labels, while being agnostic with respect to the exact notion of privacy chosen by the auditor. Our approach rather opens up a new viewpoint and further enables specifying constraints on data flow which can be automatically verified by our solution. Our case studies show that, even with this restricted toolset, vital insights in real-world systems are already possible. In the first case study, an energy monitoring system similar to Fig. 1, we could make the informal claims of the system's original architects explicit and verify them. In the second case study, a smartphone measurement framework, we demonstrate the complete audit of the real-world implementation in a fully-automated manner, uncovering previously unknown bugs. To the best of our knowledge, this is the first time that such an audit, which bridges the gap from an abstract taint analysis to complex low-level firewall rules, has been performed completely with the assurance level provided by the theorem prover Isabelle/HOL [16].

Our Mission Statement. It is not our goal to formalize the privacy protection goals of unlinkability, transparency, and intervenability. We aim for creating an environment which provides the necessary information for an auditor to start assessing those scenario-specific goals. We aim for statically analyzing distributed systems by considering their architecture specification as we found that this level of abstraction can both be mapped to the real-world implementation of a system, as well as being formally decidable. We intend to lay the groundwork to add *automatic* support for the mentioned privacy protection goals on top; our case study reveals that this is already doable today under certain circumstances.

2   Formalization and Implementation

"The architecture defines the structure of a software system in terms of components and (allowed) dependencies" [13]. We will stick to this high-level, abstract, implementation-agnostic definition for the formalization. As illustrated in Fig. 1, a graph can be conveniently used to describe a system architecture. We assume that we have a graph $G = (V, E)$ without taint label annotations which specifies a distributed architecture. Since such a graph specifies the permitted information flows and all allowed accesses, it is sometimes also called a *policy*. To analyze, formalize, and verify policies represented as graphs, we utilize the *topoS* [9,11] framework. It allows specification of predicates over a graph, which are called *security invariants*. They follow special design criteria to ensure the overall soundness of *topoS*. To define a new security invariant, *topoS* imposes strict proof obligations. In return, *topoS* offers arbitrary composability of all security invariants, generic analysis/verification algorithms, and secure auto-completion of user-defined partial attribute assignments [11]. By integrating our formalization into *topoS*, we also obtain a usable and executable tool.

We formalize tainting as a security invariant for *topoS*. To foster intuition, we first present a simplified model which does not support trust or untainting. However, we have aligned this section constructively such that all the results obtained for simple model follow analogously for the full model.

Let t be a total function which returns the taint labels for an entity, for example, t *SmartHomeBox* = {energy, location}. Given an architecture specification $G = (V, E)$, intuitively, information-flow security according to the taint model can be understood as follows: Information leaving a node v is tainted with v's taint labels, hence every receiver r must have the respective taint labels to receive the information. In other words, for every node v in the graph, all nodes r which are reachable from v must have at least v's taint labels. Representing reachability by the transitive closure (i.e. E^+), the invariant can be formalized as follows:

$$\text{tainting } (V, E) \ t \equiv \forall v \in V. \ \forall r \in \{r. \ (v, r) \in E^+\}. \ t \ v \subseteq t \ r$$

For this formalization, we discharged the proof obligations imposed by *topoS*. This enables us to make use of all generic features of *topoS*, for example, a user may specify a t which is not total.

Analysis: Tainting vs. Bell-LaPadula Model. The Bell-LaPadula model (BLP) is the traditional, de-facto standard model for label-based information-flow security. The question arises whether we can justify our taint model using BLP. *topoS* comes with a pre-defined formalization of the BLP model [11]. The labels in BLP, often called security clearances, are defined as a total order: unclassified $\leq$ confidential $\leq$ secret $\leq$ ... Let sc be a total function which assigns a security clearance to each node. Since our policy model does not distinguish read from write actions, the BLP invariant simply states that receivers must have the necessary security clearance for the information they receive:

$$\text{blp } (V, E) \ sc \equiv \forall (v_1, v_2) \in E. \ sc \ v_1 \leq sc \ v_2$$

We will now show that one **tainting** invariant is equal to BLP invariants for every taint label. We define a function project a Ts, which translates a set of taint labels Ts to a security clearance depending on whether a is in the set of taint labels. Formally, project a Ts $\equiv$ **if** $a \in Ts$ **then** confidential **else** unclassified. Using function composition, the term *project* a $\circ$ t is a function which first looks up the taint labels of a node and projects them afterwards.

Theorem 1 (Tainting and Bell-LaPadula Equivalence).

$$\text{tainting } G \ t \longleftrightarrow \forall a. \ \text{blp } G \ (\text{project } a \circ t)$$

The '$\rightarrow$'-direction of our theorem shows that one **tainting** invariant guarantees individual privacy according to BLP for each taint label. This implies that every user of a software can obtain her personal privacy guarantees. This fulfills the *transparency* requirement for individual users. The '$\leftarrow$'-direction shows that tainting is as expressive as BLP. This justifies the theoretic foundations w.r.t. the well-studied BLP model. These findings are in line with Denning's lattice interpretation [8]; however, to the best of our knowledge, we are the first to discover and formally prove this connection in the presented context.

The theorem can be generalized for arbitrary (but finite) sets of taint labels A. The project function then maps to a numeric value of a security clearance by taking the cardinality of the intersection of A with Ts.

Untainting and Adding Trust. Real-world application requires the need to untaint information, for example, when data is encrypted or properly anonymized. The taint labels now consist of two components: the labels a node taints and the labels it untaints. Let t be a total function t which returns the taints and untaints for an entity. We extend the simple tainting invariant to support untainting:

$$\text{tainting}'\ (V, E)\ t \equiv \forall (v_1, v_2) \in E.\ \text{taints}\ (t\ v_1) \setminus \text{untaints}\ (t\ v_1) \subseteq \text{taints}\ (t\ v_2)$$

For a taint label a, let $X = \text{taints}\ a$ and let $Y = \text{untaints}\ a$. We impose the type constraint that $Y \subseteq X$. We implemented the datatype such that X is internally extended to $X \cup Y$. For example in Fig. 1, t *Anonymizer* is actually taints: $\{\text{energy}, \text{location}\}$, untaints: $\{\text{location}\}$. Which merely appears to be a convenient abbreviation is actually a fundamental requirement for the overall soundness of the invariant. With this type constraint, as indicated earlier, we discharged the proof obligations imposed by *topoS* and all insights obtained for the simple mode now follow analogously for this model, in particular equivalence with a BLP model with trusted entities according to Theorem 1.

3   Conclusion

Several guidelines for verifying and auditing privacy properties of software systems exist. Yet, we found that automated tools for supporting privacy audits are still lacking. We presented a formal model based on static taint analysis which shall contribute to filling this gap. While our model is reduced to the bare minimum to facilitate adding assessment of privacy protection goals on top, the case studies show that improvements of audits are already achievable. We integrated our model into the formal policy framework *topoS* and proved soundness with Isabelle/HOL. From given system specifications or implementations, a model instance can be derived in which flow of critical data becomes explicit and data flow constraints can be verified automatically. We carried out two real-world case studies. They demonstrate the applicability of our approach, exemplifying that insights formally derived from the model are consistent with manual inspections of the architecture. In the second studied system, thanks to our tooling, auditing could be carried out in a completely automated manner.

Availability

Our formalization, case studies, and proofs can be found at https://www.isa-afp.org/entries/Network_Security_Policy_Verification.shtml. The full version of this paper is at https://arxiv.org/abs/1608.04671.

A   Case Studies

The main idea and usage of our model was already motivated by the fictional example of Fig. 1. In this appendix, we present details on two real-world case studies where we evaluate and audit two distributed systems for data collection which are deployed at the Technical University of Munich. For the sake of brevity, we only present the most interesting aspects. We will write node labels as X—Y, where X corresponds to the tainted labels and Y corresponds to the untainted labels. For example, t $Anonymizer = \{energy\}$—$\{location\}$.

A.1   Energy Monitoring System

Energy monitoring systems (EMS) have severe privacy implications: If installed in an office, such a system for example allows to draw conclusions about the effective working periods and behavior of employees by measuring the devices they use. EMS consist of at least two components: A logging unit which records energy usage locally and a server which stores and processes all recorded data. Considering privacy, storing all collected data in a single, possibly external place without fine-grained access control on the data level is critical.

We examined how to improve privacy of the data before persisting it [14]: Since the logger is an off-the-shelf component which we cannot modify, we suggest to add an additional component, called *P4S*, directly after the logger. This component separates the data by different owners, recipients, or some given predicate and applies further protection measures. The separated data can then be forwarded to (possibly different) cloud services. For the sake of brevity, we do not discuss this service, key management, and how cloud services could collaborate. Our proposed architecture is shown in Fig. 2. We modeled four different kinds of privacy-related data the logger captures by the taint labels A, B, C, and D.

As input to our tool, we provided the set of components including taint labels and system boundaries as architectural constraints. The results are as follows: Our model shows that data flow from the *Logger* to *P4S* (which crosses a system boundary physically over the network) is highly critical. For this taint label specification, *topoS* verified that our architecture is compliant with the security invariants. It also asserts that any attempt to interlink the different data processing pipelines within *P4S* would be a severe privacy violation. These insights generated by *topoS* can be further incorporated into the architecture: The designed pipelines can be separated into individual, isolated, stateless containers within *P4S* that can be instantiated on demand for each different taint label. In summary, our extended *topoS* allowed us to formally assess privacy properties of our proposed architecture before we invested time implementing it.

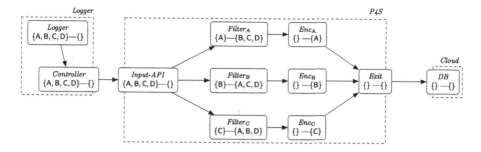

Fig. 2. Architecture of an energy monitoring system

A.2   MeasrDroid

MeasrDroid [5] is a system for collecting smartphone sensor data for research purposes. Via an app it may collect location data, information from the smartphone sensors, and networking properties such as signal strength, latency, and reliability. Ultimately, the data is stored and analyzed by a trusted machine, called *CollectDroid*. To decrease the attack surface of this machine, it is not reachable over the Internet. Instead, the smartphones push the data to a server called *UploadDroid*, which is regularly polled by *CollectDroid* for new information. Since *UploadDroid* is particularly exposed, a compromise of this machine must not lead to a privacy violation. Hence, it must be completely uncritical, i.e. not having any taint or untaint labels. This is achieved by having the smartphones encrypt the data for *CollectDroid* as only recipient. Consequently, *UploadDroid* only sees encrypted data. The model of the architecture is shown in Fig. 3. We modeled three users, each producing data with its individual tainting label A, B, or C. To model encryption of some taint label x, we create a pair of related nodes (Enc_x, Dec_x) where the first untaints and the second taints accordingly.

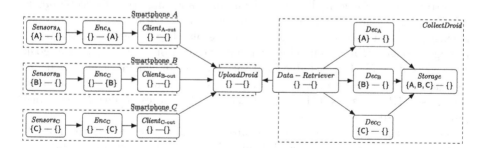

Fig. 3. MeasrDroid architecture

For this taint label specification, *topoS* verified that our architecture is compliant with the security invariants. In addition, given the taint label specification and adding an additional adversary node, *topoS* automatically computes an alternative architecture which is also compliant with the security invariants. Comparing our manually designed architecture with the *topoS*-generated architecture with adversary, we asserted that we did not overlook subtle information leaks. Our evaluation shows that our architecture is a subset of the *topoS*-generated architecture and only uncritical data can leak to an adversary. It also reveals that our architecture provides no protection against an adversary flooding *UploadDroid* with nonsensical data. We found *topoS* to be a suitable tool to formally support the previous informal privacy claims about the architecture.

Auditing the Real MeasrDroid. The previous paragraphs presents a theoretical evaluation of the architecture of MeasrDroid. The question arises how the real system, which exists since 2013, compares to our theoretical evaluation. Together with the authors of MeasrDroid we evaluate the implementation regarding our previous findings: We collect all machines which are associated with MeasrDroid. We find that they do not have a firewall set up, but instead rely on the central firewall of our lab. With over 5500 rules for IPv4, this firewall may be the largest real-world, publicly available iptables firewall in the world[1] and handles many different use cases. MeasrDroid is only a tiny fragment of it, relying on the protocols http, https, and ssh. For brevity, we focus our audit port 80 (http).

The model of the MeasrDroid architecture (cf. Fig. 3) should be recognizable in the rules of our firewall. In particular, *CollectDroid* should not be reachable from the Internet while *UploadDroid* should, and the former should be able to pull data from the latter. This information may be hidden somewhere in the firewall rule set. We used *fffuu* [10] to extract the access control structure of the firewall. The result is visualized in Fig. 4. This figure reflects the sheer intrinsic complexity of the access control policy enforced by the firewall. We have highlighted three entities. First, the IP range enclosed in a cloud corresponds to the IP range which is not used by our department, i.e. the Internet. The large block on the left corresponds to most internal machines which are not globally accessible. The IP address we marked in bold red belongs to *CollectDroid*. Inspecting the arrows, we have formally verified our first auditing goal: *CollectDroid* is not directly accessible from the Internet. The other large IP block on the right belongs to machines which are globally accessible. The IP address in bold red belongs to *UploadDroid*. Therefore, we have verified our second auditing goal: *UploadDroid* should be reachable from the Internet. In general, it is pleasant to see that the two machines are in different access groups. Finally, we see that the class of IP addresses including *CollectDroid* can access *UploadDroid* which proves our third auditing goal.

For the sake of example, we disregard that most machines at the bottom of Fig. 4 could attack *CollectDroid*. Under this assumption, we ignore this part of the graph and extract only the relevant and simplified parts in Fig. 5. So far, we presented only the positive audit finding. Our audit also reveals many problems, visualized with red arrows. They can be clearly recognized in Fig. 5: First, *UploadDroid* can connect to *CollectDroid*. This is a clear violation of

---

[1] We make them available at https://github.com/diekmann/net-network.

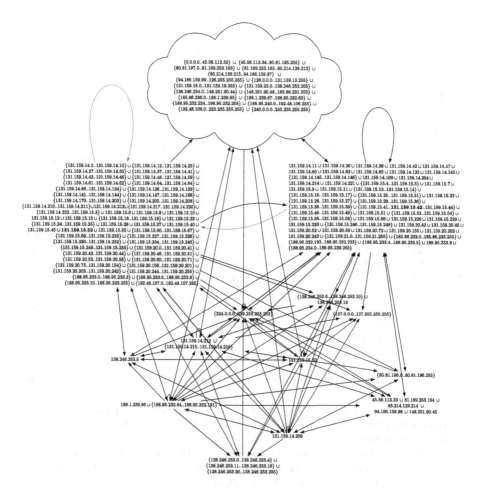

Fig. 4. MeasrDroid: Main firewall – IPv4 http connectivity matrix (Color figure online)

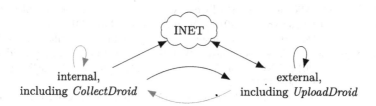

Fig. 5. MeasrDroid: Main firewall – simplified connectivity matrix (Color figure online)

234 M. von Maltitz et al.

the architecture. We have empirically verified this highly severe problem by logging into *UploadDroid* and connecting to *CollectDroid*. Second, most internal machines may access *CollectDroid*. Third, there are no restrictions for *UploadDroid* with regard to outgoing connections. In theory, it should only passively retrieve data and never initiate connections by itself (disregarding system updates).

Therefore, our audit could verify some core assertions about the actual implementation. In addition, it could uncover and confirm serious bugs. These bugs were unknown prior to our audit and we could only uncover them with the help of the presented tools. Using the firewall serialization feature of *topoS*, we fixed the problems and reiterated our evaluation to assert that our fix is effective.

References

1. Das Standard-Datenschutzmodell. Technical report, Konferenz der unabhängigen Datenschutzbehörden des Bundes und der Länder, Darmstadt (2015). https://www.datenschutzzentrum.de/uploads/sdm/SDM-Handbuch.pdf
2. Bock, K., Rost, M.: Privacy by design und die neuen schutzziele. DuD **35**(1), 30–35 (2011)
3. Cavoukian, A.: Creation of a Global Privacy Standard, November 2006, Revised October 2009. https://www.ipc.on.ca/images/resources/gps.pdf
4. Cavoukian, A.: Privacy by Design – The 7 Foundational Principles, January 2011. https://www.ipc.on.ca/wp-content/uploads/Resources/7foundationalprinciples.pdf
5. Chair of Network Architectures, Services, TUM: MeasrDroid. http://www.droid.net.in.tum.de/
6. Common Criteria: Part 3: Security assurance components. Common Criteria for Information Technology Security Evaluation CCMB-2012-09-003(Version 3.1 Revision 4), September 2012
7. Danezis, G., Domingo-Ferrer, J., Hansen, M., Hoepman, J.H., Metayer, D.L., Tirtea, R., Schiffner, S.: Privacy and data protection by design – from policy to engineering. Technical report, ENISA (2015)
8. Denning, D.: A lattice model of secure information flow. Commun. ACM **19**(5), 236–243 (1976)
9. Diekmann, C., Korsten, A., Carle, G.: Demonstrating topoS: theorem-prover-based synthesis of secure network configurations. In: 11th International Conference on Network and Service Management (CNSM), pp. 366–371, November 2015
10. Diekmann, C., Michaelis, J., Haslbeck, M., Carle, G.: Verified iptables firewall analysis. In: IFIP Networking 2016, Vienna, Austria, May 2016
11. Diekmann, C., Posselt, S.-A., Niedermayer, H., Kinkelin, H., Hanka, O., Carle, G.: Verifying security policies using host attributes. In: Ábrahám, E., Palamidessi, C. (eds.) FORTE 2014. LNCS, vol. 8461, pp. 133–148. Springer, Heidelberg (2014). doi:10.1007/978-3-662-43613-4_9
12. Enck, W., Gilbert, P., Han, S., Tendulkar, V., Chun, B.G., Cox, L.P., Jung, J., McDaniel, P., Sheth, A.N.: TaintDroid: an information-flow tracking system for realtime privacy monitoring on smartphones. ACM TOCS **32**(2), 5 (2014)
13. Feilkas, M., Ratiu, D., Jürgens, E.: The loss of architectural knowledge during system evolution: an industrial case study. In: ICPC, pp. 188–197, May 2009

14. Kinkelin, H., Maltitz, M., Peter, B., Kappler, C., Niedermayer, H., Carle, G.: Privacy preserving energy management. In: Aiello, L.M., McFarland, D. (eds.) SocInfo 2014. LNCS, vol. 8852, pp. 35–42. Springer, Cham (2015). doi:10.1007/978-3-319-15168-7_5

15. Murray, T., Matichuk, D., Brassil, M., Gammie, P., Bourke, T., Seefried, S., Lewis, C., Gao, X., Klein, G.: seL4: from general purpose to a proof of information flow enforcement. In: IEEE S&P, pp. 415–429, May 2013

16. Nipkow, T., Paulson, L.C., Wenzel, M.: Isabelle/HOL: A Proof Assistant for Higher-Order Logic. LNCS, vol. 2283. Springer, Heidelberg (2016). http://isabelle.in.tum.de/

17. Rost, M., Pfitzmann, A.: Datenschutz-Schutzziele – revisited. Datenschutz und Datensicherheit DuD **33**(6), 353–358 (2009)

18. Tromer, E., Schuster, R.: DroidDisintegrator: intra-application information flow control in Android apps (extended version). In: ASIA CCS 2016, pp. 401–412. ACM (2016). http://www.cs.tau.ac.il/~tromer/disintegrator/disintegrator.pdf

EPTL - A Temporal Logic for Weakly Consistent Systems (Short Paper)

Mathias Weber[✉], Annette Bieniusa, and Arnd Poetzsch-Heffter

University of Kaiserslautern, Kaiserslautern, Germany
{m_weber,bieniusa,poetzsch}@cs.uni-kl.de

Abstract. The high availability and scalability of weakly-consistent system attracts system designers. Yet, writing correct application code for this type of systems is difficult; even how to specify the intended behavior of such systems is still an open question. There has not been established any standard method to specify the intended dynamic behavior of a weakly consistent system.

In this paper, we present a event-based parallel temporal logic (EPTL), that is tailored to specify properties of weakly consistent systems. In contrast to LTL and CTL, EPTL takes into account that operations of weakly consistent systems are in many cases not serializable and have to be treated respectively to capture their behavior. We embed our temporal logic in Isabelle/HOL and can thereby leverage strong semi-automatic proving capabilities.

1 Introduction

To improve availability and fault tolerance, information systems are often replicated to several nodes and globally distributed. In such system scenarios, designers face a trade-off between availability, fault tolerance, and consistency. To achieve high availability, designers might weaken the consistency constraints between the nodes. In weakly consistent systems, we might refrain from making the objects consistent after each operation. For example, the replicated state might consist of several objects and communication is done via asynchronous message passing.

In such systems with weak consistency semantics, concurrent modifications of a replicated object can lead to a divergent system state as the order in which updates are applied can differ among the nodes. To avoid the divergence, these update conflicts need to be resolved e.g. using CRDTs [9]. The main idea of CRDTs is to leveraging mathematical properties of the data structure and its operations to automatically solve conflicts due to concurrent modifications of the replicated object state.

The standard notion of time as being linear is known to not work well in weakly consistent systems [6]. Instead of assuming linear time, we follow Burckhardt et al. [2] in representing time as a partial order on the events in the system.

© IFIP International Federation for Information Processing 2017
Published by Springer International Publishing AG 2017. All Rights Reserved
A. Bouajjani and A. Silva (Eds.): FORTE 2017, LNCS 10321, pp. 236–242, 2017.
DOI: 10.1007/978-3-319-60225-7_17

The topic of specifying weakly consistent systems is an open research question. LTL [8] is a classical specification language for dynamic properties of systems. It is widely used to specify properties of reactive systems. LTL is known for formulas which are easy to understand as well as its formal foundation. As we will show in Sect. 2, it can be difficult to capture the concurrent nature and asynchronous communication typical for weakly consistent systems in LTL (and CTL).

We want to decouple the specification of the behavior of the system from the behavior of the data types and want to enable to choose among different implementations based on the required properties described in the system specification. Our focus is on the understandability of the specification as well as a solid formal foundation.

Abstract Executions. Our goal is to have a specification language for properties of weakly consistent systems. The specification should be independent of the conflict resolution strategy used in the concrete implementation because this strategy partially depends on the required properties.

Weakly consistent systems are composed of multiple processes. Instead of sharing the state directly and protecting concurrent accesses using locks, each process obtains a replica of the shared object and solely interacts with this object. The values of the replicas are synchronized by asynchronously distributing the operations to all replicas. A typical data structure used in such systems is a *multi-value register (MVR)*. This datatype ensures that all written values of concurrent write operations are visible to subsequent read operations. The **put** operations allows to assign a new value to the register, the **get** operation allows to access the current state. Since the result of the **get** operation can consist of multiple concurrently written values, the operation returns a set of values. This means that if concurrently we have an operation writing the value 1 and one operation writing the value 2, the value of the register after synchronization of the operations is the set $\{1, 2\}$. Note that this property of multi-value registers usually leads to non-serializable system traces.

When formally specifying the semantics of the multi-value register, we want to abstract away from details concerning communication and process structure. Following Burckhardt et al. [2], we model the execution of a weakly consistent system as an abstract execution. An abstract execution A consists of a set of events E and a visibility relation $vis \subseteq E \times E$. The set E denotes the events representing the execution of operations on different nodes of the distributed weakly consistent system. The events have a unique identity and carry the metadata about the object and operation executed on it as well as information relevant for the specific use case (e.g. the subject executing the operation). The vis relation models the dependency between events. For two events e_1 and e_2, if $(e_1, e_2) \in vis$, then e_1 can influence the effect of e_2. The local order of events for each process is usually included in the visibility relation. To capture causality, vis must be irreflexive, transitive and antisymmetric. This corresponds to causal visibility. In addition, the visibility relation needs to be well-founded, so we can talk about the next events in the execution. The relation can also be depicted in an *event graph* where the nodes of the graph are the events and the edges represent the visibility relation. Transitive edges are left out for readability.

We annotate the nodes of event graphs with *operation expressions* as follows: $op(p_1, \ldots, p_n)$ describes that an event e represents an execution of operation op with parameters p_1 to p_n. If the returned value is relevant, we denote it as $op(p_1, \ldots, p_n) \Rightarrow retval$ where $op(p_1, \ldots, p_n)$ is defined as above and *retval* represents the returned value.

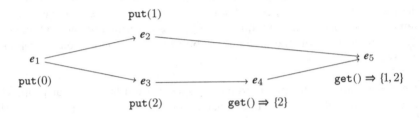

Fig. 1. Event graph of a multi-value register.

In form of an event graph, the example for the multi-value register can be depicted as in Fig. 1. Event e_1 corresponds to an initial **put** operation, which assigns the single value 0. The **put**(1) operation of e_2 happens concurrently with another operation, **put**(2) of e_3, that also modifies the state of the register. Both events are visible to event e_5 associated to the **get** operation which yields the set $\{1, 2\}$ as result. As the example shows, this abstract execution is only concerned with the partial order of events with respect to the visibility relation; the event graph abstracts away from the details of a specific implementation (e.g. which process executes an operation or how operations are distributed to the other process).

The paper makes the following contributions: (1) We show why current temporal logics are not suitable to specify the intended behavior of weakly consistent systems. (2) Our temporal logic called event-based parallel temporal logic (EPTL) based on an abstract execution of the system allows to express properties on the global partial order of the events of the system and takes into account the non-serializability of operations. (3) We have proven laws that allow to rewrite EPTL formulas while retaining the semantics. EPTL is modeled in Isabelle/HOL and all laws are formally verified.

2   Event-Based Parallel Temporal Logic (EPTL)

In this section we present a new variant of temporal logic, namely event-based parallel temporal logic (EPTL).

Why LTL and CTL are not Suitable. Traditionally, linear time logic [8] (LTL) is interpreted on Kripke structures representing the reachable states of the system. This has two implications: (1) Time is usually seen as linear thereby totally ordering the events of the system and (2) LTL formulas specify properties of the states of the system, not the events. The leads to problems when trying to use LTL to specify properties of weakly consistent systems.

If we regard the serializations of abstract executions like the one in Fig. 1 as independent event graphs, none of the executions would yield a result for a get operation that consists of more than one value since no operation would happen concurrently. We would need to encode the temporal information of the original abstract execution into the possible systems states. But this does not scale well and would typically require knowledge of the implementation of the replicated data type. Since the goal is to have a specification logic for the intended behavior of the system, this approach is not an option.

Computation tree logic [3] (CTL) allows for branching time, which solves parts of the issues discussed before. But in weakly consistent systems, the order of events forms a directed acyclic graph (DAG). Allowing to express that multiple different events can be successor of a single event and taking copies of future events is not an option. We would still loose the information that events can have happened concurrently in the past. The extended version [11] includes more details.

Syntax and Semantics. Instead of being based on possible states of the system, EPTL is directly based on events following many previous works [1,4,5,10]. For an abstract execution $A = (E, \text{vis})$, we define the partial order $e_1 \leq_A e_2 \equiv e_1 = e_2 \vee (e_1, e_2) \in \text{vis}$. When A is clear from the context, we simply write $e_1 \leq e_2$. The satisfaction relation $(A, e) \models \varphi$ is defined recursively over the structure of the formula as follows:

$$(A, e) \models Q \qquad \text{iff } Q[I](e) \text{ for variable interpretation } I$$
$$(A, e) \models \neg\varphi \qquad \text{iff } (A, e) \not\models \varphi$$
$$(A, e) \models (\varphi_1 \vee \varphi_2) \quad \text{iff } (A, e) \models \varphi_1 \text{ or } (A, e) \models \varphi_2$$
$$(A, e) \models EX\varphi \qquad \text{iff } \exists e_1.e < e_1 \text{ and } e_1 \text{ is a minimum wrt } < \text{ and } (A, e_1) \models \varphi$$
$$(A, e) \models AX\varphi \qquad \text{iff } \forall e_1.e < e_1 \text{ if } e_1 \text{ is a minimum wrt } <, \text{ then } (A, e_1) \models \varphi$$
$$(A, e) \models (\varphi \, U \, \psi) \quad \text{iff } \exists e_1.e \leq e_1 \text{ such that } (A, e_1) \models \psi) \text{ and}$$
$$\forall e_3.e \leq e_3 \text{ such that } (A, e_3) \not\models \varphi \text{ exists } e_2 \text{ such that}$$
$$e \leq e_2 \text{ and } e_2 \leq e_3 \text{ and } (A, e_2) \models \psi$$

An interpretation I assigns values to all free variables occurring in an EPTL formula. $Q[I]$ stands for the proposition Q in which all free variables are replaced by their interpretation according to I. An EPTL formula φ is said to be valid if $(A, e) \models \varphi$ for all interpretations I. An abstract execution A satisfies an EPTL property φ, $A \models \varphi$, if all starting events of the abstract execution satisfy φ. The starting events of an abstract execution A are all events that are minimal with respect to the partial order $\leq_A$ i.e. they have no predecessor events.

The logical operators $\wedge$ and $\Rightarrow$ and the remaining temporal logic operators can be defined as usual. The main difference to LTL is that we have two different step operators EX and AX and a different semantics for the until operator U

which is tailored to weakly consistent systems. Because the events in the system are ordered using a partial order, the next step is no longer unambiguous. Because of branches of concurrent events, a step might address multiple subsequent events. We want to have the possibility to address either at least one (EX) or all (AX) events that happen immediately after the current event. Also, the semantics of the until operator U has to be adapted to the partial order.

The definition of the until operation is stronger than in previous work [1,4,10] to be able to express strong properties about weakly consistent systems like the correctness of access control. Since this is a safety-critical question, we need a specification that is easy to understand and at the same time has a strong semantics on the execution of such a weakly consistent application. In general, access control is about specifying which operations are permitted to be executed by some subject or user on some object in the system. In a simple access control system we consider three types of operations: $\mathbf{grant}(op, s, o)$ gives subject s the right to perform operation op on object o. $\mathbf{revoke}(op, s, o)$ takes away the right of subject s to perform operation op on object o. $\mathbf{exec}(op, s, o)$ represents the execution of operation op performed by subject s on object o. Corresponding propositions (e.g. $\mathbf{grant}_P(op, s, o)$) are true for an event e if e represents the execution of the corresponding operation with the given parameters (e.g. $\mathbf{grant}(op, s, o)$).

Based on the given operations, we can define the properties we require from our simple access control system. We want to start with a default policy that initially no user has the right to execute any operation on the system until an administrative user grants this right to him/her. To simplify the example, we do not consider the details of rights to perform grant and revoke operations and assume that there is some administrative user in the system that has the right to perform these operations. Using the weak version of until defined as $(A, e) \models \varphi\ W\ \psi$ iff $(A, e) \models G\varphi \vee (\varphi\ U\ \psi)$, we can define the initial policy by the following property:

$$A \models \neg\mathbf{exec}_P(op, s, o)\ W\ \mathbf{grant}_P(op, s, o)$$

The dependency between grant and revoke should work like this: Whenever the right of a subject is revoked, this operation should not be executed until a subsequent grant allows the operation again. This can be specified in EPTL in the following way:

$$A \models G(\mathbf{revoke}_P(op, s, o) \Rightarrow AX(\neg\mathbf{exec}_P(op, s, o)\ W\ \mathbf{grant}_P(op, s, o)))$$

This property both models the semantics of the revoke and grant operations. A grant operation allows an operation that was previously revoked and a subsequent revoke operation disables the operation for the specified user again.

We see that the specifications are both readable and understandable as well as short. The strong semantics of the until operator ensures that revoking the right of a user disallows the operation on all future concurrent paths in the event graph.

Laws. Most of the laws of LTL can be shown to also hold in EPTL. Some implications like the distributivity of the conjunction and disjunction are only one-directional. The most important exception to the LTL laws is the induction formula for the until operator, which does not hold in EPTL.

$$\varphi \; U \; \psi \not\equiv \psi \vee (\varphi \wedge X(\varphi \; U \; \psi))$$

This makes reasoning in EPTL inconvenient. But since EPTL is mainly intended as a specification logic for the intended behavior of the system which translates to properties on abstract executions, this restriction is not a big issue.

Proofs and Extended Version. We have modeled EPTL in the theorem prover Isabelle/HOL. All laws of EPTL are formalized and verified in the interactive theorem prover and are used by the tool to simplify formulas. Even though we did not yet find an efficient automatic checking procedure for EPTL, the proofs can be done in semi-automatic fashion in HOL. Together with the strong automation of Isabelle/HOL this should make for a comfortable environment in which to show that the presented model is suitable to implement access control.

An extended version of this paper [11] includes the proven laws and extended examples.

3   Related Work

Alur et al. [1] presented a global partial order logic called ISTL. Same as we, they do not restrict the view on the system to the state sequence observed by a local process. The logic is based on a partially ordered set of local states which can also be seen as a branching structure. This branching structure represents all possible sequences of global states that may be derived from the partial order. This state based approach makes it unsuitable for reasoning about weakly consistent systems. As described in Sect. 2, encoding the events and the conflict resolution strategy into a state requires knowledge about the implementation of the conflict resolution strategy. Since the concrete implementation has to be abstracted from in the specification of the behavior of a weakly consistent system, ISTL is not suitable as a specification language for weakly consistent systems.

The other line of research about partial order semantics uses Mazurkiewicz traces [7]. The base for these traces is a finite set of actions, which can be seen as state transformations of resources of the system under investigation. Two actions are independent if they act on disjoint set of resources. Only independent actions are allowed to be performed concurrently. This restriction is the reason why Mazurkiewicz traces cannot be used to reason about weakly consistent systems in the given form. In these considered systems, the resources are replicated objects where each process performs operations on its copy. When looking at these operation from a global view, they all change the same shared object. In this sense, the operations are not independent, even though they are possibly performed concurrently. It is not obvious how to apply Mazurkiewicz traces to weakly consistent systems.

4   Conclusion

We presented the new temporal logic EPTL that is tailored to specify properties of weakly consistent systems. As the example of access control shows, it allows for a concise and readable, yet machine-checkable specification. The complete logic is modeled in Isabelle/HOL and all laws are verified using the theorem prover. All theory files are available under https://softech-git.informatik.uni-kl.de/mweber/EPTL/tree/master.

References

1. Alur, R., McMillan, K., Peled, D.: Deciding global partial-order properties. Formal Methods Syst. Des. **26**(1), 7–25 (2005)
2. Burckhardt, S., Gotsman, A., Yang, H., Zawirski, M.: Replicated data types: specification, verification, optimality. In: Proceedings of the 41st ACM SIGPLAN-SIGACT Symposium on Principles of Programming Languages, POPL 2014, pp. 271–284. ACM, New York (2014)
3. Clarke, E.M., Emerson, E.A.: Design and synthesis of synchronization skeletons using branching time temporal logic. In: Kozen, D. (ed.) Logic of Programs 1981. LNCS, vol. 131, pp. 52–71. Springer, Heidelberg (1982). doi:10.1007/BFb0025774
4. Diekert, V., Gastin, P.: Pure future local temporal logics are expressively complete for Mazurkiewicz traces. Inf. Comput. **204**(11), 1597–1619 (2006)
5. Havelund, K., Rosu, G.: Testing linear temporal logic formulae on finite execution traces. Technical report, RIACS (2001)
6. Lamport, L.: Time, clocks, and the ordering of events in a distributed system. Commun. ACM **21**(7), 558–565 (1978)
7. Mazurkiewicz, A.: Concurrent program schemes and their interpretations. DAIMI Rep. Ser. **6**(78), 1–51 (1977)
8. Pnueli, A.: The temporal logic of programs. In: 18th Annual Symposium on Foundations of Computer Science, pp. 46–57 (1977)
9. Shapiro, M., Preguiça, N., Baquero, C., Zawirski, M.: Conflict-free replicated data types. In: Défago, X., Petit, F., Villain, V. (eds.) SSS 2011. LNCS, vol. 6976, pp. 386–400. Springer, Heidelberg (2011). doi:10.1007/978-3-642-24550-3_29
10. Thiagarajan, P.S., Walukiewicz, I.: An expressively complete linear time temporal logic for Mazurkiewicz traces. Inf. Comput. **179**(2), 230–249 (2002)
11. Weber, M., Bieniusa, A., Poetzsch-Heffter, A.: EPTL - a temporal logic for weakly consistent systems abs/1704.05320 (2017). https://arxiv.org/abs/1704.05320

Author Index

Printed in the United States
By Bookmasters